Caro aluno, seja bem-vindo!

A partir de agora, você tem a oportunidade de estudar com uma coleção didática da SM que integra um conjunto de recursos educacionais impressos e digitais desenhados especialmente para auxiliar os seus estudos.

Para acessar os recursos digitais integrantes deste projeto, cadastre-se no *site* da SM e ative sua conta.

Veja como ativar sua conta SM:

1. Acesse o *site* <www.edicoessm.com.br>.
2. Se você não possui um cadastro, basta clicar em "Login/Cadastre-se" e, depois, clicar em "Quero me cadastrar" e seguir as instruções.
3. Se você já possui um cadastro, digite seu *e-mail* e sua senha para acessar.
4. Após acessar o *site* da SM, entre na área "Ativar recursos digitais" e insira o código indicado abaixo:

46K99 - 699MH - RJ6FZ - A6DEA

Você terá acesso aos recursos digitais por 36 meses, a partir da data de ativação desse código.

Ressaltamos que o código de ativação somente poderá ser utilizado uma vez, conforme descrito no "Termo de Responsabilidade do Usuário dos Recursos Digitais SM", localizado na área de ativação do código no *site* da SM.

Em caso de dúvida, entre em contato com nosso **Atendimento**, pelo telefone **0800 72 54876** ou pelo *e-mail* **atendimento@grupo-sm.com** ou pela internet <**www.edicoessm.com.br**>.

Desejamos muito sucesso nos seus estudos!

Requisitos mínimos recomendados para uso dos conteúdos digitais SM

Computador	Tablet	Navegador
PC Windows • Windows XP ou superior • Processador dual-core • 1 GB de memória RAM **PC Linux** • Ubuntu 9.x, Fedora Core 12 ou OpenSUSE 11.x • 1 GB de memória RAM **Macintosh** • MAC OS 10.x • Processador dual-core • 1 GB de memória RAM	**Tablet IPAD IOS** • IOS versão 7.x ou mais recente • Armazenamento mínimo: 8GB • Tela com tamanho de 10" *Outros fabricantes* • Sistema operacional Android versão 3.0 (Honeycomb) ou mais recente • Armazenamento mínimo: 8GB • 512 MB de memória RAM • Processador dual-core	**Internet Explorer 10** **Google Chrome 20** ou mais recente **Mozilla Firefox 20** ou mais recente Recomendado o uso do Google Chrome Você precisará ter o programa Adobe Acrobat instalado, *kit* multimídia e conexão à internet com, no mínimo, 1Mb

VOLUME ÚNICO

inglês
ensino médio

Vera Menezes
Mestre em Inglês pela Universidade Federal de Minas Gerais (UFMG).
Doutora em Linguística e Filologia pela Universidade Federal do Rio de Janeiro (UFRJ).
Professora titular de Linguística Aplicada na UFMG.

Junia Braga
Mestre em Linguística Aplicada pela Faculdade de Letras da UFMG.
Doutora em Linguística Aplicada pela Faculdade de Letras da UFMG.
Professora de Língua Inglesa da Faculdade de Letras da UFMG.

Marisa Carneiro
Mestre em Linguística Aplicada pela Faculdade de Letras da UFMG.
Doutora em Linguística pela Faculdade de Letras da UFMG.
Professora visitante de Inglês Instrumental I e II na UFMG.

Marcos Racilan
Mestre em Linguística Aplicada pela Faculdade de Letras da UFMG.
Professor de Língua Inglesa do Centro Federal de Educação Tecnológica de Minas Gerais (Cefet-MG).

Ronaldo Gomes
Mestre em Linguística Aplicada pela Faculdade de Letras da UFMG.
Professor de Língua Inglesa do Instituto Federal de Minas Gerais – Campus Ouro Preto.

São Paulo,
1ª edição 2014

Alive High — Volume único
© Edições SM Ltda.
Todos os direitos reservados

Direção editorial	Juliane Matsubara Barroso
Gerência editorial	Angelo Stefanovits
Gerência de processos editoriais	Rosimeire Tada da Cunha
Coordenação de área	Ana Paula Landi
Edição	Wilson Chequi
Apoio editorial	Cleber Ferreira de João
Consultoria	Christiane Khatchadourian, Orlando Brasil, Diego Kiam
Assistência de produção editorial	Alzira Aparecida Bertholim Meana, Flávia R. R. Chaluppe, Silvana Siqueira
Preparação e revisão	Cláudia Rodrigues do Espírito Santo (Coord.), Ana Catarina Nogueira, Angélica Lau P. Soares, Fernanda Oliveira Souza, Izilda de Oliveira Pereira, Maíra de Freitas Cammarano, Rosinei Aparecida Rodrigues Araujo, Valéria Cristina Borsanelli, Marco Aurélio Feltran (apoio de equipe)
Coordenação de *design*	Erika Tiemi Yamauchi Asato
Coordenação de arte	Ulisses Pires
Edição de arte	Felipe Repiso, Keila Grandis, Vivian Dumelle
Projeto gráfico	Erika Tiemi Yamauchi Asato, Catherine Ishihara
Capa	Alysson Ribeiro, Erika Tiemi Yamauchi Asato e Adilson Casarotti sobre ilustração de NiD-Pi
Iconografia	Priscila Ferraz, Bianca Fanelli, Josiane Laurentino
Tratamento de imagem	Marcelo Casaro, Claudia Fidelis, Robson Mereu
Editoração eletrônica	Tangente Design
Fabricação	Alexander Maeda
Impressão	EGB-Editora Gráfica Bernardi Ltda.

Dados Internacionais de Catalogação na Publicação (CIP)
(Câmara Brasileira do Livro, SP, Brasil)

Alive high, volume único : inglês : ensino médio. — 1. ed.
— São Paulo : Edições SM, 2014. — (Alive high)

"Língua estrangeira moderna."
Vários autores.
Bibliografia.
ISBN 978-85-418-0593-3 (aluno)
ISBN 978-85-418-0594-0 (professor)

1. Inglês (Ensino médio) I. Série.

14-06403   CDD-420.7

Índices para catálogo sistemático:
1. Inglês : Ensino médio 420.7

1ª edição, 2014

Edições SM Ltda.
Rua Tenente Lycurgo Lopes da Cruz, 55
Água Branca 05036-120 São Paulo SP Brasil
Tel. 11 2111-7400
edicoessm@grupo-sm.com
www.edicoessm.com.br

Apresentação

Caro aluno,

Este livro foi escrito para você, jovem do século XXI, que quer aprender inglês e usar tecnologias de interação e comunicação para agir no mundo. Ao elaborá-lo, escolhemos textos adequados à sua idade e planejamos atividades variadas que proporcionam experiências diversas com o uso da língua inglesa.

Com este livro, você terá oportunidade de rever o que já aprendeu e será desafiado a aprender outros usos da língua, essenciais ao desenvolvimento de suas habilidades orais e escritas em inglês.

Você também vai ouvir e ler textos sobre assuntos variados e interessantes, além de escutar canções em inglês. Terá oportunidade de refletir sobre experiências individuais e sociais e se sentirá motivado a exercer sua cidadania nos contextos local e global. Vai escrever textos variados e será incentivado a compartilhar sua produção com outros leitores.

Nossa proposta é que, além de aprender inglês, você amplie seu conhecimento sobre temas diversos e aprenda, também, a usar várias ferramentas da internet para publicar seus textos e interagir com usuários da língua inglesa ao redor do mundo. Evidentemente, não poderíamos deixar de incluir um trabalho que possa ajudá-lo a se preparar para o Enem ou para o vestibular, com foco em estratégias de leitura aplicadas aos tipos de questão desses exames.

Com este livro, realizamos nosso sonho de oferecer aos estudantes brasileiros um material de alta qualidade e que valoriza a capacidade dos jovens de aprender uma língua estrangeira.

Acreditamos que você vai se divertir e aprender muito com o que encontrará neste livro.

Os autores

Conheça seu livro

Seu livro é composto de doze partes, cada uma delas com duas unidades. As unidades são bastante diversificadas e estão divididas em seções. Conhecer os conteúdos e objetivos de cada uma delas o ajudará a utilizá-las de maneira mais participativa e eficaz.

Abertura das partes

Em páginas duplas, tem como objetivo ativar seu conhecimento prévio sobre os conteúdos das duas unidades que compõem cada parte. No *Learning plan*, você poderá ver os conteúdos que serão desenvolvidos nas duas unidades. Em cada abertura são ainda apresentadas ferramentas digitais gratuitas que vão ajudá-lo em seu letramento digital. As aberturas das **Parts 1**, **5** e **9** trazem também orientações sobre o projeto a ser desenvolvido durante o ano em questão.

Let's read!

Esta é a seção de leitura. Ela traz textos de diversos gêneros sobre temas relevantes para você e para a sociedade. Por meio de atividades variadas, tem como objetivo levá-lo a desenvolver habilidades de compreensão escrita (geral e/ou detalhada) e a se colocar criticamente.

Lead-in

Em página dupla, esta é a seção de abertura de cada unidade do livro. Por meio de imagens e, em alguns casos, de pequenos textos, seguidos de diversos tipos de atividades, tem como objetivo ativar seu conhecimento prévio sobre o tema que será tratado na unidade. Você também vai ter um primeiro contato com o vocabulário que será aprofundado ao longo da unidade.

Let's listen and talk!

Por meio de diferentes tipos de textos orais (diálogos, entrevistas, trechos de filmes e programas de TV, *podcasts*, trechos de palestras, etc.) e atividades variadas, nesta seção você terá oportunidade de desenvolver as habilidades de compreensão global e de compreensão de informações específicas de um texto oral. Além disso, a partir da compreensão oral, poderá discutir assuntos relacionados ao tema da unidade.

Vocabulary corner

Nesta seção, presente em algumas unidades, você terá oportunidade de desenvolver o vocabulário relacionado ao capítulo.

Profession spot

Nesta seção você vai encontrar atividades relacionadas a diferentes carreiras e profissões. Vai poder refletir e discutir sobre elas. Esta seção aparece com mais frequência nas últimas unidades do livro.

Let's focus on language!

Esta é a seção de gramática. A partir da observação de situações de uso da língua, você terá a oportunidade de deduzir as regras e empregá-las de forma contextualizada.

Let's act with words!

Esta seção, que encerra cada unidade par, propõe atividades de produção escrita (*writing*) em diferentes gêneros textuais, incluindo etapas de planejamento, escrita, avaliação e reescrita. Nela, você vai ter oportunidade de usar, de forma contextualizada, as estruturas linguísticas e o vocabulário apresentados nas unidades da parte correspondente.

5

Conheça seu livro

Learning tips & Let's reflect on learning!

Cada uma das doze partes termina com uma seção de apresentação de diferentes estratégias de aprendizagem (*Learning tips*) e outra que convida você a refletir sobre seu processo de aprendizagem (*Let's reflect on learning!*).

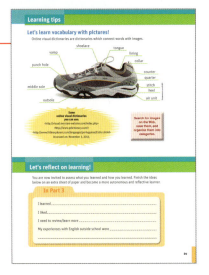

Turn on the jukebox!

Nesta seção, presente em algumas unidades, há atividades de compreensão oral com músicas, que vêm reproduzidas no DVD-ROM que acompanha o livro.

Let's study for Enem!

Seção exclusiva disponível no final de cada parte, com foco na preparação para a prova de inglês do Enem. Por meio de questões usadas em edições passadas, apresenta estratégias importantes para realizar o exame.

Exam Practice Questions (Vestibular)

Disponível no final de cada parte, esta seção tem como objetivo prepará-lo para as questões de inglês do Vestibular. Aqui também o foco é apresentar estratégias que possam ajudar você a obter bons resultados no exame.

Além dessas seções, ao longo do livro há vários **boxes** que enriquecem os conteúdos:

» **Language in action**: apresenta os objetivos de cada unidade.
» **Did you know...?**: apresenta curiosidades, informações culturais e vocabulário relacionados a uma atividade ou texto apresentado.
» **Pronunciation spot**: apresenta questões relacionadas à pronúncia e à entonação.
» **Beyond the lines...**: promove reflexões a partir dos temas dos textos com vistas ao desenvolvimento do letramento crítico.
» **Hint**: apresenta estratégias para a recepção e produção de textos orais e escritos.

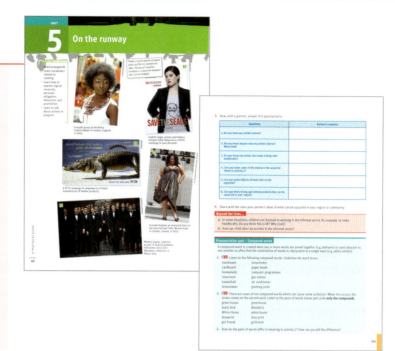

No **final** do livro, você ainda vai encontrar:

» **Workbook**: caderno de atividades integrado ao livro, composto de exercícios organizados de modo que você possa rever e aprofundar o conteúdo estudado em cada grupo de duas unidades.
» **Irregular Verb list**: lista de verbos irregulares com a transcrição fonética e tradução.
» **Glossary (inglês-português)**: itens selecionados de vocabulário, indicados em roxo ao longo do livro.

DVD-ROM

Contém o áudio necessário para a realização das atividades de compreensão oral e de pronúncia e/ou entonação. Traz também o áudio de todas as músicas.
Além disso, apresenta um conjunto de conteúdos digitais que oferecem atividades adicionais lúdicas e interativas.

Table of Contents

Part 1   **Express Yourself**   **10**
Unit 1   **What's your talent?** 12
- Let's read! 14
- Let's listen! 17
- Let's focus on language! 19
- Let's talk! 21

Unit 2   **Street art** 22
- Let's read! 24
- Vocabulary corner 26
- Let's focus on language! 27
- Let's listen and talk! 31
- Let's act with words! 32

- Learning tips & Let's reflect on learning! 33
- Let's study for Enem! 34
- Exam Practice Questions (Vestibular) 36

Part 2   **Move Your Body**   **38**
Unit 3   **You've got the moves** 40
- Turn on the jukebox! 42
- Let's read! 44
- Let's listen and talk! 46
- Let's focus on language! 47

Unit 4   **Sing it out** 50
- Let's read! 52
- Turn on the jukebox! 54
- Let's focus on language! 55
- Let's listen and talk! 58
- Let's act with words! 60

- Learning tips & Let's reflect on learning! 61
- Let's study for Enem! 62
- Exam Practice Questions (Vestibular) 64

Part 3   **Make Your Art Sparkle!**   **66**
Unit 5   **On the runway** 68
- Let's read! 70
- Vocabulary corner 71
- Let's focus on language! 72
- Turn on the jukebox! 75
- Let's listen and talk! 76

Unit 6   **Visual arts** 78
- Let's read! 80
- Vocabulary corner 83
- Let's focus on language! 84
- Let's listen and talk! 87
- Let's act with words! 88

- Learning tips & Let's reflect on learning! 89
- Let's study for Enem! 90
- Exam Practice Questions (Vestibular) 92

Part 4   **Folk Expressions**   **94**
Unit 7   **Handicrafts** 96
- Let's read! 98
- Vocabulary corner 101
- Let's listen and talk! 102
- Let's focus on language! 104

Unit 8   **Festivals and parades**   **106**
- Let's read! 108
- Vocabulary corner 110
- Let's focus on language! 111
- Let's listen and talk! 113
- Let's act with words! 116

- Learning tips & Let's reflect on learning! 117
- Let's study for Enem! 118
- Exam Practice Questions (Vestibular) 120

Part 5   **Social Networks**   **122**
Unit 9   **Making connections** 124
- Let's read! 126
- Let's listen and talk! 128
- Let's focus on language! 130
- Profession spot 133

Unit 10   **Security on the web** 134
- Let's read! 136
- Let's focus on language! 139
- Let's listen and talk! 142
- Let's act with words! 144

- Learning tips & Let's reflect on learning! 145
- Let's study for Enem! 146
- Exam Practice Questions (Vestibular) 148

Part 6   **Mobile**   **150**
Unit 11   **On the waves of the radio** 152
- Let's read! 154
- Vocabulary corner 156
- Let's listen and talk! 157
- Let's focus on language! 159
- Turn on the jukebox! 161

Unit 12   **Going mobile** 162
- Let's listen and talk! 164
- Let's focus on language! 166
- Let's read! 169
- Vocabulary corner 171
- Let's act with words! 172

- Learning tips & Let's reflect on learning! 173
- Let's study for Enem! 174
- Exam Practice Questions (Vestibular) 176

Part 7   **Print Media**   **178**
Unit 13   **Extra! Extra!** 180
- Let's read! 182
- Let's listen and talk! 185
- Let's focus on language! 186
- Profession spot 189

Unit 14   **Strike a pose** 190
- Let's read! 192
- Let's focus on language! 194
- Vocabulary corner 196

- Let's listen! ...197
- Turn on the jukebox! ...198
- Profession spot ...199
- Let's act with words! ...200
- Learning tips & Let's reflect on learning! ...201
- Let's study for Enem! ...202
- Exam Practice Questions (Vestibular) ...204

Part 8 Video ...206

Unit 15 It's on TV ...208
- Let's read! ...210
- Vocabulary corner ...211
- Let's listen and talk! ...212
- Let's focus on language! ...213
- Profession spot ...217

Unit 16 You broadcast ...218
- Let's read! ...220
- Vocabulary corner ...222
- Let's focus on language! (1) ...223
- Let's listen and talk! ...225
- Let's focus on language! (2) ...227
- Let's act with words! ...228
- Learning tips & Let's reflect on learning! ...229
- Let's study for Enem! ...230
- Exam Practice Questions (Vestibular) ...232

Part 9 Life on Earth ...234

Unit 17 Life in the countryside ...236
- Let's read! ...238
- Let's listen and talk! ...240
- Let's focus on language! ...242
- Profession spot ...245

Unit 18 Going green! ...246
- Let's read! ...248
- Let's listen and talk! ...251
- Turn on the jukebox! ...252
- Let's focus on language! ...253
- Let's act with words! ...256
- Learning tips & Let's reflect on learning! ...257
- Let's study for Enem! ...258
- Exam Practice Questions (Vestibular) ...260

Part 10 Healthy Life ...262

Unit 19 I am what I eat ...264
- Let's read! ...266
- Vocabulary corner ...269
- Let's listen and talk! ...270
- Let's focus on language! ...271
- Profession spot ...273

Unit 20 Sound body ...274
- Let's read! ...276
- Vocabulary corner ...278
- Let's listen and talk! ...279
- Let's focus on language! ...280
- Profession spot ...283
- Let's act with words! ...284
- Learning tips & Let's reflect on learning! ...285
- Let's study for Enem! ...286
- Exam Practice Questions (Vestibular) ...288

Part 11 Yes, We Can ...290

Unit 21 Intelligences and abilities ...292
- Let's read! ...294
- Let's listen and talk! ...296
- Let's focus on language! ...297
- Profession spot ...301

Unit 22 Affirmative action ...302
- Let's read! ...304
- Let's listen and talk! ...306
- Let's focus on language! ...308
- Vocabulary corner ...309
- Let's act with words! ...312
- Learning tips & Let's reflect on learning! ...313
- Let's study for Enem! ...314
- Exam Practice Questions (Vestibular) ...316

Part 12 Modern Accomplishments ...318

Unit 23 Man-made wonders ...320
- Let's read! ...322
- Let's listen and talk! ...325
- Let's focus on language! ...326
- Profession spot ...329

Unit 24 Technology advances ...330
- Let's read! ...332
- Let's focus on language! ...335
- Let's listen and talk! ...338
- Profession spot ...339
- Let's act with words! ...340
- Learning tips & Let's reflect on learning! ...341
- Let's study for Enem! ...342
- Exam Practice Questions (Vestibular) ...344

- Irregular Verbs ...346
- Workbook ...351
- Glossary ...388
- Bibliography ...392

PART

1 Express Yourself

THE TALENT

Be a clown doctor!
Bring a smile to the
faces of sick children!

Take part in the show!
Talent show! Talent show!
What's your talent?
Come on along, here we go...

Learning plan

Greeting and introducing

Understanding nonverbal signs

Giving information about you and about others

Talking about street art and reflecting on it

Talking about possibilities and abilities

Developing an art project with graffiti

Year Project - BLOG

What is a blog?

It is a journal that is available on the Web. The activity of updating a blog is "blogging" and someone who keeps a blog is a "blogger." A blog is typically updated daily using software that allows people with little or no technical background to update it and maintain it. Postings on a blog are normally arranged in chronological order with the most recent additions featured most prominently.

Adapted from: <http://www.library.yorku.ca/cms/bibblog/what-is-a-blog/>. Accessed on: May 19, 2014.

Create a blog to publish your productions in English throughout this year. See two options of free online blog platforms.

Fac-símile/Blogger

First, create a Google account. If you already have a Gmail account, use it to sign in to use Blogger. Then give a name to your blog and choose a template. It's very user-friendly and you can write your first post. It is available at <www.blogger.com> (accessed on: May 19, 2014).

Fac-símile/Brands of the World

This is another option that you can use to create a blog. This platform offers a huge range of themes and plug-ins to make your blog attractive for your viewers. This tool is available at <http://wordpress.com/> (accessed on: May 19, 2014).

You can learn how to build a WordPress blog by watching a tutorial video at <http://www.youtube.com/watch?v=H1ImndTOfC8> (accessed on: May 19, 2014).

11

UNIT 1

What's your talent?

Language in action

- Learn how to greet someone and make introductions
- Understand nonverbal signs
- Learn how to give information about you and about others

Available at: <http://www.thetalentstore.net/>. Accessed on: March 1, 2013.

Divulgação UFC/ID/BR

Claro Cortes/Reuters

Australia's Shelley Chaplin (L) celebrates with Katie Hill after winning a match against Britain during the Beijing 2008 Paralympic Games.

Brazilian MMA fighter Anderson Silva, at UFC Rio.

Luis Louro/Alamy/Glow Images

Kevin Mazur/WireImage/Getty Images

British boy-band One Direction (L to R: Niall Horan, Harry Styles, Liam Payne, Zayn Malik, and Louis Tomlinson).

1 ▪ Express Yourself

12

> Lead-in

1. Look at picture 1 and make a list of the talents represented by the silhouettes.
   _____
   _____

2. Read the text below and classify the talents into the two groups in the chart.

   Welcome to the Talent Store

   The Talent Store is a networking source for entertainment agencies, businesses, and individuals or groups who are seeking job or gig opportunities, discovery, exposure, online community support, and advice. Our services are targeted to a wide variety of people who either provide a service to, or are a part of, the entertainment industry. The list of services includes, but is not limited to: singers, dancers, actors, comedians, technicians, camera operators, stage hands, clowns, mimes, cartoonists, parade organizers, and event planners.

   Available at: <http://anndandridgepublicrelations.ning.com/profile/LithorniaLibbieHarper>. Accessed on: February 4, 2014.

Performers

Technical Crew

   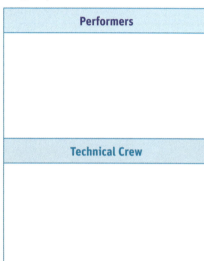

3. What other talents do the pictures on the previous page represent?
   _____
   _____

4. Which elements tell us that the person represented in picture 4 is not a "real" doctor?
   _____

5. What hand gestures can you identify in some of the photos used on the previous page? Check (✔) the corresponding options.

   (   ) high five (a celebratory gesture)   (   ) thumbs-up (approval)
   (   ) A-OK (no problem, fine)   (   ) thumbs-down (disapproval)
   (   ) crossed fingers (hope)   (   ) handshake (greeting ritual)
   (   ) V sign (victory or peace)   (   ) waving with palm facing outward (greeting)

6. What do these hand signs mean? Discuss your ideas with a classmate. Then check your guesses at the bottom of the page.

1

2

3

Answers to activity 6: 1) The "shaka" sign or "hang loose"; 2) The approval sign; 3) The loser sign.

13

› Let's read!

Before you read...
- What type of talent does the girl have in text 1?
- What does she probably do to help sick children?
- Which elements are common in both text 1 and text 2?
- Can you guess the type of talent the boy in text 3 has?
- What do the headphones tell us about this boy's hobby?

Hint
In your first contact with a text, it is possible to predict many things about it. For example, pictures, familiar words in titles, etc. tell us a lot about the topic.

1. Now, read the three texts more carefully and check (✔) the statements which are true.

Text 1

All over the world, children in hospital are being treated with a new kind of medicine: laughter. LUCY is 23 and works for Theodora Children's Trust. She is one of many clown doctors who bring a smile to the faces of sick children.

Available at: <http://media.gimnazijabb.edu.rs/2010/03/THE-CLOWN-DOCTORS.ppt>. Accessed on: October 29, 2013.

This text is part of a slide presentation available on the Internet, entitled *The Clown Doctor*. This is the seventh slide of a total of 13. In the presentation they explain in detail what clown doctors do in hospitals.

Text 2

Theodora Children's Trust brings music, magic and laughter to children in hospital and to disabled children through bedside visits from Giggle Doctors.

[…]

Our Giggle Doctors are specialist entertainers, highly trained to work both in the hospital environment and with children with disabilities. They come from a wide range of backgrounds and bring with them a variety of skills (among our team are actors, entertainers, teachers, magicians, musicians and singers).

Available at: <http://uk.blog.globalgiving.org/2012/12/12/childrens-christmas-appeal-2012-the-giggle-doctors/> (paragraph 1) and <http://uk.theodora.org/en-gb/our-mission> (paragraph 2). Accessed on: October 29, 2013.

Theodora Children's Trust is a British charity specialized in helping children recover from operations and illness. They train people to become clown doctors in order to work in collaboration with hospital professionals.

Text 3

Astro – The X Factor U.S. – Audition 1

Brian: Hello… Brian.

Steve: Brian, I'm Steve, nice to meet you. Uh, who are these people here?

Brian: Mom, stepdad. Here are my mom and my steppops. Y'know, they are both huge supporters of me. And my mom, she's… she's my number one fan.

I have er an insane love for music. I listen to music all the time, so it's in my blood.

[…]

Brian: I've always dreamed of performing at Madison Square Garden. To know that 20,000 people are here for me, that would be big.

Adapted and transcribed from: <http://www.youtube.com/watch?v=GJu_lsb2oVQ> (0:00-0:26 and 0:41-0:48). Accessed on: May 7, 2014.

American rapper Brian Bradley (stage name Astro) posing at a movie theater in California, 2011.

This text is a video transcription of an interview with Brian Bradley, also known as Astro. This young artist became famous after taking part in "The X Factor" competition (USA).

( ) Lucy and Brian are artists.

( ) Giggle doctors don't need training to entertain patients in hospitals.

( ) Lucy and Brian help sick children in the hospital environment.

( ) Both are talented people.

( ) They are entertainers.

( ) Lucy and Brian are supported by their parents.

15

2. Based on your answers in the previous activity, write correct sentences as in the example.

Giggle doctors need training to entertain patients in hospitals.

_____

_____

3. Which text presents an alternative name for "clown doctor?" What is this name?

_____

4. Read text 3 again. Can you infer who Brian is?

_____

5. Who are Brian's supporters? _____

6. Brian is talented in a specific area. What is it? Check (✔) one option.

(   ) dance   (   ) drama   (   ) clowning   (   ) DJing   (   ) music

7. Text 3 is a transcription of part of a videotaped interview. Read it again and find examples of the following characteristics of oral texts. Copy the words.

a) Hesitation particles: _____

b) Abbreviations: _____

c) Repetition: _____

d) Informal vocabulary: _____

8. Now find in the three texts sentences or words that are used to express the ideas below. Copy them here.

a) People's age: _____

b) Talking about people's occupation: _____

_____

_____

c) Names of occupations: _____

_____

_____

9. What questions would you ask Brian if you had a chance? Consider information such as hobbies, plans for the future, favorite artist, etc. Use your notebook.

10. Make a list of the talents in your family. Write sentences as in the two examples. Use your notebook for this activity.

My sister Carla plays the guitar.

My stepbrother Diego designs games.

11. Compare your list in activity 9 with a classmate's and find out if there are similar talents in both families.

> Let's listen!

1. These are dialogues related to talent shows in the USA and Nigeria. Can you predict what the *missing* parts are? Write them down based on your knowledge and the hints the texts give.

Dialogue 1

Brian: How you're feeling? Are you feeling good? Anybody from Brooklyn here?

Jury member: Hi, _____

_____

Brian: It's Brian Bradley.

Jury member: _____

_____

Brian: I'm fourteen years old.

Jury member: And _____

_____

Brian: I'm from Brooklyn, New York...

Transcribed from: <http://www.youtube.com/watch?v=GJu_lsb2oVQ> (1:08-1:22). Accessed on: October 29, 2013.

Dialogue 2

Reporter: So, how are you doing?

Interviewee: _____

_____

Reporter: I'm great.

Interviewee: Yes.

Reporter: So, are you a huge fan of Nigerian Idol?

Interviewee: Oh, I'm a very huge fan of Nigerian Idol.

Transcribed from: <http://www.youtube.com/watch?v=Lw7Nu36QXTU> (1:55-2:03). Accessed on: October 30, 2013.

Dialogue 3

Jury member: How are you?

Contestant: _____

Jury member: Are you OK? You...

Contestant: _____

Transcribed from: <http://www.youtube.com/watch?v=kAnQQ4bwRgg> (0:12-0:18). Accessed on: October 30, 2013.

17

Dialogue 4

Reporter: I'm on the district of Lagos. I'm gonna be doing a vox pop on Nigerian Idol. So, let's go talk to a few people as to what they feel about Nigerian Idol... Hello. How are you doing?

Interviewee: _____

<small>Transcribed from: <http://www.youtube.com/watch?v=Lw7Nu36QXTU> (0:03-0:13). Accessed on: October 30, 2013.</small>

Dialogue 5

Rachel: Hi.
Jury member: Hi Rachel.
Rachel: _____
Jury member: What've you chosen, Rachel?
Rachel: It's a surprise.
Jury member: Ah, I like surprises.
Rachel: OK.
Jury member: Good luck.
Rachel: Thank you.

<small>Transcribed from: <http://www.youtube.com/watch?v=7KJMOUzBDzM> (0:22-0:37). Accessed on: October 30, 2013.</small>

Did you know...?

Rachel Crow began singing as a toddler. She sang her first song, "Breathe" by Faith Hill at just 18 months. She later went on to enter talent contests at local fairs.

<small>Available at: <http://www.rachelcrowofficial.com/bio/>. Accessed on: October 30, 2013.</small>

2. 🔊1 Now listen to the recording and check if your predictions were correct. Then discuss these questions with a classmate.

a) Which of the expressions used in the dialogues are new for you?
b) How much would you understand if you didn't read the transcript?
c) Did you pay attention to different accents while listening to the dialogues?
d) Which of the five dialogues matches the picture below?

Image captured from: <http://www.youtube.com/watch?v=Lw7Nu36QXTU>. Accessed on: October 30, 2013.

> Let's focus on language!

1. Look at this excerpt from text 3 in the *Let's read!* section. Then check (✔) the right option to complete the statement.

   > *Brian*: Hello... Brian.
   > *Steve*: Brian, I'm Steve, nice to meet you. Uh, who are these people here?

   In this interaction, we can say that Brian uses
   ( ) a formal introduction,
   ( ) an informal introduction,
   and that Steve is
   ( ) more formal.
   ( ) more informal.

2. Now read a dialogue from the movie *The Express*, the story of an African-American athlete who changed the way fans looked at men of his color. Then check (✔) the right option to complete the statement.

   > *Gloria*: I'm Gloria. This is my friend... Sarah. She's visiting from Cornell.
   > *Jack Buckley*: Gloria and Sarah. OK. I'm Jack Buckley, but you call me JB.
   > *Gloria*: JB. JB.
   > *Jack Buckley*: And this is my friend, Ernie.
   > *Gloria*: How do you do?
   > *Ernie Davis*: Very well.

   In this interaction, Gloria replied to Ernie in
   ( ) a formal way.   ( ) an informal way.

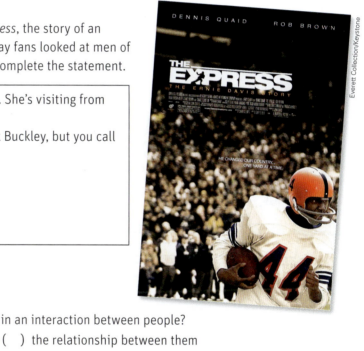

3. What factors determine the level of formality in an interaction between people?
   ( ) cultural background   ( ) the relationship between them
   ( ) age   ( ) other: _____
   ( ) the place where they are

4. Read the dialogue from the movie *The Express* again. Circle the parts in which someone introduces someone else to another person.

   Look at some other options for Jack Buckley to introduce Ernie Davis.

   > Option 1: Gloria, have you met Ernie?
   > Option 2: I'd like to introduce you to Ernie.

   Ernie could also have replied using one of the following options.

   > Option 1: Pleased to meet you.
   > Option 2: Nice to meet you.

Scene from *The Express* (from left: Rob Brown, Omar Benson Miller, Linara Washington, Nicole Beharie).

5. Practice formal and informal greetings according to each of the situations represented in the pictures. Choose expressions from the box below and complete the bubbles.

Greeting	Answering greeting	Greeting	Answering greeting
Formal	**Formal**	**Informal**	**Informal**
How do you do? Pleased to meet you. How are you? How are you doing? Nice to meet you. Good morning / afternoon /evening	How do you do? Pleased to meet you. I am fine, thank you, and you? I am fine, and you? Nice to meet you too. Good morning / afternoon / evening	How's you? Hello. Hi. Hiya. Hey! What's up?	Fine thanks. You? / Fine! Fine, and you? / I'm fine. / I'm OK. / I'm great! Hi. / Hello. / Hi there! / Hey. / Hiya.

a) Old friends meeting on the street

b) Teacher greeting students in the morning

c) Classmates meeting during the weekend

In formal situations, when you meet someone for the first time, you can say "How do you do" and shake hands. In informal situations you normally don't shake hands, but you can say and do "Give me five."

> Let's talk!

1. Let's play talent show! First, talk to your classmates using these questions.

   a) What kind of TV show is being represented in the pictures below?

   b) Do you know the woman in the picture?

   c) What questions is the man probably asking her?

   d) Do you think this contestant was successful?

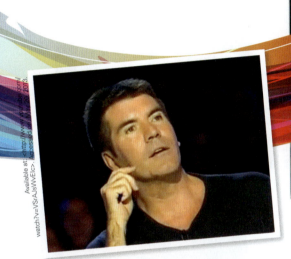

English TV producer Simon Cowell. Image captured from: <http://www.youtube.com/watch?v=JSDoPY9BOwQ>. Accessed on: October 30, 2013.

Scottish singer Susan Boyle. Image captured from: <http://www.youtube.com/watch?v=JSDoPY9BOwQ>. Accessed on: October 30, 2013.

2. Now it is your turn to interview or be interviewed. Have a similar conversation with a classmate. Use the information in the speech bubbles and vocabulary from the box.

actor	cartoonist	ceramist	clown	comedian
dancer	designer	graphic designer	gymnast	juggler
mime	musician	painter	rapper	sculptor	singer

Student A
(a member of a judging panel)
Greet your partner.
Ask his/her name.
Ask how old he/she is.
Ask where he/she is from.
Ask him/her what his/her talent is.

Student B
(a contestant)
Greet back.
Say your (artistic) name.
Say your age.
Say where you are from.
Say what your talent is.

21

UNIT

2 Street art

Language in action

- Learn about street art and reflect on it
- Learn how to talk about possibilities and abilities
- Develop an art project with graffiti

Graffiti in the borough of Brooklyn, New York City, USA.

Street art by the "guerilla" artist Banksy, London, England.

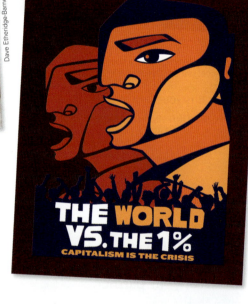

2010 Cow Parade, Manchester, England.

2011 Cow Parade, Rio de Janeiro, Brazil.

❯ Lead-in

1. Do you know a street artist? What kind of street art does he or she do?
   _____

2. Look at the images on the previous page and check (✔) the appropriate options below.
   a) The colors used in street art are
      ( ) light and soft.   ( ) vibrant and strong.
   b) The verbal element in these works is normally
      ( ) concise and short.   ( ) elaborated and long.

3. Read this blog entry and find the picture you can associate it with. Write the number.

   > Poster by Favianna Rodriguez: "As a woman of color, and as a Latina working predominantly in spaces that affect la Raza, the current moment offers me the opportunity to talk about how Wall Street has affected our families. In case you didn't see it, Pew Research Center recently released a report on how Latino Household Wealth fell by 66% from 2005 to 2009. That means we lost 2/3 of our community's assets! Now that's an important reason why Latinos should care about the Occupy movement."
   > Available at: <http://warincontext.org/2011/11/15/capitalism-is-the-crisis/>. Accessed on: October 30, 2013.

   The text refers to picture _____.

4. Based on the text in activity 3, what are the purposes of street art posters?
   ( ) to criticize society   ( ) to denounce abuse
   ( ) to decorate the walls   ( ) to promote films
   ( ) to make art popular   ( ) to address social issues

5. What do you think is (T)rue and (F)alse about the event represented in pictures 4 and 5?
   ( ) The Cow Parade is the largest and most successful public art event in the world.
   ( ) The material artists use to create these cows is bronze.
   ( ) It uses the cow as a symbol because this is a universally liked animal.
   ( ) The creators of these cows name them with funny titles using the words "cow" and "moo."
   ( ) Different artists are selected in a competition in each Cow Parade venue.
   ( ) The host cities only include places in the United States and Europe.

   > Read about the Cow Parade at <http://www.cowparade.com/our-story/> (accessed on: May 15, 2014).

▌ Did you know...?

Two Brazilian street artists are internationally famous for the quality and originality of their work. Their names are Otávio and Gustavo Pandolfo. Identical twins, the two brothers form the street art duo "Os Gêmeos."

Mural by "Os Gêmeos" installed in New York City, USA.

❯ Let's read!

Before you read...
- What do you know about the history of graffiti?
- Do you think everybody appreciates this type of work? Explain.

1. Read the first paragraph of the text below and check your answers in the previous activity.

Hint
Don't worry if the meaning of a word is unclear. The words around it and your knowledge about the topic can help you build meaning.

This text was posted on a website designed to be an online guide to life for teenagers and young adults. They provide information on other topics besides graffiti, from sex and exam stress to debt and drugs.

2. The text "Graffiti" was published on a webpage from the United Kingdom. Circle marks in the text indicating that it was created there.

3. Complete this chart with arguments for and against graffiti, based on the text. Then, on your notebook, make a similar chart adding more ideas to it.

FOR	AGAINST

4. What is the penalty in the UK if people do non-authorized graffiti?

   _____

5. Look at this illustration. Find a sentence in the text that describes this scene. Write it down.

   _____

   _____

6. Consider your answer in activity 5. Do you agree with this punishment? Tell your reasons to a classmate. You can use sentences as in these examples.

   I agree with this punishment because…

   I don't agree (disagree) with this punishment because…

7. Read these hypothetical situations in the UK and decide how much each person would probably have to pay as punishment.
   a) Someone draws graffiti on the wall of an important theater. The theater director spends £3,500 to remove the pictures and repaint the wall. £ _____
   b) A student does graffiti on a wall near his school. The police officers see him doing it and they immediately come to talk to him. £ _____
   c) The owner of a shop sells spray paint to a 14-year-old girl. He knows her age, but he doesn't hesitate to sell her the product. (up to £ _____)

   Beyond the lines…
   a) Is graffiti illegal in Brazil?
   b) How do you personally view graffiti: As art, vandalism, or what?

8. Do you agree that shopkeepers should be penalized if they sell spray paint to under-16s? Justify your answer.

   _____

9. Look at the two images below and discuss these questions with a classmate.
   a) Which scene do you consider art and which one do you consider vandalism?
   b) Based on the text "Graffiti", what punishment would you stipulate for the scene you consider vandalism here?

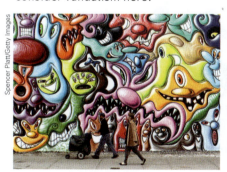

Did you know…?

Graffiti is the plural formal of *graffito*. It comes from the Italian word *graffio*, which means "a little scratch."

25

Vocabulary corner

1. Street art has many other forms of expression besides the ones presented so far. Match each form of street art (left column of the table below) to its corresponding definition.

FORMS	DEFINITIONS
a) graffiti	( ) used to propagate an image/message in public spaces with homemade stickers that commonly promote a political agenda, comment on a policy or issue
b) stencil	( ) process of digitally projecting a computer-manipulated image onto a surface via a light and projection system
c) sticker	( ) art of creating images with an assemblage of smaller parts or pieces, to resemble a single giant piece of art
d) mosaic	( ) painting on the surfaces of public or private property that is visible to the public, commonly with a can of spray paint or roll-on paint
e) video projection	( ) street art that uses 3-D objects and space to interfere with the urban environment
f) street installation	( ) painting with the use of a paper or cardboard cutout to create an image that can be easily reproduced

Adapted from: <http://artradarjournal.com/2010/01/21/what-is-street-art-vandalism-graffiti-or-public-art-part-i/>. Accessed on: October 30, 2013.

2. Now match each definition to its corresponding picture. Write the letters.

› Let's focus on language!

1. Read these excerpts from the text "Graffiti." What is the function of the words in bold?

   I. "So what are the laws around graffiti and where **can** you do it?"

   II. "[...] anyone caught doing graffiti **can** be arrested [...]"

   III. "These [fines] **can** be given out by police officers, community support officers or local authority officials."

   ( ) ability/inability   ( ) possibility/impossibility   ( ) permission/prohibition

2. Read the sentences above again. Which one(s)

   a) is/are about something that is possible to happen? _____

   b) ask(s) whether something is possible or not? _____

   > We use **can** or **can't** + **verb** to say that things are possible or impossible.
   > To ask if something is possible, we place **can** before the **subject**.

3. Now read another excerpt from the text "Graffiti" and check (✔) the function of the word in bold.

   "If a shopkeeper **can't** prove they took reasonable steps to determine the age of the person, they can be fined up to £2,500."

   ( ) inability   ( ) impossibility   ( ) prohibition

4. Read these additional sentences related to street art and check (✔) some other functions of **can**.

   a) "Anyone **can** become a street artist. A street artist is simply someone who does or displays art in public spaces."

   ( ) ability   ( ) possibility   ( ) permission

   b) "Chalk is short and thick, it is the only writing tool I **can** possibly hold [...]" (Cui Xianren, handicapped street artist)

   ( ) ability   ( ) possibility   ( ) permission

Chinese street calligrapher Cui Xianren using his damaged hands to write Chinese characters.

c) "Young adults **can** buy spray paint and markers"

( ) ability

( ) possibility

( ) permission

d) "What American street artists **can** learn from Egyptian graffiti"

( ) ability

( ) possibility

( ) permission

Sources: <http://www.wisegeek.com/how-do-i-become-a-street-artist.htm> (a); <http://www.chinadaily.com.cn/china/2011-10/25/content_13966136.htm> (b); <http://gothamist.com/2007/02/02/young_adults_ca.php> (c); <http://www.flavorwire.com/189155/what-american-street-artists-can-learn-from-egyptian-graffiti> (d). Accessed on: October 30, 2013.

5. The text "Graffiti" in the *Let's read!* section focuses on punishments involving graffiti in the UK. Read it again and answer these questions.

a) What can happen if a person is caught doing graffiti?

_____

b) What can happen if the damage costs more than £5,000?

_____

c) What can happen to owners if they don't clean up street furniture in 28 days?

_____

d) What can happen if a shopkeeper sells spray paint to under-16s?

_____

6. Look at the sentences in the previous activity. What is the function of **can** in all of them?

_____

7. Imagine you are a street artist. Decide what is possible to do with the following items. Write sentences as in the example provided.

a)

yarn

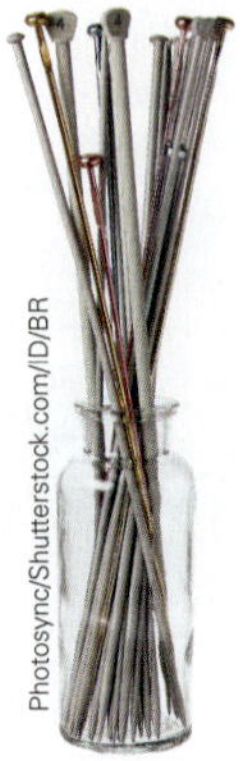

needles

I can do yarn bombing.

_____

_____

_____

b)

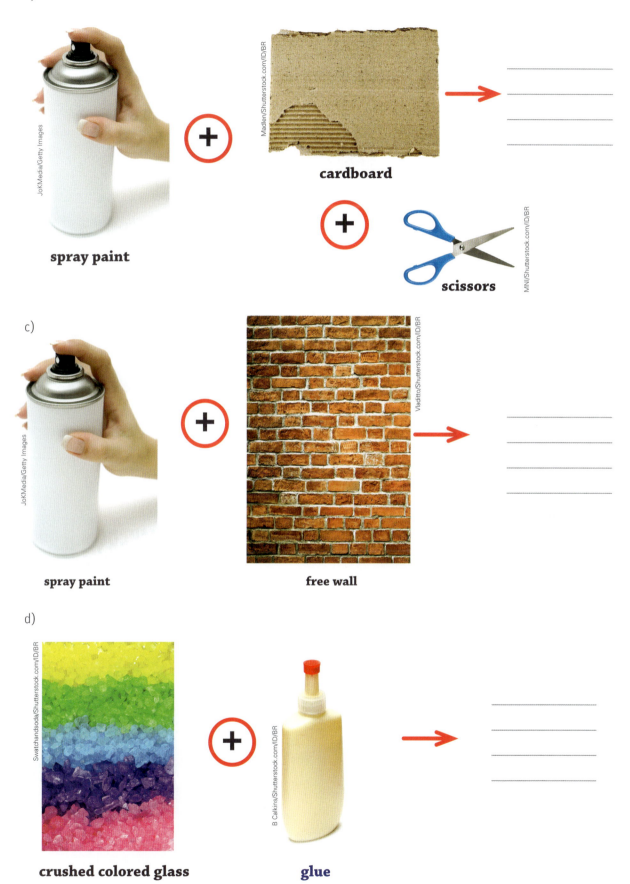

spray paint + cardboard + scissors →

c)

spray paint + free wall →

d)

crushed colored glass + glue →

e)

 + 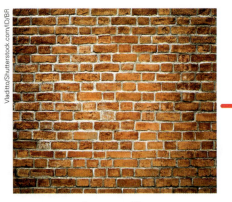 → _____

projector **free wall**

8. Look at these prohibition signs and rewrite the messages using the appropriate verb. The first one is done for you.

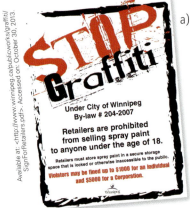

a) You can't sell spray paint to people under the age of 18.

d) _____

b) _____

e) _____

c) _____

f) _____

30

> Let's listen and talk!

Before you listen...
- Have you ever heard of moss graffiti?
- In your opinion, does moss graffiti add anything to the environment? In what ways?

1. 🔴2 In times of sustainability, some people are also using "green ideas" to do urban art. Listen to a tutorial about "moss graffiti" and answer these general questions.

   a) Who is speaking: a female presenter or a male presenter? _____

   b) Is this person a child or an adult? _____

2. 🔴2 Listen again and answer these specific questions.

   a) Which supplies are necessary for this type of art?

   ( ) some moss   ( ) a paintbrush   ( ) glue
   ( ) paint   ( ) buttermilk   ( ) chalk
   ( ) a blender   ( ) a measuring cup   ( ) butter
   ( ) milk   ( ) a spray bottle   ( ) a bucket
   ( ) water-retention gel ( ) scissors

   b) From where does the presenter get the moss? _____

   c) For how long do we have to blend the mixture?

   ( ) four to five minutes   ( ) three to five minutes   ( ) seven minutes

3. What can you do to be a clean, legal graffiti artist? Use the cues in this chart as a starting point to speak.

   | ask | consult | for permission | community representatives | free walls |
   | avoid | look for | legal graffiti initiatives | offensive language | |

   I can...

Pronunciation spot – Word stress

1. Stress is very important to English words. Put the seven words under the correct stress pattern: **sticker, permission, modernist, legibility, reasonable, manipulated, colorful, important, authorities, colored**.

●.	.●.	●..	●...	.●..	.●...	..●..
stencil	graffiti	gallery	prosecuted	ability	contemporary	possibility

   _____ _____ _____ _____ _____ _____ _____
   _____ _____ _____ _____ _____ _____ _____

2. 🔴3 Now listen and check your answers.

Let's act with words!

Create a graffiti of a cow for a Cow Parade event

First, read more about the Cow Parade event at <http://www.cowparade.com/> (accessed on: October 30, 2013).

Learn how to create graffiti and bring cow parade to your school. You can use a free online tool to design words in graffiti style. The link is <http://www.graffiticreator.net/> (accessed on: October 30, 2013).

Genre: Graffiti

Purpose: To be part of a cow parade art exhibition

Tone: Informal

Setting: School wall or blog

Writer: You or your group

Audience: School community or blog readers

Writing Steps

Organizing
- Option 1: Find a basic cow outline on the Web for you to customize.
- Option 2: Draw a big cow outline on paper and cut it with a pair of scissors. You can also use an old sheet of newspaper.
- Choose a theme for your cow.
- Think of words or short statements to create impact.
- Select adequate style and color(s) for your graffiti.

Preparing the first draft
- Make a first draft on your notebook or on an extra sheet of paper.

Peer editing
- Evaluate your work and discuss it with a classmate.
- Make the necessary corrections.

Publishing
- Paste your graffiti messages on your cow.
- Exhibit your cow on the school wall or make a digital version and publish it in your blog.

Go to Workbook, page 352, for more practice.

Learning tips

Improving your pronunciation with phonetic transcriptions

One of the ways to improve your pronunciation in English is to get more and more familiar with phonetic transcriptions. Phonetic transcriptions represent each distinct speech sound with a separate symbol. They are largely used in dictionaries. Look at some examples of phonetic symbols and some words exemplifying them.

ʊ → BOOK aɪ → MY æ → CAT θ → THINK ʒ → CASUAL ɪər → HERE ð → THE

ID/BR

You can use PhoTransEdit, an online tool that may help you improve your pronunciation. The earlier you start recognizing these symbols, the earlier you will guarantee more proficiency in English.

PHO TRANS EDIT

Fac-símile/
PhoTransEdit

This tool is available at <http://www.photransedit.com/Online/Text2Phonetics.aspx> (accessed on: May 9, 2014).

You type a word or a short text in English, then click on "transcribe" and, after a few seconds, you get the phonetic transcription. The next step is to try to pronounce the word or the sentence based on the result you get.

Let's reflect on learning!

You are now invited to assess what you learned and how you learned. Finish the ideas below on an extra sheet of paper and become a more autonomous and reflective learner.

In Part 1

I learned _____

I liked _____

I need to review/learn more _____

My experiences with English outside school were _____

_____

Let's study for Enem!

O objetivo desta seção, presente nas 12 partes do livro, é prepará-lo para o Enem. Você trabalhará com questões autênticas das últimas edições do Exame Nacional do Ensino Médio e também com questões do tipo "simulado". Nossa ideia é que você se familiarize com o tipo de questão proposta no Enem e que experimente usar estratégias de leitura para obter bons resultados.

Enem Questions

How's your mood?

Available at: <http://www.bbc.co.uk/news/magazine-17765401>. Accessed on: April 10, 2014.

Gênero
Artigo informativo

Competência de área 2
H6 - Utilizar os conhecimentos da LEM (Língua Estrangeira Moderna) e de seus mecanismos como meio de ampliar as possibilidades de acesso a informações, tecnologias e cultura.

For an interesting attempt to measure cause and effect try Mappiness, a project run by the London School of Economics, which offers a phone app that prompts you to record your mood and situation.

The Mappiness website says: "We're particularly interested in how people's happiness is affected by their local environment – air pollution, noise, green spaces, and so on – which the data from Mappiness will be absolutely great for investigating."

Will it work? With enough people, it might. But there are other problems. We've been using happiness and well-being interchangeably. Is that ok? The difference comes out in a sentiment like: "We were happier during the war." But was our well-being also greater then?

Disponível em: <http://www.bbc.co.uk>. Acesso em: 27 jun. 2011. Adaptado.

> Observe que a imagem ilustra a palavra *mood*, que significa "estado de espírito" (*happiness* = felicidade). Imagem e título já ajudam a deduzir/inferir o tema do texto. Mas não confie só na imagem! O sentido está na interação entre todos os elementos do texto: título, imagem e texto.

> As informações mais importantes no texto são parafraseadas. Por exemplo, *mood* = *people's happiness*; *situation* = *local environment*.

> Leia o enunciado com cuidado e identifique as palavras-chave que indicam o propósito da questão; no caso, "projeto *Mappiness*" e "ocupa-se". Em seguida, usando a estratégia de *scanning* (busca de informação específica), localize essas palavras ou seus sinônimos ("ocupa-se" = *offers*, *interested in*) no texto e leia os trechos onde elas são citadas para poder achar a resposta.

- O projeto *Mappiness*, idealizado pela *London School of Economics*, ocupa-se do tema relacionado

   A ao nível de felicidade das pessoas em tempos de guerra.
   B à dificuldade de medir o nível de felicidade das pessoas a partir de seu humor.
   C ao nível de felicidade das pessoas enquanto falam ao celular com seus familiares.
   D à relação entre o nível de felicidade das pessoas e o ambiente no qual se encontram.
   E à influência das imagens grafitadas pelas ruas no aumento do nível de felicidade das pessoas.

Extraído de: Exame Nacional do Ensino Médio, 2011, Caderno 7 – AZUL – Página 2 (questão 93).

Part 1 (Express Yourself)

Typical questions of Enem

Antes de resolver as questões propostas aqui e nas demais seções do livro, identifique o gênero do texto. Observe título e imagem (se houver). Ative seu conhecimento prévio sobre o tema e passe os olhos rapidamente sobre o texto para perceber as ideias principais. Em seguida, leia as instruções e o texto. Procure responder à questão antes de ler as opções. Tente inferir o significado pelo contexto, considerando que as palavras conhecidas ou com grafia parecida com a do português vão ajudá-lo a construir o sentido.

1.

Available at: <http://www.thetalentstore.net/>. Accessed on: March 1, 2013.

The Talent Store is a networking source for entertainment agencies, businesses, and individuals or groups who are seeking job or gig opportunities, discovery, exposure, online community support, and advice.

Our services are targeted to a wide variety of people who either provide a service to, or are a part of, the entertainment industry. The list of services includes, but is not limited to: singers, dancers, actors, comedians, technicians, camera operators, stage hands, clowns, mimes, cartoonists, parade organizers, and event planners. Create your FREE profile today!

Available at: <http://www.thetalentstore.net/>. Accessed on: January 14, 2013.

O serviço oferecido por esse anúncio na internet é dirigido a

( ) agências de entretenimento e pessoas que querem trabalho ou divulgar seu perfil.

( ) artistas amadores que querem se preparar para participar de um *show* de talentos.

( ) atores que querem ter o nome incluído em catálogo impresso para agenciar talentos.

( ) empresas que apoiam a indústria de divulgação e preparação de novos talentos.

( ) prestadores de serviço que trabalham como caça-talentos para a indústria de *shows*.

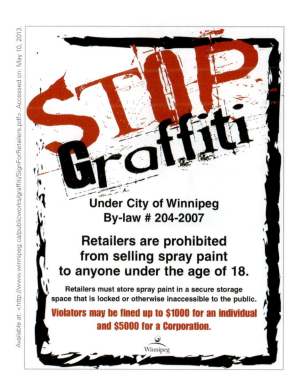

Available at: <http://www.winnipeg.ca/publicworks/graffiti/SignForRetailers.pdf>. Accessed on: May 10, 2013.

2. A prefeitura da cidade de Winnipeg tem enfrentado problemas com grafite. Este cartaz faz parte da campanha de prevenção ao vandalismo e tem por objetivo

a) ( ) alertar os comerciantes sobre a proibição de venda de tinta *spray* a menores de idade.

b) ( ) estabelecer uma política de venda de tinta *spray* a pessoas que não moram na cidade.

c) ( ) estipular o preço da multa a ser paga por todos que grafitarem na cidade de Winnipeg.

d) ( ) incentivar a população a denunciar grafiteiros que usam tinta *spray* sem permissão.

e) ( ) orientar todos os jovens com menos de dezoito anos a grafitar com responsabilidade.

Exam Practice Questions (Vestibular)

Esta seção, presente nas 12 partes do livro, traz questões de vestibular de diversas universidades. Ao resolver essas questões fazendo uso das dicas apresentadas, você vai se aprimorar em relação às questões de vestibular e Enem, além de se preparar para outros tipos de exames. Aproveite essa oportunidade e continue exercitando as estratégias de leitura que você já conhece.

Test-Taking Tips

Be a regular reader!

Read weekly magazines and newspapers, both in English and in Portuguese, on a regular basis. The more familiar you are with world events, the more chances you will have to do well on exams. That piece of news you have read in your free time may be related to a question you will find on an exam paper! Consider *Text 2*, for example. Lots of texts about the show OVO, produced by *Cirque du Soleil*, circulated in the media. Students who had previously read about it certainly found the task easier. Below are some links for you to get started:

- <http://www.newseum.org/todaysfrontpages/default.asp> The Newseum displays the front pages of more than 800 newspapers worldwide each day.
- <www.onlinenewspapers.com/> This service offers thousands of newspapers listed by country and region. (Both sites accessed on January 14, 2014.)

TEXT 1 – Questions 1 and 2
Uneb-BA, 2010

1. The girl in this cartoon
   a) (   ) is encouraging her boyfriend to be a musician.
   b) (   ) would like to go to college with her boyfriend.
   c) (   ) thinks that a career as a musician is not very promising.
   d) (   ) thinks that a musician makes more money than a lawyer.
   e) (   ) says that she won't get married with a musician.

2. About the boy in this cartoon, it's correct to say:
   a) (   ) He's got short, black hair.
   b) (   ) He's wearing modern clothes.
   c) (   ) He seems to like his girlfriend's suggestion.
   d) (   ) He looks rather sad in the second picture.
   e) (   ) He seems not to enjoy being a musician.

TEXT 2 – Questions 3 and 4
Cefet-MG, 2012

Read the text below and answer the two questions.

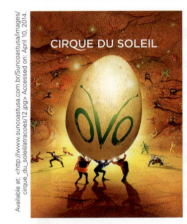

OVO is a headlong rush into a colourful ecosystem teeming with life, where insects work, eat, crawl, flutter, play, fight and look for love in a non-stop riot of energy and movement. The insects' home is a world of biodiversity and beauty filled with noisy action and moments of quiet emotion.

When a mysterious egg appears in their midst, the insects are awestruck and intensely curious about this iconic object that represents the enigma and cycles of their lives.

It's love at first sight when a gawky, quirky insect arrives in this bustling community and a fabulous ladybug catches his eye – and the feeling is mutual.

OVO is overflowing with contrasts. The hidden, secret world at our feet is revealed as tender and torrid, noisy and quiet, peaceful and chaotic. And as the sun rises on a bright new day the vibrant cycle of insect life begins anew.

Part 1 (Express yourself)

What the media say about the show:
"*Overhead and on-the-ground, OVO is a whimsical infestation.*"
"*It captivates as a vibrant, magical spectacle.*"
Chicago Now
audience reviews

 Average: 4.4 Votes: 196

Read all critics and reviews > >

Adapted from: <http://www.cirquedusoleil.com/en/shows/ovo/show/about.aspx>. Access in: September, 2011.

3. Cirque du Soleil's new show, OVO, tells the story of
   a) ( ) an insect infestation in a farmhouse.
   b) ( ) a gigantic and mysterious insect egg.
   c) ( ) insects who fall in love with a ladybug.
   d) ( ) three little insects who are best friends.
   e) ( ) an immersion into the world of insects.

4. The dash (–) in the third paragraph is used to
   a) ( ) contrast two elements.
   b) ( ) mark off a nested clause.
   c) ( ) present a word definition.
   d) ( ) provide an exemplification.
   e) ( ) introduce a person's speech.

- **TEXT 3 – Questions 5 to 7**
  UENP-PR, 2013

Painting the Fence

The sun was shining and the birds were singing and Tom was painting Aunt Polly's fence. The work was proceeding very slowly when Ben arrived.

"Do you want to go swimming?" he asked.

Tom wanted to go swimming more than anything else in the world, but he didn't answer. He stepped back and admired his painting.

"What a pity you have to work!" said Ben.

"Oh. Hello, Ben. I didn't see you," answered Tom.

"That's hard work! Poor you!" Ben sympathized.

"Work? This is fun! And only I can do it. Aunt Polly says so!"

Ben looked at what Tom was doing again. It looked different now, it looked interesting and desirable.

"Can I do some painting?" he asked.

"I am sorry, Ben. It's special work, you know. You can't do it, only I can do it."

"I'll give you my apple if you let me paint," Ben offered.

"I don't know. I really don't know. OK. But only as a special favor."

Then, Ben started to paint the fence and Tom sat and watched him work. He ate the apple, which tasted better than any apple in the world. Other friends arrived and from them he also collected a kite, a toy soldier, a kitten with only one eye, some oranges and other "valuable treasures."

Tom had a wonderful day. He rested a lot, he talked a lot, he received a lot of gifts, but he didn't paint very much; however, at the end of the afternoon, Aunt's Polly fence looked marvelous. Tom discovered a great law about human nature that day: if you want someone to do something, you must tell them that they can't do it.

Adapted from *Adventures of Tom Sawyer*, by Mark Twain.

5. De acordo com o texto, assinale a alternativa correta.
   a) ( ) Tom pediu a ajuda de Ben para pintar a cerca da casa de sua tia.
   b) ( ) Tia Polly pediu para Tom e Ben pintarem a cerca de sua casa.
   c) ( ) Tom deu aos amigos seus "tesouros" para que eles o ajudassem a pintar a cerca da casa de sua tia.
   d) ( ) Tom não podia ir nadar com seus amigos, pois tinha que pintar a cerca da casa de sua tia.
   e) ( ) Tom passou o dia pintando a cerca da casa de sua tia enquanto todos seus amigos foram nadar.

6. Qual foi a grande descoberta de Tom sobre a natureza humana?
   a) ( ) Se você quiser que alguém faça algo, deve dizer para não fazê-lo.
   b) ( ) Se você quiser evitar que alguém faça algo, deve proibi-lo de fazer.
   c) ( ) As pessoas não sentem atração pelo que é proibido.
   d) ( ) As pessoas preferem se divertir ao invés de trabalhar.
   e) ( ) As pessoas sentem curiosidade a respeito do trabalho alheio.

7. Choose the correct alternative according to the use of the ING FORM.
   a) ( ) to agree – agreing; to be – being; to shine – shining.
   b) ( ) to get – getting; to run – running; to swim – swimming.
   c) ( ) to begin – beginning; to open – openning; to prefer – preferring.
   d) ( ) to die – dying; to lie – lying; to ski – skying.
   e) ( ) to play – playing; to say – saying; to study – studing.

PART

2

Move Your Body

Learning plan

Talking about body movements

Learning to talk about things that happen regularly

Talking about and discussing music and things related to it

Learning to ask different types of questions

Creating flyers

Let's learn how to create a speaking avatar

Express yourself through **Voki**. Go to <http://www.voki.com> (accessed on: October 24, 2013) and learn how to create your own avatar.

You can record your own voice speaking or singing and your avatar will have your voice. You can also type a text and text-to-speech technology will take care of it.

Voki users have created useful tutorials to help you. Watch some of them to learn how to use this Web tool more successfully. Some options:

<http://www.youtube.com/embed/3O4rQXcBrp4> (accessed on: October 24, 2013)

<http://www.youtube.com/embed/vMSKmVhakFE> (accessed on: October 24, 2013)

Improve your oral skills and have fun!

UNIT

3 You've got the moves

Language in action

- Talk about body movements
- Discuss topics related to losing weight
- Learn to talk about things that happen regularly

Jorge Hierrezuelo Marcillis

Country
Cuba

Birth date	Gender	Classification
11/04/1983	M	B2

Sport: Judo
Men's – 90 kg

Hobbies: Music
Occupation: Teacher (Athlete, 30 Oct 2011)
Language(s) spoken: Spanish
Coach: Senen Ramos (CUB) since 2003
Handedness: Left

Adapted from: <http://www.london2012.com/paralympics/athlete/hierrezuelo-marcillis-jorge-5501069/>. Accessed on: January 20, 2013.

40

› Lead-in

1. With a classmate, identify the activities in the images on the previous page. Write the numbers.

( ) gafieira samba dancing   ( ) running   ( ) classical ballet

( ) breakdancing/b-boying   ( ) wrestling   ( ) belly dancing

( ) flamenco dancing   ( ) folk/regional dancing   ( ) capoeira playing

( ) contemporary dancing   ( ) martial arts   ( ) ritual dancing

2. How do you like to move your body? Which of the ideas below would you add to the list in activity 1?

( ) going to the gym   ( ) cycling   ( ) swimming

( ) jogging   ( ) hiking   ( ) other: _____

3. *I move my body to...* Consider the activities you do to move your body. Tell a classmate what your reasons are, using ideas from the box below.

> keep fit   have fun   socialize   stay healthy

4. Read five quotations related to the human body. Match each text to one of the topics in the box.

> (1) equality   (2) health   (3) pleasure   (4) motivation   (5) overcoming adversity

"Let us read, and let us dance; these two amusements will never do any harm to the world." – *Voltaire*

Available at: <http://www.goodreads.com/quotes/tag/dance>.
Accessed on: October 24, 2013.

"Champions aren't made in the gyms. Champions are made from something they have deep inside them – a desire, a dream, a vision." – *Muhammad Ali*

Available at: <http://sportpsych.unt.edu/resources/athletes/31>.
Accessed on: October 24, 2013.

"What's so special about dance is – everyone is equal, it doesn't matter where you are from or what background you have." – *RBS [Royal Ballet School] Student*

Available at: <http://www.royal-ballet-school.org.uk/dpa.php?s=1>.
Accessed on: October 24, 2013.

"I was slightly brain damaged at birth, and I want people like me to see that they shouldn't let a disability get in the way. I want to raise awareness – I want to turn my disability into ability." – *Susan Boyle*

Available at: <http://www.disabled-world.com/disability/disability-quotes.php#ixzz28HASi2mM>.
Accessed on: October 24, 2013.

"Dance is a song of the body. Either of joy or pain." – *Martha Graham*

Available at: <http://www.quotegarden.com/dancing.html>. Accessed on: October 24, 2013.

5. Look at the profile on the previous page. What does the information "Classification B2" suggest about Jorge?

_____

Beyond the lines...

a) Are there places offering free physical activities in your community? If so, do you use them?

b) Why do people in some cultures tend to "move their bodies" more spontaneously than people in other cultures?

▶ Turn on the jukebox!

Before you listen…

- Make a list of as many aerobic actions as you can think of.

1. 🔊 **4** Listen to the song below and check if it mentions any actions from your list.

Move Your Body
(by Beyoncé Knowles)

Whoo!
Clap your hands now! (4x)
Jump! (8x)

Mission One, let me see you run
Put your knees up in the sky 'cause we just begun
Hey! Hey!
Mission Two, this is how we do
Shuffle, shuffle to the right, to the left, let's move!
Hey! Hey!
Mission Three, can you dougie with me?
Throw your own little swag on this Swizzy beat
Hey! Hey!
Mission Four, if you're ready for more
Jump rope, jump rope, get your feet off the floor
Hey! Hey!

Chorus
I ain't worried, doing me tonight
A little sweat ain't never hurt nobody
Don't just stand there on the wall
Everybody, just move your body
Move your body (4x)
Everybody, won't you move your body? (2x)
Can you get me bodied? I wanna be myself tonight (2x)
Wanna move my body, I wanna let it out tonight
Wanna party, wanna dance
Wanna be myself tonight!

Mission Five, come here, let's go
Time to move your little hips, vámonos, vámonos
Hey! Hey!
Mission Six, bring it back real quick

Do the Running Man and then turn around like this
Hey! Hey!
Mission Seven, time to break it down
Step and touch to the dancehall sound
Hey! Hey!
Mission Eight, feel that heart beat race
Snap your fingers, tap your feet, just keep up with this pace
Hey! Hey!
(Repeat Chorus)

Fellas on the floor, all my ladies on the floor
Everybody get ready to move your body!

Baby all I want is to let it go
Ain't no worries, no
We can dance all night
Move your body
That means come closer to me
While we dance to the beat
Move your body…

Now run to the left, to the left, to the left
Now run to the left, to the left
Now run to the right, to the right, to the right
Run back to the right, to the right (Repeat)

Now wave the American flag
Wave the American flag (3x)
Hey!
[Swizz Beatz]
Now cool off, cool off
We can do it now…
Hey!

Available at: <http://www.metrolyrics.com/request.php?lyricid=1189359429&dothis=printlyrics>.
Accessed on: January 21, 2013.

Beyoncé Knowles, American singer who also starred in several films.

Did you know…?

The word "wanna" is the reduction of "want to" and it is commonly used in oral language.

2. The word "ain't" appears three times in the lyrics with different meanings. Find the sentence that corresponds to each meaning below. Write it down.

a) **ain't** = *hasn't* _____

b) **ain't** = *there aren't* _____

c) **ain't** = *am not* _____

3. ◎**4** Listen to the song again and match each "mission" below to one of its specific actions.

Mission 1	( ) shuffle to the right
Mission 2	( ) move your little hips
Mission 3	( ) break it down
Mission 4	( ) put your knees up

Mission 5	( ) snap your fingers
Mission 6	( ) dougie with me
Mission 7	( ) do the "Running Man"
Mission 8	( ) jump rope

4. Look at these illustrations. Use some of the actions in activity 3 to label each picture.

Illustrations: Estúdio Mil/IDBR

a) _____

b) _____

c) _____

d) _____

5. What other body movements can we find in the lyrics? Check (✔) the correct options.

( ) clap your hands   ( ) get ready   ( ) wave

( ) jump   ( ) dance   ( ) bring it back

( ) kneel   ( ) turn around   ( ) run

( ) get your feet off the floor   ( ) let it go   ( ) let it out

( ) stand   ( ) touch   ( ) tap your feet

6. Does your school offer any kind of physical activity after classes? If not, would you like to have it? If so, do all students take part in it?

_____

Pronunciation spot – Aspiration /k/ & /t/

The sounds /k/ and /t/ are easy consonants for you to say. Just remember that in the initial position and in stressed syllables they are explosive in English.

1. ◎**5** Listen to the words and practice their pronunciation.

| /k/ | clap | cool | 'cause | keep | come |
| /t/ | two | to | time | turn | touch |

2. ◎**6** Now, practice the aspiration in these tongue twisters. Then listen to the recording and compare.

A proper cup of coffee from a proper copper coffee pot.
If a canner can can ten cans a day, how many cans can ten canners can today?
Two toads, totally tired.
The two-twenty-two train tore through the tunnel.

43

> Let's read!

Before you read…
- What type(s) of physical activities do you do? Consider activities like dancing, doing aerobics, or practicing sports.
- Do you really believe that keeping our body active is good for our health? Why (not)?

Hint
It is helpful to learn how to **select what is relevant** when reading a text.

1. Look at the text below. Some words were highlighted in bold in it. Why did the author decide to do this? Choose the best option.

   ( ) To embellish the text
   ( ) To call our attention to central ideas
   ( ) To highlight somebody else's ideas

Dancing: A Cool Way To Lose Weight

Written By: Deva / May 6, 2012 / Posted In: Weight loss

So you want to **lose weight**, but are not ready to try out sweaty **workouts** or **yoga Asanas**. Even **Aerobics** seems tepid to you; then I have a suggestion. Start tapping your feet now. Dance is the **best way to lose weight** as you will not get bored from monotonous workouts. You can move your body freely and **burn calories** by sweating with joy. Today dancing has become the **most preferable way to lose weight** and stay fit. […]

Here are a few popular dancing styles for losing weight

Hip-hop: This is a **high intensity dancing style** mainly chosen for high workout to get a flat belly. This **style of dancing** is a very fast dance procedure, with fast movements, locking, breaking and popping. It would be more fun to move along fast beats and shed weight. At an average, a 68Kg person can burn 316 calories after an hour dance.

Belly Dancing: A very famous dancing style today, this is loved especially by girls. It helps in getting a well toned abdomen. This is a very different kind of dance where a person has to move his/her hips and the abdomen. It is **healthy for cardiac problems** and you can burn calories equivalent to **walking, bicycling or swimming**. At an average, a 68Kg person can burn 250-200 calories after an hour dance. […]

So what are you waiting for? Put on those dancing shoes and get on the floor. Pump your body with the music and let the rhythm help you lose your mental and physical stress. Lose weight and dance yourself to a fitter, slimmer you!

Available at: <http://www.thelivingwine.com/blog/dancing-a-cool-way-to-lose-weight/>.
Accessed on: October 24, 2013.

This text was posted in a blog that deals basically with ideas for people to take care of their bodies. Besides the section *Weight loss*, they offer *Yoga*, *Health & Fitness*, *Food*, *Hair styles*, among others. Most articles in this section are written by Deva.

2. Now answer these general questions about the text.

a) What kind of physical activity is the author focusing on?

_____

b) What tip does the author give readers?

_____

c) Where was this text originally published? How do you know?

_____

_____

3. Who does this text seem to be mostly addressed to? How do you know?

_____

4. Read the text more carefully now and decide if the following statements are true (**T**) or false (**F**).

a) One hour of belly dancing burns over 300 calories. (   )

b) Belly dancing evolved from workout. (   )

c) Dancing is the best activity to stay fit. (   )

d) In belly dancing, results are better for 68Kg people. (   )

e) Hip-hop is a good exercise for the abdomen. (   )

f) Dancing is a monotonous activity. (   )

5. Find words in the text with the equivalent meaning of the words below.

a) boring _____

b) in shape _____

c) strong (abdomen) _____

d) lose weight _____

e) to evaluate by experience _____

Beyond the lines...

a) The text does not mention any research which supports the statement "Today dancing has become the most preferable way to lose weight and stay fit." Is it true in the city where you live?

b) What are some of the reasons why people want to gain or lose weight?

c) Why do you think the author wants to persuade readers that dancing is a solution to lose weight?

45

› Let's listen and talk!

Before you listen...
- Look at the text below. What is it used for?
- Do you use something similar to this in your daily life?

Hint
Focus your attention on the vocabulary that may be keywords in a specific text.

1. 🔴 7 Take a look at this week organizer. Listen and complete the diary with one day in James Forbat's (English National Ballet soloist) life.

A Day in the Life of a Dancer

January 2015

8:00 am
Wake up
Have cereal for breakfast

10:30 am

12:30 pm

5:30 pm

7:30 pm

10:30 pm

English National Ballet's dancers James Forbat and Adela Ramirez, 2010.

7 monday

2. Let's play Bingo! Go around the class and find someone who answers *yes* to the questions. Complete six squares in the table below by writing in the name of your classmates.

does aerobic exercises	likes working out	knows someone with a disability
wants to learn how to dance	wants to work with sports	goes dancing regularly
takes part in live performances	has any kind of physical impairment	enjoys playing sports

❯ Let's focus on language!

1. Read the statements below taken from the transcription of the listening section. Then answer the question and read the rule.

   "I **never get up** before eight, which **sounds** really good, but we **don't finish** till late."

   "After class there**'s usually** a short break, 15 minutes when the studio**'s** available [...]"

   "After the show you **sometimes feel** exhilarated, but usually I**'m** just tired."

   Do the excerpts above refer to something that happens regularly?

   (   ) Yes, they do.

   (   ) No, they don't.

   > When we want to talk about things that happen regularly, we use the Simple Present. We add **–s** or **–es** to the verb when the subject is third person singular (e.g. My energy drop**s**).
   >
   > When we want to say how frequently something happens, we can use words such as *always* and *never*. Other possible words are *sometimes*, *often*, *usually*, among others.

2. Read one of the quotations from the *Lead-in* section again and circle the appropriate option to complete the rule to make negatives.

   "What's so special about dance is — everyone is equal, it **doesn't matter** where you are from or what background you have."

   > To make a negative statement in the Simple Present, we use **do** / **does** + *not* + verb when the subject is third person singular and use **do** / **does** + *not* + verb when the subject is any of the other persons.
   >
   > The contraction of **do** + *not* is **don't**. The contraction of **does** + *not* is **doesn't**.

3. Order the words below according to the frequency they suggest.

> usually   sometimes   seldom   hardly ever
> rarely   often   occasionally   never   frequently   always

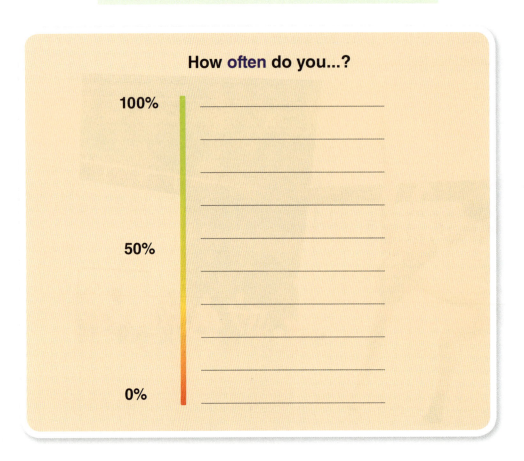

4. Work in pairs: each student reads the information from one of the cards (card A on this page and card B on the next page). Then do the activities below to find out about two athletes who overcame their physical impairments.

   a) Ask questions to complete the missing information on the first part of profiles 1 and 2. Use the information on cards A and B and the prompts below to help you.

   > Where/from?   What/type of disability/have?   How old…?
   > What/do?   Where/go to school?
   > What/main style?   What/current rank?

   b) Complete the texts of the profiles with an appropriate verb form. Choose the correct form from the options provided in the green boxes.

   Student A
   18. High school student. Hillsboro High School, Hillsboro, OR. Quadruple amputee from a blood infection at 5 years old. Wrestling.

Profile 1

DUSTIN CARTER
HOMETOWN: _____
TYPE OF DISABILITY: _____
_____
AGE: _____
OCCUPATION: _____
MAIN STYLE OF MARTIAL ART: _____
SCHOOL AFFILIATION: _____

Dustin Carter (right) in his match against Jason Ballantyne in the 103-pound bout during a championship in Virginia, USA.

Carter is a 103-pounder whose legs (1) _____ at his hips, whose right arm (2) _____ just after his elbow, and whose left arm (3) _____ even shorter. He had the rest taken from him at age 5 because of a blood infection that required extensive amputations. His life (4) _____ easy, but he (5) _____ by just fine — particularly on the wrestling mat. [...]

> am/is/are
> am not/is not/are not
> end/ends
> get/gets
> stop/stops

Adapted from: <http://martialartistwithdisabilities.blogspot.com.br/>. Accessed on: October 24, 2013.

Profile 2

JESSICA COX
HOMETOWN: _____
TYPE OF DISABILITY: _____
AGE: _____
OCCUPATION: _____
MAIN STYLE OF MARTIAL ART: _____
CURRENT RANK: _____

Jessica is recognized internationally as an inspirational keynote speaker. Born without arms, Jessica now (6) _____ airplanes, (7) _____ cars, and otherwise (8) _____ a normal life using her feet as others use their hands. She (9) _____ the title of the first person without arms in the American Taekwondo Association to get a black belt and the first woman pilot in aviation history to fly with her feet. Convinced that the way we think (10) _____ a greater impact on our lives than our physical constraints, she chose to pursue a degree in psychology while in college at the University of Arizona.

> fly/flies
> have/has
> hold/holds
> live/lives
> drive/drives

Adapted from: <http://martialartistwithdisabilities.blogspot.com.br/>. Accessed on: October 25, 2013.

Student B
25. Black Belt. Born without arms. Professional motivational speaker. Taekwondo. Tucson, AZ.

UNIT 4 Sing it out

Language in action
- Learn to talk about music
- Learn to ask different types of questions
- Learn to create a flyer

1 Music makes the people come together / Music mix the bourgeoisie and the rebel
(Madonna)

3 I blow thru here / The music goes 'round and around / Whoa-ho-ho-ho-ho-ho / And it comes out here
(Ella Fitzgerald)

2 I love rock n' roll / So put another dime in the jukebox, baby
(Guns N' Roses)

4 Cause there's country music in my soul / People music for the young and the old / I'll keep on singing a song, keep on keeping on / Cause there's country music in my soul
(Bill Anderson)

LISTEN  **PLAY**  **SING**

5 Hey mister music, sure sounds good to me / I can't refuse it, what to be got to be / Feel like dancing, dance cause we are free / Feel like dancing, come dance with me
(Bob Marley)

6 It ain't nothin' like hip hop music / Careful how you use it and please don't abuse it when you do it / Music can keep the party people dancin' and put your mind in a trance and keep you happy
(Bone Thugs-N-Harmony)

Excerpts available at: <http://letras.mus.br>. Accessed on: October 25, 2013.

> Lead-in

1. Discuss these questions with a classmate.
   a) Do you like music? What music style(s) do you usually listen to? Explain what you like about it/them.
   b) Do you prefer online radio or traditional radio to listen to music? What's your favorite radio station?
   c) Do you play any instruments? Which one? If you don't, which one would you like to play?

2. Read the excerpts of lyrics on the left page. What is the common theme in all of them?

_____

3. Below are the artists that recorded and performed the six songs on the previous page. Match each verse to its corresponding performer(s). Write the number.

Now answer: Did you already know these artists? Do you especially like any of them? Who?

_____

4. Songs often contain very informal language. This includes contracted forms, abbreviations, and non-standard grammar or dialect. Read the verses on the previous page again and find some cases of informality in the text. Write them down.

_____
_____

5. What other examples of informal language used in lyrics can you think of?

_____

6. Do a search to get more information about the songs on the previous page. You can search for the music style of each song, the title of each song, other artists that recorded and performed these songs (Did they sing them in different styles?), etc.

Let's read!

Before you read...
- Do you like concerts? How do you prefer to watch them: Live, on DVD, or online?
- What types of advertising techniques are used to promote concerts in your region? Think about flyers, blogs, radio, ads on cars, local TV channel, billboards, etc.

Hint
Notice that the **main pieces of information are salient** in the text.

Text 1

Flyer promoting Brazil Summer Fest 2012 featuring (L-R) Bebel Gilberto, DJ Dolores, Flávio Renegado, Criolo, Mauricio Pessoa, Jorge Continentino (Pifanology), Mallu Magalhães, Luísa Maita, and Sérgio Dias (Mutantes).

Available at: <http://www.brasilsummerfest.com/?page_id=384>. Accessed on: October 25, 2013.

Text 2

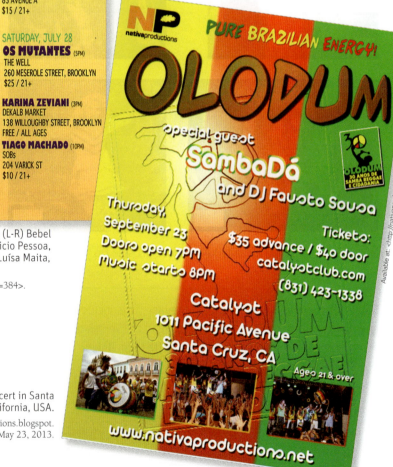

Flyer promoting an Olodum concert in Santa Cruz, California, USA.

Available at: <http://nativaproductions.blogspot.com.br/>. Accessed on: May 23, 2013.

1. Both texts 1 and 2 are examples of

( ) invitations. ( ) flyers. ( ) postcards. ( ) booklets.

2. Check (✓) the reasons why these two texts were created. More than one answer is possible.
   ( ) To promote Brazilian music festivals in the United States
   ( ) To inform about the ticket prices of each music festival
   ( ) To present biographical information about the artists
   ( ) To highlight the companies and organizations sponsoring the event
   ( ) To inform the date, place, and schedule of the events
   ( ) To describe the products and gifts that will be sold in the events
   ( ) To show images that can help interested people identify the artists quicker

3. Read these statements. Which text does each piece of information correspond to? Check (✓) the appropriate column.

	Text 1	Text 2
a) The event happens during one evening.		
b) The event consists of eight days of attractions.		
c) The ticket prices vary depending on when the ticket is bought.		
d) The ticket prices vary depending on the attraction.		
e) The event has one main attraction and two guests.		
f) The name of the event is related to a period of the year when a particular type of weather is expected.		
g) The event features different artists with different genres.		
h) The event defines an age limit.		

4. The events shown on the previous page are composed of Brazilian artists who are famous abroad. Can you think of other artists from Brazil that are also known internationally?

5. The following websites are about famous social projects that involve music. Visit these links and make notes about how these projects help children around the world. Share your notes with your classmates.

Afroreggae: <http://www.afroreggae.org/>. Accessed on: October 25, 2013.

El Sistema: <http://elsistemausa.org/el-sistema/venezuela/>. Accessed on: October 25, 2013.

Atlanta Music Project: <http://atlantamusicproject.org/>. Accessed on: October 25, 2013.

Do you know other social projects which involve music in your country or region? Use the Internet or any other source to search about this topic. Present your results to your classmates.

53

› Turn on the jukebox!

Hint
Listening to a song many times can help you understand it.

1. Look at the title of the song below. What is unusual in the way the composer wrote it? How would you pronounce this title?

2. ◎ 8 The singer tells a story in this song. Listen to it and number the stanzas in the correct order.

Sk8r boi
(by Avril Lavigne)

He was a boy, she was a girl
Can I make it any more obvious?
He was a punk, she did ballet
What more can I say?
He wanted her, she'd never tell,
Secretly she wanted him as well
And all of her friends stuck up their nose,
They had a problem with his baggy clothes.

He was a skater boy, she said
"see you later boy"
He wasn't good enough for her
She had a pretty face, but her head was up in space
She needed to come back down to earth

Sorry girl, but you missed out
Well, tough luck, that boy's mine now
We are more than just good friends
This is how the story ends
Too bad that you couldn't see
See the man that boy could be
There is more than meets the eye
I see the soul that is inside.

He was a skater boy, she said "see you later boy"
He wasn't good enough for her
Now he's a superstar, slammin' on his guitar
Does your pretty face see what he's worth? (2x)

I'm with the skater boy, I said "see you later boy"
I'll be backstage after the show
I'll be at the studio singing the song we wrote
About the girl you used to know (2x)

He's just a boy, and I'm just a girl
Can I make it any more obvious?
We are in love,
Haven't you heard how we rock each other's world?

Five years from now, she sits at home,
Feeding the baby, she's all alone
She turns on TV, guess who she sees?
Skater boy rockin' up MTV.
She calls up her friends, they already know,
And they've all got tickets to see his show
She tags along, stands in the crowd
Looks up at the man that she turned down.

Available at: <http://www.vagalume.com.br/avril-lavigne/sk8er-boy.html>. Accessed on: October 25, 2013.

Shutterstock.com/ID/BR

3. Considering the theme of the song, the title, and the layout, what age group is it aimed at? Do you think it appeals more to girls or boys? Why?

_____

4. This song is about the relationship between a girl and a boy. The girl thinks they can't be together because of the differences between them. Think about other songs (any style) that tell similar stories. You can even consider songs in your own language.

_____

2 ■ Move Your Body

54

❯ Let's focus on language!

1. The two questions below were taken from the song "Sk8r Boi". Match each one of them to its expected kind of answer.

   a) "What more can I say?" (   ) a "Yes" or "No" answer

   b) "Does your pretty face see what he's worth?" (   ) an answer that provides some information

2. Read the rules below and decide if they are about YES/NO questions or WH-questions.

   - The _____ start with an auxiliary verb followed by the subject and the verb.
   - The _____ start with a question word followed by an auxiliary verb, the subject, and the verb.

3. Get to know more about a classmate's musical interests. Sit together and ask him or her questions using the prompts below. Write out the questions and your classmate's answers in the spaces provided.

Do you…?	Questions	His/Her answers
download / music / Web		
ever / go / music / concerts		
listen / radio programs / every day		
play / any / musical instruments		
read / lyrics / Internet / usually		

4. Now sit with another classmate and ask the same questions above. After you have finished, report your findings to the class as in the example below.

TONY DOWNLOADS MUSIC ON THE WEB. HE NEVER GOES TO MUSIC CONCERTS…

5. To make WH-questions, we use different question words, depending on what we want to know. Draw a line to match each word on the left to its function on the right.

WHAT   asks about places or positions
WHERE   asks for reasons
WHEN   asks for / about people
WHO   asks for information about something
HOW   asks about time
WHY   asks about manners or conditions

Now choose three question words from the list above and write questions to a classmate you don't know very well. Then sit with this classmate and ask him or her the questions you have written.

6. Read these short biographies about two famous Brazilian singers and do the activities that follow.

Cláudia Cristina Leite Inácio Pedreira [...], known by the stage names Claudia Leitte (with double "tt") and Claudinha (born July 10, 1980 in São Gonçalo, Rio de Janeiro) is a Brazilian axé singer, and former vocalist of the group Babado Novo. Since she is one of the most popular axé singers in Brazil, she hosted MTV Brasil's Video Music Brasil 2007, in which she had been nominated as best singer in that award. Claudia Leitte has also won other awards.

Available at: <http://en.wikipedia.org/wiki/Claudia_Leitte>. Accessed on: October 25, 2013.

Ivete María Dias de Sangalo Cady [...] (born May 27, 1972 in Juazeiro, Bahia) is a Latin Grammy Award-winning Brazilian Axé and MPB singer, songwriter, and occasional actress and television show host. She is one of the most popular and best-selling Brazilian female singers of the present, with six albums released with "Banda Eva", and seven more albums in a solo career. Sangalo is most often recognized by her powerful voice, charisma and live performances. Her music is also very popular in Portugal. She has received 14 nominations for Latin Grammy Awards alongside her career.

Available at: <http://en.wikipedia.org/wiki/Ivete_Sangalo>. Accessed on: October 25, 2013.

a) Choose the appropriate word from the box to ask WH-questions related to the biographies. Add the necessary auxiliaries and other elements to build cohesive questions.

| WHAT | WHERE | WHEN | WHO | HOW | WHY | WHO | WHAT |

I) carioca axé singer come from

II) Cláudia Cristina Leite Inácio Pedreira's stage names

III) Grammy Award winner

IV) Ivete Sangalo famous for

V) Ivete Sangalo's birthday

VI) former vocalist of "Babado Novo"

VII) old Claudia Leitte now

VIII) Claudia Leitte host the MTV award

b) Now, with a classmate, ask and answer the questions based on the information in the texts.

7. Let's play *Guess who*. Follow the instructions and have fun with your classmates.
   - Get together in small groups.
   - One of the participants chooses a famous singer and writes his or her name on a piece of paper. (The other students cannot see it!)
   - Everyone else asks questions to guess who the singer is. The first round should be done with yes/no questions. For example:

Is it a woman/man?

Does she/he sing country music/samba/...?

The second round, with WH-questions. For example:

Where was this singer born?

What is his/her musical style?

Let's listen and talk!

Before you listen...
- Do you know any projects for underprivileged people in your region?
- What type of project do you think could be implemented in your neighborhood?
- Look at the images below. What kind of project do you think this is?
- Why do you think projects that involve music are always successful?

Hint
Read the questions before listening so that you can **scan for specific information.**

1. 🎧 9 Listen to a testimonial by Dantes Rameau about the Atlanta Music Project. Check (✓) the correct alternatives.

   a) Dantes Rameau is a/an
   - ( ) executive director.
   - ( ) college student.
   - ( ) history teacher.

   b) The project's philosophy (mantra) is
   - ( ) "music changes education."
   - ( ) "music for disadvantaged youth."
   - ( ) "music for social change."

   c) The qualities that the project helps children to develop are
   - ( ) confidence.
   - ( ) autonomy.
   - ( ) creativity.
   - ( ) ambition.
   - ( ) self-esteem.

   d) One way they found to raise money for the project was by selling tickets for
   - ( ) beach vacations.
   - ( ) music concerts.
   - ( ) students' presentations.

   Images captured from: <http://www.youtube.com/watch?v=BQsMfMVu174>. Accessed on: October 25, 2013.

2. 🎧 9 Listen to the recording again and take notes of other information you hear mentioned. Use your notebook. Then compare your notes to a classmate's. Are they similar?

3. Share with a classmate what you know or think about music. Use the prompts below to ask and answer WH-questions.

- queen and king of pop music
- #1 singer in your region
- origin of "sertanejo"
- favorite music style
- most famous singer in your country
- favorite band
- place of birth of your favorite singer
- favorite musical instrument
- date of the first Rock in Rio

Let's act with words!

Let's create a flyer to promote an event!

A flyer is a small printed notice that advertises an event.

Writing Steps

Organizing
- Choose a dance festival, a band or a singer to advertise.
- Observe the characteristics of a flyer and find out the main elements of this genre. You can find more examples of flyers on the Internet as well.

Preparing the first draft
- Make a first draft.

Peer editing
- Evaluate and discuss your first draft with a classmate.
- Make the necessary corrections.

Publishing
- Publish the flyer on a wall board or in a blog.

To create a flyer, you can also use an online tool available at <http://www.band-flyers.com/> (accessed on: May 13, 2014).

Go to Workbook, page 355, for more practice.

Genre: Flyer

Purpose: To advertise/promote a dance festival or a concert

Tone: Informal

Setting: A wall, a board, the Internet

Writer: You

Audience: Wall board or blog readers

Learning tips

Let's sing in English!

Karaoke is fun and can help you learn English. You can practice reading, listening, and pronunciation in a very relaxing way. You can also learn more vocabulary in context. You can listen to the song and sing it as many times as you want.

Below are some suggestions of online karaoke that you can enjoy.

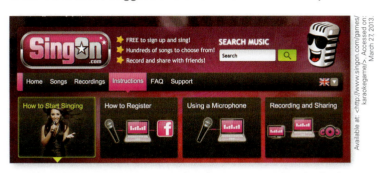

Invite some classmates to sing karaoke. Learn English and have fun...

Available at: <http://www.singon.com/games/karaokegame/>. Accessed on: October 25, 2013.

Available at: <http://tubeoke.com/>. Accessed on: October 25, 2013.

Available at: <http://www.cantanding.com/>. Accessed on: October 25, 2013.

Let's reflect on learning!

You are now invited to assess what you learned and how you learned. Finish the ideas below on an extra sheet of paper and become a more autonomous and reflective learner.

In Part 2

I learned _____

I liked _____

I need to review/learn more _____

My experiences with English outside school were _____

Let's study for Enem!

Enem Questions

Viva la Vida

I used to rule the world
Seas would rise when I gave the word
Now in the morning and I sleep alone
Sweep the streets I used to own

I used to roll the dice
Feel the fear in my enemy's eyes
Listen as the crowd would sing
"Now the old king is dead! Long live the king!"

One minute I held the key
Next the walls were closed on me
And I discovered that my castles stand
Upon pillars of salt and pillars of sand

[...]

MARTIN, C. Viva la vida, Coldplay. In: *Viva la vida or Death and all his friends.* Parlophone, 2008.

Gênero
Letra de música

Competência de área 2
H7 - Relacionar um texto em LEM, as estruturas linguísticas, sua função e seu uso social.

> O enunciado indica a repetição de trechos ou palavras; nesse caso, repete-se a forma verbal *used to*, que expressa uma ideia específica. O termo *now*, no terceiro verso, reforça essa ideia.

Letras de músicas abordam temas que, de certa forma, podem ser reforçados pela repetição de trechos ou palavras. O fragmento da canção *Viva la vida*, por exemplo, permite conhecer o relato de alguém que

A costumava ter o mundo aos seus pés e, de repente, se viu sem nada.
B almeja o título de rei e, por ele, tem enfrentado inúmeros inimigos.
C causa pouco temor a seus inimigos, embora tenha muito poder.
D limpava as ruas e, com seu esforço, tornou-se rei de seu povo.
E tinha a chave para todos os castelos nos quais desejava morar.

Extraído de: Exame Nacional do Ensino Médio, 2010, Caderno 7 – AZUL – Página 2 (questão 92).

> De algum modo, as ideias apresentadas nas alternativas se encontram no texto. Isso ocorre para que as opções sejam plausíveis. Portanto, fique atento aos elementos distrativos, os quais aparecem no texto, mas são usados de modo diferente na alternativa.

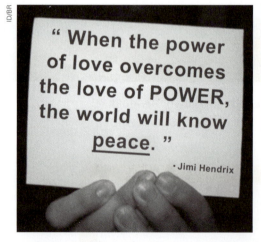

Gênero
Cartaz

Competência de área 2
H5 – Associar vocábulos e expressões de um texto em LEM ao seu tema.

> Observar marcas tipográficas, como caixa alta e sublinhado, ajuda na leitura. O autor decide marcar algum item no texto porque ele tem papel de destaque no sentido. Note também o uso de trocadilhos, como *power of love* x *love of power*. Esses recursos costumam ser usados em partes importantes do sentido pretendido pelo autor.

Aproveitando-se de seu *status* social e da possível influência sobre seus fãs, o famoso músico Jimi Hendrix associa, em seu texto, os termos *love*, *power* e *peace* para justificar sua opinião de que

A a paz tem o poder de aumentar o amor entre os homens.
B o amor pelo poder deve ser menor do que o poder do amor.
C o poder deve ser compartilhado entre aqueles que se amam.
D o amor pelo poder é capaz de desunir cada vez mais as pessoas.
E a paz será alcançada quando a busca pelo poder deixar de existir.

Extraído de: Exame Nacional do Ensino Médio, 2012, Caderno 6 – CINZA – Página 3 (questão 94).

> Leve em conta que as paráfrases que compõem as opções podem conter inversões que talvez falseiem as informações do texto.

Part 2 (Move Your Body)

Typical questions of Enem

Dancing: A Cool Way To Lose Weight
Written By: Deva

So you want to **lose weight**, but are not ready to try out sweaty **workouts** or **yoga Asanas**. Even **Aerobics** seems tepid to you; then I have a suggestion. Start tapping your feet now. Dance is the **best way to lose weight** as you will not get bored from monotonous workouts. You can move your body freely and **burn calories** by sweating with joy. Today dancing has become the **most preferable way to lose weight** and stay fit. Here are few tips that help to **shed weight** by following different procedures and **dancing styles**.

Available at: <http://www.thelivingwine.com/blog/dancing-a-cool-way-to-lose-weight/>. Accessed on: January 26, 2013.

1. O título desse texto é justificado pela afirmação de que
   a) ( ) a preferência dos atletas é pelos exercícios de dança.
   b) ( ) dançar é uma forma de perder peso e se divertir.
   c) ( ) dançar mantém a temperatura do corpo mais fria.
   d) ( ) diferentes estilos de dança nos ajudam a perder peso.
   e) ( ) só se queimam calorias transpirando durante as danças.

2. Este folheto traz a programação de um festival de música intitulado *Brasil Summer Fest*. O folheto dá destaque especial
   a) ( ) às datas e aos artistas.
   b) ( ) aos preços dos ingressos.
   c) ( ) ao endereço eletrônico do evento.
   d) ( ) aos patrocinadores.
   e) ( ) à cidade do evento.

Available at: <http://www.brasilsummerfest.com/>. Accessed on: May 23, 2013.

63

Exam Practice Questions (Vestibular)

Test-Taking Tips

Reggae, pop, and rock and roll artists – What do they have to do with examinations? The answer is: It is common to find lyrics (or bits of lyrics) as major texts on examinations. For example, lyrics by Coldplay, Bob Marley, Amy Winehouse, and The Beatles have already been used in Enem and Vestibular questions testing English skills. Other artists have also been seen on these exams, testing other teaching areas. So, it is always a good idea to look at old exams and check, for example, how lyrics are approached.

The recurrence of lyrics on recent tests might also indicate that test designers may keep on including this genre in future editions, so you can include lyrics in your reading habits. After all, they have to do with real life, with students' immediate interests. As you see, more and more, you are expected to have an active attitude and also to be curious, investigative, and eclectic.

TEXT 1 – Questions 1 and 2
Uneb-BA, 2013

Regular physical activity can help keep your thinking, learning, and judgment skills sharp as you age. It can also reduce your risk of depression and may help you sleep better. Research has shown that doing aerobic or a mix of aerobic and muscle-strengthening activities 3 to 5 times a week for 30 to 60 minutes can give you these benefits. Some scientific evidence has also shown that even lower levels of physical activity can be beneficial.

Disponível em: <www.cdc.gov/physicalactivity/everyone/health/index.html>. Acesso em: 12 out. 2012.

1. The title that best summarizes the main idea of this text is
   a) ( ) Increase your risk of diseases.
   b) ( ) Strengthen your bones and muscles.
   c) ( ) Improve your ability to do daily activities.
   d) ( ) Reduce your chances of living longer.
   e) ( ) Improve your mental health and mood.

2. Fill in the parentheses with T (True) or F (False).
   The text has answers to the following questions:
   ( ) How often should people exercise?
   ( ) What benefits does physical activity provide when people become older?
   ( ) Why is it that lower levels of physical activity don't seem to work much?
   ( ) When shouldn't people do muscle-strengthening activities?

   According to the text, the correct sequence, from top to bottom, is
   a) ( ) T T T T
   b) ( ) F T T F
   c) ( ) F F T T
   d) ( ) T F F T
   e) ( ) T T F F

Part 2 (Move Your Body)

- **TEXT 2 – Questions 3 to 7**
Unesp, 2012
Leia a letra da música, interpretada por Amy Winehouse, para responder às questões de números 3 a 7.

Tears Dry on Their Own

All I can ever be to you,
Is a darkness that we knew
And this regret I got accustomed to
Once it was so right
When we were at our high,
Waiting for you in the hotel at night
I knew I hadn't met my match
But every moment we could snatch
I don't know why I got so attached
It's my responsibility,
And you don't owe nothing to me
But to walk away I have no capacity

He walks away
The sun goes down,
He takes the day but I'm grown
And in your way
In this blue shade
My tears dry on their own.

I don't understand
Why do I stress a man,
When there's so many bigger things at hand
We could have never had it all
We had to hit a wall
So this is inevitable withdrawal
Even if I stopped wanting you,
A perspective pushes through
I'll be some next man's other woman soon
[...]

I wish I could say no regrets
And no emotional debts
'Cause as we kissed goodbye the sun sets
So we are history
The shadow covers me
The sky above a blaze
That only lovers see

http://letras.terra.com.br. Adaptado.

3. Qual das seguintes expressões indica que um relacionamento amoroso foi bom?
a) (   ) In this blue shade
b) (   ) [...] we were at our high
c) (   ) [...] I can ever be to you
d) (   ) [...] I got so attached
e) (   ) We had to hit a wall

4. Segundo a letra da música, qual das seguintes frases indica que um relacionamento amoroso acabou?
a) (   ) It's my responsibility
b) (   ) The sun goes down
c) (   ) And in your way
d) (   ) I'm grown
e) (   ) Tears dry on their own

5. A cantora afirma que
a) (   ) logo estará envolvida com outra pessoa.
b) (   ) os homens a deixam muito estressada.
c) (   ) sabia que tinha encontrado a pessoa certa.
d) (   ) não tem capacidade para viver sozinha.
e) (   ) vai chorar muito pelo fim do romance.

6. Assinale a alternativa correta.
a) (   ) A cantora gostaria de ter se envolvido bem mais no relacionamento.
b) (   ) O fim inesperado do relacionamento jamais será superado pela cantora.
c) (   ) A cantora gostaria que o fim do relacionamento não deixasse ressentimentos.
d) (   ) Uma outra mulher foi a causa do fim inesperado do relacionamento.
e) (   ) O fim do relacionamento aconteceu após uma noite em um quarto de hotel.

7. Em qual alternativa todas as palavras, conforme utilizadas na letra da música, são formas verbais?
a) (   ) *Accustomed, away, knew, met, was.*
b) (   ) *Ever, hand, match, waiting, were.*
c) (   ) *Accustomed, hand, know, owe, was.*
d) (   ) *Away, ever, met, snatch, waiting.*
e) (   ) *Attached, knew, met, owe, were.*

PART

3

Make Your Art Sparkle!

Learning plan

Reading propaganda

Learning vocabulary related to clothing and accessories

Learning to express logical necessity, personal obligation, deduction, and prohibition

Talking about actions in progress

Talking about visual arts and about the past

Writing a biography

Let's create artistic word clouds

A word cloud is a visual representation of a text. The most prominent words in a text are usually the keywords. A popular free software for word clouds is **Wordle**, available at <http://www.wordle.net/> (accessed on: May 19, 2014). Here is an example using a biography of a Ghanaian painter.

Ben Agbee, an artist from Ghana.

Watch a tutorial video at <http://www.youtube.com/watch?v=xhL5D9nz5aI> (accessed on: May 19, 2014) and learn how to work with **Wordle**.

Another free software online is **Tagxedo**, which turns different types of text into beautiful word clouds. You can create word clouds in different shapes and even upload photos to use them as forms for your work, as in the example using Ben Agbee's photo above. This tool is available at <http://www.tagxedo.com/> (accessed on: May 19, 2014).

Watch a tutorial to learn how to use **Tagxedo** at <http://www.youtube.com/watch?v=AwuB7Ub9RQU> (accessed on: May 19, 2014).

67

UNIT 5
On the runway

Language in action

- Read propaganda
- Learn vocabulary related to clothing
- Learn how to express logical necessity, personal obligation, deduction, and prohibition
- Learn to talk about actions in progress

A model poses at the Africa Fashion Week in London, England, in 2012.

"There's a reason why the European Union and the U.S. banned seal skins. The annual Canadian massacre is a shameful bloodbath and must be stopped."

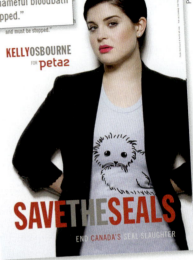

English singer, actress and fashion designer Kelly Osbourne in a PETA campaign to save the seals.

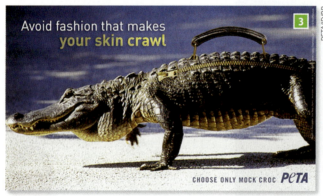

A PETA campaign in response to a French manufacturer of leather products.

A model displays an oversized dress at the International Fuller Woman Expo in Toronto, Canada, in 2012.

Models display creations as part of Dolce & Gabbana Fall-winter 2012-2013 Menswear collection, in Milan, Italy.

> Lead-in

1. Why do people wear clothes? Check (✔) the reasons you agree with.
   - (　) To protect them from the environment
   - (　) To show their social status
   - (　) To assure morality and modesty
   - (　) To cover deformities
   - (　) To identify their job or position
   - (　) To enhance beauty
   - (　) To show their values and ideas
   - (　) To show their personality
   - (　) Other: _____

2. Do men in Brazil wear clothes like the ones you see in picture 5?
   _____

3. What do men and women usually wear in your region (at school/parties, in winter/summer)?
   _____

4. Messages intended to persuade readers to accept ideas or to behave in a certain way are **propaganda**, and messages intended to persuade readers to buy services or products are **advertisements**. Read the texts in images 2 and 3 on the left page and answer.

   a) Are they propaganda or advertisements?
   _____

   b) What are their purposes?
   _____

5. Check (✔) the elements of propaganda that you can find in the examples on the left page.
   - (　) Strategic use of color is used.
   - (　) The central message is highlighted.
   - (　) Lots of words are used.
   - (　) A specific group's agenda is represented.
   - (　) New information comes on the right.
   - (　) Emotions and feelings are evoked.
   - (　) Humorous tones are used.
   - (　) They obscure reasoning.

6. In this kind of discourse, we can find images that associate two or more concepts, blending them into one image. What are the concepts involved in the PETA campaign that you can see in text 3?
   _____

7. Look at these images and find the blended elements.

   a)
   Body painting by Brazilian artist Guido Daniele.

   b)
   Image from "Make it Possible" video at <http://vimeo.com/51837094> (accessed on: October 31, 2013).

69

> Let's read!

Before you read...

- Look at the title and picture of the propaganda below. It is against

  ( ) keeping animals in cages.   ( ) using animals for clothing.
  ( ) using animals for research.   ( ) keeping animals in zoos

Available at: <http://www.mediapeta.com/peta/Images/Main/Sections/MediaCenter/PrintAds/Fox_fur.pdf>. Accessed on: October 30, 2013.

Hint
Identify the **purpose of the text** by paying special attention to its theme and details.

1. Read the text above and answer these questions.

a) What animal is being used to illustrate their campaign? Check (✔) the answer.

   ( ) a bear   ( ) a snake   ( ) a mink
   ( ) a seal   ( ) a raccoon   ( ) a rabbit
   ( ) a fox   ( ) a chinchilla   ( ) an otter

b) Is the animal shown in its own habitat or not? Does it look happy or sad?

_____

c) Who do you think the intended audience of this PETA campaign is?

_____

d) What can you gain from reading this campaign?

_____

e) Why must we stop buying fur, according to the text?

_____

f) How many animals are needed to make a fur coat?

_____

2. Besides the reasons presented in the text, are there any others for not using animal furs? Work in groups and list as many reasons as you can. Ask your science teacher to help you.

_____

_____

Beyond the lines...

a) How can this kind of propaganda influence people's opinions?
b) In your opinion, is this PETA campaign a case of ethical or unethical propaganda? Explain.

Vocabulary corner

What are these models wearing? Choose words from the box to label the items. Some words will be left out.

1. belt   2. miniskirt   3. T-shirt   4. sweater   5. leggings   6. dress   7. pants   8. shoes
9. sweatshirt   10. scarf   11. hat   12. pantyhose/nylons   13. sneakers   14. jeans   15. sunglasses
16. jacket   17. sandals   18. socks   19. shirt   20. shorts

a)

b)

c)

d)

e)

› Let's focus on language!

1. Read again some excerpts taken from the *Lead-in* and *Let's read!* sections. Then check (✔) the correct option to complete the statement.

   "But the fact is, to make a single coat, dozens of animals **must** pay with their lives."
   "The annual Canadian massacre is a shameful bloodbath and **must** be stopped."

   The word **must** in the sentences above indicates that the action in both cases is

   ( ) a necessity/an obligation.   ( ) an ability/a possibility.   ( ) a deduction.

2. Now read this statement and check (✔) the correct option to complete the statement.

   *Kelly Osbourne posed for the PETA campaign... She **must** be really engaged in this cause.*

   The word **must** in this case indicates

   ( ) an obligation/a necessity.   ( ) a deduction.   ( ) an ability/a possibility.

   > We use **must + verb** to express deduction, personal obligation, or logical necessity. If you use **must** in the negative (**must not = mustn't**), you are expressing prohibition.

3. Read this text and write what people and/or the fashion industry must do to be ethically fashionable. Use the prompts in the box to help you.

   WHAT IS ETHICAL FASHION?

   Ethical Fashion is an umbrella term to describe ethical fashion design, production, retail, and purchasing. It covers a range of issues such as working conditions, exploitation, fair trade, sustainable production, the environment, and animal welfare. [...]

   Some of the issues around Ethical Fashion

   Ethical Fashion aims to address the problems it sees with the way the fashion industry currently operates, such as exploitative labour, environmental damage, the use of hazardous chemicals, waste, and animal cruelty.
   - Serious concerns are often raised about exploitative working conditions in the factories that make cheap clothes for the high street.
   - Child workers, alongside exploited adults, can be subjected to violence and abuse such as forced overtime, as well as cramped and unhygienic surroundings, bad food, and very poor pay. [...]
   - Cotton provides much of the world's fabric, but growing it uses 22.5% of the world's insecticides and 10% of the world's pesticides [...].
   - Current textile growing practices are considered unsustainable because of the damage they do to the immediate environment. [...]
   - The low costs and disposable nature of high street fashion means that much of it is destined for incinerators or landfill sites. [...]
   - Many animals are farmed to supply fur for the fashion industry, and many people feel that animal welfare is an important part of the Ethical Fashion debate. [...]

   Adapted from: <http://www.vam.ac.uk/content/articles/w/what-is-ethical-fashion/>. Accessed on: November 1, 2013.

> be incinerated • have good food and good pay • offer good working conditions • be sustainable • use insecticides • farm animals to supply fur for the fashion industry • recycle high street fashion • exploit children • damage the immediate environment

a) Factories _____
b) Factories _____
c) Factory workers _____
d) Cotton farmers _____
e) Current textile practices _____
f) Current textile practices _____
g) People _____
h) High street fashion _____
i) People _____

4. Now, read the following excerpts taken from the text in the *Let's read!* section. Then underline the one which expresses an action in progress.

"Just think, you only need 29 more to make a coat."

"So, if you're thinking about buying a fur – don't."

"Most people don't realize the true cost of a fur."

> If you want to say that an action is in progress, use the Present Continuous. You need to use a form of the verb *be* in the present (*am*, *is*, or *are*) + a verb in the *–ing* form.
> For the negative, use *am*, *is* or *are* + *not* + verb in the *–ing* form.
> To make a question, use *am*, *is*, or *are* + **SUBJECT** + verb in the *–ing* form.

5. What are they wearing? Match five of the descriptions below to the two photos on this page and the three photos on the next page. Write the corresponding letter.

( ) She's wearing a white tank top and sunglasses.

( ) He is wearing a checked blue shirt and red glasses.

( ) She is wearing a short dress and white sandals.

( ) She's wearing black pants and a blue blouse.

( ) He's wearing a purple sweater, a purple and black scarf, pants, and boots.

( ) She's wearing a light green dress and a brown leather belt.

( ) He's wearing a checked red shirt, a white long-sleeve shirt, a black tie, a vest, and black pants.

( ) She's wearing khaki pants, an orange parka, and a khaki scarf.

73

6. What are these people doing? Complete the descriptions using the items in the box.

> look in a store window • sew • sketch a design for a dress • try on a suit • walk down the catwalk • put on sneakers

a) The two women _____

b) The woman _____

c) The boy and his girlfriend _____

d) The model _____

e) The man _____

f) The fashion designer _____

> Turn on the jukebox!

Hint
Use **clues** in the text and your own knowledge to fill in the gaps.

New Shoes (by Paolo Nutini)

Woke up cold one Tuesday,
I'm looking tired and _____ quite sick
I felt like there was something missing in my day-to-day life
So I quickly opened the wardrobe
Pulled out some jeans and a T-shirt that seemed clean
Topped it off with a pair of old shoes that were ripped around the seams,
And I thought these shoes just don't suit me.

CHORUS
Hey, I put some new shoes on, and suddenly everything's right,
I said, hey, I put some new shoes on and everybody_____,
It's so inviting, oh, short on money,
But long on time,
Slowly strolling in the sweet sunshine,
And I'_____ late, and I don't need an excuse,
'Cause I'_____ my brand-new shoes.

Woke up late one Thursday,
And I'_____ stars as I'_____ my eyes
And I felt like there were two days missing, as I focused on the time
And I made my way to the kitchen
But I had to stop from the shock of what I found
A room full of all my friends all _____ round and round
And I thought hello new shoes, bye bye 'em blues.

CHORUS
Take me wandering through these streets,
Where bright lights and angels meet,
Stone to stone they take me on,
I _____ to the break of dawn. (2x)

CHORUS (2x)

Available at: <http://letras.mus.br/paolo-nutini/695798/>. Accessed on: November 1, 2013.

Miguel Medina/AFP

1. **◎10** Listen to the song and complete it with an appropriate form of the verbs below. The first one is done for you.

> feel   rub   run   see   ~~look~~   smile   walk   wear   dance

2. Now, answer these questions about the song.

   a) How is the speaker feeling in the first stanza? _____

   b) How is the speaker feeling in the second stanza? _____

   c) What made him change his mood? _____

75

Let's listen and talk!

Before you listen...
- Look at the images below. Which words and sound effects will you probably hear in the recording? Why?
- Based on these images, what do you think the topic of this recording is?

Images captured from: <http://www.3news.co.nz/Fashion-show-for-big-women/tabid/372/articleID/253139/Default.aspx>. Accessed on: November 1, 2013.

1. 🎧11 Listen to the first part of a news broadcast about a fashion show and check (✔) the correct options.

   a) According to the text, society expects women these days to

   ( ) look healthy. ( ) look fashionable.
   ( ) look good. ( ) look happy.

   b) The fashion show in South Auckland features

   ( ) plus size models. ( ) skinny models.

   c) For Cat Pause, Massey University fat studies lecturer, there is a myth that fat people are

   ( ) sad. ( ) lazy. ( ) unmotivated.
   ( ) untalented. ( ) unhealthy. ( ) happy.

2. ⊚**12** Now listen to the second part of the recording and number the items below in the order you hear them mentioned.

( ) ***Reporter Adrien Taylor***: But True South isn't your regular fashion show. There's the glitz, there's the glamour and the catwalk, but there's also a unique Pacific flavour.

( ) ***Reporter Adrien Taylor***: Regular fashion shows are glitzy and glamorous affairs. Stick-thin models put on their best pouts and the audience claps politely.

( ) ***Reporter Adrien Taylor***: The clear message: if you've got it, flaunt it, even if you've got three times as much as Kate Moss. Adrien Taylor, 3 News.

( ) ***Reporter Adrien Taylor***: And there was a serious message behind all the smiles.

Auckland Council Pacific arts coordinator Ema Tavola: We're celebrating Pacific women and big women, and bigness is kind of the norm here in South Auckland, so tonight is really a celebration of all things big and bold and Poly-fabulous.

( ) ***Reporter Adrien Taylor***: And while big people are often portrayed as ticking health time-bombs who should know better, the models were relishing their moment in the spotlight.

Model Loretta Aukuso: It made me feel beautiful, it made feel hot out there. I felt sexy out there. And, you know, it's about time that we had this kind of fashion line. It's so good for us to kind of wear clothes that accentuate the bits that we usually wanna hide. I love my body! I love to show it off now.

( ) ***Reporter Adrien Taylor***: The clothes are designed to look good and feel good.

Stylist: My clothes are all that fun, they're about attitude, they're about loving who you are, owing it and rocking it.

3. With a classmate, give your opinion about the following questions.

a) Is beauty in the eye of the media? Does the exposure to the media have any influence on people's perception of beauty?

b) Can you notice this difference in the clothing items you choose to wear every day?

c) Do the advertisements give every information consumers need before buying clothes?

d) What are some of the things consumers must do before buying clothes? Make a list in your notebook.

> ■ **Useful language**
>
> I think...
> I find...
> Consumers must...

UNIT 6

Visual arts

Language in action

- Talk about visual arts
- Talk about the past
- Read about visual artists
- Write a biography

Work by Kim Smith depicting a dog staring at a crescent moon.

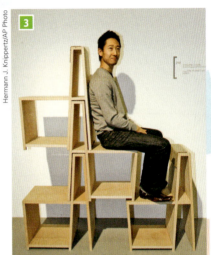

Japanese designer Jun Murakoshi and his "shelving chairs" at the International Furniture Fair in Cologne, Germany, 2008.

Sunrise, 1872 (oil on canvas), by French artist Claude Monet (1840-1926) at the Musée Marmottan Monet, Paris, France.

The Thinker, by French artist Auguste Rodin (1840-1917), in a museum in Paris, France.

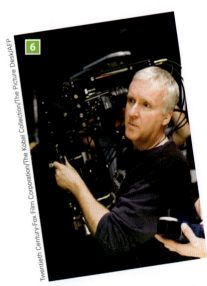

Canadian movie director James Cameron during the Avatar production in 2009.

Let's Rock, a photo exhibition at Oca, São Paulo, Brazil, 2012.

3 ■ Make Your Art Sparkle!

78

› Lead-in

1. Visual arts are all forms of art which are predominantly visual in their nature. Read a more complete definition of visual arts. Then label each picture on the left page using vocabulary from the text.

> The **visual arts** are art forms that create works that are primarily visual in nature, such as ceramics, drawing, painting, sculpture, printmaking, design, crafts, photography, video, filmmaking, and architecture. These definitions should not be taken too strictly as many artistic disciplines (performing arts, conceptual art, textile arts) involve aspects of the visual arts as well as arts of other types. Also included within the visual arts are the applied arts such as industrial design, graphic design, fashion design, interior design and decorative art.
>
> Available at: <http://en.wikipedia.org/wiki/Visual_arts>. Accessed on: November 2, 2013

Picture 1: _____   Picture 5: _____

Picture 2: _____   Picture 6: _____

Picture 3: _____   Picture 7: _____

Picture 4: _____

2. What are your favorite types of visual arts?

_____

3. Take a look at the pictures of artistic expressions on the previous page again and decide which one(s) is/are created

a) with the use of advanced technological resources: _____

b) with precise manual skills: _____

c) using different types of paint: _____

d) with different types of materials such as marble, steel, wood, stone, glass, bronze, ivory, etc.: _____

e) mainly with pencil, crayon, pen, ink, chalk, and other materials: _____

f) basically with the use of cameras: _____

4. Read the excerpts of two famous visual artists' biographies. Do they mention any of the kinds of art represented on the previous page? If so, what are they?

_____

> "Although he was a relatively poor student, Picasso displayed a prodigious talent for drawing from a very young age. According to legend, his first words were 'piz, piz,' his childish attempt at saying 'lápiz', the Spanish word for pencil."
>
> Available at: <http://www.biography.com/people/pablo-picasso-9440021>. Accessed on: November 2, 2013.

> "Famed French artist Paul Gauguin, born on June 7, 1848, created his own unique painting style, much like he crafted his own distinctive path through life. Known for bold colors, simplified forms and strong lines, he didn't have any art formal training."
>
> Available at: <http://www.biography.com/people/paul-gauguin-9307741>. Accessed on: November 2, 2013.

5. Do you know any famous visual artists? Try to think about artists from the past and contemporary times. Write their names.

_____

⟩ Let's read!

Before you read...
- Do you know any Brazilian visual artists who are famous abroad? What do you know about their lives?
- Have your ever seen famous paintings or other pieces of visual art in person?

Hint
Scan the texts to search for **keywords** and the main ideas.

TEXT 1: Ben Agbee's Biography

Ben Agbee, born in 1966 in Ghana, is one of the most successful Ghanaian artists. He has over the years carved a niche for himself with extremely evocative works. Ben majored in art, graduating in 1989, and worked for four years in advertising and design before starting to paint and discovering his talent that is markedly original and vigorous. His acrylic paintings are in vibrant and earthy colors, mainly of women in attractive clothing, and incorporate unusual shapes. His works, with all kinds of figures, images, and symbols, border on abstracts, impressionism, landscapes, and realism, which lead to a myriad of interpretations. Since his first exhibition at the Loom Gallery in Accra, Ben has displayed his works in Ghana, Europe, Canada, the United States, and New Zealand.

Ben Agbee (full name Benjamin Agbenyega)

Adapted from: <http://www.africanafrican.com/negroartist/ben%20agbee/Ben%20Agbee%20biography%20final.pdf>. Accessed on: November 2, 2013.

Did you know...?

An autobiography is a history of a person's life written or told by that person. A biography is a history of a person's life written or told by someone else. A famous autobiography is *The Diary of Anne Frank*, by Anne Frank. A famous biography is *Diana: Her true story*, by Andrew Morton.

TEXT 2: Louise Holgate's Autobiography

ABOUT
In the right light, at the right time, everything is extraordinary.

I live in Birmingham with my husband and four-year-old daughter. I've been a primary school teacher for more years than I care to admit to, but am now following my dreams and developing a career in photography.

I was a keen photographer as a teenager but it fell by the wayside as I got older and life got busier. I picked up a camera again after my daughter was born, then bought a DSLR and started a Photo-a-Day project. I quickly became hooked. I've always enjoyed being creative and with digital photography I have finally found my form.

Available at: <http://louiseholgate.wordpress.com/about/>. Accessed on: November 2, 2013.

Photo titled *Angelique*, by Louise Holgate.

TEXT 3: Zena Santos's Biography

ZENA SANTOS
ABOUT

Zena Santos is a graphic illustrator living in Sydney, Australia. She's most at home with a wacom pen in one hand and typing keyboard shortcuts in Adobe Illustrator with the other.

Zena graduated from Billy Blue College of Design in 2010 and immediately started working at www.thedmci.com.au, where she was exposed to the world of broadcast design, motion graphics and animation.

But her true passion was in design and illustration, using her weapons of choice, Adobe Illustrator, Photoshop and a wacom tablet.

She loves creating vector worlds, characters and illustrated type for any application, from advertising to animation and of course motion graphics.

Available (with corrections) at: <http://www.behance.net/zena_santos>. Accessed on: November 2, 2013.

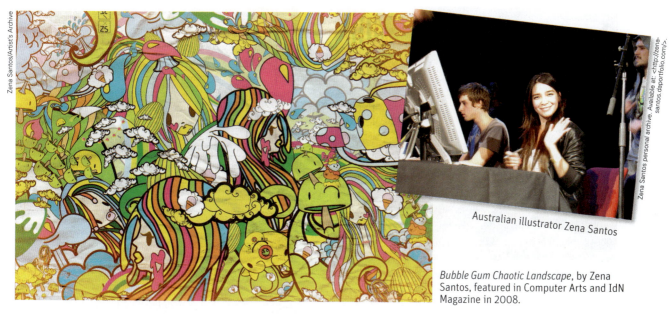

Australian illustrator Zena Santos

Bubble Gum Chaotic Landscape, by Zena Santos, featured in Computer Arts and IdN Magazine in 2008.

1. A biography is a description of a person's life which comprehends personal facts and experiences. Read the three texts and mark **B** if the facts (or experiences) below refer to Ben Agbee, **L** if they refer to Louise Holgate, and **Z** if they refer to Zena Santos.

   ( ) born in Ghana   ( ) loves photography
   ( ) lives in Australia   ( ) is a graphic illustrator
   ( ) works in advertising   ( ) worked in advertising
   ( ) lives in Birmingham   ( ) has a daughter
   ( ) has works exhibited in different   ( ) graduated in 1989
       countries

2. Read the three texts again and answer the following questions.

   a) Who became an artist after being married? _____
   b) Who is the youngest artist of the three? _____
   c) Who is originally from Africa? _____
   d) Which artist has no degree in art? _____
   e) Which artists use digital technologies? _____

3. Look at some of Ben Agbee's paintings and label them according to the titles assigned by the artist.

A. **Contemplation**   B. **Hornblowers**

C. **We can fly**   D. **Wait a minute**

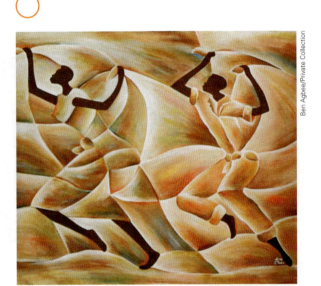
Oil on canvas (2008), by Ghanaian artist Ben Agbee. 46 x 36 inches.

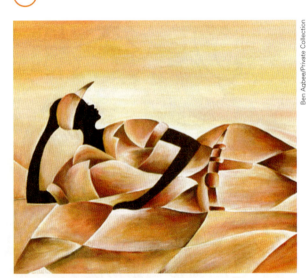
Oil on canvas (2007), by Ghanaian artist Ben Agbee.

Oil on canvas (2009), by Ghanaian artist Ben Agbee. 30 x 30 inches.

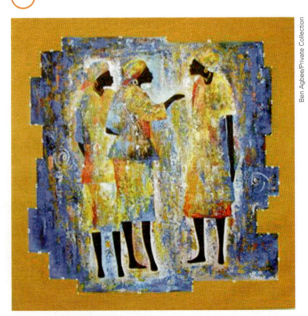
Oil on canvas (2009), by Ghanaian artist Ben Agbee.

Vocabulary corner

1. Do you know how to refer to people who create visual art? Normally, we add the ending –er (and in some cases –or) to the verb associated with the artistic expression. Some spelling changes are sometimes necessary. Look at these examples.

artistic expression	related verb	professional
painting	paint	paint**er**

What about the artistic expressions below? Complete the table.

artistic expression	related verb	professional
printmaking		
design		
photography		
sculpture		
filmmaking		
illustration		

2. All the materials in the box are used in visual arts. Write their names under the corresponding pictures.

| chalk | crayons | eraser | glass | ink | marble |
| paint | pen | clay | wood | steel | soapstone |

❯ Let's focus on language!

1. Read the following excerpts. Then check (✔) the correct option.

I. "McKenna's exhibit of 36 oil paintings and photographs **opened** last week at the museum."
Available at: <http://www.thealpenanews.com/page/content.detail/id/522308/Museum-exhibit-now-open-for-last-year-s-Juried-Art-Exhibition-winner.html?nav=5042>. Accessed on: November 2, 2013.

II. "The Cultural Arts Guild of Mastic Beach **held** their annual Art Show yesterday at the gazebo on Neighborhood Road."
Available at: <http://trihamletnews.com/archives/1207>. Accessed on: November 2, 2013.

III. "Ben **majored** in art, graduating in 1989, and **worked** for four years in advertising and design before starting to paint..."

IV. "I **was** a keen photographer as a teenager but it **fell** by the wayside as I **got** older and life **got** busier."

V. "Zena **graduated** from Billy Blue College of Design in 2010 [...]"

The words in bold tell us that the actions, states and events happened

( ) in a continuous period of time in the past.

( ) in a specific time in the past.

( ) in an undefined time in the past.

> We use the Simple Past to talk about actions, states, and events that happened and finished at a specific time in the past. Although the time is not necessarily mentioned, it can be imagined by the speaker. When we want to mention the time, we use expressions such as "last week", "yesterday", "in (year)", among others.

2. The words in bold in sentences I, III, and V are

( ) regular verbs. ( ) irregular verbs.

3. The words in bold in sentences II and IV are

( ) regular verbs. ( ) irregular verbs.

> In the Simple Past, regular verbs always end in *–ed*. Irregular verbs have several different endings.

4. Notice the main verb in the sentence about Paul Gauguin and answer.

"... he didn't have any art formal training."

Is it modified for Simple Past?

( ) Yes, it is. ( ) No, it isn't.

> To make negatives, use *did + not + verb in the infinitive*:
> "[...] he **didn't have** any art formal training."
> To make interrogatives, use *did + SUBJECT + verb in the infinitive*:
> **Did** Zena **graduate** in 2010?

5. Read the biographies and autobiographies in the *Let's read!* section again and underline or circle all the verbs in the Simple Past.

6. The following answers are related to the texts in the *Let's read!* section. Complete the questions accordingly.

a) When _____

Ben graduated in 1989.

b) What _____

Louise bought a DSLR.

c) What project _____

Louise started a Photo-a-Day project.

d) Where _____

Zena graduated from Billy Blue College of Design.

e) Where _____

Zena started working at www.thedmci.com.au.

7. Pieces of art can cost a lot of money. The more famous a piece of art is, the more money it costs. As other valuable things, pieces of art are stolen more and more. Read about the disappearance of Leonardo da Vinci's *Mona Lisa* and do the activities below.

a) Fill in the gaps with the appropriate form of the verbs in the boxes.

How could someone **steal** a painting from a museum?
by Julia Layton

assume	be	call	disappear	see

When Leonardo da Vinci's *Mona Lisa* _____ from the Louvre museum in Paris in 1911, the world _____ shocked. The theft went undetected for days. Museum staff _____ the empty space on the wall and _____ the painting had been moved to the Louvre's restoration center for upkeep. But by the second day, the Louvre _____ the police.

Mona Lisa, c. 1503-1506 (oil on panel), by Leonardo da Vinci (1452-1519). 77 cm × 53 cm. Louvre, Paris, France.

Musée du Louvre, Paris. Fotografia: Stuart Dee/ Photographer's Choice/Getty Images

be	end	leave	remove	stick	take	use	walk

The theft of the *Mona Lisa* by museum worker Vincenzo Perugia _____ brilliant in its simplicity. It's unclear what type of security the museum _____ at the time, but some facts are known for sure. After Perugia's shift _____ on Sunday, he hid in a room. When everyone had gone home, he _____ his hiding place, _____ the *Mona Lisa* off the wall, _____ it from its frame, _____ the priceless work under his shirt and _____ out into the night. […]

Read more at: <http://people.howstuffworks.com/steal-painting-from-museum.htm>. Accessed on: November 3, 2013.

b) The Mona Lisa was stolen from the Louvre because security

( ) did not call the police immediately.

( ) thought the Mona Lisa had been moved to the Louvre's restoration center.

( ) did not check if all the employees had gone home.

Beyond the lines...

a) What makes a piece of art cost so much money?

b) What should define the price of a piece of art?

8. Several time expressions can be used to refer to past time. Underline the time expressions you can recognize in the sentences in activity 1. Then copy them here.

_____

9. Read the statements below and complete the rule with *in* or *on*.

Ben Agbee, born in 1966 [...].

Famed French artist Paul Gauguin, born on June 7, 1848 [...].

> We use _____ for complete dates or days of the week; we use _____ to refer to a specific month or year.

10. Complete the lines below with information about time. Consult a calendar if necessary.

a) Today is _____

b) Last Carnival was _____

c) Last month was _____

d) Brazil's Independence Day last year was _____

e) I was born _____

f) I _____ two weeks ago.

g) Yesterday, I _____

11. The exercises below are based on a past calendar of events at the National Gallery of Art. When could you see each of the following events at the National Gallery of Art if you were there in that year? Finish the sentences with correct information.

a) On Sunday, November 25, there were two _____ at 11:30.

b) The gallery talk on Renaissance prints and drawings was _____

c) There was a guided tour of the French collection on _____

d) There were two guided tours on _____

PROGRAMS & EVENTS

NATIONAL GALLERY OF ART

CALENDAR OF EVENTS

What's New
Newsletters
Calendar
Recent Acquisitions
Videos & Podcasts
About the Gallery
Pre-Raphaelites
Albrecht Dürer
Global Navigation
Pre-Raphaelites
Albrecht Dürer
The Collection

Previous Week   Next Week

SUNDAY, NOVEMBER 25

11:30   **Guided Tour:** Early Italian to Early Modern: An Introduction to the West Building Collection
         Guided Tour: 1900 to Now: An Introduction to the East Building Collection

MONDAY, NOVEMBER 26

10:30   **Guided Tour:** Early Italian to Early Modern: An Introduction to the West Building Collection
11:30   **Guided Tour:** 1900 to Now: An Introduction to the East Building Collection
12:30   **Guided Tour:** French Collection: Eighteenth and Nineteenth Centuries
1:00   **Gallery Talk:** Imperial Augsburg: Renaissance Prints and Drawings, 1475-1540

EVENTS BY DATE

‹‹ **December 2012** ››

S	M	T	W	T	F	S
25	26	27	28	29	30	1
2	3	4	5	6	7	8
9	10	11	12	13	14	15
16	17	18	19	20	21	22
23	24	25	26	27	28	29
30	31	1	2	3	4	5

Events will be added as they are scheduled. Please check back regularly for the most up-to-date calendar of events information.

Available at: <http://www.nga.gov/programs/>. Accessed on: November 2, 2013.

12. Would you like to attend any of these events? Why (not)?

_____

Let's listen and talk!

Before you listen...
- What does the poster of *The Artist* tell you about the movie?

1. 🔊13 Now listen to the movie trailer and do the activities below.

    a) Complete the sentence.

    George Valentine was Hollywood's big star until _____ stole his spotlight _____

    b) Check (✔) the expressions the speaker uses to describe the film.

    ( ) exciting   ( ) unexpected gift
    ( ) beautiful   ( ) elegant
    ( ) magnificent creation   ( ) rich production

    c) What does the speaker say to invite listeners to watch the film?

    _____

2. Invite a friend to the movies. Use these prompts to help you.

Student A makes the invitation	Student B answers the invitation
Greet your partner. Invite him/her. Make a suggestion. Suggest a date and time. Decide on a meeting point.	Greet back. Ask what movie. Ask what day and time. Accept or decline the invitation. Say good-bye.

Useful language

Making invitations
Do you want to go to the movies tonight?
Would you like to go to the movies tomorrow?
How about going to the movies?

Accepting invitations
Sure. What time?
I'd love to, thanks.
That's awesome.
Great. When can we go?

Declining invitations
I can't. I have work to do.
I'm sorry. Can I take a rain check on that?
I'm really sorry, but I've got something else going on.

Pronunciation spot – Letters vs Syllables

1. 🔊14 Listen to these words. Write down the number of letters and syllables in the correct columns.

	Number of letters	Number of syllables
stole		
heart		
head		
glass		

	Number of letters	Number of syllables
movie		
miss		
chalk		
steel		

	Number of letters	Number of syllables
spotlight		
crayons		
stone		
disappear		

2. Based on activity 1, we can say that

    ( ) usually, there are less syllables than letters.   ( ) double consonants (-ss, -pp) have a single sound.
    ( ) all the letters in a word are always pronounced.   ( ) some letters are not pronounced.

87

Let's act with words!

Let's write a biography

A biography is an account of a person's life. This is the type of text you are invited to create here.

Writing Steps

Organizing
- Choose an activist, a fashion designer or a visual artist from your community. He or she can be living or dead.
- Interview the person, his or her relatives or friends to gather information about him or her.
- Find or take a picture of the person (or even draw one).

Preparing the first draft
- Make a first draft highlighting what makes this person so special.
- Include information about place and date of birth; some major facts about his/her life; general description of his/her work and the importance of his/her work. If the person is dead, you can tell why, when, where.
- Use verbs in the past and adverbs of time.

Peer editing
- Evaluate your text and discuss it with a classmate.
- Make the necessary corrections.

Publishing
- Publish it in your blog or on a wall newspaper.

Genre: Biography

Purpose: To make an account of the life of a person

Tone: Formal

Setting: Blog or wall newspaper

Writer: You

Audience: Blog readers or wall newspaper readers

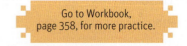
Go to Workbook, page 358, for more practice.

Learning tips

Let's learn vocabulary with pictures!

Online visual dictionaries are dictionaries which connect words with images.

Labels: shoelace, tongue, lining, collar, vamp, counter, quarter, stitch, heel, air unit, punch hole, middle sole, outsole

Shutterstock.com/ID/BR

Some online visual dictionaries you can use:
<http://visual.merriam-webster.com/index.php>
<http://www.pdictionary.com/>
<http://www.littleexplorers.com/languages/portuguese/Eisfor.shtml>
Accessed on: November 3, 2013.

Search for images on the Web, save them, and organize them into categories.

Let's reflect on learning!

You are now invited to assess what you learned and how you learned. Finish the ideas below on an extra sheet of paper and become a more autonomous and reflective learner.

In Part 3

I learned _____

I liked _____

I need to review/learn more _____

My experiences with English outside school were _____

_____

89

Let's study for Enem!

Enem Questions

Disponível em: http://politicalgraffiti.wordpress.com.
Acesso em: 15 maio 2014.

> A identificação do gênero textual e de suas características pode ser um elemento importante na compreensão do texto. Repare que, tipicamente, o "pulo do gato" em cartuns vem no último quadrinho.

Gênero

Cartum

Competência de área 2

H7 – Relacionar um texto em LEM, as estruturas linguísticas, sua função e seu uso social.

> Note que as opções de resposta descrevem aspectos presentes no texto. Para não cometer erros, é preciso identificar exatamente o que a questão está pedindo (no caso, o que "a linguagem evidencia") e onde essa informação é encontrada no texto.

Os cartuns são produzidos com o intuito de satirizar comportamentos humanos, possibilitando, assim, a reflexão sobre nossos próprios comportamentos e atitudes. Nesse cartum, a linguagem utilizada pelas personagens em uma conversa em inglês evidencia a

Ⓐ predominância do uso da linguagem informal sobre a língua padrão.

Ⓑ dificuldade de reconhecer a existência de diferentes usos da linguagem.

Ⓒ aceitação dos regionalismos utilizados por pessoas de diferentes lugares.

Ⓓ necessidade de estudo da língua inglesa por parte das personagens.

Ⓔ facilidade de compreensão entre falantes com sotaques distintos.

Extraído de: Exame Nacional do Ensino Médio, 2012, Caderno 6 – CINZA – Página 3 (questão 95).

Part 3 (Make Your Art Sparkle!)

Typical questions of Enem

1. PETA é um acrônimo para uma organização não governamental intitulada "People for the Ethical Treatment of Animals". Nesta propaganda, a artista Kelly Osbourne apoia PETA em uma campanha para
   a) ( ) convidar para um espetáculo em prol das focas.
   b) ( ) demonstrar que eles não usam peles de focas.
   c) ( ) denunciar os países que usam peles de focas.
   d) ( ) impedir que a Europa compre peles de focas.
   e) ( ) protestar contra a matança de focas no Canadá.

2. A expressão SAVE THE SEALS tem a função de
   a) ( ) apresentar uma justificativa.
   b) ( ) comover o leitor emotivo.
   c) ( ) descrever um problema ético.
   d) ( ) pedir ao leitor uma doação.
   e) ( ) persuadir o leitor a fazer algo.

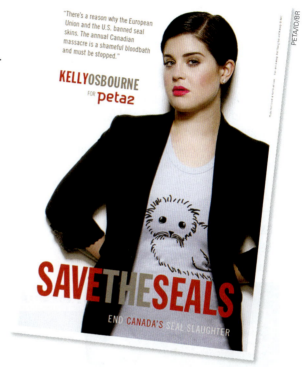

> I live in Birmingham with my husband and four-year-old daughter. I've been a primary school teacher for more years than I care to admit to, but am now following my dreams and developing a career in photography.
>
> Available at: <http://louiseholgate.wordpress.com/about/>.
> Accessed on: January 31, 2013.

3. O trecho acima foi retirado da biografia da fotógrafa Louise Holgate. Ele nos informa que ela
   a) ( ) admite ter deixado de ser professora.
   b) ( ) é professora primária há muitos anos.
   c) ( ) foi professora, mas agora é fotógrafa.
   d) ( ) gosta de ser professora de fotografia.
   e) ( ) sempre sonhou em ser professora.

4. Esta peça de uma campanha publicitária faz uma crítica a
   a) ( ) criadores de crocodilo em cativeiro da PETA.
   b) ( ) fabricantes de acessórios de grifes famosas.
   c) ( ) fabricantes de produtos de couro.
   d) ( ) modismos da manufatura de acessórios caros.
   e) ( ) pessoas que usam bolsas de crocodilo falsas.

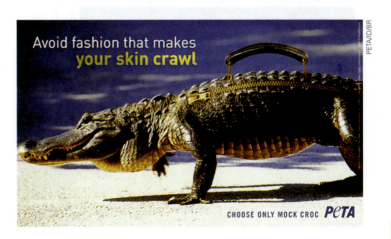

Exam Practice Questions (Vestibular)

Test-Taking Tips

Understand the question!

Many of the tests we take include short answer questions and, sometimes, essay questions. Make sure you really understand what type of answer the examiner wants. Notice that questions 1 and 2 demand answers of varying sizes. Determine every element the questions explore and address each one thoroughly but objectively. Write legibly or you risk having an answer marked "wrong" only because the grader cannot understand you! Pace yourself so that you have enough time to proofread the answers and make sure that what you mean is clear. Study the links below and learn some other strategies to always employ.

- <http://www.uwlax.edu/biology/communication/answeringessayquestions.htm>
- <http://www.monash.edu.au/lls/llonline/study/exam-it/3.2.xml> (both accessed on: January 15, 2014)

TEXT 1 – Questions 1 and 2
UEL-PR, 2014

Leia o anúncio a seguir.

Disponível em: <http://www.redcmarketing.net/wp-content/uploads/2011/02/DIVA-magazine-press-ad_F.jpg>. Acesso em: 12 jul. 2013.

1. Um dos objetivos do texto é divulgar um evento. Responda que evento é esse, onde e quando ele acontece.

_____

_____

_____

2. Estabeleça a relação entre a imagem veiculada, o nome da organização e a frase "Save future generations of girls from hating their bodies".

_____

_____

_____

_____

_____

_____

_____

_____

_____

_____

_____

TEXT 2 – Question 3
UnB-DF, 2012

Girl with a Pearl Earring is a quiet movie about things not said, opportunities not taken, potentials not realized, lips unkissed. All of these elements are guessed at by the filmmakers as they regard a painting made in about 1665 by Johannes Vermeer. The painting shows a young woman looking at us over her left shoulder. She wears a simple blue headband, a modest smock and a pearl earring. Her red lips are slightly parted. Is she smiling?

Not much is known about Vermeer, who left about 35 paintings. Nothing is known about his model. You can hear that it was his daughter, a neighbor, a tradeswoman, but not his lover, because Vermeer's household was under the iron rule of his mother-in-law, who was vigilant as a hawk. The painting has become as intriguing in its modest way as the *Mona Lisa*. The girl's face turned toward us from centuries ago demands that we ask, "Who was she? What was she thinking? What was the artist thinking about her?"

Tracy Chevalier's novel speculating about the painting has now been filmed by Peter Webber, who cast

Part 3 (Make Your Art Sparkle!)

Scarlett Johansson as the girl and Colin Firth as Vermeer. The girl's name is Griet, according to this story. She lives nearby and is sent by her blind father to work in Vermeer's house.

Roger Ebert. *Review of Girl with a Pearl Earring*. Internet: <www.rogerebert.suntimes.com>. Adapted.

3. De acordo com o texto acima, marque, para cada item: o campo designado com o código C, caso julgue o item CERTO; ou o campo designado com o código E, caso julgue o item ERRADO.

	C	E
a) In the writer's opinion, the girl's facial expression is ironic.		
b) In the sentence "You can hear that it was his daughter" (line 19), "it" can correctly be replaced with she.		
c) It is likely that Vermeer's mother-in-law met the girl shown in the painting.		
d) In the text, the word "iron" (line 21) can correctly be replaced with strict.		
e) The painting is compared to the *Mona Lisa* because of the mystery which surrounds it.		
f) The movie answers the questions raised by the painting.		
g) Griet's father did not realize that she was in love with Vermeer.		
h) The filmmakers had more information than Tracy Chevalier about the girl in the painting.		
i) The text contains many details about the girl's clothes.		

- **TEXT 3 – Questions 4 to 6**
Unesp, 2013

Examine os anúncios para responder às questões de números 4 a 6.

Anúncio 1

(www.hongkiat.com. Adaptado.)

Anúncio 2

(www.crookedbrains.net. Adaptado.)

4. O anúncio 1 refere-se
   a) ( ) a uma campanha para economia do consumo de água.
   b) ( ) à divulgação de uma nova tinta para bancos de jardim.
   c) ( ) a uma campanha para embelezar a cidade de Denver.
   d) ( ) à divulgação de reformas nos jardins públicos em Denver.
   e) ( ) a uma campanha contra a destruição de patrimônio público.

5. O anúncio 2 refere-se
   a) ( ) a um incentivo para anúncios mais iluminados.
   b) ( ) a uma empresa de eletricidade chamada Wisely.
   c) ( ) a um incentivo ao uso de lâmpadas fluorescentes.
   d) ( ) ao uso mais consciente de energia elétrica.
   e) ( ) à falta de iluminação suficiente em locais públicos.

6. Os dois anúncios têm em comum o fato de
   a) ( ) terem sido produzidos para empresas de pequeno porte.
   b) ( ) terem sido produzidos para duas empresas concorrentes.
   c) ( ) estimularem o uso de recursos alternativos.
   d) ( ) terem sido produzidos pela mesma agência de publicidade.
   e) ( ) estimularem ações embasadas na sustentabilidade.

93

PART 4: Folk Expressions

Learning plan

Talking about handicrafts

Learning how to express possessive relations

Talking about future plans and making predictions for the near future

Learning vocabulary related to festivals and parades

Planning a festival at school

Adding comments to posts on the Web

Let's learn how to add oral comments to texts and images with VoiceThread.

What is VoiceThread?

An online application to share and discuss texts, slide presentations, images, audio files, and videos.

What can I do with VoiceThread?

· Share texts, photos, slide presentations, and videos;
· Add audio to your texts;
· Draw on top of video clips on the fly (video doodling);
· Pre-record your voice or record it online;
· Have a conversation with your audience;
· Collaborate and share ideas.

What do I need to do?

· Register for VoiceThread by clicking on "Sign in or Register" at their homepage: ‹http://voicethread.com/› (accessed on: May 21, 2014);
· Upload images, slide presentations, videos, or texts;
· Make comments and share your work.

You can learn more about VoiceThread by reading a tutorial at: ‹http://globallyconnectedproj.wikispaces.com/file/view/VoiceThreadTutorial.pdf› (accessed on: May 21, 2014).

95

UNIT

7 Handicrafts

Language in action

- Talk about handicrafts
- Follow instructions on how to make a handicraft
- Learn how to express possessive relations

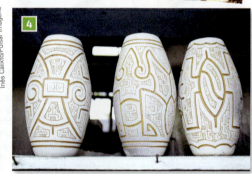

4 ■ Folk Expressions

96

> Lead-in

1. Match each of the handicraft picture on the previous page to one of the categories below. Write the numbers.

   Home Decor: _____ Personal accessories: _____

2. Now find the picture which matches each of the following captions below.

   Brazilian figureheads from the São Francisco River are placed on the prow of the boats. Some people believe they have the power to scare away river demons.

   Lampshades made of recycled plastic bottles are sophisticated handicrafts.

   Brazilian seeds and their beautiful colors can be arranged to make a tray.

   These pairs of earrings look like gold, but their material is "golden grass." Golden grass is found in Tocantins, in the heart of Brazil.

   Filet lace is a very old hand embroidery technique found in the Northeast of Brazil.

   Can you imagine how many cans one needs to make this handbag?

   Marajoara art in ceramics is famous in the state of Pará.

   Her beautiful necklace is made of recycled bottle caps.

   Clay ladies can be found in Caruaru market in Pernambuco and in handicraft shops in different parts of Brazil.

3. Do you (or anyone in your family) make handicrafts? If so, describe the work.

   _____

4. Which handicrafts on the left page were made from natural materials? Which ones were made using recycled objects? Write the names of the pieces.

   Natural materials: _____

   _____

   Recycled objects: _____

   _____

5. Let's create an innovative handicraft project! Look around your environment and see what materials you can use and what objects you could create. Illustrate your project with pictures. Use your notebook.

■ Did you know...?

You can either write **lampshade** or **lamp shade**.

Beyond the lines...

Is every handicraft activity beneficial to the environment? Are there any examples that represent a menace to it?

97

❯ Let's read!

Before you read...
- Do you have handicraft objects in your house? If you do, what objects do you have?
- Can you make handicraft objects? If not, would you like to learn this art?

Hint
It is helpful to learn how to **select what is relevant** when reading a text.

1. Read this announcement for an event and complete the missing information in the table on the next page.

Upcycling fashion and craft workshop

Date: 10-Nov-12
City: South Melbourne Vic
Category: National Recycling Week Event
Venue: South Melbourne Commons, 217 - 239 Montague St, South Melbourne
Date and Time: 10 November 2012, 11am - 1pm

There are five different workshops on offer, you can pick the two you most want to do:

✓ **"Spin it right round"**
Mixed Media Collage Art – Create a magnificent mixed media artwork on reclaimed vinyl LPs or plywood offcuts. Use vintage op-shopped dictionaries, album covers, retro books, poetry, novels and multiple stencil cuts to create amazing multi-layered mixed media works. Art in an instant.

✓ **"Plarn it"**
Make "plarn" (yarn) from used plastic bags, then learn how to weave a square using a homemade cardboard loom. Take your new skills home to make a bag!

✓ **"Breakfast beads"**
Recycled paper beads on zero craft budget. Upcycle your cereal boxes into marvellous beads!

✓ **"The Treasury"**
Based on the simple ethos that everything has potential and nothing is trash, The Treasury is a jewellery fixing and re-creation workshop. Bring along your old or broken jewellery to fix or remake it into something new.

✓ **"Love skin"**
Learn to make your own natural face and body scrub from common kitchen ingredients and take home in recycled kitchen jars.

Bookings required - call 9209 6548 or email enviro@portphillip.vic.gov.au

Did you know...?
The word *plarn* is a blend of **pl**astic + y**arn**.

Available at: <http://recyclingweek.planetark.org/events/display/373>. Accessed on: November 4, 2013.

Planet Ark is an Australian not-for-profit environmental organization, founded in 1992. It aims to teach people and businesses how they can reduce their impact on the planet, at home, at work and in the community. In 1996, Planet Ark founded National Recycling Week to bring a national focus to the environmental benefits of recycling.

Adapted from: <http://planetark.org/about/>. Accessed on: November 4, 2013.

a) Name of the event:	
b) What is being offered:	
c) Number of workshops you can take:	
d) Where to go to learn how to make art:	
e) Material you will use to make beads:	
f) What you will make with kitchen ingredients:	
g) Workshop to attend to learn to fix/recreate jewelry:	

2. What are the social concerns of the organizers?

____

3. What kind of audience would attend the workshops?

____

4. The event mentioned in the text takes place in Melbourne. Where is it located? Check (✔) the correct map.

Maps: Estúdio Mil/ID/BR

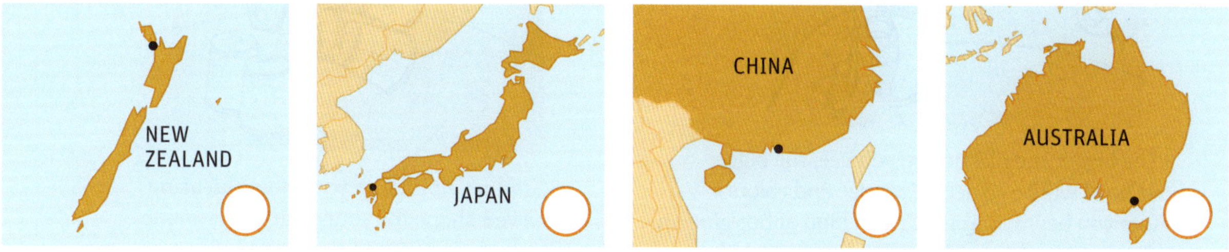

5. What are the other cities indicated in the maps above?

____

6. According to the text, the event starts at 11am. Do you know the time difference between Melbourne and Brasília? Complete the sentence below.

When it is 11am in Melbourne, it is ____________ in Brasília.

7. In which of the workshops mentioned in the text can you learn to make a bowl like the one in this photo?

____

____

Rosa Say/Flickr

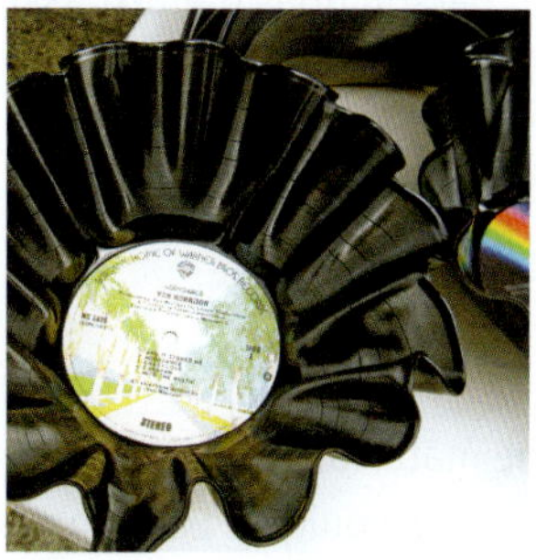

8. Which of the workshops offered in the text would you like to attend? Why?

____

____

9. Are there any similar events in your city/town?

____

10. Do you know any projects that teach people to recycle in order to provide them some extra money? If so, describe it/them.

_____
_____

11. What about trying a simple handicraft project? Look at these instructions on how to make a plastic cup fruit bowl and answer the questions.

How to make a plastic cup fruit bowl

Make a bright and colourful fruit bowl from plastic cups in this fun craft project that's ideal for beginners.

You will need…
· Plastic cups (yogurt cups, for example!)
· Glue gun

Interior designer Gordon Whistance shows you how to make a modern fruit bowl from left over plastic cups.

Step 1: Choose your cups

The bigger the plastic cup you use, the bigger your bowl will be so decide on size and colours before you begin. Carefully put a blob of hot glue on the top and bottom of the side of each cup, where you want to add your next cup.

Step 2: Build a sphere

Gradually build up your bowl, creating a curved shape for your fruit to sit inside. Check for any excess glue and you're ready to add your fruit!

Adapted from: <http://uktv.co.uk/home/item/aid/651314>. Accessed on: May 21, 2014.

a) What is the purpose of the DIY text above?

_____

b) What sort of person does the text assume you are?

_____

c) Why is the text organized in steps?

_____

d) Based on the materials you consume in your community, discuss with a classmate what other things could be used to make a fruit bowl.

_____

> **Did you know…?**
>
> A *do-it-yourself* (DIY) text is a kind of text which teaches you to do something.

12. Suppose you are going to organize some recycling workshops. What workshops would you offer?

_____

Vocabulary corner

Besides recycled objects, handicrafts involve other materials and tools. Look at the items in the pictures and label them using words from the box.

| beads | ceramic tiles | clay | fabric | glass | glue | needle |
| nylon | paint | scissors | seeds | stone | yarn | wood | handsaw |

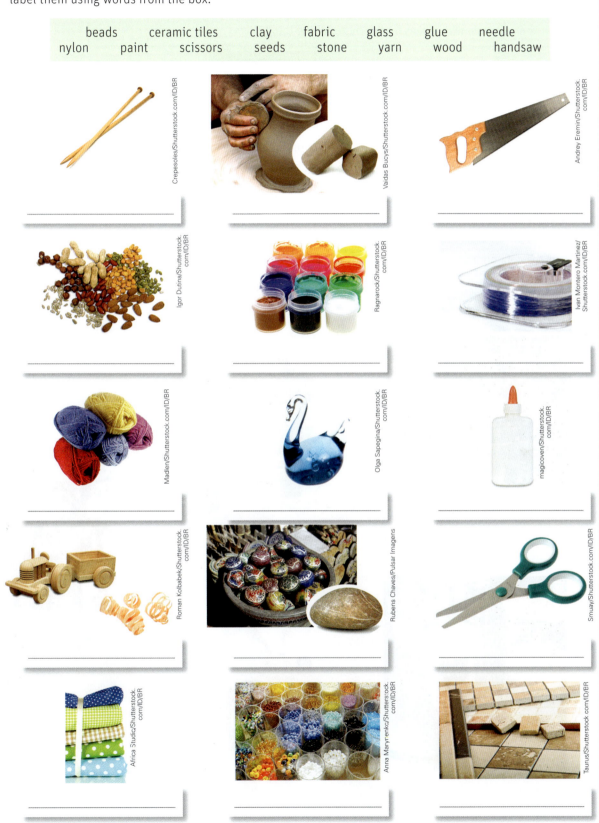

▶ Let's listen and talk!

Before you listen...
- Do you have any objects that are made with recycled material? If so, what?
- Do you know anyone who makes money by recycling things?

1. 🔘15 Listen to the recording and do the following activities.

   a) The main idea of the text is to
      - ( ) inform about how a community turns coconut shells into a commercial activity.
      - ( ) inform about the impact of coconut production in the tourist sector in Phuket.
      - ( ) inform about the beaches and sightseeing in Phuket and its surroundings.

   b) The words *attractive*, *outstanding*, *valuable*, and *delicate* are used to qualify
      - ( ) the waste.
      - ( ) the products.
      - ( ) the community.

2. Look at these upcycled items. Which of them is related to the type of handicraft mentioned in the recording? Check (✔) the option.

3. Now, with a partner, answer this questionnaire.

Questions	Partner's answers
1. Do you have any artistic talents?	
2. Do you know anyone who has artistic talents? What kind?	
3. Do you know any artists that make a living with handicrafts?	
4. Can you name some of the objects in the upcycled items in activity 2?	
5. Can you name objects at home that can be upcycled?	
6. Can you think of any agricultural products that can be upcycled in your region?	

4. Share with the class your partner's ideas of what can be upcycled in your region or community.

Beyond the lines...

a) In some situations, children are involved in working in the informal sector, for example, to make handicrafts. Do you think this is OK? Why (not)?

b) How can child labor be avoided in the informal sector?

Pronunciation spot – Compound words

A compound word is created when two or more words are joined together (e.g. *bedroom*) or used adjacent to one another so often that the combination of words is interpreted as a single noun (e.g. *police station*).

1. 🔘**16** Listen to the following compound words. Underline the word stress.

handmade	lampshades
cardboard	paper beads
homemade	computer programmer
classroom	gas station
basketball	air conditioner
dressmaker	greeting cards

2. 🔘**17** There are cases of non compound words which can cause some confusion. When this occurs, the stress comes on the second word. Listen to the pairs of words below and circle **only the compounds**.

green house	greenhouse
black bird	Blackbird
White House	white house
blueprint	blue print
girl friend	girlfriend

3. How do the pairs of words differ in meaning in activity 2? How can you tell the difference?

› Let's focus on language!

1. Take a look at these statements and do the following activities.

    I. "Bring along **your** old or broken jewellery to fix or remake it into something new."

    II. "[...] they also have so much material in **their** local area."

    III. "Rawai is one of Phuket's famous tourist locations and **our** community in particular [...]"

a) Who do the words in bold refer to? Match the columns and find out.

    I. *"your [...] jewellery"*   (   ) a plural element in the text

    II. *"their [...] area"*   (   ) the people in the neighborhood

    III. *"our community"*   (   ) the readers in general

b) What relationship do the words in bold above establish with the elements they refer to?

_____

> The words *your*, *their*, and *our* tell us **who** or **what** the noun belongs to.

c) Complete this chart with the words in the box.

singular	I	
	You	Your
	He	
	She	
	It	
plural	We	Our
	You	
	They	Their

Its   **Her**   **My**   **Your**   **His**

2. Complete the spaces with the most appropriate words from the chart above and learn about some Brazilian artists.

a) Cornélio was born in 1955 in the small village of Campo Maior, state of Piauí. He started to work very early, helping his father in the joinery. _____ work is mainly related to wood carving.

b) Anna and Julia Salgueiro are mother and daughter and were born in Recife, Pernambuco. They create artistic and decorative items using several paper recycling techniques. _____ work is marked by good humor. They use colors and strong motifs.

c) "Each ballerina has _____ own personality and dances to _____ own music." Dividing _____ time between the Guignard School of Plastic Arts in Belo Horizonte and her own studio in Sabará, Juliana Queiroz de Lima has been creating the Juli Buli Ballerinas since 2002.

d) José Silvano was born in Caruaru, Pernambuco, in 1959. He learned to paint and mold clay from _____ father. _____ works depict the people around him.

Adapted from: <http://www.brasilecia.com.br/>. Accessed on: February 10, 2013.

3. Another way of saying that something belongs to someone or something else is by adding *'s*. Read an example taken from the transcription of the listening section.

"*Rawai is one of Phuket's famous tourist locations and our community in particular [...]*"

In this case, "*Phuket's famous tourist locations*" means "the famous tourist locations located in Phuket."

> If the possessor is a singular noun, add **'s**, like in *girl's handicraft*. If the possessor is a plural noun, just add an apostrophe ('), like in *workers' project*.
>
> If we have more than one possessor of the same item we add **'s** to the last noun, like in *Carol and Pedro's art teacher*.
>
> For irregular plurals add **'s**, like in *the children's crafts*.

4. Based on what you learned about the five artists in activity 2, identify who made the following crafts. The first one is done for you.

a) This ballerina is *Juliana's craft.*

b) This work done with recycled paper is
_____

c) This wood sculpture is _____

d) This craft made of clay is _____

105

UNIT 8

Festivals and parades

Language in action

- Talk about future plans and make predictions for the near future
- Learn vocabulary related to festivals and parades
- Plan a festival at school
- Add a comment to a post on the Web

Image captured from: <http://www.cheltenhamtownhall.org.uk/dyn/_newsletters/august-2012-enewsletter.html>. Accessed on: May 28, 2013.

Bali Food Festival, Bali, Indonesia, 2009.

Duanwu Festival, Beijing, China, 2010.

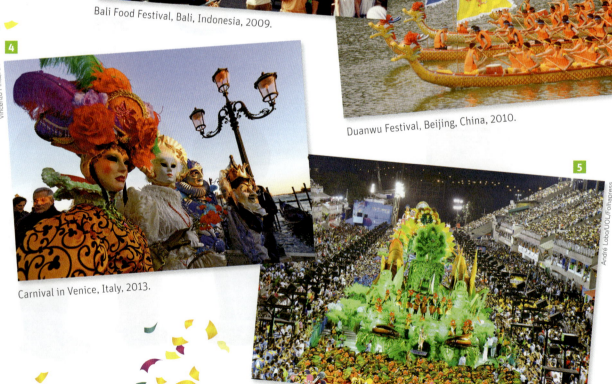

Carnival in Venice, Italy, 2013.

Carnival in Rio de Janeiro, Brazil, 2013.

> Lead-in

1. What is the most famous festival in Brazil? And in your state? _____

2. Match each image on the left page to its corresponding text below. Write the number.

( ) Brazil is world-famous for its Carnival celebrations. Carnival is celebrated all around the country, but the most famous celebrations happen in Rio, Bahia and Pernambuco.

Available at: <http://leilamelquiades.blogspot.com.br/2011/03/carnival-in-brazil.html>. Accessed on: November 4, 2013.

( ) *Wednesday 14 November 2012*

The Boy with Tape on his Face promises a comedy evening like no other: mime with noise, stand-up with no talking, and drama with no acting, when he performs live at Parabola Arts Centre.

Available at: <http://www.soglos.com/comedy/33233/Hobgoblin-Cheltenham-Comedy-Festival>. Accessed on: February 11, 2013.

( ) Dragon boats are giant sized boats painted attractively and embellished with a dragon head and tail. The race begins with the rowing of boats to the rhythm of pounding drums. Once the night falls the breath-taking Dragon Lanterns and brightly lit creations come alive and truly steal the show.

Available at: <http://www.funonthenet.in/festivals/unique-festivals-world.html>. Accessed on: November 4, 2013.

( ) *Sept 29-Oct 3, 2010*   Kuta Karnival Bali Food Festival [...]

You are invited to take part in this year's event, where you will be able to show-off your culinary delights or products whilst being part of a truly fun weekend. We expect over 30,000 visitors for the three days.

Available at: <http://www.foodreference.com/html/indonesia-food-shows.html>. Accessed on: November 4, 2013.

( ) Venetian masks were worn first in the 15th century to remove social and sexual differences. During the Carnival, Venice comes alive with masked Venetians and tourists. Bands, jugglers and entertainers are everywhere and the canals are full of colorful boats.

Available at: <http://www.funonthenet.in/festivals/unique-festivals-world.html>. Accessed on: November 4, 2013.

3. Look at the picture of Sam Wills on the right and answer these questions.

a) In what festival can we find this man?

_____

b) What is he called?

_____

c) What is Sam's profession?

_____

d) What are his main means of communication with his public?

( ) gestures   ( ) voice   ( ) facial expressions

4. Look at picture 2. Based on the clothes people are wearing, what was the weather probably like on that day?

( ) warm   ( ) cold   ( ) freezing

107

> Let's read!

Before you read...
- Do you like going to music festivals or concerts? What is the last one you went to?
- Who would play at your "ideal" music festival?

Hint
Anticipate what you may find in the text by identifying the magazine and section it was published in, as well as the pictures, videos, and links associated with it.

1. The text below was published during the organization of Reading and Leeds Festivals in 2013. Quickly read the piece of news about their plans and answer the questions.

Reading & Leeds organisers have revealed that they are looking to add three new stages to the event in 2013.

The festival, which currently boasts six stages and was headlined by Kasabian, Foo Fighters and The Cure in 2012, would increase to nine in 2013 but keep its capacity at the same level. Festival Republic boss Melvin Benn has revealed that the plan is to "add more music" to the festivals, especially for fans of dance music.

Foo Fighters with Dave Grohl at the center.

Speaking to BBC Newsbeat, Benn stated: "We're changing the arena at Reading and Leeds quite significantly. I've got quite a strong buzz and feeling in myself in the changes that I'm making there. I'm still formulating the ideas." He adds: "There will be quite a bit more dance music, quite a bit more other bits and pieces."

Benn also revealed that he is hoping to name the first of the festivals' three headliners before Christmas.

It was confirmed at this year's Reading Festival that two of the three headliners for 2013 are already confirmed, though The Stone Roses are unlikely to feature. Similarly, Benn also expressed a belief that The Black Keys and Florence and The Machine will be headliners in years to come.

COMMENTS

Available at: <http://www.nme.com/news/various-artists/66939>. Accessed on: November 4, 2013.

The Reading and Leeds Festivals are a pair of music events that occur simultaneously every year in Reading and Leeds, two cities in England.

a) Who is the intended audience?

_____

_____

b) What is the purpose of the text?

_____

2. Read the text again and find out the answers for the following pieces of information.

a) The number of stages in the 2012 edition of the festival: _____

b) The possible number of stages in the 2013 edition of the festival: _____

c) The bands/artists that headlined the 2012 festival: _____

d) The number of headliners that were already confirmed for 2013: _____

e) The preferred music style for the 2013 edition: _____

f) Possible artists in future festivals: _____

3. Read the comments that two readers left after reading the piece of news. Which reader

a) believes the festival will need more land? _____

b) thinks there will be a DJ and acoustic tent? _____

c) believes prices for the festival will increase? _____

d) thinks the festival has sound problems? _____

4. Has anyone ever organized a festival similar to Reading and Leeds Festivals in your state or country? If so, what was it?

_____

5. Read about the TIFF Next Wave Film Festival and answer the questions on the next page.

http://tiff.net/nextwave/about

tiff. Toronto International Film Festival Inc./ID/BR

The TIFF Next Wave Film Festival is the new annual festival exclusively for youth aged 14 to 18. This exciting event includes twenty films made for youth – and in some cases by youth – along with an array of activities in which students are exposed to the world of cinema and to life behind the lens. From February 15 through 17, TIFF Bell Lightbox will be turned over to the next generation of movie lovers!

With films from across the globe and spanning all genres, TIFF Next Wave Film Festival brings the world of cinema to Toronto's youth audiences. The festival also includes an exciting slate of special guests, seminars and showcases for young filmmakers. Select screenings are accompanied by Q&A sessions with directors and special guests.

Find out about the TIFF Next Wave Committee

Available at: <http://tiff.net/nextwave/about>. Accessed on: February 11, 2013.

The Toronto International Film Festival (TIFF) is a Canadian event for film lovers. It offers screenings, lectures, discussions, workshops, and industry support.

Adapted from: <http://tiff.net/about>. Accessed on: November 4, 2013.

a) Who is the TIFF event for?

_____

b) What is the purpose of this Canadian festival?

_____

c) Who are the people in the picture?

_____

6. Read the text about the TIFF Next Wave Film Festival again and match the items in the left column to the corresponding information in the right column.

a) festival venue ( ) Bell Lightbox
b) city where the festival takes place ( ) 14 to 18
c) age of target audience ( ) Q&A sessions with directors and special guests
d) number of films in the festival
e) what is also part of the festival ( ) 20
f) what select screenings also include ( ) Toronto
( ) special guests, seminars, and showcases

Did you know...?
Q&A means **Q**uestion and **A**nswer.

7. The two texts you have just read are about music and film festivals. Make a list of different festivals in your region and ask your classmates if they have plans to go. See an example.

> Are you going to the Ora-Pro-Nobis Festival in May in Sabará?

> Yes, I am. / No, I am not. I live too far away. / No, I am going to (name of another festival).

Vocabulary corner

Label the images using words from the box.

| Carnival float | costume | crowd | Venetian mask | face paint kit | Mardi Gras beads |

_____   _____   _____

_____   _____   _____

> Let's focus on language!

1. Read these three statements. Two of them were taken from the first text in the *Let's read!* section.

> I. […] they **are looking** to add three new stages to the event in 2013.
>
> II. Unless they **are getting** more land, adding more stages **is** just **going to make** the problem even worse.
>
> III. Tonight I **am going** to Budapest – for the Sziget Music Festival!
> Available at: <http://www.imperatortravel.com/2012/08/tonight-i-am-going-to-budapest-for-the-sziget-festival.html>.
> Accessed on: November 4, 2013.

The parts in bold express

( ) a prediction.   ( ) an ongoing event.   ( ) a future plan.

2. Complete the rules and learn about how to speak of the future. Use words from the box.

> interrogative   future plans/intentions   negative   predictions   Present Continuous

When we want to express _____ or _____,
we use the structure **am/are/is** + **going to** + **verb**.

To make the _____, we add **not** after **am/are/is**.

To make the _____, we use **am/are/is** + **SUBJECT** + **going to** + **verb**.

We can also use the _____ when we want to talk about the near future.

3. Imagine you are attending the TIFF event. Look at four films made by post-secondary students from across Canada. Decide which one(s) you are(not) going to watch and give reasons. Write your plans in your notebook, as in the example on the next page.

Venue	**Friday**									
	10:00am	11:00am	12:00pm	1:00pm	2:00pm	3:00pm	4:00pm	5:00pm	6:00pm	7:00pm
Theater 1			**Basic Space** *by Carrie Mombourquette* — Two roommates find a novel solution to the tiny confines of their apartment in this unique paper-based animation.							
Theater 2	10:00 AM-11:27 AM (*FAT*) Read more...		12:45 PM-2:01 PM (*FAT*) Read more...				**FAT** *by Margaret Donahoe* — A bold and personal documentary combining interviews and self-portraits, *FAT* unflinchingly explores issues of self-image and stereotype.			
Theater 3		10:30 AM-11:30 AM (*Basic Space*) Read more...	**Pale Blue Dot** *by Adam Winnik* — Fall into this contemplative animation that considers our place in the vast universe. Narrated by Carl Sagan.							
Theater 4	10:00 AM-11:00 AM (*Make Treks*) Read more...		12:15 PM-1:30PM (*Pale Blue Dot*) Read more...	**Make Treks** *by Chris Chami* — *Make Treks* is a raw profile of a not-for-profit that harnesses the power of social media in bringing awareness to the plight of Toronto's homeless.						
Theater 5			12:00 PM-1:00 PM (*Basic Space*) Read more...							

Adapted from: <http://tiff.net/nextwave/films/2013/schedule/day>. Accessed on: February 17, 2013.

> *I'm going to... (and...) because...*
>
> *I'm definitely not watching... (or...) because...*

4. You and your classmates need to organize a school festival. What are you going to need? You have a budget of 500 dollars to spend on the general cost of the event. Make a list, choosing items to prepare for the party and calculate costs for 150 people. Check prices in local markets. If you need more money, decide on an adequate price for the tickets. Include prices in dollars or "reais."

Public health
Toilet paper – $_____
Liquid soap – $_____
Paper towel – $_____
Trash cans – free

Incident management plan
Lost property – free
First aid – $_____
Fire extinguishers – free

Traffic and pedestrian management
Parking – free
Tickets – $_____
(decide on a price)

Furniture
Rental (tables, chairs, stools) – $_____
Food stalls - $_____

Entertainment
Live band – $_____
Dance performance – $_____
DJ - $_____

Food
Finger food – $_____
(decide on kind of food & price - include typical food from your region)

You can add more ideas to the options above and include items the school can offer free of charge.

Ask and answer questions as in the examples below.

> **Let's listen and talk!**

Before you listen...
- Does your school or community promote any festival regularly? If so, what kind of festival is it? Does it take place annually?

1. ⊙18 Listen to the recording and do the activities.

    a) This text is
       ( ) an interview about a festival.   ( ) a commercial about a festival.
       ( ) a news report about a festival.

    b) Based on your experience with English, what variant do you recognize in this passage: British or American English?

    _____

    c) How many speakers take part in this recording?

    _____

2. ⊙18 Listen again and choose the correct option to complete the statements.

    a) The name of the food festival is
       ( ) Savor Food Festival.   ( ) Sample Food Festival.

    b) The day of the festival is
       ( ) Saturday, October 6.   ( ) Friday, October 5.

    c) At this festival, you can find
       ( ) live music.   ( ) local shops.
       ( ) soft drinks.   ( ) children's activities.
       ( ) tasting plates.   ( ) producer and lifestyle exhibitors.

3. Look at this picture captured from the video and write appropriate answers.

Image captured from: <http://www.youtube.com/watch?v=qN-UaMWMcYA>.
Accessed on: November 5, 2013.

a) What are they doing?

_____
_____
_____

b) What are they going to do?

_____
_____
_____

113

4. Imagine you are holding a food festival. With a classmate, make a to-do list to guide your steps. Use the prompts below, if necessary. Present your plans to the class.

Organization	Things to do
Venue/site plan	Choose a location
Date and time	Set a date and time
Equipment	List the necessary equipment
Kinds of food	Choose the kinds of food
Participants	Decide who to invite to participate
Advertisement/media	Decide how to advertise the event
Decoration/music	Choose the decoration/music, etc.

Useful language

The festival is going to be... at school/the school courts/the gymnasium

We... serve...   Brazilian/regional dishes   finger food   regional desserts

We... decorate the table/the walls with balloons/pictures of food/banners of typical dishes, etc.

The band/DJ is going to play...   good music/country music/jazz/rock.

We... use posters/flyers...   to advertise.

Pronunciation spot – Sounds /m/ and /n/

The sounds /m/ and /n/ aren't commonly pronounced in final position in Brazilian Portuguese. Instead, we nasalize the final vowel sound.

1. ⊚**19** Listen and compare how these proper names would be usually pronounced by a Brazilian and an American.

Melvin Benn	Kasabian	Sean Penn	Ann Sheridan
Cheltenham	Sam	Liam Neeson	Jason Statham

2. ⊚**20** Listen and repeat the words and proper nouns below. Pay attention to the final sounds /m/ and /n/.

yum	from	some
ma'am	Eminem	Kim Kardashian
can	been	an
one	One Direction	Owen Wilson

The "explain yourself" game

Copy the words below on separate pieces of paper. Put the 16 pieces of paper in a bag. Pass this bag around the class so that each student takes one item at a time. The class asks, for example:

Why do you have an electric bug racket in your bag? Explain yourself!

The student thinks of a good reason and explains, for example:

I'm going to go hunting mosquitoes at night.

If another student takes the same item, he or she should give a different reason. The more creative, the better!

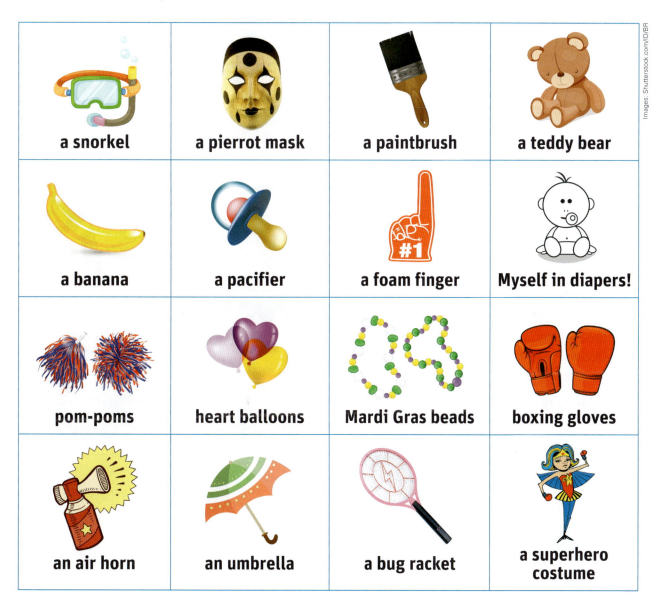

a snorkel	a pierrot mask	a paintbrush	a teddy bear
a banana	a pacifier	a foam finger	Myself in diapers!
pom-poms	heart balloons	Mardi Gras beads	boxing gloves
an air horn	an umbrella	a bug racket	a superhero costume

■ **Useful language**

| eat | hug | sleep | propose | lick | support | wake up | save |
| paint | | scuba diving | cheerleader | cockroach | | costume party | parade |

Example: *I have a superhero costume because I am going to a parade/costume party.*

Let's act with words!

Let's write a comment to post on a website

Comments are used to express personal opinion, join a debate, or add more information about the post under discussion.

Splashing out for Carnival 2012

Though Brazil is the sixth largest economy in the world, the largely unbalanced distribution of wealth means the average citizen is generally not wealthy. Despite this, at Carnival time, no expense is spared even amongst many of the poorest people in the country.

For example, one of the most expensive costumes that will be flaunted at events *throughout* Brazil for Carnival 2012 can be purchased ready to wear for the price of R$800 (£296 GBP/$465 USD).

Adapted from: <http://www.therealbrazil.com/blog/2012/02/15/splashing-out-for-carnival-2012/>. Accessed on: May 21, 2014.

Writing Steps

Organizing
- Read the excerpt of a blog above and identify the problem.
- Decide if you agree or disagree with the author.
- List arguments to justify your opinion.

Preparing the first draft
- Make a first draft of a comment in your notebook.
- Use first person to show your voice. For example: *I think… / My opinion…*

Peer editing
- Evaluate your text and discuss your first draft with a partner.
- Make the necessary corrections.

Publishing
- Access the blog at <http://www.therealbrazil.com/blog/2012/02/15/splashing-out-for-carnival-2012/> (accessed on: May 21, 2014).
- Insert your comment in the form under the news and submit it.
- Alternatively, if you do not have access to the Internet, you can make a summary of the news, add your comment, and publish it on a wall newspaper.

Genre: Comment

Purpose: To reflect about a piece of news

Tone: Informal

Setting: Blog or a wall newspaper

Writer(s): You

Audience: School community or blog readers

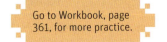

Go to Workbook, page 361, for more practice.

Learning tips

Playing a memory game to associate words to images

Memry is a memory game that uses Flickr pictures as cards. You write a tag and the game cards suit the word. You work with only one concept at a time. Here are some basic guidelines for you to play and learn with this Web tool.

- Go to <http://www.pimpampum.net/memry> (accessed on: May 21, 2014).
- Choose a tag and type it. Example: **parades**.
- Press *Play!* to begin the game.
- Click on the squares to find the right matches.
- The game is over when all photos have been matched.
- If you want to enlarge the picture, click on it and it will open in Flickr.

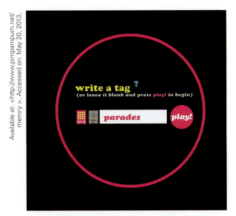 

Images captured from: <http://www.pimpampum.net/memry/enter.php>. Accessed on: November 5, 2013.

Alternatively, you can make this memory game in paper with a collection of words and images taken from old magazines, for example. Have fun!

Let's reflect on learning!

You are now invited to assess what you learned and how you learned. Finish the ideas below on an extra sheet of paper and become a more autonomous and reflective learner.

In Part 4

I learned _____

I liked _____

I need to review/learn more _____

My experiences with English outside school were ____

117

Let's study for Enem!

Enem Questions

Do one thing for diversity and inclusion

The United Nations Alliance of Civilizations (UNAOC) is launching a campaign aimed at engaging people around the world to *Do One Thing* to support Cultural Diversity and Inclusion. Every one of us can do ONE thing for diversity and inclusion; even one very little thing can become a global action if we all take part in it.

Simple things YOU can do to celebrate the World Day for Cultural Diversity for Dialogue and Development on May 21.

1. Visit an art exhibit or a museum dedicated to other cultures.

2. Read about the great thinkers of other cultures.

3. Visit a place of worship different than yours and participate in the celebration.

4. Spread your own culture around the world and learn about other cultures.

5. Explore music of a different culture.

There are thousands of things that you can do, **are you taking part in it**?

United Nations Alliance of Civilizations. Disponível em: <www.unaoc.org>. Acesso em: 16 fev. 2013. Adaptado.

Gênero

Artigo informativo

Competência de área 2

H6 - Utilizar os conhecimentos da LEM e de seus mecanismos como meio de ampliar as possibilidades de acesso a informações, tecnologias e culturas.

Os títulos dos textos nem sempre oferecem uma visão clara do assunto. Em alguns casos, eles se limitam a apresentar o tema geral. Procure sempre usar os títulos como estratégia de leitura, mas avalie o seu valor informacional.

Questões que envolvem síntese e julgamento demandam maior atenção por parte do leitor.
Se necessário, leia as alternativas e a parte relevante do texto mais de uma vez para ter certeza da sua resposta.

Internautas costumam manifestar suas opiniões sobre artigos *on-line* por meio da postagem de comentários. O comentário que exemplifica o engajamento proposto na quarta dica da campanha apresentada no texto é:

A "Lá na minha escola, aprendi a jogar capoeira para uma apresentação no Dia da Consciência Negra."

B "Outro dia assisti na TV uma reportagem sobre respeito à diversidade. Gente de todos os tipos, várias tribos. Curti bastante."

C "Eu me inscrevi no Programa Jovens Embaixadores para mostrar o que tem de bom em meu país e conhecer outras formas de ser."

D "Curto muito bater papo na internet. Meus amigos estrangeiros me ajudam a aperfeiçoar minha proficiência em língua estrangeira."

E "Pesquisei em *sites* de culinária e preparei uma festa árabe para uns amigos da escola. Eles adoraram, principalmente, os doces!"

Extraído de: Exame Nacional do Ensino Médio, 2013, Caderno 6 – CINZA – Página 4 (questão 95).

Part 4 (Folk Expressions)

Typical questions of Enem

"The Treasury"

Based on the simple ethos that everything has potential and nothing is trash, The Treasury is a jewellery fixing and re-creation workshop. Bring along your old or broken jewellery to fix or remake it into something new.

Available at: <http://recyclingweek.planetark.org/events/display/373>. Accessed on: May 21, 2014.

1. Esse excerto foi retirado do anúncio de um evento sobre artesanato, realizado em 2012 na Austrália. O anúncio apresentava uma lista de oficinas de reciclagem de objetos usados. A oficina "The Treasury" teve como objetivo

    ( ) consertar e recriar ornamentos pessoais.
    ( ) contribuir para formação de joalheiros.
    ( ) discutir o potencial da criação de joias.
    ( ) fixar e difundir a recriação de bijuterias.
    ( ) transformar lixo em peças artesanais.

Splashing out for Carnival 2012

Though Brazil is the sixth largest economy in the world, the largely unbalanced distribution of wealth means the average citizen is generally not wealthy. Despite this, at Carnival time, no expense is spared even amongst many of the poorest people in the country. For example, one of the most expensive costumes that will be flaunted at events throughout Brazil for Carnival 2012 can be purchased ready to wear for the price of R$800 (£296 GBP/$465 USD).

Adapted from: <http://www.therealbrazil.com/blog/2012/02/15/splashing-out-for-carnival-2012/>. Accessed on: May 21, 2014.

2. O trecho acima, uma adaptação de um texto publicado no blog *The Buzz from Brazil*, fala sobre o preço de uma determinada fantasia de Carnaval no Brasil. O autor procura mostrar a contradição entre

    ( ) a distribuição de riqueza e a exibição de fantasias durante o ano.
    ( ) as despesas com as fantasias e a poupança feitas pelos mais pobres.
    ( ) as fantasias mais caras e a diminuição dos preços no período da festa.
    ( ) o perfil econômico do cidadão médio brasileiro e o preço das fantasias.
    ( ) os costumes dos mais pobres no Brasil e a escolha de trajes mais caros.

Exam Practice Questions (Vestibular)

Test-Taking Tips

Don't let long texts intimidate you!

Feeling a bit nervous on this day is normal. It can even help you focus. But don't let anxiety interfere with your performance on test day. Many factors can intimidate us when we take tests. For example, sometimes the texts are too long or too numerous! What you can do is take a deep breath and relax. Focus on what you know, and remember that reading strategies can help you interact with any text more efficiently. Notice how information is organized. A text usually presents information in a logical or chronological order, so if you pay attention to its organization you may locate what you need to find the answers faster. Concentrate on your test, pace yourself, and don't worry if others finish before you.

TEXT 1 – Questions 1 to 3

UNIOESTE-PR, 2014

Embratur will Release a Term for Promoting Brazilian *Junina* Parties Abroad

Advertising interventions are part of strategy to publicise popular parties in the country, making the most of the visibility provided by the World Cup

Turning the June folk parties into a Brazilian cultural icon abroad is the new challenge being faced by the Brazilian Tourism Agency (Embratur) in the next few months. Embratur is developing interventions together with states in Brazil's northern and northeast regions, where these parties are a tradition and attract a lot of tourists. One of them will be the terms for bidding, worth R$ 3 million, which should be ready in September, when states and municipalities will be able to submit projects aimed at publicising the parties. In 2014, these parties will be held at the same time as the 2014 World Cup.

"We need to provide the world with an additional image of Brazil in relation to the June parties. We want foreign tourists to associate Brazil to these parties also, as they do with carnival", stated Embratur president Flavio Dino.

"We want to turn these June parties into a strong and consolidated tourist product. We are going to play host to around 600 thousand foreign tourists, who will visit the country as a result of the World Cup. We have to make the most of this moment to strengthen Brazilian tourist culture and products", stated the head of Embratur Executive Office, Katia Bitencourt.

Katia also explained that the intervention will also promote other parties normally held in June, such as the Parintins Festival. "We don't want to restrict ourselves to the São João parties by encompassing all cultural celebrations held in the country at that time". Embratur is also developing a set of marketing, digital communication interventions, press trips and is aiming to take part in international trade shows to promote the parties.

Last June, Embratur brought journalists from South America, Europe and the United States to these parties in north and northeast regions. In addition, campaigns were conducted on social networks such as Instagram and Facebook, encouraging those going to the parties to publish their pictures and impressions about them.

Adapted from: http://www.copa2014.gov.br/en/noticia/embratur-will-release-a-terms-bidding-promotingbrazilian-junina-parties-abroad.

1. De acordo com o texto, qual é o <u>novo</u> desafio enfrentado pela Embratur?

a) ( ) Desenvolver intervenções nos Estados brasileiros onde há muitos turistas.

b) ( ) Promover o festival de Parintins – Amazonas – internacionalmente.

c) ( ) Promover campanhas de divulgação pela internet.

d) ( ) Encorajar as pessoas a publicarem suas participações nas redes sociais.

e) ( ) Fazer com que as festas juninas se transformem em um ícone no exterior.

2. Ainda, de acordo com o texto, somente é CORRETO afirmar que

a) ( ) para divulgar a realização de festas populares no Brasil, como estratégia para promover a Copa Mundial de 2014, somente as redes sociais Instagram, Facebook e Twitter serão utilizadas.

b) ( ) as festas populares atraem mais turistas nas regiões Sul e Norte do Brasil.

c) ( ) Katia Bitencourt e Flávio Dino são os principais organizadores da Copa Mundial de 2014.

d) ( ) somente os órgãos estaduais poderão submeter projetos para a realização das festas na Copa Mundial.

e) ( ) as festas juninas brasileiras acontecerão juntamente com as atividades da Copa Mundial em 2014.

Part 4 (Folk Expressions)

3. Sobre a última sentença do texto: "encouraging those going to the parties to publish their pictures and impressions about them", é CORRETO afirmar que

a) (   ) "those" refere-se às pessoas em geral.

b) (   ) "those" refere-se às campanhas para a Copa Mundial de 2014.

c) (   ) "them" refere-se às redes sociais da internet.

d) (   ) "those" e "their" referem-se às festas populares.

e) (   ) "them" refere-se às redes sociais.

- **TEXT 2 – Questions 4 to 7**

UFTM-MG, 2010

Brazil... Life is a Carnival

Iman Kurdi, 23 March 2010

Visiting Brazil is my first experience of being in a BRIC country. I have never been to Russia, India or China, the other three countries that make up the BRIC acronym, so I was intrigued to see what an economic success story looks like.

My first port of call is Rio de Janeiro, possibly the most beautiful city I have ever visited but also in some respects the most disconcerting. As a tourist you are warned to be not just careful but weary, making you constantly aware of potential danger, and consequently it is hard to feel entirely relaxed. As a human being it is hard not to feel distressed at the sight of the sprawling Favelas where hundreds of thousands live in enduring misery. I was shocked to see that there are now Favela Tours on the tourist trail. I find the idea that the Favelas have now become a tourist attraction somewhat obscene. And though the middle class is growing fast, one in four remains below the poverty line.

All the stereotypes are quickly confirmed. First, of course, there is the beach culture with the women wearing the tiniest bikinis I have seen. Then there is the national passion for football. In Rio, I saw them play on the beach, in the street, in parks, anywhere they could kick a ball. In Brasilia I noticed how the villas of the rich often have their own football fields. Then there is the samba and the capacity to party. Brazilians are a fun-loving people. It is just as you expect it to be.

What you don't expect are the prices. The days when Brazil was a cheap place to visit are long gone. A cup of coffee in Rio is as expensive as New York or Paris. Entrance prices to the main tourist attractions are priced in the same range as tourist attractions in London.

The Brazilian economy is thriving. It was one of the last countries to be hit by the financial crisis and has been one of the first to emerge from recession. However, poverty and income inequality remain serious problems in Brazil, with the crime and security issues that naturally follow.

www.khaleejtimes.com/DisplayArticle.asp?xfile=data. Adaptado.

4. Responda em português, de acordo com o texto.

a) Quais países BRIC a autora do texto visitou?

b) No trecho do primeiro parágrafo, a qual país a autora se refere como *an economic success story*?

5. Responda em português, segundo as informações do texto.

a) Por que os turistas não ficam totalmente relaxados no Rio de Janeiro?

b) Que impressão a autora teve das favelas do Rio de Janeiro?

6. Responda em português, segundo as informações do texto.

a) Mesmo com o crescimento da classe média, que dado o texto apresenta sobre a pobreza?

b) Que estereótipos sobre os cariocas a autora confirmou ao visitar o Rio de Janeiro?

7. Answer the following in English, according to the text.

a) What didn't the author expect about Brazil?

b) Although the economy is growing, what are the challenges Brazil has to overcome?

121

PART 5
Social Networks

Learning plan

Reading infographics and posters

Talking about things that are always true and things that happen regularly

Talking about things happening around now and actions in process

Making recommendations and warnings, giving orders and instructions

Talking about safety on the web

Making infographics

Year Project – My Portfolio

What is a portfolio?

In the context of school, a portfolio is a collection of all the activites developed by the student.

What are some of the benefits of a portfolio?
- You can observe your personal growth.
- You have better attitudes towards your work.
- You start thinking of yourself as a writer.
- You identify weak spots in your work.

Source: <http://712educators.about.com/od/portfolios/a/portfolios.htm>. Accessed on: May 19, 2014.

Steps to create a student portfolio

1. **Collect:** You can collect your drafts and finished works on a computer, in a folder, or in a box.

2. **Reflect:** Select the best version of each work and write a presentation with your opinion about it.

3. **Publish:** You can publish the final versions on your wiki*. If you don't have your own wiki, you can create one at <http://www.wikispaces.com/> (accessed on: May 19, 2014) or you can join an existing group.

*__Wiki__: a website which allows its readers to freely add and edit content and to create links between different pieces of content. Available at: <http://www.macmillandictionary.com/dictionary/british/wiki>. Accessed on: May 19, 2014.

123

UNIT 9
Making connections

Language in action

- Learn to read infographics
- Learn how to give tips and instructions
- Talk about things that are always true and things that happen regularly
- Talk about things happening around now and actions in process

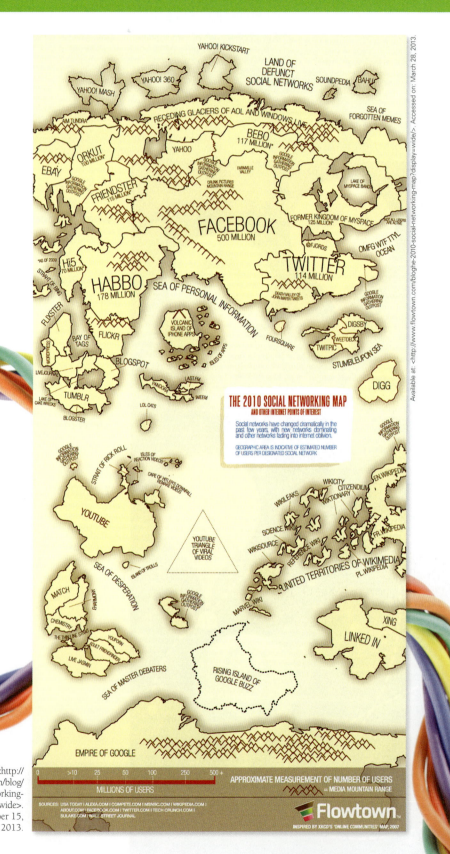

Adapted from: <http://www.flowtown.com/blog/the-2010-social-networking-map?display=wide>. Accessed on: November 15, 2013.

> Lead-in

1. Take a look at the text on the previous page. Which words are you familiar with? What do you know about them?

   _____

2. Look at the text on the previous page again and answer these questions orally.

   a) What does it seem to be?

   b) What is the purpose of this text?

   c) Who is the intended audience for this text?

   d) What does it represent?

   e) How is this similar to or different from a world map?

3. The elements that make up this text allow us to say that

   (   ) it is a graph.

   (   ) it is an infographic.

   (   ) it is a map.

4. Below are some typical features of this textual genre. Check (✔) the ones you can find on the previous page. Then find examples from the text to support your choices.

   (   ) It communicates complex ideas in a clear and often attractive way.

   (   ) It doesn't integrate images and words in its creation.

   (   ) The aesthetic design draws the viewer in.

   (   ) It is a type of visualization easier to understand than words alone.

   (   ) The size of the letters isn't so important to convey message.

   (   ) Graphics are integrated to reveal information, patterns or trends.

   (   ) It tells a story by means of easy-to-read illustrations.

   (   ) It doesn't mention data sources.

   (   ) It aims at twisting the facts by means of dubious images.

   Adapted from: <http://visual.ly/what-is-an-infographic>. Accessed on: November 15, 2013.

5. Now read the text on the previous page more carefully. Which social networks seem to be on the rise and which ones are in decline? Justify your answer.

   _____
   _____
   _____
   _____

   ## Beyond the lines...

   Are all Internet users represented in this infographic?

Shutterstock.com/ID/BR

125

> Let's read!

Before you read...
- Are you a network addict?
- Look at the image below and name the networks you are a member of.

Managing Your Social Network Addiction
By Ibrahim Husain

Facebook, LinkedIn, MySpace, Twitter [...] the list goes on and on. And if you are any sort of tech savvy, there is good chance you are a member of multiple social networks. Even I have accounts with at least 5 of these. While there is a lot to be gained by using these services, there is also a lot to be lost.

[...]

Here are a few tips that can help you monitor your social network use, and ensure that you are being productive instead of wasting time.

- **Track Your Time Online**
  The simplest way to ensure you aren't wasting time in any one place is to monitor your time. Use a stopwatch and set a limit. When time is up, log out, regardless of what's left. There is always tomorrow.

- **Remember the Telephone**
  I know, it's so primitive. But a call to a friend works just as well as a Facebook message, and it is real human interaction, something we are losing touch with.

- **Go Outside**
  Get away from your portal to the network. Get some sunshine, chances are you need it.

Ibrahim Husain is from Texas, USA, and writes motivational and self development works for many online publications.

- **Limit Your Memberships**
  There is no need for memberships to 15 different networks. In fact, there is no need for even 2 memberships of sites which do the same thing. Choose Facebook or Myspace, but not both. Digg, or StumbleUpon. This will probably cut your memberships in half, and hopefully cut the time spent on them down also.

  [...]

- **Spend More Time With Close Friends and Family**
  You aren't the only one who suffers when you spend countless hours on MySpace. Your family and friends don't see you, because you are too busy learning how to customize your backgrounds and take crazy pictures from all different angles for your profile pic. [...] get back to friends and family. [...]

  Available at: <www.lifehack.org/articles/productivity/managing-your-social-network-addiction.html>. Accessed on: November 15, 2013.

1. Who is the intended audience for this text?

2. What is the purpose of this text?

3. According to the text, what can be an indication of social network addiction?

4. Do you agree with the author's opinions? Support your answer.

5. In pairs, rank the five suggestions given by the author according to what you consider more or less effective. Give reasons for your judgement.

Suggestions	Reason(s)
1st	
2nd	
3rd	
4th	
5th	

127

› Let's listen and talk!

Before you listen...
- With a classmate, read the title of the text below and guess possible answers for the question.

1. 🔴21 Read and listen to the text below. Then answer the questions.

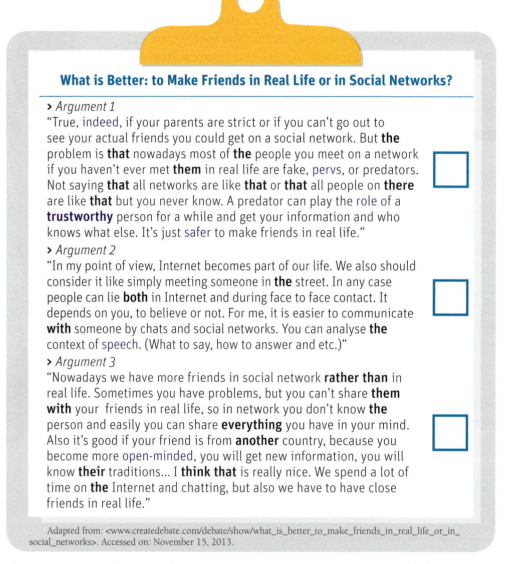

What is Better: to Make Friends in Real Life or in Social Networks?

› *Argument 1*
"True, indeed, if your parents are strict or if you can't go out to see your actual friends you could get on a social network. But **the** problem is **that** nowadays most of **the** people you meet on a network if you haven't ever met **them** in real life are fake, pervs, or predators. Not saying **that** all networks are like **that** or **that** all people on **there** are like **that** but you never know. A predator can play the role of a **trustworthy** person for a while and get your information and who knows what else. It's just safer to make friends in real life."

› *Argument 2*
"In my point of view, Internet becomes part of our life. We also should consider it like simply meeting someone in **the** street. In any case people can lie **both** in Internet and during face to face contact. It depends on you, to believe or not. For me, it is easier to communicate **with** someone by chats and social networks. You can analyse **the** context of speech. (What to say, how to answer and etc.)"

› *Argument 3*
"Nowadays we have more friends in social network **rather than** in real life. Sometimes you have problems, but you can't share **them with** your friends in real life, so in network you don't know **the** person and easily you can share **everything** you have in your mind. Also it's good if your friend is from **another** country, because you become more open-minded, you will get new information, you will know **their** traditions... I **think that** is really nice. We spend a lot of time on **the** Internet and chatting, but also we have to have close friends in real life."

Adapted from: <www.createdebate.com/debate/show/what_is_better_to_make_friends_in_real_life_or_in_social_networks>. Accessed on: November 15, 2013.

a) Which argument best describes your opinion about the question? Check (✓) the box.
b) Who's the text addressed to?

_____

c) Is friendship online for real? Do you have any close virtual friends?

_____

2. 🔴21 Listen to the text above again. Pay attention to how the "th" is pronounced in the words in bold.

Pronunciation spot – /θ/ and /ð/

1. **◉22** Listen to eight words taken from the texts of this unit and pay attention to the different pronunciations of **th**.

A	
thing	math
both	with

B	
there	that
either	another

> **Group A words**: the "th" sounds like /θ/. To produce this sound, place the tip of your tongue just below the upper teeth as you blow the air out.
> **Group B words**: the "th" sounds like /ð/. This sound is very similar to /θ/, but your vocal cords vibrate when you produce /ð/.

2. **◉23** Now listen again and repeat the words after the recording.

3. **◉21** Listen to the texts in activity 1 again. As you do this, underline all the words with the sound /ð/ and circle the words with the sound /θ/.

3. In groups, look at this comic strip and discuss the questions.

   a) In what ways does the comic strip reflect **your parents'** nights (or some of your friends' nights)?

   b) Do social networks change our lives for better or for worse? Support your answer.

   c) What are the advantages and disadvantages of making friends in "real life" and in social networks?

"I love our nights in together, just you, me, and our 756 friends."

4. Based on your discussion in activity 3, try to come to a consensus about which is better: making friends in "real life" or in social networks. Report your group opinion to the class.

> ### Useful language
> Make your point by using some of these expressions:
> - I think that…
> - I somewhat disagree…
> - I totally disagree…
> - From my point of view…
> - I agree…
> - I consider both…

Let's focus on language!

Verb tense review

1. Read the following sentences and decide whether they present (**A**) an action in progress or a temporary action or (**B**) statements that are always true.
   - ( ) "The simplest way to ensure you **aren't wasting** time in any one place [...]."
   - ( ) "[...] something we **are losing** touch with."
   - ( ) "But a call to a friend **works** just as well as a Facebook message [...]."
   - ( ) **Is** social media **changing** the way we communicate?
   - ( ) "Nowadays we **have** more friends in social network rather than in real life."

> **Let's remember!**
>
> To form the Simple Present, add **–s** (**–es** or **–ies**) to the verb for **he**, **she**, and **it**.
> To make the negative, use **doesn't** for **he**, **she**, and **it** and **don't** for **I**, **you**, **we**, and **they**.
> To ask questions, use **does** when the subject is **he/she/it** and **do** when the subject is **I/you/we/they**.

2. Check (✓) the options that best describe how the structures are used.

   a) We use the Present Continuous with
   - ( ) things happening around now.
   - ( ) actions in progress.
   - ( ) habitual actions.

   b) We use the Simple Present for
   - ( ) things that are always true.
   - ( ) things that happen regularly.
   - ( ) actions in progress.

3. Let's conduct surveys in the classroom. In groups, create questions for one of the topics below. Go around the class and invite two classmates to answer your survey. Add up your results and figure out the **yes** and **no** percentages. Report your results to the class.

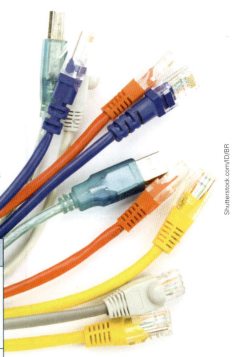

Topics
Broadband Internet
Do you subscribe for a paid broadband service?
Do you ever use a broadband wireless connection?
Social networking
Do you buy things online?
Do you share something online that you created yourself?
Mobile learning
Do you ever use your cell phone to access a social network site?
Do you ever use your cell phone to send or receive e-mails?

4. Take a good look at this cartoon and answer the questions.

a) What social networks are represented in the logo "flitterin?"

b) Why did the author use a different letter for "litter?"

c) What does "litter" mean?

d) In your opinion, what was the cartoonist's intention? Do you agree with it?

5. Use some of the words in the box to write sentences describing what the people are doing in the cartoon above.

carry	read	eat	type	drink	text	pizza
books	web	juice		soda	cell phone	

a) _____

b) _____

c) _____

d) _____

6. In pairs, think of what is currently going on in your social networks. Share with the class what people are doing. Use the language below whenever appropriate.

A friend of mine is discussing…   People are talking about…
My friends are sharing…   People are using…   Another friend is…

7. Read the text below and eliminate the verb forms that don't make sense in the context.

http://teenadvice.about.com/od/datingrelationships/tp/making-new-friends.htm

Ways to Make New Friends and Meet People

(1) Listen and Ask Questions

[...] By being a good listener, you let others know that you **are valuing / value** what they have to say [...]. You can let others know you **are paying / pay** attention by making eye contact while they **are speaking / speak**, then asking a question or two about what they **are saying / say.** [...]

(2) Give a Compliment

Everyone **is loving / loves** an ego boost. Noticing something you like about someone and sharing it with him or her is a great way to forge a connection and **is starting / start** a conversation. When giving a compliment, be honest and genuine. [...]

(3) Join a Club or Team

Having an interest in common with another person **gives /are giving** both of you something to talk about. No matter if that interest is reading, rugby or rock'n'roll, pursuing it with other people is fun and gives you a sense of meaning and belonging. Clubs, teams and other groups also **are working / work** toward common goals, [...] **are teaching / teach** you how to solve problems and **are helping / help** you bond with others.

[...]

(4) Form a Study Group

Does / Is your math teacher give super-hard exams? [...] Round up a few others from your class to study together each week. Ask your teacher if you could pass around a sign-up sheet or make an announcement about the group after class. [...] Make flash cards together or quiz one another. Bring snacks and **is sharing / share** what **is going on / goes on** in your life. You'll have new friends before you know it.

[...]

Available at: <http://teenadvice.about.com/od/datingrelationships/tp/making-new-friends.htm>. Accessed on: November 15, 2013.

8. Focus on the four subtitles used in the text above. They are used for

( ) talking about actions in progress.   ( ) giving instructions.   ( ) giving tips.

9. Go back to the text "Managing Your Social Network Addiction," in the *Let's read!* section. What are the subtitles in bold used for?

Profession spot

> ## Careers in the Internet world

Match the names of the following Internet careers to their corresponding definitions. The first exercise is done for you.

- ~~blogger~~
- Internet judge
- network engineer
- social media consultant
- user operations analyst
- web designer
- web developer
- webmaster

a) _____A blogger_____ writes articles and/or posts for online publications.

b) _____ is responsible for installing, maintaining and supporting computer communication networks within an organization or between organizations.

c) _____ is an individual who is employed by a search engine to review and rate websites.

d) _____ is someone who creates web-based applications by using programming languages.

e) _____ is someone who works with the visual elements of a web page.

f) _____ can be either a web developer or a web designer. He or she, usually, works alone doing both jobs as he or she maintains a web site. In addition, a webmaster may be responsible for search engine optimization (SEO), web content writing, and/or marketing.

g) _____ is someone who sets up and maintains accounts on Twitter, Facebook, MySpace and any other social media site that pops up. He or she might work for a public relations director or alongside a branding consultant. Whatever the case, this person needs to keep the content fresh, monitor user feedback and create a persona for the company – all through the click of a mouse.

h) _____ monitors how users interact with the site, answers users' questions or listens to their feedback to see what they want in a site and reports the results to the site owner.

Sources: <http://edition.cnn.com/2010/LIVING/worklife/02/10/cb.jobs.internet.addicts/index.html>; <http://www.webreference.com/internet/jobs/careers/index.html>; <http://voices.yahoo.com/google-jobs-work-as-internet-judge-googles-7819988.html?cat=15>; and <http://www.prospects.ac.uk/network_engineer_job_description.htm>. Accessed on: November 15, 2013.

UNIT

10 Security on the web

Language in action

- Learn how to read posters
- Learn how to make recommendations and warnings, give orders and instructions
- Learn to talk about safety on the web

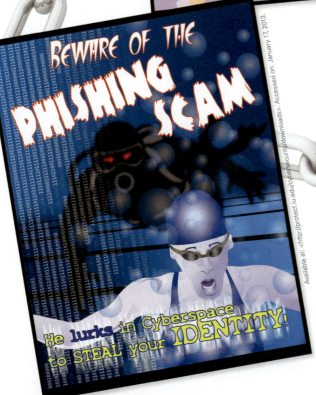

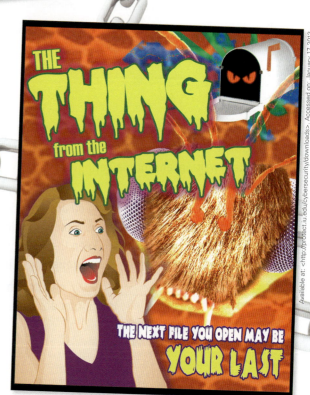

› Lead-in

1. Look at the posters on the previous page and answer orally.

   a) What do they have in common?

   b) What is their purpose?

   c) Where did the creators of these posters get inspiration to produce them?

   d) In your opinion, what kind of reaction does the producer of these posters want to create in the viewers?

   e) Do you think this was an original idea?

2. How much do you know about security on the web? Talk to a classmate using these questions as a guide.

   a) What can viruses and worms do to your computer?

   b) What are the risks of opening files from the e-mails you receive?

   c) What can someone do after stealing your identity?

   d) What are the risks of someone discovering your passwords?

3. What type of visual effects are used in posters?

4. How is the information in posters normally conveyed?

5. What kind of information do people usually find in posters?

Shutterstock.com/ID/BR

135

> Let's read!

Before you read...
- How do you keep your privacy and personal information safe?
- How do you normally protect yourself against potential online dangers?

Hint
Use your **previous knowledge** about the subject of the text to help you understand it.

1. Read the article and find out how safely you are browsing on the web.

Your Guide to Safe Web Browsing

Get tips on keeping your computer (and your personal information) safe while on the Internet.

Here are some tips for keeping your computer, your data and your personal information safe while browsing the web:

The Basics:

- **Use anti-virus software on your computer.** Anti-virus software will detect and remove viruses or prevent them from ever entering your computer. [...]

- **Use a firewall on your computer.** [...] A personal firewall will protect your computer against viruses, worms and other Internet threats.

- **Create and use strong passwords.** [...] To create a strong password, use both upper and lower case letters. Also, incorporate numbers or punctuation marks to make your password at least eight characters long. A good password is NOT your name, phone number, [...]. [...] don't use a word that uses digits in place of letters or passwords that are simply a group of keys right next to each other on the keyboard (asdfghjkl) or one letter or number repeated (44444444444).

- **Update your security software and change your passwords often.** [...] It isn't enough just to download and install security software one time. To keep your computer safe, you must update your protective software regularly. Also, even if your passwords are strong, change them every six months or so. Never use one password [...] for multiple online accounts. If one of these systems is compromised, your password from one system may be used to try to enter other systems.

- **Beware** of instant message links and e-mail attachments. A good rule to follow when communicating online is to never open an attachment that you aren't expecting, even if you know the person who sent it. [...] The sender may not even be aware that the link or attachment contains a virus. [...] Before you click on that ad for free software or for an online game demo, know that you may also be downloading spyware. [...] With spyware, identity theft is just a few clicks away for the intruder.

Available at: <www.utexas.edu/its/secure/articles/safe_browsing_tips.php>. Accessed on: November 16, 2013.

The Information Technology Services (ITS) is an organization which supports the University of Texas community in improving its research, education, and public service.

2. Do you follow the tips presented in the article? Which ones? Do you know any other tips that were not included in this text?

_____

_____

_____

3. Notice the tips in the text on the previous page. They express

( ) instructions.

( ) warning.

( ) orders.

( ) advice.

( ) recommendations.

( ) suggestions.

4. Refer to the article again and check (✔) the option that best completes each sentence.

a) A strong password

( ) is no more than eight characters long.

( ) has more lower case than upper case letters.

( ) includes numbers and punctuation marks.

b) While we are connected, some unscrupulous Internet users can steal our

( ) identity.

( ) research information.

( ) unpaid bills.

c) To keep your computer safe,

( ) change security software passwords every year.

( ) update security software on a regular basis.

( ) use a strong password for all online accounts.

d) Open an e-mail attachment

( ) even if it was sent by someone you don't know.

( ) only if it was sent by someone you know well.

( ) only if you are expecting someone to send it.

e) The aim of the article "Your Guide to Safe Web Browsing" is to

( ) give people advice on how they can be safe online.

( ) teach people how to install anti-virus software.

( ) tell people what to do in case of identity theft.

5. Have you ever had problems similar to the ones mentioned in the text? What happened? Tell a classmate what the problem was.

Vocabulary corner

Do you know the meaning of these words used in the article "Your Guide to Safe Web Browsing?" If necessary, find them in the text and use the context to help you choose the best option here.

a) **theft**:

( ) robbery

( ) change

b) **often**:

( ) frequently

( ) rarely

c) **threats**:

( ) sites for hackers

( ) sources of danger

d) **keep**:

( ) maintain

( ) prevent

e) **be aware**:

( ) to allow something to happen

( ) to know that something exists

6. Read the following problems. What advice would you give to these students?

❶ Some girls are sending me mean texts and Facebook messages. I don't respond, but it's starting to hurt. What do I do?

❷ My friend and I said some bad things about another girl on Twitter and she found out. We didn't mean for her to see it – were we wrong?

Available at: <http://www.athinline.org/real-stories>. Accessed on: November 16, 2013.

Beyond the lines...

a) What message does the cartoon convey?
b) What advice would you give the Three Little Pigs?
c) In what ways does the cartoon criticize people who use the Internet? Do you agree?

❯ Let's focus on language!

1. Which of these sentences taken from the text "Your Guide to Safe Web Browsing" express a recommendation?

( ) "Use anti-virus software on your computer."

( ) "Hundreds of new viruses are discovered every month [...]."

( ) "Don't use a word that uses digits in place of letters [...]."

2. Go over the text again. Which recommendations do you find more useful? What else would you recommend to a friend?

_____

_____

3. When we want someone to do (or not to do) something, or when we want to make a recommendation, we use the Imperative. Read your examples in activity 2 and check (✔) the appropriate options.

The Imperative

( ) describes a recent event.   ( ) is used to give instructions.

( ) uses the base form of the verb.   ( ) expresses an action in progress.

( ) has no subject.

4. Look at the incomplete infographic below. Help finish it by writing the tips that are missing. Choose from the box.

| Share the love | Be social | Be helpful | Be present | Pay it forward |

5 Ways to Cultivate an Active Social Network

1 _____ – offer your network advice or suggest people that can help.

2 _____ – participate and contribute.

3 _____ – engage with as many people as possible... not to be confused with just pushing out messages to a list.

4 _____ – make it about them... talk about your network.

5 _____ – build equity by contributing to your network before asking for anything in return... and never take out more than you put in.

©Mark Smicklas, Digital Strategist, IntersectionConsulting.com

Available at: <http://www.wikihow.com/Image:5-Ways-to-Cultivate-an-Active-Social-Network.jpg>. Accessed on: November 16, 2013.

Beyond the lines...

Compare the recommendations in activity 4 to what happens in your social networks. Do the participants behave according to these "rules"?

5. There are **Dos** and **Don'ts** when using the computer. Make recommendations with the verbs in the box. You may have to use the negative in some sentences. Then create your own recommendation under the empty box in *e*.

leave   talk   throw   scan

a) _____ batteries in designated places.

b) _____ your computer on standby.

c) _____ for computer viruses.

d) _____ to strangers.

e) _____

6. Read the following webpage. Write the instructions on how to open an account on Twitter.

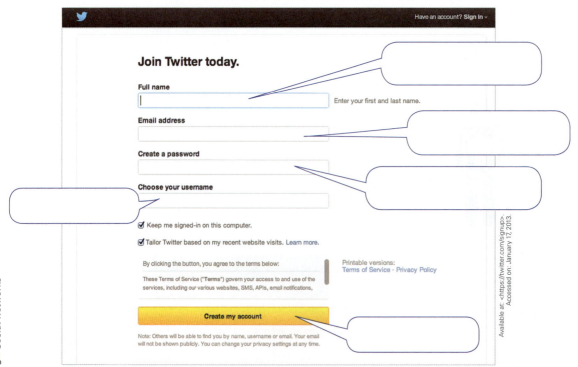

7. What does each sign express: **warning** or **order**?

a) _____ b) _____ c) _____

8. We can use the Imperative to **give orders**, **instructions**, **warnings**, or **to make recommendations**. Read these sentences and identify what they express. The first one is done for you.

	USE
a) If you're not sure of the IP address to use, open your router's setup page and look in its quick-start guide for the correct address.	instruction
b) Save paper when printing.	
c) Don't accept unknown friend requests.	
d) Monitor what your friends are sending and sharing with you.	
e) Turn on https:// browsing on your Facebook settings.	
f) Don't click on suspicious links.	
g) Don't you dare touch my mouse.	
h) Download Facebook security server.	
i) Do not respond to cyber-bullying messages.	
j) Look out for moving vehicles!	
k) Don't ever give out any personal information.	

Let's listen and talk!

Before you listen…
- Have you ever felt you were at risk when using a social network?

1. 🔘24 Listen to the first two minutes of a newscast and answer the questions.

    a) Which image best describes the main topic of this newscast? Justify your answer.

    ( )

    _____
    _____

    ( )    ( )

    _____   _____
    _____   _____
    _____   _____
    _____   _____

    b) What is this newscast about?
    - ( ) a debate
    - ( ) a survey
    - ( ) a cyber crime

Hint
Listening for the **general idea** of the text can help you **infer** some of its details.

2. ⊙25 Listen to the whole recording now and match the statements according to what you hear.

a) 2/3 of teens interviewed

b) 10% of teens interviewed

c) 40% of the teens interviewed

d) 43% of the teens interviewed

( ) have an open profile.
( ) have been contacted by a stranger.
( ) are keeping their profiles closed.
( ) share both their first and last names online.

Information based on: <http://www.youtube.com/watch?v=_tqWbcFi-d0&feature=related>. Accessed on: November 16, 2013.

3. What other information can be problematic when shared online?
_____

4. Make a survey in your classroom and compare the results to the survey in the newscast. Think of interesting questions to find out how your classmates use social networking safely. Add up your results and figure out the **yes** and **no** percentages.

	Questions	Yes %	No %
1			
2			
3			
4			
5			

Useful language

Do you...
- have an open profile?
- share your name online?
- choose a strong password?

Pronunciation spot — /æ/

1. ⊙26 Listen and repeat these words. Make sure you open your mouth wider when producing the sound /æ/.

   hacker   scam   add   password

2. ⊙27 Listen to the words and underline the ones with the /æ/ sound.

   last   fast   spam   alarm   have   are
   farm   am   after   ask   market   start

3. ⊙28 Now listen to the words again with a British accent. Notice the difference.

143

Let's act with words!

Create an infographic

Your task is to create an infographic in order to instruct your classmates about making connections or keeping their computer safe while on the Internet. As a quick reference, use the infographics in units 9 and 10, as well as the example below, which teaches us how to develop a good podcast.

Simple Steps to Podcast Optimization

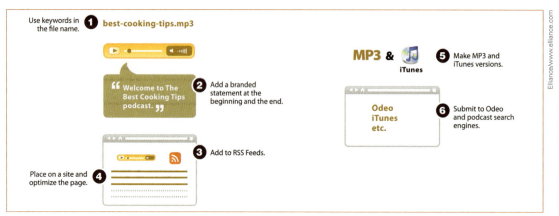

Available at: <http://www.elliance.com/aha/infographics/podcast-optimization.aspx?page=4>. Accessed on: November 16, 2013.

Remember to consider the following:

Typical grammar patterns: *imperative*
Structure: *facts and instructions in frames; visual information; colors*
Suggested themes: *instructions on making connections / keeping our computer safe while on the Net*

Writing Steps

Organizing
- Before you start, find more infographics in magazines, newspapers and, of course, on the Internet. Observe their characteristics. These websites may be useful: <http://www.makeuseof.com/tag/awesome-free-tools-infographics/>; <http://www.theprcoach.com/infographics-how-to-make-them-work-best/> (both accessed on: May 20, 2014).
- Make a collection of the examples you have and read them.
- Make a list of elements to include in your infographic.

Preparing the first draft
- Make a first draft.
- Use a glossary or dictionary to help you.
- Find icons to illustrate it.

Peer editing
- Evaluate and discuss it with a classmate.
- Make the necessary corrections.

Publishing
- Write the final version of your infographic and include it in your portfolio or publish it on Wikispaces.

Genre: Infographic
Purpose: To instruct your classmates about making connections/keeping their computer safe while online
Tone: Informal
Setting: Wikispaces
Writer: You or your group
Audience: Classmates or wiki readers

You can also build an online infographic with Creately, at <http://creately.com/> (accessed on: May 20, 2014).

Go to Workbook, page 364, for more practice.

Learning tips

How to learn more vocabulary

Learning vocabulary means knowing not only the meaning of the words, but also how to use them in context. To know a word also implies spelling, pronunciation, collocation, register or style, changes in form, and grammar information.

How to learn new words:

- Read a lot.
- Listen to music and pay attention to the lyrics.
- Watch movies and pay attention to the new words.
- Use a good dictionary.
- Build a personal glossary.
- Use vocabulary graphic organizers.

Ever considered recording new words in graphic organizers? Find several kinds of graphic organizers to help you learn new vocabulary at <http://www.enchantedlearning.com/graphicorganizers/vocab/> (accessed on: November 16, 2013).

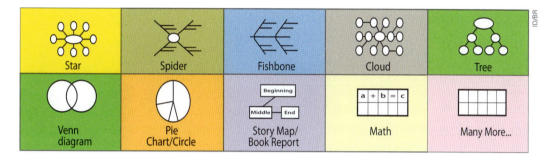

Let's reflect on learning!

You are now invited to assess what you learned and how you learned. Finish the ideas below on an extra sheet of paper and become a more autonomous and reflective learner.

In Part 5

I learned _____

I liked _____

I need to review/learn more _____

My experiences with English outside school were _____

145

Let's study for Enem!

Enem Questions

The death of the PC

The days of paying for costly software upgrades are numbered. The PC will soon be obsolete. And *BusinessWeek* reports 70% of Americans are already using the technology that will replace it. Merrill Lynch calls it "a $160 billion tsunami." Computing giants including IBM, Yahoo!, and Amazon are racing to be the first to cash in on this PC-killing revolution.

Yet, two little-known companies have a huge head start. Get their names in a free report from The Motley Fool called, "The Two Words Bill Gates Doesn't Want You to Hear..."

Click here for instant access to this FREE report!
BROUGHT TO YOU BY THE MOTLEY FOOL

Disponível em: <http://www.fool.com>. Acesso em: 21 jul. 2010.

Gênero

Reportagem

Competência de área 2

H7 – Relacionar um texto em LEM, as estruturas linguísticas, sua função e seu uso social.

Procure identificar no enunciado da questão palavras ou expressões que possam encaminhar você ao trecho do texto onde a informação desejada pode ser encontrada. Quando ler esse trecho no texto, observe bem recursos de referenciação, como o uso de pronomes, paráfrases, repetição, etc. Observe como foi usado um tipo de recurso de referenciação nesta questão (*two companies* › duas palavras).

Ao optar por ler a reportagem completa sobre o assunto anunciado, tem-se acesso a duas palavras que Bill Gates não quer que o leitor conheça e que se referem

A aos responsáveis pela divulgação desta informação na internet.

B às marcas mais importantes de microcomputadores do mercado.

C aos nomes dos americanos que inventaram a suposta tecnologia.

D aos *sites* da internet pelos quais o produto já pode ser conhecido.

E às empresas que levam vantagem para serem suas concorrentes.

Extraído de: Exame Nacional do Ensino Médio, 2010, Caderno 7 – AZUL – Página 2 (questão 91).

Part 5 (Social Networks)

Typical questions of Enem

1. Uma nuvem de palavras é uma representação visual de um texto. A leitura da nuvem de palavras abaixo indica que o tema do texto ao qual ela se refere é

a) ( ) amigos em visita a Chicago.
b) ( ) conexões em redes sociais.
c) ( ) mapas de trabalho na web.
d) ( ) oportunidades de negócios.
e) ( ) problemas de conectividade.

2. "In my point of view, Internet becomes part of our life. We also should consider it like simply meeting someone in the street. In any case people can lie both on the Internet and during face-to-face contact. It depends on you, to believe or not. For me, it is easier to communicate with someone by chats and social networks. You can analyse the context of speech. (What to say, how to answer and etc.)"

Available at: <http://www.createdebate.com/debate/show/what_is_better_to_make_friends_in_real_life_or_in_social_networks>. Accessed on: November 15, 2013.

O texto acima foi retirado de um fórum de discussões sobre redes sociais. O ponto de vista do autor desse texto sobre a mentira é o de que

a) ( ) chats e redes sociais são facilitadores da mentira.
b) ( ) é mais fácil mentir quando se está conectado na Web.
c) ( ) mente-se na Internet ou na interação fora da rede.
d) ( ) mentir faz parte de nossa vida cotidiana.
e) ( ) o contexto da fala induz alguém a mentir.

3. Em 2005, a Universidade de Indiana (EUA) distribuiu pelo *campus* um conjunto de cinco cartazes em uma campanha sobre segurança no ciberespaço. O cartaz abaixo, que fez parte dessa campanha, está associado ao tema

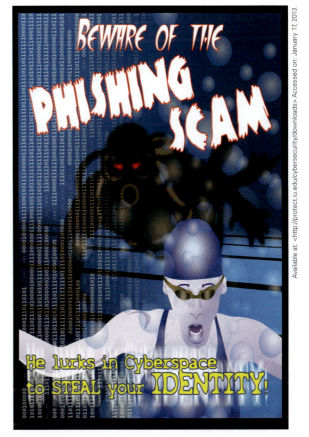

a) ( ) anexos roubados.
b) ( ) fraude eletrônica.
c) ( ) programa espião.
d) ( ) senha confiável.
e) ( ) propagação de vírus.

4. O cartaz mostrado no exercício anterior alerta sobre um tipo de e-mail que

a) ( ) engana usuários desatentos no ciberespaço.
b) ( ) identifica as pessoas que cometem furtos.
c) ( ) impede que a pessoa tenha todo o cuidado.
d) ( ) parece vir de uma empresa como um banco.
e) ( ) rouba identidades de agentes comerciais.

147

Exam Practice Questions (Vestibular)

Test-Taking Tips

Practice speed-reading!

Comprehension is usually better when you can maintain a good rhythm to your reading. When you feel comfortable, practice speeding up your reading in English. Time yourself and try to read a little faster each time. Remember: The further on we move in school life, the more reading we need to do. Reading faster will help you improve comprehension on exams and be more efficient in your school assignments in general.

- Understand how speed-reading works at <http://www.wikihow.com/Learn-Speed-Reading>.
- Test your reading speed at <http://www.freereadingtest.com/> and <www.readingsoft.com/>.
- Finally, practice speed-reading at <http://www.spreeder.com/>.

Links accessed on: January 16, 2014.

TEXT 1 - Questions 1 to 6
PUC-RS, 2010

1   Over the past 5 years, social-networking sites have evolved from a preoccupation of high-school and college students to a mainstream form of social interaction that spans divisions of age, profession, and socioeconomic
5   status. At the hospital where I'm in training, medical students, nurses, residents, fellows, attending physicians, and service chiefs can all be found linked to one another as active members of social-networking sites. The technology facilitates communication,
10   with personal Web pages that permit users to post information about events in their lives, advertise social activities, and share photographs. Users are prompted by Facebook to carve out a digital identity by disclosing their political affiliations, sexual orientation, and
15   relationship status.

Physicians, medical centers, and medical schools are trying to keep pace with the potential effects of (such) networking on clinical practice. In an e-mail to students and faculty of Harvard Medical School, Dean
20   for Medical Education Jules Dienstag wrote: "Caution is recommended in using social networking sites such as Facebook or MySpace. Items that represent unprofessional behavior that are posted by you on such networking sites reflect poorly on you and the
25   medical profession. Such items may become public and could subject you to unintended exposure and consequences." At the Drexel University College of Medicine, medical students are warned about the possibility that information placed on social-networking
30   sites might influence the fate of their applications for postgraduate training. Although legal questions surrounding the relationship between clinical medicine and social networking are as yet undefined, there are obvious concerns for individuals and institutions, since

35   their Internet presence makes clinicians' attitudes and activities increasingly visible.
Source: The New England Journal of Medicine, number 7, August 13, 2009.

1. According to the information from the text, we assume that the author is
a) (   ) a professor of a medical school.
b) (   ) a physician in training.
c) (   ) a medical journalist.
d) (   ) a doctor of a medical school.
e) (   ) a college student.

Answer question 2 based on statements I, II and III.

I. Doctors encourage their patients to learn about them on sites.
II. Social networking sites are creating new challenges for those who work in clinical settings.
III. The use of paging beepers is recommended for doctors to become visible.

2. The only statement(s) which has/have support from the text is/are
a) (   ) I.   d) (   ) I and III.
b) (   ) II.
c) (   ) I and II.   e) (   ) II and III.

3. The best title for this text would be
a) (   ) The various uses of Facebook and other web sites.
b) (   ) Practicing Medicine in the age of social-networking web sites.
c) (   ) The role of technology in medical practice.
d) (   ) Crossing boundaries in clinical medicine in the 21st century.
e) (   ) The advantages of sharing medical knowledge.

4. The issue raised in the second paragraph is that, through access to online media, physicians and medical institutions
a) (   ) can have a close relationship with their patients.
b) (   ) use services which are meant to shield physicians from their patients.
c) (   ) ought to develop a network of friends to improve their services.
d) (   ) should consider maintaining professional distance.
e) (   ) would rather use Facebook to rapidly mobilize doctors and share their views on health policies.

Part 5 (Social Networks)

5. The respective meaning of the verbs *to prompt* and *to carve*, according to their use in the text (lines 12 and 13) is
a) (   ) to volunteer / to engrave
b) (   ) to start / to struggle
c) (   ) to urge / to shape
d) (   ) to dare / to execute
e) (   ) to mention / to insert

6. De acordo com o segundo parágrafo, a atuação dos médicos nas redes sociais NÃO deve ser
a) (   ) cuidadosa
b) (   ) precavida
c) (   ) profissional
d) (   ) discreta
e) (   ) indefinida

- **TEXT 2 – Questions 7 to 10**
  Unimontes-MG, 2013

Instagram

1   Since it launched in October 2010, Instagram has surpassed 100 million active users and rapidly changed the way we organize and access the photos of our lives. Instagram is an "app". What's an "app"? "App" is the
5   abbreviation for the word application. An application is a programme which you can install onto your smartphone. Instagram is a programme which permits you to take pictures, apply some special effects to them, share them with the other Instagram users and receive
10 comments on them. Instagram is also a social network, like Facebook or Twitter. You can have friends, you can follow people, and people can follow you.

Rules and Regulation

Instagram was originally for Apple phones and
15 devices such as iPods and iPads, but it is now possible to have this programme on Android phones, too. There are Terms of Use that users must follow. For example: You must be 13 years old or older. You can't post nude, partially nude, or sexually suggestive photos. You must
20 be responsible for your own account and all its activity.

Did you know that...

Instagram development began when Kevin Systrom and Mike Krieger started working on a project on mobile photography. In January 2011, Instagram added hashtags[1]
25 to help users discover pictures they could find interesting, and discover other users with similar tastes and interests. In February 2011 Instagram's value was $25 million.

Facebook

In April 2012 Facebook bought Instagram for
30 $1 billion. In contrast to many other programmes and social networks, Instagram does not claim[2] any ownership rights in the text, files, images, photos, video or any other materials that users post.
(...)

Speak Up. Ano XXVI, nº. 313, setembro 2013.
1. **hashtags**: palavra (ou frase)-chave precedida pelo símbolo #
2. **claim**: reivindicar

7. Sobre o Instagram, pode-se afirmar, de acordo com o texto, que
a) (   ) não possui uma política de privacidade.
b) (   ) foi projetado e desenvolvido, inicialmente, para uso no sistema Android.
c) (   ) não exige uma idade mínima para se usar o aplicativo.
d) (   ) é uma rede social de fotografia que permite, no mesmo aplicativo, tirar fotos, editá-las e compartilhá-las.

8. Assinale a única alternativa que apresenta uma ideia que NÃO pode ser comprovada pelo texto.
a) (   ) O Instagram permite que o usuário insira legendas nas imagens postadas.
b) (   ) O Instagram, como aplicativo e rede social, também está disponível para computadores pessoais.
c) (   ) O Instagram é uma rede social para usuários de Android e iPhone.
d) (   ) O Instagram segue regras para evitar conteúdos impróprios como, por exemplo, a pornografia.

9. Assinale a única alternativa INCORRETA quanto ao que se afirma a respeito do uso do verbo modal.
a) (   ) Em "There are Terms of Use that users must follow." (linha 17), *must* expressa obrigação.
b) (   ) Em "You can't post nude..." (linha 18), *can't* expressa proibição.
c) (   ) Em "You can have friends..." (linha 11), *can* expressa habilidade.
d) (   ) Em "... they could find interesting..." (linha 25), *could* expressa possibilidade.

10. Analisando os vocábulos retirados do texto, assinale a alternativa CORRETA.
a) (   ) "ownership" (linha 32) apresenta o sufixo *-ship*, usado para formar substantivos em inglês.
b) (   ) "some" (linha 8) refere-se sempre a um substantivo em sua forma plural.
c) (   ) O verbo "lives" (linha 3) está empregado no *Simple Present*.
d) (   ) "similar" (linha 26) é um falso cognato que não significa *similar*.

149

PART

Mobile

Learning plan

Asking questions

Telling and describing past events

Talking about things that happened at an unspecified time

Learning how to create an answering machine message and how to leave a message

Reading and writing texting abbreviations

Creating interviews

Let's learn how to create a podcast.

What is a podcast?
Read the definitions below to learn.

> **pod·cast** /ˈpɒdˌkæst, -ˌkɑst/
> **noun**
> 1. a digital audio or video file or recording, usually part of a themed series, that can be downloaded from a Web site to a media player or computer: *Download or subscribe to daily, one-hour podcasts of our radio show.*
>
> **verb** *(used without object)*, **verb** *(used with object)*
> 2. to record and upload as a podcast: *He podcasts once a week on various topics. She podcasts her lectures.*

Available at: <http://dictionary.reference.com/browse/podcast>.
Accessed on: November 11, 2013.

Add audio to Wikispaces. Here are some tips:
1. Record a simple welcome message.
2. Record yourself singing or reading a poem.
3. Record a short news report about your school or town.

You can use two free online tools to record your podcast:
Audacity, available at <http://audacity.sourceforge.net/>.
Podomatic, available at <http://www.podomatic.com/login>.

See detailed instructions on how to produce and publish a podcast at <http://www.wikihow.com/Make-an-Easy-Podcast>.
All links accessed on: November 11, 2013.

151

UNIT

11 On the waves of the radio

Language in action

- Learn how to create interviews
- Learn how to tell and describe past events
- Learn how to ask questions

› Lead-in

1. What do the images on the previous page portray?

2. Number the stages in the history of the radio according to the pictures.

( ) People can now listen to radio stations when they are online.

( ) The radio became portable and reduced in size.

( ) People can listen to the radio wherever they are on their mobile devices.

( ) People got together to listen to the news or the soaps on the radio.

( ) People used to listen to the radio only in their houses.

( ) Almost every car has a radio.

3. This text is an excerpt of a transcription from a radio program. What kind of show is it?

Radio host: Time now for music. And our guest today made some news this past week when she seemed to endorse Ron Paul for president. Pop singer Kelly Clarkson saw her record sales jump 422 percent in a day as a result. [...] She burst onto the scene in 2002 when she became the first winner of "American Idol." She'd go on to win Grammys, break records on the charts and earn the affection of critics. One called her voice the best in pop music history. But unlike many of her contemporaries, Kelly Clarkson has managed to retain her authenticity, and you can trace that back to early 2000 when, on the strength of her voice, Kelly Clarkson was offered a record deal. She was unknown at the time, just 18 years old. She moved to L.A. from Texas to pursue her dream, and yet when that deal came around, she turned it down.

Kelly Clarkson: The one contract that I was offered - this was my favorite thing 'cause I deal with it on the daily now [...].

Transcribed from: <http://www.wbur.org/npr/144839981/kelly-clarkson-a-pop-star-survives>. Accessed on: November 11, 2012.

( ) a sitcom   ( ) The top 10 hits

( ) an interview   ( ) a commercial

4. The text was taken from a podcast of an online radio. In which type(s) of radio presented on the previous page can you listen to it?

5. We can say that the excerpt is

( ) the introduction of the text.

( ) the body of the text.

( ) the closure of the text.

6. Are oral and written interviews organized the same way?

❯ Let's read!

Before you read...

- Look at the text below. Pay attention to the titles, subtitles, tabs, and pictures. What kind of information do you expect to find here?

Hint
Trying to **predict** what you are going to read can help you deal with new vocabulary.

1. Read the text more carefully now to check your predictions. Then do the activities on the next two pages. Alternatively, you can have an interdisciplinary project with your history teacher.

ORACLE ThinkQuest — Projects by Students for Students
EDUCATION FOUDATION Library | FAQ | Privacy Policy | Terms of Use   About this Site

The Invention of the Radio

Radio is the **branch** of telecommunication that involves the propagation of electromagnetic **waves through** space.

How did the Radio Originate?

Many scientists dreamed of discovering a way to wireless communication, but didn't succeed until the late nineteenth century. James Clerk Maxwell developed the first radio-wave theorem in 1864.

Heinrich Hertz experimented with Maxwell's thesis in 1888. He demonstrated that "waves traveled in straight lines and that they could be reflected by a metal sheet." He tested with two conductors separated by a short gap (5ft). This idealism was advanced by the Italian physicist Guglielmo Marconi, who repeated Hertz's experiments with a **spark** gap of 30ft and succeeded.

Guglielmo Marconi in 1896 – at age 22

Augusto Righi, an Italian physicist, continued and refined Hertz's work establishing the equality between electrical and optical vibrations. Another scientist, Temistocle Calzecchi-Onesti, constructed, in 1888, a "tube" **due to** his **belief** that electrical discharges of atmospheric perturbations influence **iron filings**.

Replica of Marconi's wireless telegraph, 1899

In 1894, Oliver Lodge named Temistocle's famous "tube" the "coherer" and increased the reception gain of the hertzian waves. All that was left was the Russian, Alexander Popoff, to create a vertical metal pole by using Lodge's coherer and collecting atmospheric disturbances in a rudimentary antenna. The invention of these instruments helped Guglielmo Marconi's discovery. Marconi verified that electromagnetic waves travel between two points separated by an obstacle. This **led** to the creation of the first radio transmitter... This experiment was repeated with larger spark gaps (started with 5ft; expanded to 100 km). Radiotelegraphy was born.

Available at: <http://library.thinkquest.org/27887/gather/history/radio.shtml>. Accessed on: November 13, 2013.

This text is part of the project section of a platform for online learning sponsored by Oracle Education Foundation.

a) What is the purpose of the text?

b) Who was the website developed by?

c) Who was it developed for?

d) Who sponsored the website?

e) Do you think the information on the website is reliable? How do you check information when you search the web?

2. Many scientists were involved in the creation of the radio. Match the names in **A** to the facts in **B**.

A - SCIENTISTS

1) Heinrich Hertz
2) Guglielmo Marconi
3) Oliver Lodge
4) James Clerk Maxwell
5) Temistocle Calzecchi-Onesti
6) Alexander Popoff
7) Augusto Righi

B - FACTS

( ) created the first radio-wave formula.

( ) proved that radio waves are transmitted in straight lines.

( ) discovered that radio waves travel through an obstacle.

( ) established the equality between electrical and optical vibrations.

( ) believed in the influence of electrical discharges of atmospheric perturbations.

( ) came up with the name "coherer."

( ) incorporated a rudimentary antenna.

Did you know...?

The plural of "antenna" can be *antennas* or *antennae*.

3. The text "The Invention of the Radio" is mostly written in the

( ) past.

( ) present.

( ) future.

4. Underline the verbs in the text that justify your previous answer. What do most of them have in common?

_____

5. What was the most relevant information for you in this text that you have read?

_____

Vocabulary corner

Read the text "The Invention of the Radio" again and find the correct word for the definitions below.

a) Having no wires (*adj*):

b) An electronic device consisting of a system of electrodes (*n*):

c) Presenting magnetism produced by electric charge (*adj*):

d) Electromagnetic radiations (*n*):

e) Tests, trials (*n*):

f) A device that sends and receives waves (*n*):

> Let's listen and talk!

Radio still plays an important role in the world of communication, especially when we consider the music industry. This medium is a very important tool for the career of music artists. Be prepared to listen to part of an online radio interview with a famous singer.

Kelly Clarkson onstage at *VH1 Divas 2012*.

Before you listen…

- What do you already know about Kelly Clarkson?
- What kind of music does she sing?

1. ⊙29 Listen to the interview with Kelly Clarkson and answer the questions.

   a) What's the general tone of the interview?

   _____

   b) Why can she be considered a strong woman?

   _____

   c) Why did her single "Stronger" jump 422% in a day?

   _____

   d) Where is Kelly Clarkson from?

   _____

   e) When did she get famous?

   _____

   f) What was demanded of her when she was invited to sign her first contract?

   _____

   g) Who does Simon Cowell compare Kelly Clarkson to?

   _____

   h) What other question(s) would you ask Kelly Clarkson?

   _____

Hint
Use the **prediction** strategy to help you **maintain your focus** and not to get distracted.

Did you know…?

- **Celine Dion** is a Canadian singer who became famous with the song "My heart will go on", theme of the film *Titanic*.
- **Simon Cowell** is an English entrepreneur, famous in the UK and in the US for his role as a talent judge on TV shows such as *Britain's Got Talent* and *American Idol*.

2. 🔴29 The phrase "you know" is a very common *gap filler*. Listen to the recording again and identify other examples of gap fillers.

_____
_____
_____

3. Now discuss these questions with a classmate.
   a) Do you know any other famous singer who has also started his/her career in a TV show? List the ones you know.
   b) What advice would you give to a person who faced the same problems that Kelly Clarkson had?

Pronunciation spot – Final -ed

In the Simple Past, the **-ed** sound is pronounced differently depending on the preceding sound.

Verbs preceded by...		
voiced sounds -ed → /d/	voiceless sounds -ed → /t/	/t/ or /d/ -ed → /ɪd/

🔴30 Listen to the verbs below and put them in the appropriate column.

developed   experimented   constructed   occurred

played   improved   helped   verified   continued

repeated   succeeded   proved   demonstrated

	-ed
/d/	
/t/	
/ɪd/	

Beyond the lines...

a) How can beauty standards affect one's career, job or life?
b) In what ways do the media play a role in keeping these standards?
c) How do beauty standards influence your own choices?
d) What can you do to change these standards?

> Let's focus on language!

1. Let's remember! Read these sentences and pay attention to the words in bold.

> "She **moved** to L.A. from Texas to pursue her dream [...]."
>
> "And I **had**, like, an eating disorder in high school [...]."
>
> "[...] they **didn't allow** us to use their kitchen."
>
> "[... those months you lived in L.A.] **were** kind of a disaster, right?"
>
> "How **did** the radio originate?"
>
> "All that **was** left **was** the Russian, Alexander Popoff, to create a vertical metal pole [...]"

2. Check (✔) the options that best describe how the structure is used in the sentences above.
We use the Simple Past to talk about

( ) completed actions in the past.   ( ) unspecified time actions.

( ) actions in progress in the past.   ( ) facts and habits in the past.

( ) uncompleted actions.   ( ) a sequence of events in the past.

3. Complete these rules based on the sentences in activity 1.

a) Add _____ to the end of regular verbs.

b) The Simple Past of the verb *be* is _____ (I, he, she, it) and
_____ (you, we, they).

c) Use _____ for the interrogative and _____ for the
negative forms.

d) _____ verbs have a special form which we need to know by heart.

4. Are these sentences about the radio (T)rue or (F)alse? Correct the false statements.

a) ( ) The invention of the radio was possible at the beginning of the 19th century.

_____

b) ( ) James Clerk Maxwell invented the first radio.

_____

c) ( ) In 1888, Heinrich Hertz tested Maxwell's assumption.

_____

d) ( ) Hertz's experiment was replicated by Marconi without much success.

_____

e) ( ) Temistocle named the coherer in 1888.

_____

f) ( ) Scientists found that radio communication involves the transmission of
electromagnetic waves.

_____

_____

5. Match the questions to the answers, according to the text "The Invention of the Radio."

a) Where was Guglielmo Marconi born?   ( ) In straight lines

b) When was the first radio-wave formula created?   ( ) Because many inventors were involved

c) Who created the name "coherer?"   ( ) In 1864

d) What was constructed in 1888?   ( ) Oliver Lodge

e) How do radio waves travel?   ( ) A "tube"

f) Why can we say that the radio was collaboratively invented?   ( ) In Italy

6. The following text is about the history of podcasting. The most important words in this kind of text are the verbs in the past, because they express actions and facts that happened. Complete the gaps with the past form of the verbs in the box.

> allow   become (2x)   explode   help   include   start   decide

A Brief History of Podcasting

Podcasting _____ part of the general lexicon almost overnight. The technology behind podcasting comes from RSS news feeds, which were developed by programmer and blogging pioneer Dave Winer. Former MTV VJ Adam Curry had been pushing for a new way to do RSS with multimedia, and _____ encourage Winer to develop RSS with enclosures.

That technology _____ people to publish RSS feeds with audio or video, but it took a few years before regular podcasts were launched. In the summer of 2004, Winer _____ a proto-podcast called Morning Coffee Notes and Curry started his Daily Source Code show. Curry _____ to start coding his own podcast software called iPodder, and was hoping to get other programmers to join in on the open source software project. Eventually, iPodder _____ the basis for other "podcatching" software programs, which help you manage and subscribe to podcasts. In 2005, when Apple's iTunes _____ podcatching software as well as a podcast directory, the medium _____. [...]

Available at: <http://www.pbs.org/mediashift/2007/02/your-guide-to-podcasts059.html>. Accessed on: November 14, 2013.

7. The pieces of information below were taken from another text about the history of podcasting, available at <http://www.how-to-podcast-tutorial.com/history-of-podcasting.htm> (accessed on: November 14, 2013). Ask questions. The answers should be the underlined parts.

a) _____

Weblogs started to appear <u>after the appearance of the Internet</u>.

b) _____

The next step in the history of podcasting was <u>audio blogging</u>.

c) _____

The problem with audio blogs was that <u>readers had to check for new MP3 files</u>.

d) _____

The spoken word added <u>a new personal element</u> to the media of blogging.

Turn on the jukebox!

Before you listen...

Read this quotation from Friedrich Nietzsche, a German philosopher and poet. Then answer.

"That which does not kill us makes us stronger."

- Is there an equivalent saying in Portuguese?
- How do you think it is related to the song?

Caricature of the German philosopher Friedrich Nietzsche (1844-1900)

1. 🔊31 Read and listen to the song and check your prediction.

Stronger
By Kelly Clarkson

You know the bed feels warmer
Sleeping here alone
You know I dream in color
And do the things I want

You think you got the best of me
You think you've had the last laugh
Bet you think that everything good is gone
Think you left me broken down
Think that I'd come running back
Baby you don't know me, 'cause you're dead wrong

What doesn't kill you makes you stronger
Stand a little taller
Doesn't mean I'm lonely when I'm alone
What doesn't kill you makes you a fighter
Footsteps even lighter
Doesn't mean I'm over 'cause you're gone
What doesn't kill you makes you stronger, stronger.
Just me, myself, and I

What doesn't kill you makes you stronger
Stand a little taller
Doesn't mean I'm lonely when I'm alone

You heard that I was starting over with someone new
They told you I was moving on, and over you

You didn't think that I'd come back
I'd come back swinging
You try to break me but you'll see

(Chorus)

Thanks to you I got a new thing started
Thanks to you I'm not the broken hearted
Thanks to you I'm finally thinking 'bout me
You know in the end the day you left was just my beginning
In the end...

Available at: <http://musica.com.br/artistas/kelly-clarkson/m/stronger/traducao.html>. Accessed on: November 14, 2013.

2. How does the quotation above fit the song?

_____

3. Which expressions refer to how the speaker feels after the end of the relationship?

_____

4. How would you describe the speaker's feelings?

_____

5. 🔊31 Listen to the song again and sing along!

161

UNIT 12 Going mobile

Language in action

- Learn to talk about things that happened at an unspecified time
- Learn how to create an answering machine message and how to leave a message
- Read and write texting abbreviations

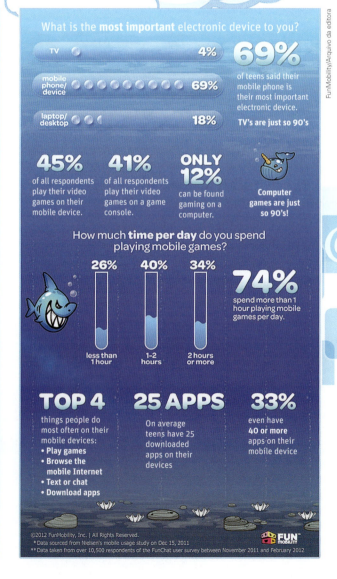

GENERATION OMG
How Teens Use Mobile Devices
By FunMobility

> Lead-in

1. Take a look at the infographic on the previous page. What's it about?

_____

2. The teenagers are surrounded by lots of clouds in this infographic. What do they represent?

_____

_____

3. Match the abbreviations from the text and their meanings.

a) OMG   (   ) Quarter 3 (July/August/September)

b) Q3   (   ) Multimedia Messaging Service

c) SMS   (   ) Oh, my God/Gosh/Goodness!

d) MMS   (   ) Short Message Service

e) avg   (   ) applications

f) APPS   (   ) average

g) MB   (   ) television

h) TV   (   ) December

i) Dec   (   ) megabyte

4. Why do you think teenagers are referred to as "Generation OMG?"

_____

5. Do you think the use of mobile devices has changed since the survey was made?

_____

6. How do you think these results are similar or different in your country?

_____

7. Do you use any applications on your cell phone to send free text messages? If so, which one(s)?

_____

> **Did you know...?**
>
> While in American English we say "cell phone," in British English the term is "mobile phone."

Shutterstock/ID/BR

163

› Let's listen and talk!

1. **◉32** Listen to the messages that some people recorded on their voicemail. What is the common characteristic in all of them?
   - ( ) They are all serious.
   - ( ) They are all very long.
   - ( ) They are all funny.

> **Hint**
> Keeping the **immediate context** in mind can help you guess possible words for a gap.

2. Below is the transcript of the messages you have just heard. What words are missing? Work in pairs and fill in the blanks with as many words as you can according to the context.

Message 1
"Hello? Hello? Hello? Hello? Hello? Must be having _____ difficulties, so _____ a message."
Available at: <http://www.ahajokes.com/funny_audio.html>. Accessed on: November 14, 2013.

Message 2
"Hi. I'm not _____ to come to the _____ right now, so please leave a _____ for my cat who will return your _____ as soon as he finishes a six-hour _____, has a two-hour _____, sharpens his claws on my fine _____ modern couch, makes a _____ in his little _____ and finds some poor unsuspecting _____ to kill and leave on my front step. _____ for the meow. Meow!"
Available at: <http://www.ahajokes.com/funny_audio.html>. Accessed on: November 14, 2013.

Message 3
"Hello. I'm home _____ now, but I can't find the _____. Please leave a long, loud _____ to help me locate _____."
Available at: <http://www.ahajokes.com/funny_audio.html>. Accessed on: November 14, 2013.

Message 4
[Oh, baby baby]
Hi, this is Britney Spears
and sometimes
my _____ can't
_____ to the phone,
and this is one
of _____ times.
So leave a _____
at the _____
and baby
they'll _____ you back
one more _____.
And _____ for calling!
[Hit me baby one _____ time]

Adapted from the song "Baby One More Time," from the album "Born To Make You Happy" (Europe/Australia Single CD/UK Cassette). Available at: <www.youtube.com/watch?v=R16RQdv45tY>. Accessed on: November 14, 2013.

3. ⊙**32** Listen to the messages again and check if your predictions in activity 2 were correct.

4. ⊙**33** Listen to messages 3 and 4 again and notice how "can't" is pronounced. Which one indicates American English and which one indicates British English?

_____

5. What messages would you leave if you called someone and heard these voicemail messages?

6. Get ready to record two different messages for a cell phone. The structures below may help you think of what you are going to say.

    Message 1: Prepare the text of a message **being yourself**.

- Greeting:

_____

- Excuse for not being able to answer:

_____

_____

- Request for a message:

_____

_____

    Message 2: Prepare the text of a message **being a politician**. Hint: Use formal language.

- Greeting:

_____

- Excuse for not being able to answer:

_____

_____

- Request for a message:

_____

_____

Now you're ready to record the two messages!

7. What does your ringtone say about you (*headbanging rocker*, *gamer*, *sci-fi nerd*, *TV addict*, etc.)? Think of the last ones you chose and share with your classmates what they say about you.

Pronunciation spot – Final *-e*

1. ⊙**34** Listen to these words and underline the last sound you hear.

take	message	phone	time
leave	creature	able	

2. What did you notice? Complete the hint.

    When "_____" is the last letter of the word, it is usually silent; the consonant is actually the last sound.

› Let's focus on language!

1. Read this excerpt of an Internet article and answer the questions.

Medicos may have used mobiles to cheat: Cops

Pushpa Narayan, TNN May 16, 2012, 04.15AM IST

[...]

The Tamil Nadu Dr MGR Medical University had withheld results of nine students and lodged a complaint with cyber crime in March after they received complaints from two final year students that nine of their classmates cheated during the exam. The students gave their names and roll numbers. A faculty member also supported the letter. "Police have given us an interim report that suggests there could have been malpractice. We are now waiting for the final report," said university vice-chancellor Dr Mayil Vahanan Natarajan.

Adapted from: <http://articles.timesofindia.indiatimes.com/2012-05-16/chennai/31725192_1_cyber-crime-exam-hall-s-arif-mohammed>. Accessed on: November 14, 2013.

a) What does the police report suggest? _____

b) Does the text mention when cheating happened? _____

c) What is more important in this text, the fact itself or the time it happened?
_____

d) Underline in the text examples of actions which happened at an unspecified time in the past. Which tense is used in these sentences?
_____

Did you know...?

Medico: a physician or doctor; a medical student.

2. Check the best alternative to complete the rule.

We use the Present Perfect when we want to

( ) talk about past experiences without mentioning when they happened.

( ) talk about past experiences which happened at a specified time in the past.

( ) talk about a past event that has present consequences.

> **To make the Present Perfect, use *has/have* + verb in the Past Participle.**
>
> For questions, use *have/has* + subject + verb in the Past Participle.
> A: *Have you ever used a tablet?*
> B: *No, never.*
> We often use *ever* and *never* to emphasize experiences or lack of experiences before the present time respectively.

3. Work in pairs. Use the prompts below to ask questions. Take notes of your classmate's answers to report back to the class.

a) use / a tablet – Have you ever used a tablet?

b) send / e-mail with a smartphone – Have you ever sent an e-mail with a smartphone?

c) access / wireless Internet on a tablet –

d) play / online games –

e) buy / anything online –

f) make / new friends online –

g) download / content in your cell phone –

h) use / cell phone in class –

i) tweet / famous person –

Use *never*, *already*, or *yet* to answer the questions.

Examples:

Yes, I have already used a tablet.
No, I have never used a tablet.
No, I haven't used a tablet yet.

4. Look at this timeline of social media. Then study the two sentences on the next page.

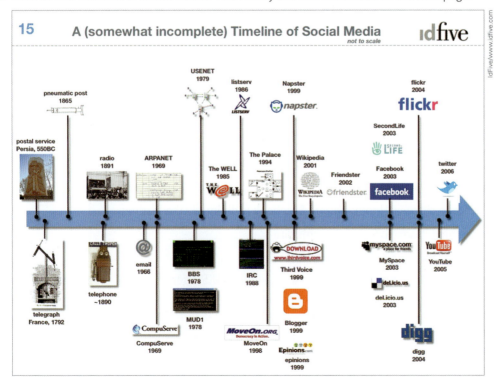

Available at: <http://webdeliciousness.blogspot.com/2010/11/social-media-timeline.html>.
Accessed on: November 14, 2013.

a) *Del.icio.us has been available for several years.*

b) *Wikipedia has been available since 2001.*

Based on the two examples above, complete the rule for the use of *for* and *since*.

> - When we want to refer to a period of time, we use _____ as in example _____.
> - When we want to refer to a point in time, we use _____, as in example _____.
>
> We use the Present Perfect followed by *for* or *since* to talk about events or states which started in the past but are still true now.

5. Below is a text about how long some social media have been available. To find out the exact information, complete the spaces using *for* or *since* or the correct form of the verbs in parentheses.

a) Also known as "snail mail," the postal service has been available _____ (*for/since*) 550 BC. More recently electronic mail _____ (*make*) communication quicker and easier. In fact, people _____ (*be able*) to send e-mails for more than 50 years.

b) _____ (*For/Since*) Guglielmo Marconi first transmitted signals more than a century ago, radio _____ (*become*) one of the world's most common sources of news and entertainment.

c) _____ (*For/Since*) its invention in 1890, the telephone _____ (*change*) significantly over the years. It _____ (*come*) a long way from two cups and a string. Today's phones are technological wonders, constantly getting smaller, more sophisticated, and less expensive.

d) _____ (*For/Since*) 2003, social networking sites such as Facebook and MySpace allow visitors to create networks of friends and contacts and to upload images, music, videos, and news stories. Facebook _____ (*grow*) into a website with millions of users who share vital information. Facebook is definitely the leading contender. At the beginning it was MySpace, but this site _____ (*be*) in decline for quite a few years now. Over the past two years, MySpace _____ (*lose*), on average, more than a million U.S. users a month.

e) Twitter _____ (*be*) around _____ (*for/since*) a while. A "tweet" is a text-based post comprised of up to 140 characters. Tweets _____ (*evolve*) from more simple, everyday experiences, to shared links to web content, hot topic conversations, photos, videos, and songs.

Let's read!

Before you read...
- Can you write or read texting abbreviations?
- Do you find abbreviations helpful? Why or why not?

Hint
Words that are **similar to Portuguese** in form and meaning can make reading easier.

1. Read the text below and answer the questions that follow.

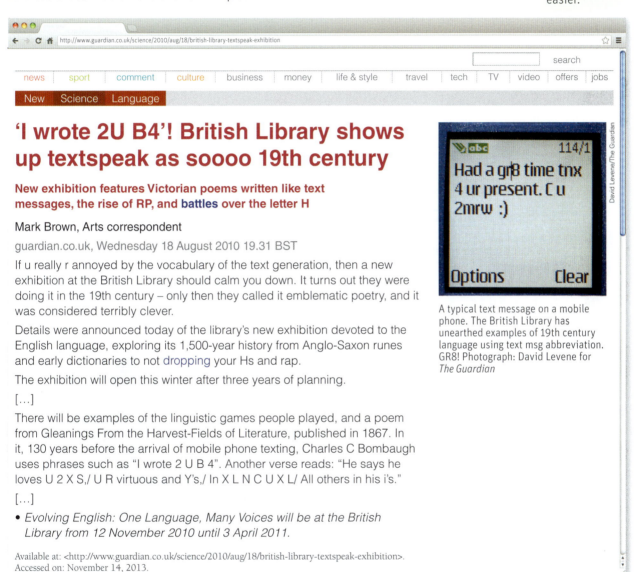

'I wrote 2U B4'! British Library shows up textspeak as soooo 19th century

New exhibition features Victorian poems written like text messages, the rise of RP, and **battles** over the letter H

Mark Brown, Arts correspondent

guardian.co.uk, Wednesday 18 August 2010 19.31 BST

If u really r annoyed by the vocabulary of the text generation, then a new exhibition at the British Library should calm you down. It turns out they were doing it in the 19th century – only then they called it emblematic poetry, and it was considered terribly clever.

Details were announced today of the library's new exhibition devoted to the English language, exploring its 1,500-year history from Anglo-Saxon runes and early dictionaries to not **dropping** your Hs and rap.

The exhibition will open this winter after three years of planning.

[…]

There will be examples of the linguistic games people played, and a poem from Gleanings From the Harvest-Fields of Literature, published in 1867. In it, 130 years before the arrival of mobile phone texting, Charles C Bombaugh uses phrases such as "I wrote 2 U B 4". Another verse reads: "He says he loves U 2 X S,/ U R virtuous and Y's,/ In X L N C U X L/ All others in his i's."

[…]

- Evolving English: One Language, Many Voices will be at the British Library from 12 November 2010 until 3 April 2011.

Available at: <http://www.guardian.co.uk/science/2010/aug/18/british-library-textspeak-exhibition>. Accessed on: November 14, 2013.

A typical text message on a mobile phone. The British Library has unearthed examples of 19th century language using text msg abbreviation. GR8! Photograph: David Levene for *The Guardian*

The Guardian is a British national daily newspaper with web presence.

a) What kind of text is it?

_____

b) What does this text tell us about texting?

_____

c) Based on the text, what is the relationship between SMS speak (texting abbreviations) and a type of literature of the past?

d) Do you think a poem written in this format can be considered "literature?" Why (not)?

e) Mark Brown, the author of the article, uses some abbreviations in some parts. Why do you think he chose to use them?
   ( ) To make comprehension a bit more difficult.
   ( ) To show that abbreviations convey a message.
   ( ) To flirt with the reader by showing that his own text is a type of code.
   ( ) Other: _____

2. Read the poem *Essay to Miss Catharine Jay*, by Charles C. Bombaugh, and rewrite it in your notebook decoding the abbreviations and numbers. Saying the letters and numbers aloud can help in some cases. For example: "U" sounds like "You".

Essay to Miss Catharine Jay by Charles C. Bombaugh (~1847)

An S A now I mean 2 write
2 U sweet K T J,
The girl without a ||,
The belle of U T K.

I 1 der if U got that 1
I wrote 2 U B 4
I sailed in the R K D A,
And sent by L N Moore.

My M T head will scarce contain
A calm I D A bright;
But A T miles from U I must
M ⁓ this chance 2 write.

And 1st, should N E N V U,
B E Z, mind it not;
Should N E friendship show, B true;
They should not B forgot.

From virt U nev R D V 8;
Her influence B 9
A like induces 10 dern S,
Or 40 tude D vine.

And if you cannot cut a —
Or cut an !
I hope U 'll put a .
2 1 ?.

R U for an X ation 2,
My cous N? — heart and ☞
He off R's in a ¶
A § 2 of land.

He says he loves U 2 X S,
U R virtuous and Y's,
In X L N C U X L
All others in his i's.

This S A, until U I C,
I pray U 2 X Q's,
And do not burn in F E G
My young and wayward muse.

Now fare U well, dear K T J,
I trust that U R true—
When this U C, then you can say,
An S A I O U.

Charles Carroll Bombaugh (1828-1906)

Available at: <http://www.bl.uk/learning/timeline/large126809.html>. Accessed on: November 14, 2013.

3. Write a poem in text message style or choose a poem you like and rewrite it in this style. Then invite a classmate to decode it. You can also post your text on your wiki. Remember to include a copy of it in your portfolio.

4. Read another text and then do the activity that follows.

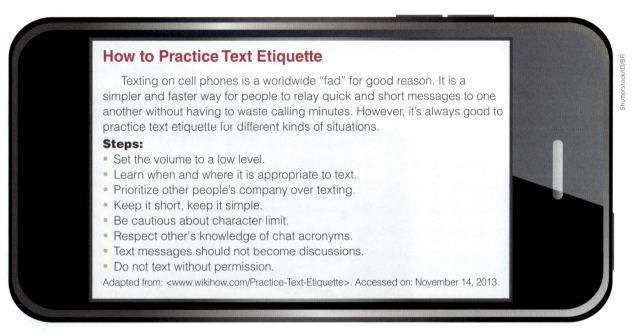

How to Practice Text Etiquette

Texting on cell phones is a worldwide "fad" for good reason. It is a simpler and faster way for people to relay quick and short messages to one another without having to waste calling minutes. However, it's always good to practice text etiquette for different kinds of situations.

Steps:
- Set the volume to a low level.
- Learn when and where it is appropriate to text.
- Prioritize other people's company over texting.
- Keep it short, keep it simple.
- Be cautious about character limit.
- Respect other's knowledge of chat acronyms.
- Text messages should not become discussions.
- Do not text without permission.

Adapted from: <www.wikihow.com/Practice-Text-Etiquette>. Accessed on: November 14, 2013.

Work in groups. Interview a classmate about texting. Follow these steps.

a) Talk about attitudes that annoy you regarding the use of cell phones. Create some questions based on your discussion to find out your interviewee's behavior when talking on the cell phone or texting. You can use ideas from the steps above to help you.

b) Interview a classmate and find out if she or he practices text etiquette. Share your findings with the class and identify as a group which etiquette items could be improved.

Vocabulary corner

1. Do you know any chat acronyms or abbreviations in English?
2. Complete the abbreviation chart. The first one is done for you.

Top 18 most popular texting abbreviations

asap: as soon as possible	**jk:** _____
b4: _____	**l8r:** _____
BF: _____	**lol:** _____
btw: _____	**oxox:** _____
cos: _____	**rofl:** _____
cya: _____	**sup:** _____
fyi: _____	**thx :** _____
GF: _____	**w/:** _____
gtg: _____	**zzzz:** _____

Available at: <www.textingadvice.com/abbreviations/top20_most_poular_texting_abbreviations.htm>. Accessed on: November 14, 2013.

171

Let's act with words!

An interview about radio or telephone

What about interviewing elderly people about their experience with radio or telephone? Before you do that, look at some features found in written and oral interviews. Sort out the features according to the interview type. Some features may be found in both.

1 written interview
2 oral interview

(2) hesitation noises
(   ) quotations
(   ) gap fillers
(   ) open questions
(   ) title
(   ) "yes" and "no" questions
(   ) multimedia texts
(   ) false starts
(   ) images

Elvis Duran (L) interviews Nicki Minaj, 2012.

Writing Steps

Organizing
- Get basic information about your interviewee.
- Make a list of questions in Portuguese.
- Interview elderly people (you can record it or take notes).

Preparing the first draft
- Write a short text to introduce your interviewee.
- Write the interview in Portuguese and ask your interviewee if he or she approves it.
- Choose some interesting questions and answers and translate them into English.
- Use online translators to help you. (Read about this tool on the *Learning tips* page)
- Edit the translation and make the necessary corrections.

Peer editing
- Evaluate and discuss the interview with a classmate.
- Make the necessary changes.

Publishing
- Write the final version of your interview and publish it on Wikispaces. Keep a copy in your portfolio.

Read more about interviewing at <http://www.ehow.com/how_2059751_interview-someone-story.html> and <http://www.right-writing.com/steps.html> (both accessed on: November 15, 2013).

Typical grammar patterns:
WH-questions, past tense

Key vocabulary items (radio):
radio, soap opera, news, ads, interviews, artists, like, prefer, etc.

Key vocabulary items (telephone):
telephone, communication, operator, phone company, price, etc.

Structure: Questions and answers

Genre: Written interview

Purpose: To know about someone's experience

Tone: Informal

Setting: Wikispaces

Writer: You or your group

Audience: Classmates or wiki readers

Go to Workbook, page 367, for more practice.

Learning tips

How to use Google Translate

Google Translate is an online tool available at <http://translate.google.com.br/> (accessed on: May 21, 2014). It can help you with translations, but it has limitations and you must revise the text to make it more accurate. See an example below.

> *Você ouve rádio?*
> *— Muito pouco.*
> *Você costumava ouvir rádio quando era criança?*
> *— Sim, eu gostava muito de rádio. Eu adorava os programas de humor e as novelas.*

Now, read the translation and pay attention to the interrogative form.

> You listen to the radio?
> — Very little.
> You used to listen to the radio as a child?
> — Yes, I loved the radio. I loved sitcoms and soap operas.

Observe the suggested final version below.

> Do you listen to the radio?
> — Very little.
> Did you use to listen to the radio as a child?
> — Yes, I loved the radio. I loved sitcoms and soap operas.

Let's reflect on learning!

You are now invited to assess what you learned and how you learned. Finish the ideas below on an extra sheet of paper and become a more autonomous and reflective learner.

In Part 6

I learned _____

I liked _____

I need to review/learn more _____

My experiences with English outside school were _____

_____

Let's study for Enem!

Enem Questions

Gênero
Cartaz

Competência de área 2
H7 - Relacionar um texto em LEM, as estruturas linguísticas, sua função e seu uso social.

Disponível em: http://www.chris-alexander.co.uk/1191. Acesso em: 28 jul. 2010. Adaptado.

> A interação de texto (elemento verbal) e imagem (elemento não verbal) sempre contribui para a produção de sentido no momento da leitura. Portanto, não se atenha apenas aos pequenos textos deste cartaz. É importante que você observe também as imagens (no caso, os ícones usados para ilustrar cada item da peça).

> A estratégia de *scanning* (busca por informação específica num texto) pode ser uma boa maneira de responder às questões de exames que avaliam a compreensão de informação pontual. Procure identificar essa informação nas alternativas apresentadas e busque pelo seu equivalente no texto.

Definidas pelos países membros da Organização das Nações Unidas e por organizações internacionais, as metas de desenvolvimento do milênio envolvem oito objetivos a serem alcançados até 2015. Apesar da diversidade cultural, esses objetivos, mostrados na imagem, são comuns ao mundo todo, sendo dois deles:

A O combate à AIDS e a melhoria do ensino universitário.
B A redução da mortalidade adulta e a criação de parcerias globais.
C A promoção da igualdade de gêneros e a erradicação da pobreza.
D A parceria global para o desenvolvimento e a valorização das crianças.
E A garantia da sustentabilidade ambiental e o combate ao trabalho infantil.

Extraído de: Exame Nacional do Ensino Médio, 2010, Caderno 7 – AZUL – Página 3 (questão 94).

Part 6 (Mobile)

Typical questions of Enem

> *Billboard* is a weekly American magazine devoted to the music industry, and is one of the oldest trade magazines in the world. It maintains several internationally recognized music charts that track the most popular songs and albums in various categories on a weekly basis. The two most notable charts are the Billboard Hot 100, which ranks the top 100 songs regardless of genre and is based on physical sales, digital sales and radio airplay; and the Billboard 200, the corresponding chart for album sales.
>
> Available at: <http://en.wikipedia.org/wiki/Billboard_(magazine)>. Accessed on: May 22, 2014.

1. De acordo com o texto acima, *Billboard* é
   a) ( ) a venda *on-line* dos melhores álbuns de canções produzidos pela indústria estadunidense.
   b) ( ) um programa de rádio que toca as 100 canções mais populares da indústria musical.
   c) ( ) uma indústria musical que publica semanalmente partituras musicais em inglês.
   d) ( ) uma loja que se dedica a divulgar produtos internacionais da indústria da música.
   e) ( ) uma revista semanal especializada em informações sobre a indústria musical.

> Wireless networking could allow you to offer new products or services. For example, many airport departure lounges, train stations, hotels, cafes and restaurants have installed "hot spot" wireless networking services to allow mobile users to connect their equipment to their "home" offices while travelling.
>
> Available at: <http://www.nibusinessinfo.co.uk/content/pros-and-cons-wireless-networking>. Accessed on: February 6, 2014.

2. Esse excerto sobre redes sem fio fala sobre as vantagens desse tipo de conexão à internet. De acordo com o texto, *hot spots* são
   a) ( ) equipamentos móveis que servem para mapear meios de transportes, hotéis e restaurantes.
   b) ( ) instalações em escritórios domésticos conectados com pessoas em trânsito nos aeroportos.
   c) ( ) produtos ou serviços oferecidos em redes sem fio para pessoas com permissão de uso móvel.
   d) ( ) redes sem fio que ainda não permitem a oferta de novos produtos e serviços a passageiros.
   e) ( ) serviços que permitem que portadores de equipamentos móveis se conectem à internet.

> Mobile computing can improve the service you offer your customers. For example, when meeting with customers you could access your customer relationship management system – over the Internet – allowing you to update customer details whilst away from the office. Alternatively, you can enable customers to pay for services or goods without having to go to the till. For example, by using a wireless payment terminal diners can pay for their meal without leaving their table.
>
> Available at: <http://www.businesslink.gov.uk/bdotg/action/detail?itemId=1074298219&type=RESOURCES>. Accessed on: July 16, 2012.

3. Este texto sobre computação móvel tem por objetivo
   a) ( ) alertar os leitores sobre a necessidade de atualizar seus dados na web.
   b) ( ) capacitar compradores a usar terminais de pagamento em restaurantes.
   c) ( ) informar os comerciantes sobre os benefícios da computação móvel.
   d) ( ) oferecer serviços de transação comercial mediada por internet sem fio.
   e) ( ) orientar os consumidores a fazer pagamentos seguros na internet móvel.

175

Exam Practice Questions (Vestibular)

Test-Taking Tips

Identify the principles behind a test!

Official tests usually have characteristics that we can identify. This depends on the principles defended by the institutions. Some of them focus on problem-solving questions, while others focus on reading comprehension or on grammar. Some may even mix different types of questions in their exams. As you practice taking tests from different universities, pay attention to the format of the test and try to identify its features. The more you know about the tests and institutions, the better prepared you will be. This awareness may also help control your anxiety and help you have better results.

- **TEXT 1 – Questions 1 and 2**
Mackenzie-SP, 2014

London in your Pocket

Smartphone applications are transforming the tourism experience. The latest development is called Streetmuseum, or "the museum in your pocket." It can be downloaded __(I)__ any Iphone or Android tablet and it enables you to explore the streets of London, both past and present.

Streetmuseum unites 200 images __(II)__ the Museum of London collection with actual locations __(III)__ the capital. It uses the smartphone's geo-tagging facility: as you walk the streets of London, satellite technology will give the phone's "geoposition." The phone will produce an image of that place in the past and you can compare this with what you see there today. So far the app has been downloaded by __(IV)__ 150,000 people around the world.

Skyline

The collection shows how much the London skyline has changed __(V)__ recent decades. Until 1962 St Paul's Cathedral (which was completed in 1710 and is 110 metres high) was London's tallest building. Today that honour goes to "One Canada Square," the Canary Wharf Tower in the Docklands. It is 230 metres high, but it will soon be overtaken __(VI)__ the 87-storey tower "Shard London Bridge," which will be 310 metres high. Designed by architect Renzo Piano, it should be completed in May.

By Linda Ligios
www.speakup.com.br

1. The prepositions that properly fill in blanks I, II, III, IV, V and VI, in the text, are
   a) (   ) in / of / around / more / on / in
   b) (   ) for / from / in / than / on / by
   c) (   ) for / all around / through / about / about / for
   d) (   ) on / from / across / over / in / by
   e) (   ) out of / of / in / around / over / from

2. According to the text,
   a) (   ) Streetmuseum can show you what London used to look like.
   b) (   ) the pictures shown in Streetmuseum can be downloaded on any IPhone or Android tablet.
   c) (   ) the London skyline today is made up of the tallest buildings in the world.
   d) (   ) the Canary Wharf Tower has been overtaken by the Shard London Bridge in terms of their height.
   e) (   ) satellite technology has been used by more than 150,000 people in recent decades.

- **TEXT 2 – Question 3**
UFSC, 2012

Marque, para cada item: o campo designado com o código C, caso julgue o item CERTO; ou o campo designado com o código E, caso julgue o item ERRADO.

Part 6 (Mobile)

"My wife doesn't let me bring my BlackBerry on vacation. If you need to reach me, call my shellphone."

1   Through the advancement of technology nowadays, many things were invented to make our lives easier than it has usually been. Communication is now at its best. The mobile phone is a vital and integral part of
5   our everyday life in this modern age. More than luxury, it is indeed a necessity.
    The mobile phone industry is changing fast. The early years were ruled by smartphones based on a simple operating system. These old smartphones did not
10 have advanced features, and they were limited in their functions. The history of the mobile phone has taken a new turn with the introduction of a new generation of smart mobile phones which have replaced old types of smartphones. These new smartphones use adapted
15 operating systems for mobile applications. Just like computers, they allow us to use text and image editors.
    The new mobile smartphones offer a wide choice of configurations. They have both a physical keypad and touch screen pads. Typing on these smart phones is
20 much easier when compared to typing on a laptop or PC. With the push of the button or a slight touch, it also allows you to explore mobile phones. It only takes some days of practice to be an expert user of these mobiles. Internet access is the main function of these mobiles.
25 You can download different browsers and browse with the hand set. The new smart phones can be used as a modem which does not require any wires to connect.

Internet: <ezinearticles.com> and <www.articlesnatch.com>. Adapted.

3. Judge the following items according to the cartoon.

	C	E
a) It satirizes people who cannot live without using mobile phones.		
b) It criticizes the fact that people need to be connected all the time.		
c) The man is lost and he is trying to make contact with his wife through a shell.		
d) The name BlackBerry is used in the cartoon as a synonym for mobile phone.		
e) The man's wife doesn't allow him to be on vacation without a mobile phone.		

- **TEXT 3 – Question 4**
  UnB-DF, 2011

Marque, para cada item: o campo designado com o código C, caso julgue o item CERTO; ou o campo designado com o código E, caso julgue o item ERRADO.

4. Judge the following items according to the text above.

	C	E
a) Outmoded mobile phones have long been a common substitute for the previously existing smartphones.		
b) New smartphone typing is not as difficult as that of a laptop or PC.		
c) One needs but some days to become a skillful user of the new smart mobile phones mentioned in the text.		
d) "Browse" (line 25) means *access*.		
e) Nowadays mobile phones are in fact one of the basic amenities.		
f) At first smartphone operating systems were unable to perform tasks now available in the more up-to-date apparatus.		

PART

7

Print Media

Learning plan

Talking about news stories

Understanding printed and online newspapers

Talking about completed actions in the past

Describing actions in progress in the past

Reading magazine covers critically

Distinguishing facts from opinions and giving opinions

Writing headlines and making newspaper clippings

Let's learn how to create cool photo effects

Nowadays it is possible to create cool effects for your images easily. It's not something that only professionals can do. Would you like to try?

There are free tools to transform your pictures into interesting images. One of them is PhotoFunia, available at <http://www.photofunia.com/> (accessed on: May 22, 2014).

The photo montage below was generated with the help of this tool.

179

UNIT 13
Extra! Extra!

Language in action

- Learn how to talk about news stories
- Understand printed and online newspapers
- Talk about completed actions in the past and describe actions in progress in the past

www.sentinelsource.com/news/national_world/tech-titan-dies/article_f6eaafdf-e2ea-5fc2-a54e-bf1c3fc84fa8.html

Home | News | Sport | Community | Entertainment | Life & Style | Features

TECH TITAN DIES

Apple co-founder Steve Jobs dies of cancer at 56; tributes pour in

By Brandon Griggs CNN News Service

Apple co-founder Steve Jobs, seen in June, 2008 introducing the iPhone 3G, died Wednesday. Jobs was 56.

Steve Jobs, the visionary who led a mobile computer revolution with the creation of wildly popular devices such as the iPhone, was mourned today by admirers and competitors as much of the world awoke to news of his death.

Jobs' death was announced Wednesday by Apple, the Silicon Valley company he co-founded with Steve Wozniak. He was 56.

"Apple has lost a visionary and creative genius, and the world has lost an amazing human being," Apple said in a statement on its website.

"Those of us who have been fortunate enough to know and work with Steve have lost a dear friend and an inspiring mentor."

The hard-driving executive pioneered the concept of the personal computer and of navigating them by clicking onscreen images with a mouse.

In more recent years, he introduced the iPod portable music player, the iPhone and the iPad tablet all of which changed how digital content was consumed.

More than one pundit, praising Jobs' ability to transform industries with his inventions, called him a modern-day Leonardo da Vinci.

"Steve Jobs is one of the great innovators in the history of modern capitalism," *New York Times* columnist Joe Nocera said in August. "His intuition has been phenomenal over the years."

Others championed his leadership skills.

"He was a historical figure on the scale of a Thomas Edison or a Henry Ford, and set the mold for many other corporate leaders in many other industries," wrote Walter Mossberg, a tech columnist for *The Wall Street Journal*.

"He did what a CEO should: Hired and inspired great people; managed for the long term, not the quarter of the short-term stock price; made big bets and took big risks."

Jobs' death, while dreaded by Apple's legions of fans, was not unexpected. He had battled cancer for years, took a medical leave from Apple in January and stepped down as chief executive in August because he could "no longer meet (his) duties and expectations."

[...]

Available at: <www.sentinelsource.com/news/national_world/tech-titan-dies/article_f6eaafdf-e2ea-5fc2-a54e-bf1c3fc84fa8.html>. Accessed on: November 18, 2013.

7 ■ Print Media

180

› Lead-in

1. Notice how the news story on the left page is organized. Complete this text with the parts of a news story.

> Most news stories have a clear organization and contain a headline, a strapline, a lead, a body (content) and an image with a caption. The _____ sums up the main newspaper story to attract the reader. The _____ adds a little more detail to the _____. The opening paragraph of the news story is known as the _____. The _____, the strapline, and the _____ tell you the main ideas of the news article. The _____ of the story is where you find detailed information to help you better understand the story. An image is another element often used in news stories. It is usually followed by a _____ which integrates the image to the news story.

2. In what ways does the headline differ from the other parts of the article?
_____

3. Relate the parts of a newspaper to their definitions.

a) Local and Foreign News Section ( ) comes on the front page and contains the most important news.
b) Obituary Page ( ) contains domestic and international news.
c) Sports Page ( ) contains news about sports events in and out of the country.
d) Business and Finance Section ( ) gives views or opinions of the editor or publisher on certain issues or events.
e) General News ( ) contains advertisements of various types.
f) Art and Entertainment Section ( ) provides information on banking and business in general.
g) Travel and Tourism Section ( ) provides a guide to enjoyable travel.
h) Editorial Page ( ) provides information about people who died and the time and place of their burial.
i) Classified Ads Section ( ) contains information about movies, radio, TV, etc.

4. Discuss in pairs in which part of a newspaper these headlines can be found. Answer using the letters in activity 3.

I. ( ) **MEN WALK ON MOON**
ASTRONAUTS LAND ON PLAIN; COLLECT ROCKS, PLANT FLAG
The New York Times
Available at: <http://www.nytimes.com/learning/general/onthisday/big/0720.html\>. Accessed on: November 18, 2013.

II. ( ) **theguardian** — Huge quake devastates Japan
• 1,000 dead, many missing; commuter train and ship lost • State of emergency at nuclear plant over leak risk • Tsunami alerts and evacuations across Pacific
Available at: <http://www.politicshome.com/images/guardian11.JPG>. Accessed on: November 18, 2013.

III. ( ) **OBAMA TO SEE CONTROVERSIAL 'GANGNAM STYLE' SINGER**
Available at: <http://www.usatoday.com/story/theoval/2012/12/09/obama-psy-gangnam-style-christmas-in-washington/1756667/>. Accessed on: November 18, 2013.

IV. ( ) **Revealed: How the cost of a degree is now £100,000**
Available at: <http://www.independent.co.uk/news/education/education-news/revealed-how-the-cost-of-a-degree-is-now-100000-8395989.html>. Accessed on: November 18, 2013.

V. ( ) **In Rust Belt, a teenager's climb from poverty**
Available at: <http://www.washingtonpost.com/national/in-new-castle-pa-trying-to-break-free-of-poverty/2012/12/08/f41f20ec-3985-11e2-8a97-363b0f9a0ab3_story.html?tid=pm_pop>. Accessed on: November 18, 2013.

▶ Let's read!

Before you read...
- What does the photo below tell us about this article?
- What kinds of devices are being shown?

> **Hint**
> Pay attention to the **nonverbal information** before reading a text.

1. Read the headline and the strapline below. Who is the article addressed to?

January 23, 2012

It was hard for these teens to give up Facebook, YouTube and texting while doing their homework

Distractions are all around us – Facebook, YouTube, texting, TV. It's sometimes so overwhelming that it can be hard to focus on homework. So we challenged teens to do their homework without distractions for three days. They were allowed to take breaks to do things like check their Facebook, go on YouTube, talk to their friends or watch TV, but they couldn't do those things while doing their homework.

Photo by Elizabeth Vidar, 17, North Hollywood HS Zoo Magnet.

Elizabeth Vidar/Available at: <http://www.layouth.com/too-much-temptation/>. Accessed on: March 2, 2013.

L.A. Youth is an online newspaper "by and about teens," according to its editor. It publishes first-hand accounts of teens' experiences with college stress and personal troubles like racial identity, broken families, teen pregnancy, and drug addiction, among other issues.

[...]

By Jazmine Mendoza
16, Valley Regional HS #5 (San Fernando)

[...]

I was confident the first day. I left my computer and phone on because I wanted to challenge myself by keeping temptations nearby. I felt more focused because I wasn't thinking about checking my Facebook every five minutes. I spent only three hours doing homework instead of the six to seven hours I usually take. I even had time to read for pleasure before going to bed. The following day at school I felt better prepared because without distractions, I had fully understood the homework.

During the second night I found myself dozing off and getting bored since I was used to going online or calling a friend when my homework got hard. I didn't want to cave in though, so I dedicated myself to doing portions of my homework for about an hour and then taking five-minute breaks. I didn't use the breaks to go online though, because I knew that I'd stay on longer than five minutes. Instead I cleaned my room, got a snack or saw what my family was doing. Then I continued my homework more refreshed.

I repeated the same routine the third day, and will try to keep that routine from now on. Spending less time on Facebook made it less important. I knew I wasn't missing out on much because I could go on later and nothing had changed. It feels good being on the computer less.

Available at: <http://www.layouth.com/too-much-temptation/>. Accessed on: November 18, 2013.

By Jessica Marin
17, Culver City HS

The first day, I forgot that I had to be distraction free until I realized it took me 30 minutes to come back to a government question because I was texting my friends and checking my email. When I stopped replying to texts, I finished my homework in less than 20 minutes. I was able to work on college applications the rest of the night and go to sleep before 11.

I usually stay up until midnight and spend about four hours doing homework.

The next two days were not as successful. I tried not to get distracted by my phone but I couldn't help it. I could have moved it away from my desk, but what if I missed an important call or text? Like what if my friend broke up with her boyfriend? I'm so attached to my phone that if I don't have it near me I feel like a part of me is missing, which is not normal – it is just an object. Text messages would come in, I would ignore them but then another message would come in and another one after that one. I gave in and texted and called my best friend. We didn't even talk about anything important, just the usual rundown of how our day went and complaints about our homework.

My mom said she knew I would fail this challenge because according to her I'm "addicted" to my phone. In my defense, the challenge worked for one day but then I went back to how things usually are, staying up until midnight. But I'm OK with that because I feel like I need mini-distractions during homework or else I'd go crazy.

Available at: <http://www.layouth.com/too-much-temptation/>. Accessed on: November 18, 2013.

183

2. What challenge was proposed to the students?

( ) To do homework listening to music all the time.

( ) To do homework without electronic distractions for three days.

( ) To avoid friends for three days.

3. Fill in the table according to the testimonials given by Jazmine and Jessica.

What did Jessica and Jazmine do each day?

	First day	Second day	Third day
Jazmine			
Jessica			

4. Is there any newspaper like this in your city/state/country? What kind of issues could be reported by you and your colleagues if there were one?

5. Would you accept the challenge of doing homework without distractions? In pairs, discuss your studying habits.

6. Do you prefer reading the news in print or online? What websites do you read?

_____

7. Discuss with a partner the advantages and disadvantages of printed and online newspapers.

■ **Useful language**

Expressing opinion		Useful words/expressions
In my opinion...	I think...	allow/store/borrow/sell
To me...	I believe...	multimedia options/availability/sustainability

Beyond the lines...

a) Who chooses what is published in newspapers? What do you think they base their choices on?

b) How do you check the reliability of your source of news?

c) Do you think the news in and about your local community represents people from different social and economical backgrounds equally?

> Let's listen and talk!

Hint
Taking notes
while you
listen may
help you focus
on what you
understand.

Before you listen...

- What are the most popular newspapers in your town or state?
- Besides newspapers, what other media do you resort to when you want to know the news?
  - ( ) video-sharing websites
  - ( ) radio
  - ( ) TV
  - ( ) online newspapers
  - ( ) magazines
  - ( ) podcasts
  - ( ) tabloids

1. ◎**35** Listen to some newscasts. Focus on the general ideas and take notes of words and expressions which helped you understand the texts.

> **Newscast 1**
> Available at: <http://www.guardian.co.uk/film/audio/2012/jan/12/film-weekly-podcast-ralph-fiennes-coriolanus>. Accessed on: November 19, 2013.

> **Newscast 2**
> Available at: <http://www.youtube.comwatch?v=AXBdIBgl7to>. Accessed on: November 19, 2013.

> **Newscast 3**
> Available at: <http://www.youtube.com/watch?v=DJb-_VvfllE&playnext=1&list=PL3AE53E53CC17E299&feature=results_video>. Accessed on: November 19, 2013.

2. ◎**35** Listen to the newscasts again. Mark in what part of a newspaper these pieces of news would be found.

( ) General news   ( ) Entertainment section   ( ) Sports page

3. ◎**36** The following words from newscast 1 can be pronounced in different ways. Listen to the American and British pronunciations of these words. Which sound marks the variation?

> guardian   war   horse   power

4. ◎**37** Listen to more information about the Haitian team. Decide which statements are true (**T**) and which are false (**F**).

( ) The Haiti soccer team is made up of people who have lost either a leg or an arm.

( ) The players lost their legs and arms in accidents.

( ) The newscast talks about a team that has participated in the Paralympic Games.

( ) The coach is proud of the team's accomplishment.

( ) The interviewed players talked about how soccer has changed their lives.

( ) The players have to pay for the mechanical legs.

5. In groups, make a list of news stories about disasters that have affected different communities including yours. With help from the geography and history teachers, research on how communities worked together to overcome local difficulties and report in English next class.

185

▸ Let's focus on language!

› Verb tense review

1. We use the **Simple Past** to talk about completed actions in the past, and we use the **Past Continuous** to describe an action in the past that was in progress. Based on this, read the excerpts and do the following activity.

Jazmine Mendoza, 16

"I was confident the first day. I left my computer and phone on because I wanted to challenge myself by keeping temptations nearby. I felt more focused because I wasn't thinking about checking my Facebook every five minutes."

Available at: <http://www.layouth.com/too-much-temptation/>. Accessed on: November 18, 2013.

Jessica Marin, 17

"The first day, I forgot that I had to be distraction free until I realized it took me 30 minutes to come back to a government question because I was texting my friends and checking my email."

Available at: <http://www.layouth.com/too-much-temptation/>. Accessed on: November 18, 2013.

a) Write **A** for the statements that describe complete, finished actions in the past and **B** for the ones that describe an action in the past that was in progress.

( ) I wanted to challenge myself by keeping temptations nearby.

( ) I felt more focused [...].

( ) [...] because I wasn't thinking about checking my Facebook every five minutes.

( ) I forgot that I had to be distraction free [...].

( ) [...] because I was texting my friends and checking my email.

b) Brian Yu also accepted the challenge of doing his homework without distractions. Review verb tenses by completing the missing gaps on the next page. Then swap books with a classmate for peer correction.

Elizabeth */icar/Available at: <http://www.layouth.com/too-muchtemptation/>. Accessed on: March 2, 2013.

I knew the challenge would for the most part be a piece of cake. Last year I would go on Facebook or Tumblr while I _____ (do) my homework. I would also go on YouTube for a lecture and get distracted by the sidebar, wasting an hour or two on random links. So I _____ (install) an app on my browser called Stayfocus. I _____ (give) myself 50 minutes a day for browsing and once those minutes _____ (be) up, the sites were blocked. My only distraction now _____ (be) instant messaging my friends about girls, classes and schoolwork.

For the challenge I _____ (choose) the Stayfocus option that _____ (let/neg.) me browse at all, and I _____ (log/neg.) in to AIM (AOL Instant Messenger) until I was done with my homework. I _____ (come) home from band practice at 7 p.m. and napped for two hours before starting my homework. I got bored while working on my essay about Fidel Castro and I _____ (have) the urge to use AIM or check out videos on YouTube. However, I _____ (do) the challenge so I _____ (make) myself a sandwich and _____ (go) back to work. After I _____ (finish) my stuff, it was around 2 a.m. Not bad for a school night; I usually _____ (finish) around 3.

On Day 2, I _____ (go) home after band practice and woke up around 8. I _____ (put) on my headphones and started my AP Spanish homework. It wasn't hard staying off the Internet.

On Day 3, I _____ (study) for my history test and _____ (do) my homework for my other classes. Occasionally I would wonder what my friends were up to and how they were doing. I _____ (like) to have AIM open on my browser window to have a friend to talk to while I _____ (work). You can only focus so much before you get distracted. Taking breaks _____ (help) keep me refreshed.

Available at: <http://www.layouth.com/too-much-temptation/>. Accessed on: November 19, 2013.

2. Choose five situations and share what you were doing when/before they happened. Look at the example.

When	my parents arrived last night, my favorite team won a game, I went to bed yesterday, a relative came to my house unannounced,	I was...
Before	the telephone rang the last time, I met my best friend, I did my homework,	

When I met my best friend, I **was playing** soccer with my neighbors.

_____

_____

_____

3. Now check with a classmate if you have any similarities of actions that happened while others were in progress.

187

4. Study these headlines and straplines on the introductory pages. Complete the statements with the words **headlines** and **straplines** and learn more about their characteristics.

Massive Study Says Earth Getting Warmer

More than a billion temperature readings from around the world say the mercury has gone up by one degree over the past half-century.

Available at: <http://pioneers.themarknews.com/articles/7149-massive-study-says-earth-getting-warmer/>. Accessed on: November 19, 2013.

Referee 'challenge' could be added to NRL rules

National Rugby League captains may eventually be empowered to challenge controversial refereeing decisions [...].

Available at: <http://www.stuff.co.nz/sport/league/6294212/Referee-challenge-could-be-added-to-NRL-rules>. Accessed on: November 19, 2013.

a) _____ are formed by full sentences.

b) _____ are formed by reduced sentences or phrases.

c) _____ normally use the Present to suggest they convey recent news.

5. Read the following headlines. Write **S** when they are formed by reduced sentences or **P** when they are formed by phrases.

(   ) Massive Study Says Earth Getting Warmer

(   ) The Economics of Art

(   ) Referee 'challenge' could be added to NRL rules

(   ) Funeral for a Tuskegee Airman

(   ) White House Kills Keystone Pipeline

(   ) Drummer Jimmy Cobb still tears it up

6. Notice that both the reduced sentences and the phrases are formed by "groups of meaning" (verbal and nominal). It is easy to understand them if you make a pause between these groups.

A Massive Study / Says / (That) Earth / (Is) Getting / Warmer

Funeral / for a Tuskegee Airman

7. Use slashes (/) to identify the groups of meaning in the ambiguous headlines below. They were taken from real newspapers.

Hospitals Are Sued By 7 Foot Doctors

Miners Refuse To Work After Death

Milk Drinkers Are Turning To Powder

Complaints About NBA Referees Growing Ugly

Man Eating Piranha Mistakenly Sold As Pet Fish

Astronaut Takes Blame For Gas In Spacecraft

INCLUDE YOUR CHILDREN WHEN BAKING COOKIES

HERSHEY BARS PROTEST

Available at: <http://www.fun-with-words.com/ambiguous_headlines.html>. Accessed on: November 19, 2013.

Hint
Make a **pause** in the right places and notice how these pauses help you understand the text.

Profession spot

> **Newspaper staff positions**

A typical day in a Brazilian newsroom, 2011.

Match the columns and find out what each professional does at a newspaper company.

1. Advertising manager ( ) reviews all photos and graphics in the paper and edits them to fit layout.
2. Business manager ( ) reads and edits feature stories, assigns stories to writers, and manages the layout of the features section.
3. Copy editor ( ) determines the layout of all ads, sells advertisement spots, and designs some ads.
4. Editor-in-chief ( ) is in charge of the news section, reads and edits all news stories, works out the layout of the sections, and assigns specific stories to writers.
5. Features editor ( ) reads and edits the entire sports section, manages layout, and occasionally writes an article for the section.
6. Managing editor ( ) proofreads the entire paper, edits copy and photos to fit layout.
7. News editor ( ) reads and edits the entire opinion section, usually writes his or her own column, and manages the layout of the opinion section.
8. Opinion editor ( ) oversees all phases of the production of the paper, reviews all articles and sections, and assigns staff with their stories, along with the section editors.
9. Photo/Graphics editor ( ) manages money of the newspaper and is in charge of marketing, salaries, and the overall budget.
10. Sports editor ( ) helps the editor-in-chief decide content of the issue, designs overall layout and section layout with section editors.

Adapted from: <http://quizlet.com/3170822/staff-positions-of-a-newspaper-flash-cards/>. Accessed on: November 19, 2013.

UNIT 14 Strike a pose

Language in action

- Learn how to read magazine covers critically
- Learn how to distinguish facts from opinions
- Learn how to give opinions

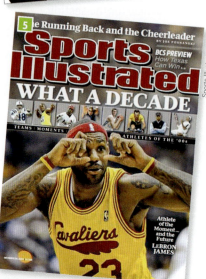

> Lead-in

1. Look at the magazine covers on the previous page. Choose which category they fit in. There are nine extra categories!

( ) Current Affairs, Culture & Politics ( ) Sports & Hobbies ( ) Education ( ) Lifestyle

( ) Science, Geography & History ( ) Business & Finance ( ) Computer Games ( ) Fashion

( ) Design, Architecture & Construction ( ) Health & Medical ( ) Youth Issues ( ) Travel

( ) Art, Literature & Music ( ) Cars & Motorbikes ( ) Agriculture & Gardening

2. Think of other magazines you know. What categories do they fit in?

_____

3. Do you read magazines (both in print and online)? What kinds of magazines do you like reading?

_____

4. Which seems to be the most important news for you on these six covers? How is it highlighted?

_____

5. Check (✔) words from the covers that convey the positive idea of happiness and perfection.

( ) amazing ( ) blood ( ) provocative ( ) amazingly ( ) unexpected ( ) pretty

( ) good ( ) extraordinary ( ) popular ( ) pathetic ( ) surprising ( ) friendship

6. Read the headlines below and decide which category of magazine they were probably taken from.

a) **YOU CAN STILL GET RICH IN REAL ESTATE**

_____

Available at: <https://www.forbesmagazine.com/backissues/august-8-2009-real-estate-rich-war.html>. Accessed on: November 19, 2013.

b) **A NEW SECRET TO LASTING WEIGHT LOSS**

_____

Available at: <http://theprobar.com/archives/2008/05/26/health-magazine-food-awards-superfood-slam-a-winner/>. Accessed on: November 19, 2013.

c) **THE 100 GREATEST PC GAMES OF ALL TIME**

_____

Available at: <http://www.pcgamer.com/2013/07/24/pc-gamer-us-issue-243-the-100-greatest-pc-games-of-all-time/>. Accessed on: November 19, 2013.

d) **50 GREAT ADVENTURES: TURKEY, ISRAEL, EGYPT, INDIA, SPAIN AND MORE**

_____

Available at:<http://www.witnessmyscience.com/pages/magazine_cover.html>. Accessed on: November 19, 2013.

e) **FUTURE CARS: WHAT'S NOW, WHAT'S NEXT**

_____

Available at: <http://downmagaz.ws/car_magazine_moto/page/8/>. Accessed on: November 19, 2013.

f) **CITIES OF TOMORROW ENVISIONING THE FUTURE OF URBAN HABITAT**

_____

Available at: <http://www.evolo.us/category/magazine/>. Accessed on: November 19, 2013.

> Let's read!

Before you read...

- Look at the excerpts in activity 1. From which section of a magazine do you think they were taken? Choose from these options.

    Home   Business & Tech   Health & Science   Life & Style
        Arts & Entertainment   Contributors   Letters

- Why do you think magazines normally include this section?

Hint
Thinking of the most **common features** of a genre can help you identify the text's relevant information.

1. Read the three excerpts more carefully now. Decide if the highlighted sentences refer to a fact (F) or an author's opinion (O).

1

The Language of Flowers: Latin No More?

To the Editor:

The botanist James S. Miller ("Flora, Now in English," Op-Ed, Jan. 23) thinks it is a cause for celebration (   ) that the International Code of Botanical Nomenclature no longer requires that a new species be described in Latin; English and other languages can now be used (   ).

What if Mr. Miller were Chinese; would he prefer English to Latin?

What if a Chinese botanist described a new species in his own language? Would that suit English-speaking scientists? […]

In short, I think that it's a mistake to substitute modern languages for an ancient universal one that does not bear the stamp of cultural hegemony (   ). By the way, I am also a Latin teacher (   ) (fair disclosure, you know).

EDWARD D. LASKY

Chicago, Jan. 23, 2012

Available at: <http://www.nytimes.com/2012/01/26/opinion/the-language-of-flowers-latin-no-more.html?ref=letters>. Accessed on: November 20, 2013.

2

Teen Magazines Lack Substance

I agree with Natascia L.(   ) I sometimes wish I could read about topics other than Paris Hilton or how to apply eyeliner correctly. I think that if we had a magazine that talked about actual news, it would sell.(   ) Most teenagers need to be more informed about politics and world issues.(   ) Teenagers today need a magazine with substance.

Available at: <http://www.teenink.com/hot_topics/letters_to_the_editor/article/17328/Teen-Magazines-Lack-Substance/>. Accessed on: November 20, 2013.

3

Tortoise power

March 8, 2012

Re "The solar desert: An uneasy coexistence," March 4

I was utterly amazed, though not surprised, (   ) by the attempts to "save" the desert tortoise at such a tremendous expense of dollars, personnel, programs, sacrifices and concessions.

There is a severe shortage of renewable clean energy on this planet. (   ) There are millions of children who go to bed hungry each day. (   ) There are millions of humans who do not have access to clean drinking water. (   ) But by all means let's have a private company spend in excess of $56 million to provide food, housing, medical care and security for the desert tortoise. (   )

Available at: <http://articles.latimes.com/keyword/desert-tortoise>. Accessed on: November 20, 2013.

---

7 ■ Print Media

192

2. Read the three texts again and write their corresponding numbers.

(　) The author does not agree with the article s/he read.

(　) The author asks questions to make his/her point.

(　) The author mentions the change in a code.

(　) The author mentions his/her profession.

(　) The author makes a suggestion to the magazine.

(　) The author mentions a few problems on the planet.

(　) The author agrees with the author of the article.

Shutterstock.com/ID/BR

3. Talk to a classmate about the reasons that make someone write a letter to the editor of a magazine or newspaper. Then read this Wikipedia definition and compare.

> **Letter to the editor**
>
> A letter to the editor is a letter sent to a publication about issues of concern from its readers. Usually, letters are intended for publication. In many publications, letters to the editor may be sent either through conventional mail or electronic mail. Letters to the editor are most frequently associated with newspapers and news magazines. [...]
>
> The subject matter of letters to the editor varies widely. However, the most common topics include:
>
> - Supporting or opposing a stance taken by the publication in its editorial, or responding to another writer's letter to the editor.
>   [...]
> - Remarking on materials (such as a news story) that have appeared in a previous edition. Such letters may either be critical or praising.
> - Correcting a perceived error or misrepresentation. [...]
>
> Available at: <http://en.wikipedia.org/wiki/Letter_to_the_editor>. Accessed on: November 20, 2013.

4. Now that you know what a letter to the editor is and what topics it may cover, go back to the texts on the previous page. What is/are the topic(s) of these letters?

_____

5. In pairs, discuss these questions orally.

a) Do you like reading other people's opinions?

b) Have you ever written a letter to a magazine or newspaper? If so, what was it about?

c) Do you share your opinions about something that you have read in a magazine/ newspaper with other people? How do you prefer to do it (comments, social networks, personally)?

d) If you were to write a letter to the editor, which magazine and category would you choose?

e) How could you check the facts before giving your opinion on a subject?

> **Beyond the lines...**
>
> a) Do you think magazines are reliable sources of information?
>
> b) Why do you think some magazines use celebrities on their covers? What do they want to sell?
>
> c) In pairs, analyze the covers on the first page of this unit. What lifestyles, values, physical features are represented or omitted on them?
>
> d) Do these images reinforce any stereotypes – preconceptions about what it means to be beautiful, interesting, etc?

193

› Let's focus on language!

1. Take a look at the following excerpts from the previous reading. How do you know they refer to a fact or an opinion? Check the correct alternative.

> "I think that it's a mistake to substitute modern languages for an ancient universal one that does not bear the stamp of cultural hegemony."

> "There are millions of humans who do not have access to clean drinking water."

> "I agree with Natascia L."

> "I was utterly amazed, though not surprised [...]."

> "But by all means let's have a private company spend in excess of $56 million to provide food, housing, medical care and security for the desert tortoise."

In facts,

( ) the sentence begins with certain verbs, such as "think," "imagine," "agree," and "believe."

( ) it is possible to check that what is being said is true.

( ) the author mentions how he or she felt when reading the text.

2. Now complete with **fact** or **opinion**.

a) A/An _____ is something that is true about a subject and can either be tested or proven.

b) A/An _____ is what somebody thinks about that subject.

3. Read the excerpts above again and find out:

a) The verbs used to express opinion.

_____

b) The words or expressions used to express how the author felt.

_____

4. Read these sentences taken from texts 1 and 2 in the *Let's read!* section and check the correct alternatives.

> "The botanist James S. Miller [...] **thinks** it is a cause for celebration [...]."
> "I **agree** with Natascia L."

( ) "think" and "agree" were used to express opinion.

( ) "think" and "agree" referred to an action in progress or temporary situations.

( ) verbs of opinion are usually used in the simple form (not in the continuous form).

5. Now circle the correct words to complete the rules.

   Verbs that express **opinion/action** are called "stative verbs." Other verbs in this group include *imagine, remember, believe, doubt, know, understand, like, love, dislike, guess, realize*. They **are/are not** usually used in the continuous form.

6. Read the letters below and insert the correct form of the verbs to complete the sentences.

   a) *Mission Viejo*

   Everyone _____ (agree) on the fact that education is important. The Cal State system _____ (plan) to freeze spring 2013 enrollment, and more cuts will happen if voters reject the proposed initiative to raise taxes. Obviously, the Cal State system _____ (try) to push voters to help fund education, but is this really the best idea?

   Adapted from: <http://www.latimes.com/news/opinion/letters/>. Accessed on: July 24, 2012.

   b) I am 20 years old and have recently started to be disgusted with what I _____ (see) on the covers of the teen magazines at the grocery checkout. Did I really read that crap when I was 15? Yep, I sure did. Now that I've grown up a bit, I _____ (realize) that these teen magazines are ridiculous. Anyways, I _____ (think) what your magazine _____ (do) is great. It's real, honest and integral.

   — Natalie S.

   Adapted from: <http://www.fazeteen.com/issue23/letters_to_editor.html>. Accessed on: November 20, 2013.

   > **Hint**
   > **Planning** what to say can help you organize your thoughts before speaking.

7. Talk to a classmate: Do you agree with Natalie S.'s opinion about teen magazines? Do you read this kind of magazine? Why (not)?

8. Read the following excerpts from a magazine. Work in pairs and prepare a 5-minute presentation giving your opinion on one of the subjects.

   > **Useful language**
   > I believe…
   > I think…
   > I agree that…
   > In my opinion, …
   > I don't like…

   ### EDUCATION | TECHNOLOGY
   From Issue #1

   Death of the Classroom: The New Wave of Online Education
   By Scott Reekie

   Picture a society where learning can happen at any time, in any place and can be completed without ever going to class. This could be the new wave of education and the Internet technology now exists to support such a system. […]

   Available at: <http://www.fazeteen.com/issue01/death_of_classroom.html>. Accessed on: November 20, 2013.

   ### SPORTS & FITNESS
   From Issue #5

   Is Wrestling a Sport?
   By Karen Coyle

   Blood, broken bones, lies, conspiracy, vulgar language and half naked women. You guessed it, pro-wrestling. In the "old days" wrestling was merely a way of saying, "I'm stronger than you". Now, some call it a soap opera for guys, some call it entertainment and others call it crap. But can we call it a sport? […]

   Available at: <http://www.fazeteen.com/issue05/is_wrestling_a_sport.html>. Accessed on: November 20, 2013.

Vocabulary corner

Take a look at the back of a typical digital camera. Relate the parts of the camera to their functions.

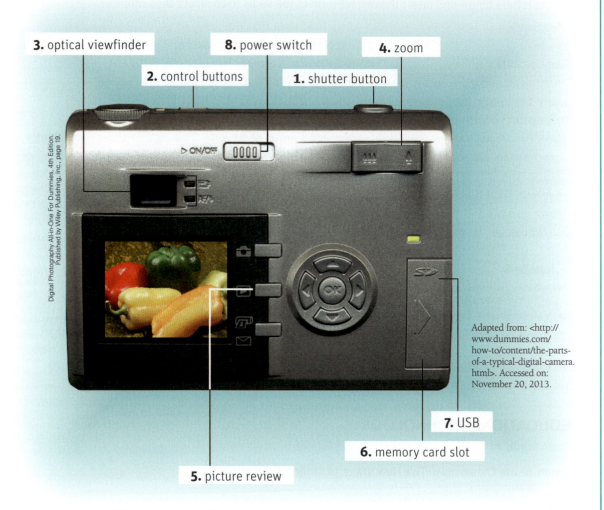

Adapted from: <http://www.dummies.com/how-to/content/the-parts-of-a-typical-digital-camera.html>. Accessed on: November 20, 2013.

( ) Used to accept digital memory cards

( ) Used to adjust various camera settings

( ) Used to frame and compose a picture

( ) Used to take a picture

( ) Used to magnify or reduce the size of the image

( ) Used to turn the camera on or off

( ) Used to review the pictures one has already taken

( ) Used to connect a USB cable

› Let's listen!

Before you listen...

Take a look at this magazine cover and answer.
- What is the target audience of the magazine?
- What do you think this edition is about?

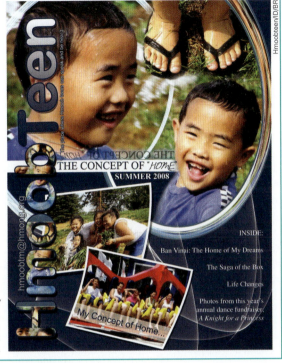

Available at: <http://hmoobteen.hmong.org/page17739.aspx>. Accessed on: November 20, 2013.

Did you know...?

The Hmong are an Asian ethnic group from the mountainous regions of China, Vietnam, Laos, and Thailand. A number of Hmong people fought against the communist Pathet Lao during the Laotian Civil War. Hmong people were singled out for retribution when the Pathet Lao took over the Laotian government in 1975, and tens of thousands fled to Thailand seeking political asylum. Thousands of these refugees have resettled in Western countries since the late 1970s.

Source: <http://en.wikipedia.org/wiki/Hmong_people>. Accessed on: November 20, 2013.

1. ⊚38 Listen to the audio and find out.

   a) What social networks are mentioned in the audio?
   _____

   b) What kind of support is the editor asking for?
   _____

   c) Why do the Hmong teens want to continue with the magazine?
   _____

2. Are there people from other states or ethnic groups in your region? What do you know about their culture?
   _____

Pronunciation spot – The /ɪ/ and /i/ sounds

1. ⊚39 Listen to the sounds /ɪ/ and /i/ in these words.

/ɪ/	/i/
ed**i**tor th**i**s **i**t	t**ea**chers thr**ee** p**eo**ple
s**i**x w**i**thout sk**i**ll	agr**ee** bel**ie**ve
y**ea**r	

2. ⊚40 Listen carefully to the words and write /ɪ/ or /i/ in the adequate places.

   drink   see   these   think   severe   missed
   / /   / /   / /   / /   / /   / /

   mistake   tips   give   since   seek
   / /   / /   / /   / /   / /

› Turn on the jukebox!

1. 🔴41 Read the lyrics below. Circle the words with the /i/ sound and underline the words with the /ɪ/ sound. Then listen to the song and check your answers.

Vogue (by Madonna)

Strike a pose
Vogue, vogue, vogue (2x)

Look around, everywhere you turn is heartache
It's everywhere that you go (look around)
You try everything you can to escape
The pain of life that you know (life that you know)

When all else fails and you long to be
Something better than you are today
I know a place where you can get away
It's called a dance floor, and here's what it's for, so

(Chorus)
Come on, vogue
Let your body move to the music
Hey, hey, hey
Come on, vogue
Let your body go with the flow
You know you can do it

All you need is your own imagination
So use it that's what it's for
Go inside, for your finest inspiration
Your dreams will open the door
It makes no difference if you're black or white
If you're a boy or a girl
If the music's pumping it will give you new life
You're a superstar, yes, that's what you are, you know it

(Chorus, substituting "groove" for "move")

Beauty's where you find it
Not just where you bump and grind it
Soul is in the musical
That's where I feel so beautiful
Magical, life's a ball
So get up on the dance floor (Chorus)
Vogue,
Beauty's where you find it (2x)

Greta Garbo, and Monroe
Dietrich and DiMaggio
Marlon Brando, Jimmy Dean
On the cover of a magazine

Grace Kelly; Harlow, Jean
Picture of a beauty queen
Gene Kelly, Fred Astaire
Ginger Rodgers, dance on air

They had style, they had grace
Rita Hayworth gave good face
Lauren, Katherine, Lana too
Bette Davis, we love you

Ladies with an attitude
Fellows that were in the mood
Don't just stand there, let's get to it
Strike a pose, there's nothing to it

Vogue, vogue

Oooh, you've got to
Let your body move to the music
Oooh, you've got to just
Let your body go with the flow
Oooh, you've got to Vogue

Available at: <http://letras.mus.br/madonna/63190/traducao.html>. Accessed on: November 20, 2013.

2. 🔴42 Listen to the words in boxes **A** and **B**. What will happen if you mispronounce these words?

A	eat	reach	feel	feet	peel
B	it	rich	fill	fit	pill

Profession spot

> **Photographers**

1. There are different types of photos in magazines. Most professional photographers have their areas of specialization. Look at the pictures below and decide what each photographer's specialization is. The first one is done for you.

a) Yousuf Karsh was a _____ portrait photographer.

b) David Munns is a _____

c) Richard Avedon is a _____

d) Daniel Rouse is a _____

e) Charles O'Rear is a _____

2. Can you name other areas of expertise or specialization in photography?
_____
_____

3. Would you like to be a professional photographer? Which area would you choose? Why?
_____
_____

199

Let's act with words!

Make a news report!

Inform your readers about something which happened in your community and which has not been reported in the daily newspapers.

Make a **newspaper clipping** with your own news report.

Go to <http://www.fodey.com/generators/newspaper/snippet.asp> (accessed on: May 26, 2014) and create a newspaper clipping similar to the example below. Fill in the form to do it online or make a similar one in paper.

First: Choose a name for your "newspaper."
Second: Write the date, including day of the week, month, and year.
Third: Write the headline.
Fourth: Paste or type your news report with four to six short paragraphs.
Fifth: Press the button "generate" and you will get an image similar to the one above.
Sixth: Download your newspaper clipping as a JPG image by clicking on the "Download Your Image" link.
Seventh: Publish the image on Wikispaces. You can also include a copy in your portfolio.

Read more about this web tool at:

<http://www.scrappersguide.com/tips_el/nifty-newspaper-clipping-el/>. Accessed on: November 20, 2013.

Go to Workbook, page 370, for more practice.

Learning tips

How to learn with online newspapers and magazines

Newseum is a museum of news in Washington D.C. It offers an online service which displays more than 800 newspaper front pages each day. The service is available at <http://www.newseum.org/todaysfrontpages> (accessed on: November 20, 2013).

You can view today's page or archived pages with events of historical significance. Choose a page and click on it to read the news. You can find two links: Readable PDF and Website. You can open the PDF file and read or save the front page, or you can go to the website of the newspaper and read more news.

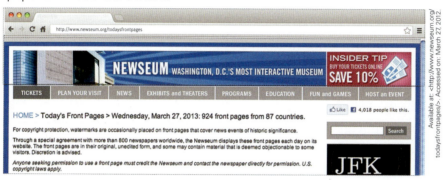

Suggestions to improve your English with newspapers

1. Start with headlines and make a glossary for the new words. You can use an online dictionary (example: <www.dictionary.com>) to learn more about the words.
2. Then read the leads and try to find answers to questions beginning with *when*, *why*, *who*, *whom*, *what*, *where*, *how*.
3. Build a grammar pattern bank with examples from the news.
4. Answer a daily news quiz at *The New York Times* and do the exercises in its special learning section available at <http://learning.blogs.nytimes.com/>.
(All sites accessed on: November 20, 2013.)

Let's reflect on learning!

You are now invited to assess what you learned and how you learned. Finish the ideas below on an extra sheet of paper and become a more autonomous and reflective learner.

In Part 7

I learned _____

I liked _____

I need to review/learn more _____

My experiences with English outside school were _____

201

Let's study for Enem!

After prison blaze kills hundreds in Honduras, UN warns on overcrowding

15 February 2012

A United Nations human rights official today called on Latin American countries to tackle the problem of prison overcrowding in the wake of an overnight fire at a jail in Honduras that killed hundreds of inmates. More than 300 prisoners are reported to have died in the blaze at the prison, located north of the capital, Tegucigalpa, with dozens of others still missing and presumed dead. Antonio Maldonado, human rights adviser for the UN system in Honduras, told UN Radio today that overcrowding may have contributed to the death toll. "But we have to wait until a thorough investigation is conducted so we can reach a precise cause," he said. "But of course there is a problem of overcrowding in the prison system, not only in this country, but also in many other prisons in Latin America."

Disponível em: www.un.org. Acesso em: 22 fev. 2012. Adaptado.

Gênero

Notícia de jornal

Competência de área 2

H6 - Utilizar os conhecimentos da LEM e de seus mecanismos como meio de ampliar as possibilidades de acesso a informações, tecnologias e culturas.

Não se deixe impressionar por palavras novas. Faça uma leitura estratégica delas também: procure sinônimos, tente inferir significado pelo contexto, observe bem a formação da palavra (prefixo, sufixo).

O nível de leitura a ser aplicado dependerá da questão explorada no enunciado. Se o enunciado requerer apenas uma compreensão geral, muitas vezes a leitura do *lead* da notícia já basta; se for necessária a compreensão das ideias centrais, será preciso ler a maior parte do texto; se for explorada a compreensão de detalhes do texto, em geral podemos aplicar a estratégia de *scanning* e procurar no texto somente o que precisamos. Lembre-se disso antes de responder a uma questão.

Os noticiários destacam acontecimentos diários, que são veiculados em jornal impresso, rádio, televisão e internet. Nesse texto, o acontecimento reportado é a

A ocorrência de um incêndio em um presídio superlotado em Honduras.

B questão da superlotação nos presídios em Honduras e na América Latina.

C investigação da morte de um oficial das Nações Unidas em visita a um presídio.

D conclusão do relatório sobre a morte de mais de trezentos detentos em Honduras.

E causa da morte de doze detentos em um presídio superlotado ao norte de Honduras.

Extraído de: Exame Nacional do Ensino Médio, 2013, Caderno 6 – CINZA – Página 3 (questão 91).

7 ■ Print Media

202

Part 7 (Print Media)

Typical questions of Enem

Too much temptation

It was hard for these teens to give up Facebook, YouTube and texting while doing their homework.

Distractions are all around us – Facebook, YouTube, texting, TV. It's sometimes so overwhelming that it can be hard to focus on homework. So we challenged teens to do their homework without distractions for three days. They were allowed to take breaks to do things like check their Facebook, go on YouTube, talk to their friends or watch TV, but they couldn't do those things while doing their homework. (...)

Available at: <http://www.layouth.com/too-much-temptation/>. Accessed on: May 26, 2014.

1. O texto mostra o parágrafo inicial de uma notícia sobre uma experiência feita com adolescentes. Durante essa experiência, que durou três dias, os participantes deveriam

    ( ) buscar dados das redes sociais e da TV para resolver as tarefas escolares.

    ( ) concentrar-se nos deveres escolares com acesso apenas à Internet e à TV.

    ( ) dividir o tempo livre entre o acesso à Internet e o uso do celular e da televisão.

    ( ) fazer os deveres escolares sem, ao mesmo tempo, usar aparelhos eletrônicos.

    ( ) manter a TV desligada ao tentarem resolver as tarefas escolares com amigos.

2. O Titanic sempre foi motivo de interesse popular. Podemos inferir pela manchete ao lado que, em Belfast, foi

    ( ) aberto um museu no local da construção do Titanic.

    ( ) criada uma página na web para visitantes do Titanic.

    ( ) iniciada uma viagem semelhante à do Titanic.

    ( ) lançada uma réplica do Titanic para novas viagens.

    ( ) produzido um filme sobre o naufrágio do Titanic.

> Titanic Belfast, the world's largest Titanic visitor attraction, has finally opened in Belfast on the site where the ship was designed, built and launched.
>
> Available at: <http://insideireland.ie/>. Accessed on: April 2, 2012.

Teen Magazines Lack Substance

By Alysha S., Dell Rapids, SD

I agree with Natascia L. I sometimes wish I could read about topics other than Paris Hilton or how to apply eyeliner correctly. I think that if we had a magazine that talked about actual news, it would sell. Most teenagers need to be more informed about politics and world issues. Teenagers today need a magazine with substance.

Available at: <http://www.teenink.com/hot_topics/letters_to_the_editor/article/17328/Teen-Magazines-Lack-Substance/>. Accessed on: May 26, 2014.

3. Este texto é uma carta de uma leitora publicada na *Teen Ink*, uma revista mensal que divulga textos e trabalhos de arte de adolescentes. Na carta, a autora critica

    ( ) a ausência de outros tópicos sobre Paris Hilton.

    ( ) a imprensa por divulgar notícias sobre celebridades.

    ( ) Natascia por escrever sobre futilidades na revista.

    ( ) os temas das notícias que são publicadas nas revistas de adolescentes.

    ( ) Paris Hilton por não usar delineador de forma correta.

Exam Practice Questions (Vestibular)

Test-Taking Tips

Don't get stuck on a question

The level of dificulty in tests may be determined by the content explored in the question and also by the length and complexity of the texts. It is always a good idea to start with the questions and texts you find easier. Time is a factor in tests, so don't get stuck on a particular question. Normally, tests include both multiple-choice questions, as you have seen in the previous sections, and short answer questions, as in the example below. In any case, decide which type is easier for you and start from there. Always be careful with the instructions, especially when they are very specific, as in the question you are going to deal with here.

- **TEXT 1 – Questions 1 to 4**
UFBA, 2011

INSTRUÇÕES:

- Leia cuidadosamente o enunciado de cada questão e formule suas respostas com objetividade e correção de linguagem.

- Responda às questões, <u>em português</u>, de forma clara e legível. Entretanto, haverá uma questão envolvendo construção e/ou transformação de frases <u>em inglês</u>.

- Caso utilize letra de imprensa, destaque as iniciais maiúsculas.

- Será atribuída pontuação zero à questão cuja resposta
  - não se atenha à situação ou ao tema proposto;
  - apresente texto incompreensível ou letra ilegível.

Baby Talk

What similarities are there between the way that infants acquire their first language and the way that adults acquire a second or foreign language? [...]

5 To give an adequate answer, we should start by considering some characteristics of our adult minds and the minds of infants. First, what do we have in common? We all have ears and auditory memory and we are all able to imitate sounds. We make connections in our brains between words and the persons, things, 10 situations and actions around us. Subconsciously, we find and develop a theoretical map of the structure of the language.

But a little more thought reveals that the situation of a baby is quite different from ours as adults. First of 15 all, for a baby, the parents are the principal language teachers, while older children and adults can learn a language by themselves, or from any other teacher. You will not learn English from another adult as you learned your language as a baby because your teacher 20 is not your mother, and you are not a baby anymore. Babies are learning about the whole world around them at the same time they are absorbing language, while older children and adults can take advantage of their rational minds and many diverse situations and 25 experiences during the process of learning a language. Babies do not have another mother tongue in their minds that can interfere with the language being studied. What's more, babies talk about a different set of experiences, which is a very limited set of things. It 30 usually takes two years or more before a baby starts making sense.

Babies hear language for more than a year before forming their first words, and their ability to enunciate words grows very gradually. But adults can 35 start speaking in a matter of days under the right circumstances. What's more, in adults there are many variables, such as motivation, attitude about the language and its culture, which are not present in babies. There are even many differences in our abilities 40 as we grow up: younger children, older children and adults of all ages experience many different levels of ability and accomplishment.

Students often feel frustrated with English lessons and teaching materials that seem to take all the fun out 45 of learning the language, which should be a perfectly natural and pleasant process. Natural language learning in adults is one thing, but it is absurd to make the leap to saying that it is anything like the way babies learn their first language. With all the differences 50 between the mental processes of learning a first and a second language, you should be wary of teachers and books that promise you will learn as easily as a baby, because, even if it were true, that could actually complicate the process for you!

DIMATTEO, Christopher. Baby Talk. *Speak up*, São Paulo, Peixes, ano XV, n. 188, p. 39, s.d. Adaptado.

1. According to the text,
- mention the characteristics which are common to adult minds and the minds of infants when learning a language.

_____

_____

_____

_____

_____

Part 7 (Print Media)

• concerning their language teachers, explain how the situation of a baby differs from the situation of adults.

————————————————————

————————————————————

————————————————————

————————————————————

————————————————————

————————————————————

2. Summarize what the author says about
• the role of the mother tongue in the process of language learning.

————————————————————

————————————————————

————————————————————

————————————————————

————————————————————

————————————————————

• babies' ability to enunciate words in comparison with adults' ability when learning a second language.

————————————————————

————————————————————

————————————————————

————————————————————

————————————————————

• the idea of adults learning a second language the same way babies learn their first language.

————————————————————

————————————————————

————————————————————

————————————————————

————————————————————

————————————————————

————————————————————

3. Rewrite the following sentences according to the instructions below. Make all the necessary changes.
• "We [...] have ears and auditory memory and we are [...] able to imitate sounds. (lines 7-8)

Make this sentence **negative**.

————————————————————

————————————————————

————————————————————

"It usually takes **two years or more** before a baby starts making sense." (lines 29-31)

Ask a question so that the **boldfaced** phrase is the answer.

————————————————————

————————————————————

————————————————————

• "There are even many differences in our abilities as we grow up: [...]" (lines 39-40)

Change the verb forms into the **Simple Past Tense**.

————————————————————

————————————————————

————————————————————

• "you will learn as easily as a baby [...]" (lines 52-53)

Rewrite this sentence in the **comparative degree of superiority**.

————————————————————

————————————————————

————————————————————

4. Analyze the uses of "that" in these sentences and indicate their grammatical functions.

a) "But a little more thought reveals **that** the situation of a baby is quite different [...]" (lines 13-14)

————————————————————

b) "Students often feel frustrated with English lessons and teaching materials **that** seem to take all the fun out of learning the language [...]" (lines 43-45)

————————————————————

205

PART

Video

Learning plan

Talking about the future, offering help, and expressing decisions, willingness, consequences, predictions, and promises

Talking about the weather

Giving instructions

Talking about likes/dislikes and presenting reasons

Using linking words

Writing a weather script

Let's learn how to make a video

You can use one of the programs below:

Dvolver moviemaker, available at: <http://www.dvolver.com/moviemaker/make.html> (accessed on: May 23, 2014).

Muvee Cloud, available at <http://cloud.muvee.com> (accessed on: May 23, 2014).

You can also make movies with a cell phone or a digital camera.

207

UNIT 15 It's on TV

Language in action

- Learn how to talk about the future, offer help, and express decisions, willingness, consequences, predictions, and promises
- Talk about the weather

'Mummy...one of my friends says you can watch films and cartoons and stories on T.V as well.'

Available at: <http://www.cartoonstock.com/directory/e/egotistic.asp>. Accessed on: November 20, 2013.

"I realize you're upset that Oprah hasn't reviewed your new book on her show. You've mentioned it several times. But you are on MY show, so why don't you tell us what inspired you to write 'Overcoming Disappointment and Resentment.'"

Available at: <http://www.cartoonstock.com/directory/p/publishing.asp>. Accessed on: November 20, 2013.

"Your father kicked in the screen and threw the set out the window. He feels violence on TV is a bad influence."

Available at: <http://www.cartoonstock.com/directory/v/violence_on_tv.asp>. Accessed on: November 20, 2013.

> Lead-in

1. Read the cartoons on the previous page and answer these questions.

Cartoon 1

a) What kind of TV channel is the mother watching?

( ) a sales channel ( ) a documentary channel ( ) a sports channel ( ) a travel channel

b) Where is this program broadcast? Look at the price on the TV screen for a hint.

_____

c) What is the boy trying to do with his ironic utterance?

_____

d) What is the stereotype of women in this cartoon?

_____

Cartoon 2

a) Why is the writer upset?

_____

b) How many times did the writer talk about her disappointment?

_____

c) Why is "MY" written with capital letters?

_____

d) The title of the book suggests that the author teaches people to

( ) defeat disappointment and resentment. ( ) welcome disappointment and resentment.

e) Why is there a contradiction between the writer's behavior and the name of her book?

_____

Cartoon 3

a) What did the boy's father do? Why?

_____

b) What is the irony conveyed by the cartoon?

_____

2. What is a common purpose for cartoons?

_____

3. Take a look at the three cartoons again. What features do they have in common?

( ) They use text and image.   ( ) They are colored.

( ) They convey meaning implicitly.   ( ) They use formal language.

( ) Drawings are intended for caricature, satire, or humor.   ( ) The text is short.

> Let's read!

Before you read...

- What is the weather like in your region?

  ( ) It's dry and warm.   ( ) It's wet and hot.   ( ) It's cold.   ( ) It's...
- What do you know about the weather in the United States?
- Do you watch the weather forecast on TV?
- What does forecast mean?

1. Read the weather forecast for two regions in the United States on March 27, 2012 and answer the questions.

Storms target Northeast and Northwest

M. Ressler, Lead Meteorologist, The Weather Channel

Mar. 27, 2012 11:08 am ET

Northeast

- As a storm slides eastward along the Canadian border midweek, showers will dampen western New York, a shot of wintry mix and snow will change to rain from northeast New York to New Hampshire and snow will develop over much of Maine.

South

- Wednesday will be dry and warm for most of the region.
- A very few thunderstorms are possible in parts of Texas, Oklahoma, northern Arkansas, Tennessee, southern Louisiana and central Florida.
- A couple of the thunderstorms could turn severe in northern Oklahoma and northern Tennessee.
- Temperatures will vary from average to 16 degrees above average.

Available at: <http://www.weather.com/newscenter/nationalforecast/index.html>. Accessed on: March 27, 2012.

a) Who may be interested in this weather forecast?

_____

_____

b) Where was it broadcast?

_____

c) What was happening during that week along the Canadian border?

_____

2. Find in the text a prediction for

a) the Northeast concerning showers:

_____

b) the South about the temperature:

_____

3. Look at the map on the previous page. What do the colors represent?

_____

_____

4. Read the following predictions and check (✔) the one(s) which is(are) true for your region this week.

( ) It will be warm and dry.

( ) Rain will fall during the night.

( ) It will be sunny.

( ) Thunderstorms are possible.

( ) It will be hot and wet.

( ) Temperature will be high.

( ) It will be cold.

( ) It will be windy.

( ) It will be cloudy.

( ) There is just a small chance for an isolated shower.

Shutterstock.com/ID/BR

Vocabulary corner

Match the weather idioms to their meanings.

a) A snowball's chance =   ( ) a disturbance about little or nothing
b) A storm in a teacup =   ( ) to chat casually
c) Come rain or shine =   ( ) to postpone something
d) Every cloud has a silver lining = ( ) very little chance
e) Take a rain check =   ( ) there is usually a good aspect of a bad situation
f) Shoot the breeze =   ( ) whatever happens

211

> **Let's listen and talk!**

Before you listen...
- What do you think the future of TV will be?

Hint
Think of what you already know about the theme.

1. 🔴43 Listen to the audio with predictions about TV and answer the question: What kind of program is this?

   _____

2. 🔴43 Listen again and answer (T)rue or (F)alse according to the interviewee's opinions.

   a) TV will continue to change and will continue to evolve. ( )
   b) TV will disappear in the long term. ( )
   c) TV will be replaced by the Internet. ( )
   d) TV will absorb Internet and will keep on moving. ( )
   e) People don't love TV anymore like they used to. ( )

3. Are your predictions and the interviewee's the same? Justify your answer.

4. In groups, ask and answer questions. Each participant asks 3-4 questions. In your notebook, take notes of the answers and then make a summary of the results to report to your class.

   1. How many television sets are there in your home?
   2. Do you have cable TV in your house?
   3. Do you have a television set in your bedroom?
   4. Are you a couch potato?
   5. When do you watch the most television?
   6. When you watch TV, are you a remote control freak?
   7. What types of shows do you watch?
   8. How much television do you watch per day on average?
   9. How many television shows do you watch regularly without fail and would never EVER miss an episode?
   10. What is your favorite television soap opera?
   11. Do you record TV shows or films?
   12. Do you watch DVDs on TV?
   13. Do you use the TV set to play video games?
   14. If you could go on a dream date with a television character, with whom would it be?
   15. What is your favorite television theme song?
   16. What is your favorite television actor or actress?
   17. Free question: _____
   18. Free question: _____

Beyond the lines...
a) Does TV influence human behavior? If so, how?
b) In your opinion, what are the positive aspects of TV?

> Let's focus on language!

1. Read the text and complete the sentence below by checking (✔) the right option.

   > The Internet is about to swallow the television, a development that will change the nature of global media. Soon hundreds of thousands, and eventually hundreds of millions of viewers around the world will be on a path back from being passive couch potatoes into actively engaged citizens again, the way we were before mass media radio and then television arrived in our homes in the 1920s, nearly a century ago.
   > Available at: <http://accelerating.org/articles/televisionwillberevolutionized.html>. Accessed on: May 23, 2014.

   The text above presents a set of

   ( ) decisions.   ( ) consequences.   ( ) predictions.   ( ) promises.

2. Analyze the following statements with **will** and write (**1**) for decision, (**2**) for consequence, (**3**) for prediction, and (**4**) for promise.

   ( ) "I will always love you."

   ( ) "If you walk away/Everyday, it will rain, rain, rain."

   ( ) "Obama says he will help unemployed engineer find job…"

   ( ) "People will cease distinguishing between computers and televisions."

   ( ) "Starting in two weeks, Fox will no longer offer free access to its TV-shows the day after they air on television."

   ( ) Will I need a DTV Converter Box if I buy a High Definition television?

   Excerpts available at: <http://letras.terra.com.br/whitney-houston/18488/>; <http://letras.terra.com.br/bruno-mars/1968932/traducao.html>; <http://www.guardian.co.uk/world/2012/jan/31/obama-unemployed-engineer-video-hangout>; <http://graphics.stanford.edu/~bjohanso/cs448/>; <http://torrentfreak.com/fox-will-boost-u-s-tv-show-piracy-110728/>; <http://tv.about.com/od/frequentlyaskedquestions/f/dtvconverterHD.htm>. All accessed on: November 21, 2013.

3. Look at the image below and write predictions about the weather. One is done for you.

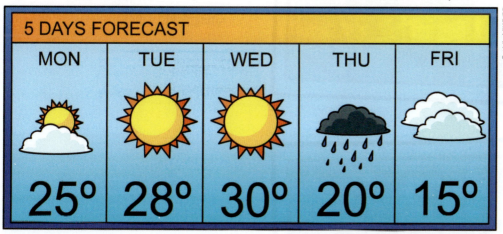

   a) _____

   b) _____

   c) Wednesday will be a hot day.

   d) _____

   e) _____

> We use the **Simple Future** tense to say something will happen in the future. We also use it to express decisions, willingness, consequences, predictions, and promises.

4. Complete the sentences to describe the predictions depicted in Villemard's pictures. The first one is done for you. Use the key words in parentheses, as in the example.

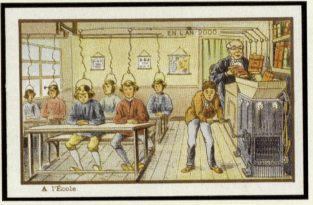

a) In the 21st century, in order to control traffic jams in the air, <u>there will be more and more flying police officers</u>. (flying police officers)

b) Students _____
_____.
(audio books)

c) People _____
_____
_____ just by
dictating it into a loudspeaker. (mail)

d) Women _____
_____
_____ just by
pressing buttons. (make up)

e) We _____. (audio newspapers)

f) We _____. (video-telegraphs)

> World in 2000 as Predicted in 1910: Illustrations by French artist Villemard in 1910 of how he imagined the future to be in the year 2000.
> Available at: <http://www.sadanduseless.com/2011/03/world-in-2000/>. Accessed on: May 23, 2014.

5. What are your predictions for the world in 3000?

_____

_____

6. What would you say in the following situations to show willingness to help? Use the verbs in parentheses. The first one is done for you.

a) A visitor: It's cold because the window is open.

You: I'll close it. (close)

b) A relative: The phone is ringing.

You: _____ (get)

c) A friend: The TV set is too loud.

You: _____ (turn down)

d) Your teacher: I need help with the computer.

You: _____ (help)

7. The song below by The Beatles presents some love promises. Complete the lyrics with the correct form of the verbs in the box.

| feel | fill | find | love | wait | love |

I will
By The Beatles

Who knows how long I' _____ you,
You know I _____ you still,
_____ I _____ a lonely lifetime,
If you want me to I will.

For if I ever saw you,
I didn't catch your name,
But it never really mattered,
I _____ always _____ the same.

Love you forever and forever,
Love you with all my heart;
Love you whenever we're together,
Love you when we're apart.

And when at last I _____ you,
Your song _____ the air,
Sing it loud so I can hear you,
Make it easy to be near you,
For the things you do endear you to me,
you know I will.
I will.

Available at: <http://letras.terra.com.br/the-beatles/208/>. Accessed on: May 23, 2014.

8. 📀**44** Listen to the song and check your answers.

Pronunciation spot – The / l / sound

1. Notice the / l / sound while you listen to the recording.

2. Practice producing this sound reading lines of the song above as well as other sentences that you can find in this unit.

9. Based on the song above, what love promises would *you* make to someone?

_____

_____

_____

_____

Profession spot

> **Careers in television**

Careers in television involve workers in front of the cameras and behind the cameras. Read the definitions for some TV careers and mark (**F**) if the work is in **front** of the cameras and (**B**) if it is **behind** it.

Control room operators at Fox News studios, NY, USA, 2011.

Singer Usher with Jimmy Fallon during an interview in 2013.

- ( ) **Actors** interpret others' words in order to bring a script to life, and to put flesh and blood on the characters they portray.
- ( ) **Camera operators** capture images, which involves receiving camera directions (usually over a headset) from the **director**.
- ( ) **Directors** are responsible for the look and sound of a production and its technical standards; they interpret the **producer**'s and/or **writer**'s vision.
- ( ) **Location managers** research and assess suitable locations, negotiate contracts and payments, and present their findings to **producers** and other decision makers.
- ( ) **Network operations assistants** co-ordinate the movements of program materials in and out of satellite and cable broadcasting organizations.
- ( ) **Presenters** work at the front line of television and radio. They introduce and host programs, read the news, interview people and report on issues and events.
- ( ) **Production managers** are responsible for all the organizational aspects of production scheduling and budgeting.
- ( ) **Puppeteers** bring inanimate objects to life in order to make them perform and interpret scripts with the same degree of integrity as **actors**.
- ( ) **Researchers** originate or develop program ideas, drawing on their knowledge and understanding of industry requirements, and present their findings to decision makers.
- ( ) **Stand up comedians** usually write, direct, and perform their own material.
- ( ) **Stunt performers** are employed to take **actors**' places when dangerous or specialised actions are specified in the script, or to perform roles requiring specific skills.
- ( ) **Transmission engineers** (or **operations managers**) supervise the transmission of all genres of television programs, working in the Master Control Room (MCR).
- ( ) **Vision mixers** edit programs live (as they are being transmitted or recorded), using a variety of transition methods, such as cuts, mixes, wipes, frame manipulation, etc.

Source: <http://www.creativeskillset.org/tv/jobs/>. Accessed on: May 23, 2014.

UNIT 16
You broadcast

Language in action
- Learn how to give instructions
- Talk about likes/dislikes and present reasons
- Learn how to use linking words

Personal broadcasting and **Personal mobile broadcasting** are terms for participatory journalism that focuses on television webcasting over the Internet and mobile Internet. The term is akin to "personal publishing" which is synonymous with blogging. However, personal broadcasting is not the same as "vlogging" (a portmanteau of "video web logging"), as vlogging does not stream live material.
Available at: <http://en.wikipedia.org/wiki/Personal_broadcasting>. Accessed on: November 22, 2013.

1. Julia Petit in Jan. 2012. Available at: <https://www.youtube.com/watch?v=5PNW7watnEs>. Accessed on: April 16, 2013.

2. Available at: <https://www.youtube.com/watch?v=aHthFwZ4eiU>. Accessed on: April 16, 2013.

3. Recipe on Web a Milanesa. Available at: <https://www.youtube.com/watch?v=fr vw7Fg5WF1>. Accessed on: April 16, 2013.

4. Justin Bieber. Available at: <https://www.youtube.com/watch?v=Zjp-Zd EKFVg>. Accessed on: April 16, 2013.

5. Available at: <https://www.youtube.com/watch?v=o7M1m6rPijLk>. Accessed on: April 16, 2013.

6. Movie review of The Avengers, by Hugo Dias. Available at: <http://youtube.com/watch?v=soAeWB OtEXs>. Accessed on: April 16, 2013.

> Lead-in

1. Look at the snapshots on the previous page. What types of video do they show? Match them to some of the categories below. Write the corresponding numbers.

   (   ) tutorials   (   ) performances

   (   ) trailers   (   ) complaints

   (   ) advertisements   (   ) reviews

   (   ) babies   (   ) recipes

2. Refer to the images on the previous page and to your own experience with the Internet. Which type(s) of video do you usually watch? Which ones do you *never* watch? Explain your choices to a classmate.

   _____

   _____

   _____

   _____

3. In pairs, discuss the questions below.

   a) Do you know any video-sharing websites? Do you use them?

   b) Why do you think people post videos on video-sharing websites?

4. Do you know what viral videos are? Make a list of the five most popular viral videos in Brazil.

   _____

   _____

   _____

   _____

   _____

5. Do you know any famous people whose careers are associated with personal broadcasting? Write their names and their professional activities.

   _____

   _____

   _____

   _____

6. Do you trust all the informative videos you watch online? How do you select the videos you watch? Discuss this question as a group.

> Let's read!

Before you read...
- Have you ever broadcast yourself singing on a video-sharing website?
- Do you know any famous people whose careers are associated with personal broadcasting?

1. Read the title of the text below and look at the images. What do you think the text is about?

_____

2. Now read the text to confirm your hypothesis.

Fame and Fortune: The Power of YouTube

3 jan. 2012/ 4 Comments / in Social Media, Social Networking, YouTube/ by admin

By Julie Lamb | @juliedlamb

1   What do Justin Bieber, Colbie Caillat, Soulja Boy, and Sean Kingston all have in common? Aside from being celebrities/singers, they all started out simply by posting amateur videos of
5   themselves on the Internet, and after developing a large following online, were fortunate enough to "get discovered" by important people in the music industry.

   It may be easy to discount these stories as pure
10 luck and claim that such successes don't justify all the time that many YouTubers spend making videos. But the truth is that the path from YouTube sensation to professional musician is becoming more and more common, and this trend does not
15 show signs of slowing down any time soon.

   As long as there are people willing to post their talent online, music executives now have an easy, free way to search for budding new stars without ever leaving their couches. More importantly, they
20 no longer have to be limited to their city, state, or even their country.

   Take the story of Arnel Pineda, who has been the lead singer of the band Journey since 2007. Prior to 2007, Pineda performed in various groups at
25 nightclubs in Hong Kong and the Philippines but finally got his big break when his friend posted

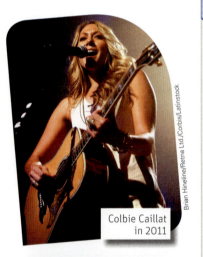

Colbie Caillat in 2011

Sean Kingston in 2011

Hint
Reading the **first sentence** of each paragraph in an article can help you grasp its main topics.

Julie Lamb is one of the contributors to Social Media Delivered, a company that offers social media training, consulting, and services for organizations.

videos of his performances on YouTube. At that time, Journey was looking for a new lead singer, and after holding
30 numerous unsatisfying auditions, they turned to YouTube as their last hope… and found exactly what they were looking for in Arnel Pineda.

You could still say that Pineda was
35 lucky, since in order to find the "diamonds in the rough" on YouTube, one must sift through a huge amount of bizarre, inappropriate, or clearly talentless videos. However, between the number of views, "likes," the comment section, and the ease of
40 finding videos that have gone viral by posts on Facebook and Twitter, YouTube is still a relatively easy and efficient way to discover the next big star, in music or otherwise. Plus, with its global popularity, YouTube puts the world at your fingertips, which increases the chances
45 that any talent-seeking executive will find someone who fits exactly what they are looking for. […]

Soulja Boy in 2010

Every YouTube sensation, from Justin Bieber to Arnel Pineda, understands that it is not
50 enough to simply post a video or two, find some success, and then expect it to last. In order to maintain and continue to grow your fan base in this fast-paced, social media-obsessed world, you have to be willing to
55 put in the time and effort to interact with your followers on Twitter and continually post new content on Facebook and YouTube. The minute you stop, your content appears old and you become a "has-been." Remember, there is
60 always going to be some budding new star or innovative business only one upload away from taking your place.

Available at: <http://www.socialmediadelivered.com/2012/01/03/fame-and-fortune-the-power-of-youtube-2/>. Accessed on: November 22, 2013.

Justin Bieber in 2012

3. How can fame and fortune be associated with personal broadcasting?

4. In your opinion, why is personal broadcasting becoming a more and more common marketing technique nowadays?

221

5. Read the text on the two previous pages again and do the activities below.

a) What is the central idea of the text?

_____

b) How did the singers mentioned in the text achieve a successful career?

_____

c) What are other important actions for achieving success online besides posting a video on YouTube, according to the text?

_____

_____

d) Find out more about the text "Fame and Fortune" by matching the columns below.

I. Who?	( )	Social networks
II. To whom?	( )	3 Jan 2012
III. When?	( )	By Julie Lamb / @juliedlamb
IV. Where from?	( )	Social Media Delivered website
V. Forwarded to?	( )	Famous-to-be artists

6. What does it mean to find "diamonds in the rough" on YouTube? Explain the expression in your own words. What strategy did you use to understand this expression?

_____

_____

7. Try to infer the meaning of each expression below according to the context.

A. budding new stars (line 18)	( ) a forgotten person
B. big break (line 26)	( ) rising talents
C. the world at your fingertips (line 43)	( ) moving quickly
D. fast-paced (line 53)	( ) great opportunity
E. a "has-been" (line 59)	( ) something which is easily reached

Vocabulary corner

On video-sharing sites there are some peculiar and specific words. Match the terms below to their correct description.

A. account	( ) the amount of screen space available for the video
B. profile	( ) the affiliation to a certain channel you enjoy
C. caption	( ) a personal area where you can group all your videos together
D. definition	( ) the quality of the image defined by the amount of pixels
E. screen size	( ) the formal relationship between the user and the video-sharing site
F. channel	( ) an outline of your personal characteristics
G. subscription	( ) the text of a speech, etc., superimposed on the film and projected onto the screen

Beyond the lines...

a) Does fame on the Internet always mean success? Explain.

b) Do you know any examples of a YouTube video which interfered negatively in one's career?

› Let's focus on language! (1)

The underlined words in the excerpts below are called "linking words." They help us organize what we say or write. Most of these linking words are often used in writing or more formal speech.

1. Read these excerpts and choose the options with the same meaning.

a) "<u>Aside from</u> being celebrities/singers, they all started out simply by posting amateur videos of themselves on the Internet (...)."

( ) moreover ( ) in addition to ( ) except for

b) "<u>However</u>, between the number of views, (...) and the ease of finding videos that have gone viral by posts on Facebook and Twitter, YouTube is still a relatively easy and efficient way to discover the next big star (...)."

( ) nevertheless ( ) for example ( ) in conclusion

c) "It may be easy to discount these stories as pure luck and claim that such successes don't justify all the time that many YouTubers spend making videos. <u>But</u> the truth is that the path from YouTube sensation to professional musician is becoming more and more common (...)."

( ) such as ( ) nevertheless ( ) in brief

All excerpts above available at: <http://www.squidrootbeer.com/>. Accessed on: May 26, 2014.

2. Read the excerpts and decide what ideas from the box the underlined words convey.

> adding   showing result   summing up   giving examples   making contrast

a) "<u>Although</u> the company says it plans to add 5 to 15 HD titles per month, their HD offerings will still lag severely behind the availability of film and TV on Blu-ray. <u>Also</u>, new HD rentals cost $6, <u>while</u> catalog rentals are $4. (...)"

Available at: <http://pcworld.about.net/od/dvdplayers/Now-Playing-High-Def-Movies.htm>. Accessed on: November 29, 2012.

---

b) "<u>Since</u> the introduction of the modern computer, obtaining information has been increasingly simple, especially with the help of the Internet, online encyclopedias and other various CD-ROMs. The computer can also accomplish smaller chores with ease. <u>For example</u>, the built-in calculator in Windows comes in handy when figuring calculations. <u>In brief</u>, computers are remarkably important in finishing trivial everyday tasks."

Available at: <http://www.customessaymeister.com/customessays/Entertainment/13766.htm>. Accessed on: November 23, 2013.

---

c) "The monthly charge for a new PC typically is less than the monthly fee to finance the cost of a new TV. <u>Moreover</u>, consumers who choose the monthly repayment option on the purchase of a television often must use the company's store credit card to do so. This is not typically the case with "free PCs." <u>Thus</u>, as the cost of the average entry-level personal computer continues to fall well below that of the average television set, American households should have fewer problems affording new computers."

Available at: <http://www.heritage.org/research/reports/2000/04/how-free-computers-are-filling-the-digital-divide>. Accessed on: November 23, 2013.

223

3. Read the following excerpts taken from the text "Fame and Fortune: The Power of YouTube" and answer the questions.

"Aside from being celebrities/singers, they all started out **simply** by posting amateur videos of themselves on the Internet (…)"

"(…) they turned to YouTube as their last hope… and found **exactly** what they were looking for in Arnel Pineda."

"(…) one must sift through a huge amount of bizarre, inappropriate, or **clearly** talentless videos."

"(…) YouTube is still a **relatively** easy and efficient way to discover the next big star, in music or otherwise."

"(…) you have to be willing to put in the time and effort to interact with your followers on Twitter and **continually** post new content on Facebook and YouTube."

a) Which word or words in bold describe how you do something?

_____

b) Which word or words modify another word/phrase?

_____

> The words in bold are called "adverbs of manner." These adverbs can modify another word (adjectives and other adverbs) or describe an action (verb).

4. Complete the excerpt below with the adverbs *carefully, extremely, historically, relatively, relentlessly, seriously,* and *suddenly*.

For Teenage Girls, Facebook Means Always Being Camera-Ready

By Randye Hoder

It used to be that the only people _____ concerned about getting caught in grungy sweat pants, sans makeup, were starlets stalked by the paparazzi. But in today's hyper-public Internet age, young teenagers are _____ living their lives camera-ready – and it's not a pretty picture. I first noticed this while looking over my 14-year-old son's shoulder at photos of his "friends" on Facebook. Girls, in particular, seemed to be always posing for the camera: hair swept back, hand on hip, dressed just so. Creating a persona via Facebook is nothing new. Kids have been doing this since the site was first launched eight years ago. By _____ selecting their own profile pictures, younger teenagers have become quite adept at managing their image. But what is _____ new is that the glare of the camera is never far away. And that is _____ affecting how adolescent girls conduct themselves in their actual, everyday lives. Girls this age, who have felt pressured _____ to look their best most of the time, _____ seem to feel as if they need to look their best all of the time.

Adapted from: <http://parenting.blogs.nytimes.com/2012/03/07/for-teenage-girls-facebook-means-always-being-camera-ready/>. Accessed on: November 24, 2013.

> Let's listen and talk!

1. 🔴45 Listen to instructions on how to make a sandwich. Check (✔) the ingredients you hear.

( ) tuna   ( ) mustard   ( ) bread   ( ) tomato

( ) lettuce   ( ) mayonnaise   ( ) butter

2. Match the actions in the box to the pictures below. One has been done for you.

| ~~put~~   complete   mash   spread (2x)   slice   mix |

3. 🔴45 Now listen to the recording again and put the instructions in sequence.

_____ ( )   _____ ( )   _____ ( )   _____ ( )

_____ ( )   put ( )   _____ ( )

Available at: <http://www.youtube.com/watch?v=XmFsa7mquZY&feature=endscreen&NR=1>. Accessed on: November 24, 2013.

225

4. This oral text is
   ( ) a review,   ( ) a recipe,
   probably broadcast as
   ( ) a video.   ( ) a podcast.

5. What time expressions are used to show the sequence of actions in the instructions?
   _____
   _____

6. 🔊45 The audio was recorded by a Malaysian girl. Listen to it again and notice her foreign accent.

7. Work alone. List five things you have watched on YouTube that you *like, love, couldn't care less about, hate*.
   _____
   _____

8. Now think about reasons for each choice in activity 7. Draft your ideas using language from the *Useful language* box. Then talk to a classmate using your draft notes as a guide.

Pronunciation spot – The schwa vowel / ə /

The schwa vowel / ə / is a very short, quick sound.
🔊46 Listen and repeat. Notice how the syllable with the schwa vowel / ə / receives less stress than the other syllables in the words.

am<u>a</u>teur   in<u>a</u>ppropriate   <u>a</u>side   col<u>u</u>mn   <u>a</u>mount
p<u>e</u>rform<u>a</u>nce   op<u>e</u>n   typic<u>a</u>l   less<u>o</u>n

Useful language

I hated watching... since...
I couldn't care less about... because...
I love... as...
I like... because...

❯ Let's focus on language! (2)

1. Read the following excerpt from the listening passage on the previous page.

   "**First**, mash the tuna. **Then**, put in the mayonnaise and mix evenly. **Next**, spread butter on the bread and slice off the edges. **Lastly**, spread the tuna on the bread."

   The words in bold are used to
   ( ) introduce an opinion.
   ( ) indicate the sequence of events.
   ( ) make a pause to think.

   > We use the following words to show the order of instructions:
   > First   Then   After that
   > Next   Lastly   Finally

2. The sentences below are used in the instructions for creating a "mangatar." Match the first column to the second to make complete sentences. One is done for you.

   A. Log in   ( ) the gender of your manga.
   B. Choose   ( ) to select skin tone.
   C. Click   ( ) facial expressions by clicking the smileys.
   D. Change   ( ) at your account.
   E. Navigate   ( ) changes to your manga and give it a nickname.
   F. Click   ( ) through the tabs to choose different features.
   G. Save   (C) "Create" to continue.

3. Use the sentences from the previous activity to write the sequence of instructions to create a manga. Follow the numbers in the boxes and use the sequence words from activity 1.

First, log in at your account. Then, _____

_____

_____

Available at: <http://faceyourmanga.com/>. Accessed on: November 24, 2013.

Let's act with words!

A weather script

In this activity you are going to have the opportunity to deal with topics you saw in Unit 15 (weather forecast) and 16 (personal broadcasting). Do your best and, who knows, an important executive recognizes your talent online.

Writing Steps

Organizing
- Choose a weather forecast website on the Internet.
- Decide on a specific area for your forecast. You can pick a town or village in your area or even create a forecast specific to your school.
- Consider all the data you have carefully, one piece at a time. Which pieces of data are most important that day to tell the weather story?

Preparing the first draft
- Make a first draft of your weather script.
- Decide if you are going to use a formal or an informal tone. Take into consideration the target public you have in mind.

Peer editing
- Ask a classmate to revise your first draft.
- Make the necessary corrections.

Publishing
- Record a video or a podcast and publish it on Wikispaces. You can post your video on video-sharing websites as well.
- Remember to keep the script in your portfolio.

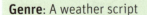

Genre:	A weather script
Purpose:	To build a weather forecast
Tone:	Formal or informal
Setting:	Wikispaces/Video-sharing websites
Writer:	You
Audience:	Portfolio, wiki readers or video-sharing site viewers

Images: Shutterstock.com/ID/BR

Go to Workbook, page 373, for more practice

Learning tips

How to learn with TV and videos

Did you know...?

Programme is British English and *program* is American English.

HD TV

Television is great for learning English. The pictures make it easier to understand than radio and because you can see who's talking, you get a better idea of what people mean. Just watch their "body language!"

Watch programs that you find enjoyable and entertaining – whatever you watch will help you to improve your English.

Here's a guide to learning as much as possible while watching English television:

Only watch programs you find interesting. Learning English should be fun – not something you have to force yourself to do. If you have a passion for football, watch matches or the sports news.

Keep a notebook near your television, so that you can jot down any new words or expressions that you hear. This is especially useful if the program you are watching has been subtitled into your language.

Try to watch English television regularly. Even if you can only watch 15 minutes a day, you'll be amazed how much you learn.

Don't worry if you don't understand everything. English television is normally aimed at native English language speakers. Programs often include difficult words and expressions. If the program you're watching is full of unknown words, just concentrate on understanding the general meaning.

Even cartoons and children's programs are useful when learning English, and quiz shows are useful for learning how to ask and answer questions in English.

Keep a note of television programs and presenters that you find easy to understand and try to watch them regularly. Doing this will increase your confidence and give you a sense of achievement.

Available at: <http://www.english-at-home.com/business/learn-english-with-television/>. Accessed on: November 24, 2013.

Let's reflect on learning!

You are now invited to assess what you learned and how you learned. Finish the ideas below on an extra sheet of paper and become a more autonomous and reflective learner.

In Part 8

I learned _____

I liked _____

I need to review/learn more _____

My experiences with English outside school were _____

_____

Let's study for Enem!

Enem Questions

Gênero
Tira

Competência de área 2
H7 - Relacionar um texto em LEM, as estruturas linguísticas, sua função e seu uso social.

Procure sempre identificar o gênero textual usado na questão e suas características. Pense, por exemplo, em que parte do texto cada tipo de informação é apresentada. Verifique onde o efeito de sentido explorado no enunciado da questão apareceria em uma tira.

Disponível em: <www.gocomics.com>.
Acesso em: 26 fev. 2012.

Não se deixe intimidar com palavras novas e desconhecidas. As imagens, as palavras cognatas e o uso de prefixos ou sufixos podem nos ajudar em boa parte dos casos. Note como o segundo quadro da tira do Calvin traz vários exemplos de palavras formadas com sufixo e prefixo. Se você já sabe o significado deles poderá inferir o significado das palavras das quais eles estão fazendo parte.

A partir da leitura dessa tira, infere-se que o discurso de Calvin teve um efeito diferente do pretendido, uma vez que ele

A decide tirar a neve do quintal para convencer seu pai sobre seu discurso.
B culpa o pai por exercer influência negativa na formação de sua personalidade.
C comenta que suas discussões com o pai não correspondem às suas expectativas.
D conclui que os acontecimentos ruins não fazem falta para a sociedade.
E reclama que é vítima de valores que o levam a atitudes inadequadas.

Extraído de: Exame Nacional do Ensino Médio, 2013, Caderno 6 – CINZA – Página 4 (questão 94).

Part 8 (Video)

Typical questions of Encm

1. Nesta charge, que critica os hábitos televisivos, a fala do menino tem por função, de forma indireta e irônica,

    a) ( ) convidar a mãe a ler histórias.
    b) ( ) criticar o que seu amigo vê na TV.
    c) ( ) impedir a mãe de comprar pela TV.
    d) ( ) pedir à mãe para assistir a um filme.
    e) ( ) persuadir a mãe a mudar de canal.

    Available at: <http://www.cartoonstock.com/directory/o/obsessive_behaviour.asp>. Accessed on: November 20, 2013.

'Mummy...one of my friends says you can watch films and cartoons and stories on TV as well.'

Storms target Northeast and Northwest
M. Ressler, Lead Meteorologist, The Weather Channel
Mar. 27, 2012 11:08 am ET

Northeast
As a storm slides eastward along the Canadian border midweek, showers will dampen western New York, a shot of wintry mix and snow will change to rain from northeast New York to New Hampshire and snow will develop over much of Maine. (...)

Available at: <http://www.weather.com/newscenter/nationalforecast/index.html>. Accessed on: March 27, 2012.

---

2. O texto registra previsões meteorológicas para a cidade de Nova York em março de 2012. Assim, tomamos conhecimento que, em 27 de março de 2012,

    a) ( ) a chuva estava se encaminhando para a fronteira do Canadá.
    b) ( ) a neve atingiu alvos do nordeste ao sudeste de dois países.
    c) ( ) a tempestade de neve cobriria todo o estado de Nova York.
    d) ( ) estava nevando em Nova York e choveria em seguida.
    e) ( ) haveria muita chuva ao longo do Canadá no meio da semana.

Fame and Fortune: The Power of YouTube
by Julie Lamb (3 jan. 2012)

What do Justin Bieber, Colbie Caillat, Soulja Boy, and Sean Kingston all have in common? Aside from being celebrities/singers, they all started out simply by posting amateur videos of themselves on the Internet, and after developing a large following online, were fortunate enough to "get discovered" by important people in the music industry.

It may be easy to discount these stories as pure luck and claim that such successes don't justify all the time that many YouTubers spend making videos. But the truth is that the path from YouTube sensation to professional musician is becoming more and more common, and this trend does not show signs of slowing down any time soon. (...)

Available at: <http://www.socialmediadelivered.com/2012/01/03/fame-and-fortune-the-power-of-youtube-2/>. Accessed on: November 22, 2013.

---

3. Este texto fala do poder das tecnologias em nossa sociedade e nos informa que os cantores Justin Bieber, Colbie Caillat, Soulja Boy e Sean Kingston

    a) ( ) postaram seus vídeos no YouTube antes de fazerem sucesso.
    b) ( ) fazem sucesso porque alimentam o YouTube com seus vídeos.
    c) ( ) foram descobertos no YouTube porque são bons profissionais.
    d) ( ) são músicos profissionais que anunciam seus *shows* no YouTube.
    e) ( ) descobriram a indústria da música nos vídeos do YouTube.

231

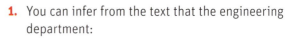

Exam Practice Questions (Vestibular)

Test-Taking Tips

Answer the question yourself first!

As you have noticed, in most of the cases, tests are composed of multiple-choice questions. To do well with this type of question, you can use a strategy that might be helpful. Try to answer the question yourself without reading the options provided. (You can cover them with your hand!) Remember that there is only one correct choice and that the others are "distractors." Pay attention and check if the choices go beyond the text. If they do, they are not the correct answer. Keep in mind that just the fact that an option contains words from the text doesn't make it the correct one. Sometimes the right answer is the one that has synonyms or other words that convey the idea in the text. Be alert!

- **TEXT 1 – Questions 1 and 2**
  ESPM-SP, 2011

1. You can infer from the text that the engineering department:
   a) ( ) ignored the video as soon as it arrived for appreciation.
   b) ( ) spent three months preparing the video.
   c) ( ) considered the video funny.
   d) ( ) said the video had to be technically improved.
   e) ( ) said the video was technically inaccurate.

2. The e-mail she got back from Wally most likely read:
   a) ( ) "The script had been great."
   b) ( ) "I think the script is humorless."
   c) ( ) "It was funny."
   d) ( ) "I thought the script would be great."
   e) ( ) "It is great."

- **TEXT 2 – Questions 3 to 5**
  Fuvest-SP, 2013

Time was, advertising was a relatively simple undertaking: buy some print space and airtime, create the spots, and blast them at a captive audience. Today it's chaos: while passive viewers still exist, mostly we pick and choose what to consume, ignoring ads with a touch of the DVR remote. Ads are forced to become more like content, and the best aim to engage consumers so much that they pass the material on to friends – by email, Twitter, Facebook – who will pass it on to friends, who will… you get the picture. In the industry, "viral" has become a usefully vague way to describe any campaign that spreads from person to person, acquiring its own momentum.

It's not that online advertising has eclipsed TV, but it has become its full partner – and in many ways the more substantive one, a medium in which the audience must be earned, not simply bought.

Newsweek, March 26 & April 2, 2012. Adaptado.

3. De acordo com o texto, a indústria publicitária
   a) ( ) passou a criar anúncios mais curtos.
   b) ( ) deixou de comprar tempo na TV devido ao aumento de custo por minuto.
   c) ( ) foi forçada a se modificar em função das novas tecnologias.
   d) ( ) aumentou sua audiência cativa.
   e) ( ) começou a privilegiar a forma em vez de conteúdos.

4. No texto, a palavra "viral" refere-se a
   a) ( ) campanhas publicitárias divulgadas entre usuários de mídias eletrônicas.

Part 8 (Video)

b) ( ) vírus eletrônicos acoplados a anúncios publicitários.

c) ( ) mensagens de alerta aos consumidores para os riscos de determinados produtos.

d) ( ) mídias eletrônicas que têm dificuldade em controlar a disseminação de vírus.

e) ( ) quantidades de anúncios que congestionam as caixas postais dos usuários de correio eletrônico.

5. Afirma-se, no texto, que, diferentemente da TV, na publicidade *online* a audiência tem de ser

a) ( ) partilhada. d) ( ) multiplicada.

b) ( ) valorizada. e) ( ) conquistada.

c) ( ) comprada.

- **TEXT 3 – Questions 6 to 8**

ITA-SP, 2011

TV Will Save the World

In a lot of places, it's the next big thing

By Charles Kenny

FORGET TWITTER AND FACEBOOK, Google and the Kindle. Forget the latest sleek iGadget. Television is still the most influential medium around. Indeed, for many of the poorest regions of the world, it remains the next big thing – poised, finally, to attain truly global ubiquity. And that is a good thing, because the TV revolution is changing lives for the better.

Across the developing world, around 45% of households had a TV in 1995; by 2005 the number had climbed above 60%. That's some way behind the U.S., where there are more TVs than people, but it dwarfs worldwide Internet access. Five million more households in sub-Saharan Africa will get a TV over the next five years. In 2005, after the fall of the Taliban, which had outlawed TV, 1 in 5 Afghans had one. The global total is another 150 million by 2013 – pushing the numbers to well beyond two-thirds of households.

Television's most transformative impact will be on the lives of women. In India, researchers Robert Jensen and Emily Oster found that when cable TV reached villages, women were more likely to go to the market without their husbands' permission and less likely to want a boy rather than a girl. They were more likely to make decisions over child health and less likely to think that men had the right to beat their wives. TV is also a powerful medium for adult education. In the Indian state of Gujarat, *Chitrageet* is a hugely popular show that plays Bollywood song and dance clips. The routines are subtitled in Gujarati. Within six months, viewers had made a small but significant improvement in their reading skills.

Too much TV has been associated with violence, obesity and social isolation. But TV is having a positive impact on the lives of billions worldwide, and as the spread of mobile TV, video cameras and YouTube democratize both access and content, it will become an even greater force for humbling tyrannical governments and tyrannical husbands alike. ■

Kenny, a development economist, is the author of a forthcoming book on innovation, ideas and the global standard of living
Time, March 22, 2010.

6. De acordo com o texto, o argumento que melhor justifica o título *TV Will Save the World* é:

a) ( ) a TV se tornará um meio ainda mais importante para enfraquecer governos e maridos tirânicos.

b) ( ) a TV possibilitará melhoras na educação dos adultos, principalmente no desenvolvimento das habilidades de leitura.

c) ( ) a TV continuará exercendo um impacto positivo nos países em desenvolvimento.

d) ( ) a TV propiciará a diminuição da obesidade, da violência e do isolamento social.

e) ( ) a TV trará melhoras para a vida de mulheres afegãs.

7. Sobre a presença da TV no mundo, o texto informa que,

a) ( ) em países em desenvolvimento, haverá mais aparelhos de TV do que pessoas até 2013.

b) ( ) até 2013, mais de 2/3 das famílias, em todo o mundo, terão aparelhos de TV.

c) ( ) depois da queda do Talibã, a TV foi declarada ilegal e poucos afegãos possuem um aparelho.

d) ( ) em 2005, nos países em desenvolvimento, o número de televisores diminuiu drasticamente.

e) ( ) nos países que possuem o maior número de televisores, o acesso à Internet também é proporcionalmente maior.

8. Segundo o texto, um dos impactos que a TV a cabo trouxe para a vida das mulheres indianas foi que elas

a) ( ) passaram a gostar de ir ao mercado sem a permissão de seus maridos.

b) ( ) ficaram menos propensas a preferir ter um filho a uma filha.

c) ( ) se mostraram mais dispostas a fazer compras sozinhas.

d) ( ) ainda acham que os maridos têm o direito de agredir suas esposas, apesar de já criticarem esta prática.

e) ( ) não gostam mais de tomar decisões sobre os cuidados com a saúde das crianças.

233

PART

9 Life on Earth

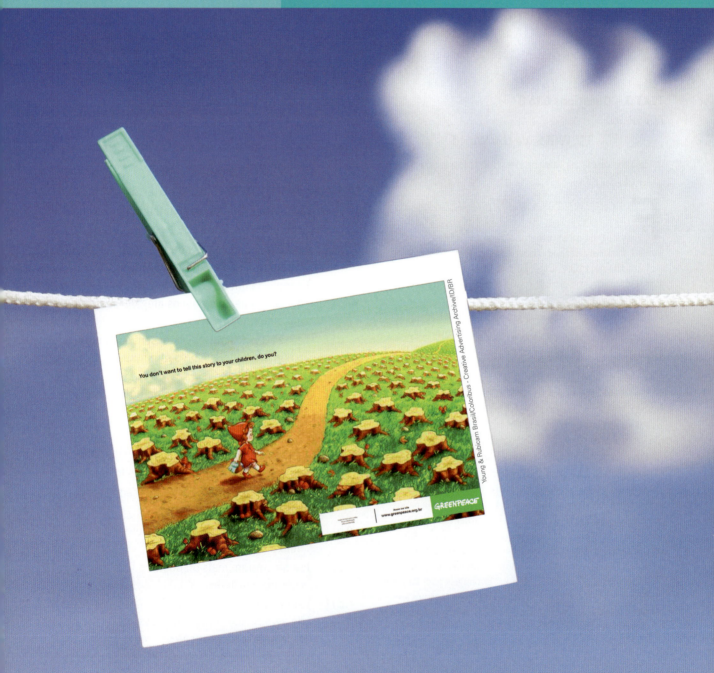

Learning plan

Understanding the characteristics of a painting description

Learning how to make comparisons

Talking about advantages and disadvantages of life in the city and in the countryside

Learning how to ask questions and check information

Reading campaigns and comic strips critically

Understanding and producing slogans and campaigns

Learning how to indicate the location of people and things

Year Project – MY WALL

What is Padlet?
It is a free online tool to build a virtual wall panel.

Build a wall for your English production this year
You can post texts, pictures, YouTube videos, web page links, and documents (PDF, PowerPoints, etc.) inside "post-it notes."

Your visitors can also post comments, but they are limited to 160 characters. You can edit your posts and delete posts and comments. You can move the posts with the help of the mouse.

Follow the steps below to start using this web facility throughout the year.

Steps
1. **Go** to Padlet website at <http://padlet.com/> (accessed on: May 25, 2014).
2. **Click** on the "Build a Wall" button.
3. **Choose** a wallpaper for your wall.
4. **Start** creating your wall by posting some information about you. Then post your productions along the year. To delete a post-it, click on the "X" in the top right hand corner.
5. **Add** comments to your classmates' walls and read their comments on yours.

235

UNIT 17 Life in the countryside

Language in action

- Understand the characteristics of painting descriptions
- Make comparisons and use the superlative
- Talk about advantages and disadvantages

Poppies, near Argenteuil, by Claude Monet, 1873. Oil on canvas, 50 cm × 65 cm. Musée d'Orsay, Paris.

1. Monet, *Poppies; near Argenteuil*

In the countryside, a vivid splash of poppies seems to move in a gentle breeze. Monet has made the red poppies and the green field effectively equiluminant. The position of the poppies seems uncertain. To many viewers, they appear to quiver.

If you remove the color, most of the poppies cannot be seen in the field. The poppies and field are equiluminant. As has been noted, the Impressionists painted not a landscape but the impression of a landscape. Nothing here is painted exactly; rather, everything is suggested. Monet unforgettably evokes a mood by choosing these shades of green and red. If he painted flowers of another color, the hillside would be stagnant.

Available at: <http://www.webexhibits.org/colorart/monet2.html>. Accessed on: December 5, 2013.

2. Degas, *Race Horses at Longchamp*

Edgar Degas said regarding his painting: "In painting you must give the idea of the true by means of the false."

Available at: <http://www.1artclub.com/racehorses-in-a-landscape-by-edgar-degas/>. Accessed on: December 5, 2013.

Race Horses at Longchamp, by Edgar Degas, 1871. Oil on canvas, 34 cm × 41.9 cm. Museum of Fine Arts, Boston, USA.

3. Renoir, *Red boat, Argenteuil*

Renoir landscape beautifully illustrates the rise of landscape painting as the dominant genre of the avant-garde – one of the great dramas of 19th-century painting. Throughout art history, landscape paintings were considered less ambitious than history paintings or portraits. Between 1850 and 1900, however, artists like Renoir introduced exciting innovations in the art of landscape. Landscape paintings were increasingly in demand by middle-class patrons wishing to decorate their urban apartments with paintings of the countryside.

Available at: <http://www.allartclassic.com/pictures_zoom.php?p_number=113&p=&number=REP074>. Accessed on: December 5, 2013.

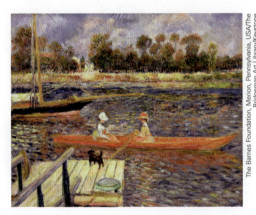

Red boat, Argenteuil, by Pierre-Auguste Renoir, 1888. Oil on canvas. The Barnes Foundation, Merlon, USA.

> **Lead-in**

1. What is the relationship between the paintings on the left page and the title of the unit?
   _____

2. Had you already heard about Monet, Degas, and Renoir? _____

3. Look at the three paintings and read the statement below. Do you agree with this conclusion? Explain.
   "IF MONET IS REGARDED AS THE IMPRESSIONIST par excellence, one must admit that both Degas and Renoir also have their own special qualities."
   Available at: <http://www.artchive.com/artchive/M/monet.html>. Accessed on: December 5, 2013.
   _____

4. Which text presents a description? _____

5. Check (✔) the characteristics of a descriptive text for a painted picture.
   ( ) It appeals to the reader's senses.   ( ) It presents arguments for and against something.
   ( ) It presents differing points of view.   ( ) It includes information about style.
   ( ) It uses adjectives (color, size, etc.).   ( ) It points out details of the object being described.
   ( ) It uses third person pronoun forms (he, she, it).   ( ) It includes specific instructions.
   ( ) It quotes famous people's opinions.   ( ) It describes the characteristics of something.

6. Look at Degas' painting. Has he managed to "give the idea of the true by means of the false?"
   _____
   _____

7. Look at a black and white version of *Poppies; near Argenteuil*. Then read the two hypotheses from text 1 again and answer the question.

   I. "If you remove the color, most of the poppies cannot be seen in the field."
   II. "If he painted flowers of another color, the hillside would be stagnant."

   Which of the two conditions above proved to be real in the edited image on the right side? _____

> **Beyond the lines...**

a) According to the statement in activity 3, which of the three painters is considered the "number one?" Who do you think determines this "hierarchy of quality:" ordinary people or art critics?

b) Based on text 3, would the demand for landscape have risen if the middle class were not willing to decorate their houses in the second half of the 19th century?

> Let's read!

Before you read...

- Do you prefer life in the city or in the countryside? Think about the pros and cons of living in each place. Use a table like this to organize your ideas in your notebook.

CITY		COUNTRYSIDE	
Pros	Cons	Pros	Cons

1. Read this text and compare your perceptions to the author's. Are they similar? Are they very different?

Hint
Paratextual elements such as the title, the images used, the author's background, the institution responsible for the publishing, among others, help us predict what an article is about.

---

http://www.topics-mag.com/edition21/life/city-country.htm

Why Should People Put Up with Life in the City?

Sylvia Wang from Hong Kong

Can you imagine exchanging the glamour of city life for a quiet life in the countryside?

Many people want to move from the country to the city because they think that life in the city is more exciting and better than in rural areas, especially younger people who like new, modern things.

Often people like to be fashionable and feel they can find the latest styles only in the city.

Other people are interested in technological things and high tech jobs and think they can find them only in a big city. If they want to find a job, especially a good position in a company, they feel they have to live in a city. To enjoy these jobs, they are willing to put up with many of the disadvantages of city life such as crime, high traffic, and pollution.

However, it is now possible to enjoy a higher quality of life in the countryside and still enjoy some of the advantages of living in the city.

Nowadays, travel is fast and information is available on the Internet, so many people are able to do their work in home offices.

Because they have e-mail and personal computers, they don't have to be in big cities to conduct their business. It is not important where they *actually* work because the results of their work can be sent everywhere with technology. So, why should they put up with all the disadvantages of the city any longer? Now they can escape *hectic* city life to enjoy life in the countryside and still be able to do good business and have successful careers.

Available at: <http://www.topics-mag.com/edition21/life/city-country.htm>. Accessed on: December 5, 2013.

Topics-mag.com is an online magazine for learners of English. It offers learners the opportunity to express and publish their ideas in English to an online audience. This is what happened to Sylvia Wang. She had her text published in Issue 21 (Reflecting on Life).

2. The phrasal verb **put up with**, in the title of the text, could be replaced by

   ( ) install
   ( ) move
   ( ) tolerate
   ( ) place
   ( ) endure

Rural scene in Ouro Fino, Minas Gerais, 2009.

3. According to Sylvia Wang, what are some of the reasons why people decide to live in cities?

   _____
   _____
   _____

4. What are some of the negative aspects of living in the city, based on the text?

   _____
   _____

Traffic jam in Kathmandu, Nepal, 2012.

5. These sentences are captions of the pictures that illustrate the text on the previous page. Match each caption to its corresponding image. Write the Roman numeral next to it.

   > I. It is now possible to enjoy a higher quality of life in the countryside and still enjoy some of the advantages of living in the city.
   >
   > II. Many people think that life in the city is more exciting than in rural areas.

6. Which argument is used by the author to convince us that it is now possible to have the advantages of both the city and rural life?

   _____
   _____

7. What is the author's final conclusion about living in cities and in the countryside?

   _____
   _____

Beyond the lines...

a) The author is from Hong Kong. Do you think country life and city life in China are the same as here in Brazil?

b) Do you notice any stereotypes in the way you and your friends refer to people who live in the city or people who live in the countryside?

8. After thinking about the topic and reading the author's point of view, decide which of the sentences below best describes your opinion. Share your ideas with a classmate.

   a) I live in the city and I **want/don't want** to move to the country.
   b) I live in the country and I **want/don't want** to move to the city.
   c) I haven't made up my mind yet.

> **Let's listen and talk!**

Before you listen...
- What do you know about organic farming?
- Take a quick look at the text below. What kind of problem does it address?

Could Organic Farming Solve the World's Food Problems?

The world's food problem is not that there isn't _____ food. It's the fact that, the problem lies within the distribution of food. And, where there are food problems, (*1) arguably, you could (*2) say there are food problems in this country with obesity, (*3) but generally, the problems where there isn't enough food tends to be in _____ countries, _____ countries. (*4) It is much more sustainable to have farmers using (*5) nature (*6) as a way of building their fertility and controlling their pests, (*7) than getting them _____ on expensive pesticides and other chemicals. And what happened in India, during the _____ revolution, was that (*8) chemical companies (*9) marketed their products at these poor, poverty stricken farmers, (*10) promising them increased yield. But, actually, what happened was, they then got locked into this cycle of dependence on chemicals, and they couldn't afford to buy them, and then they couldn't afford to feed their families, and send their children to school. (*11) It is a much more _____ way of farming to use _____ methods. And, certainly, what's happening in Ethiopia, (*12), the poster boy of poverty and famine, is that the agriculture minister is encouraging farmers to use _____ methods because they see that as the most _____, surefire way to feed their population.

Available at: <http://www.videojug.com/interview/organic-farming>. Accessed on: May 28, 2014.

1. 🔴47 You are going to listen to Melissa Kidd, Soil Association Information Officer, giving advice on an important current issue: organic farming. Listen to the recording and do the activities.

    a) Fill in the missing adjectives.

b) 🔴47 In this recording, there are some typical features of spoken language. We have numbered in the transcription on the previous page some of the moments where they can be identified. Listen again and number the cases and expressions below accordingly.

Repetition of words: _____

"I mean": _____

"and so on": _____

"so": _____

"you know": _____

"uhm": _____

Hesitation: _____

2. In pairs, come up with some ideas on organic products you could grow. Brainstorm the type of garden (greens? herbs? medicinal? etc.). Exchange ideas on where you would grow your products. Make a short oral presentation to your classmates.

Useful language

Growing... could be a good idea because...

I think we could grow... in our... (backyard, clay pots, recycled containers...)

The type of garden I would choose is...

A good idea is to grow...

One possibility is to grow...

We decided to choose this type of garden because...

Pronunciation spot – Syllables

1. 🔴48 Listen to the recording and write down the number of syllables in the following words.

quiet ___	young ___	sustainable ___	poor ___	green ___
important ___	natural ___	high ___	organic ___	enough ___
long ___	dependent ___	late ___		

2. In English, we find out the number of syllables in a word by counting

( ) the number of orthographic vowels in the word.

( ) the number of phonetic vowels or vowel clusters in the word.

241

> Let's focus on language!

1. Read these excerpts from the text "Why Should People Put Up with Life in the City?" and answer the questions.

"Many people want to move […] to the city because they think that life in the city is **more exciting** and **better than** in rural areas, especially **younger** people who like new, modern things."

"However, it is now possible to enjoy a **higher** quality of life in the countryside […]."

a) Does the author mean that life in the city is the same as life in rural areas?

_____

b) Is the quality of life in the countryside the same as before?

_____

c) Which structures are used to state that they are different?

_____

> We use **comparatives** (superiority and inferiority) when we want to say how a person or thing is different from another.

Did you know...?

Good and **bad** have irregular comparative and superlative forms: for *good* the forms are **better** and **best** while for *bad* the forms are **worse** and **worst**, respectively.

d) Complete these rules by writing **longer**, **than**, or **one-syllable** in the appropriate spaces.

How to make comparatives

With _____ adjectives, add **-er**.

With adjectives ending in **-y**, replace **-y** with **-ier**.

With _____ adjectives, use **more/less** before them.

Use _____ when the two people or things compared are explicit.

2. Read another excerpt from the text "Why Should People Put Up with Life in the City?" and answer the questions.

"Often people like to be fashionable and feel they can find the latest styles only in the city."

a) Does the author compare one style to another?

_____

b) To what does she compare the style?

_____

> We use **superlatives** when we want to compare a person or thing with the entire group they are in.

c) Complete these rules by writing **longer**, **the**, or **one-syllable** in the appropriate spaces.

How to make superlatives

With _____ adjectives, add **-est**.

With adjectives ending in **-y**, replace **-y** with **-iest**.

With _____ adjectives, use **the most/the least** before them.

Start a superlative with _____.

9 ▪ Life on Earth

3. Look at some facts about our world. Complete the sentences with a superlative form of the adjectives in the box. Then circle the correct option to complete the statements.

| deep | high | large | low | old |
| populous | small | large | spoken | tall |

a) _____ language in the world is **English/Spanish/Chinese Mandarin**, with over one billion speakers.

b) The continent with _____ number of countries is **Europe/Africa/North America**, with 54 countries.

c) **Mongolia and Namibia/Malta and Monaco** are the two countries with _____ _____ density. There are only two people per square kilometer.

d) _____ country in the world is **China/Canada/Russia**, with 17,075,400 square kilometers.

e) **The Pacific/Indian/Arctic** Ocean is _____ one in the world, with 14,056,000 square kilometers.

f) _____ ocean in the world is the **Pacific/Atlantic/Indian** Ocean.

g) **France/San Marino/Bulgaria** is _____ country in the world.

h) **Kangchenjunga/Mount Everest/K2** is _____ mountain, with 8,850 meters.

Mount Everest   Mount K2   Mount Kangchenjunga

i) South America is the fifth _____ continent, after Asia, Africa, Europe, and **Australia/North America**.

Adapted from: <http://www.worldatlas.com/geoquiz/thelist.htm>. Accessed on: December 5, 2013.

243

4. Below is a text contrasting the cost of living in different cities. Complete the spaces with a comparative or a superlative form of the words in parentheses, according to the context.

London Cheaper to Live Than Rio, Beijing and South Korea

A new survey has revealed that the cost of living in London is _____ (cheap) a number of other places in the world – 24 to be exact.

The study carried out by consultancy group, Mercer, places London as the 25th _____ _____ (expensive) city, behind countries such as Hong Kong, Chad, Brazil and Russia.

But which city was crowned with the dubious honour of being _____ (pricy) place?

According to this study, the Japanese city of Tokyo is _____ (expensive) place to live, with Luanda in Angola coming a surprising second. Another Japanese location was third (Osaka), whilst Moscow in Russia was named fourth.

In the study of 214 cities across the world, London was deemed to be the 25th _____ _____ (expensive) place to live, down seven places in the last 12 months from 18th. However, despite it now being a _____ (cheap) place to live according to the survey, it still ranks _____ (high) many other European cities, including Paris and Rome.

Belfast was _____ (cheap) UK city, coming in at 165th place, _____ (high) by 13 places than in the same poll last year. Birmingham also moved up, jumping by 17 places into 133rd position.

_____ (cheap) location identified was Karachi in Pakistan, with the cost of living just a third of what those in Tokyo have to pay.

The drop in the position of London is partially due to how the results were worked out. The cost of living was calculated from a US perspective and the conversion rate of dollars played a part. The relatively weak pound compared to the dollar pushed the cost of living _____ (low) for London. The position of African cities was bumped up, primarily as a result of the cost of expatriate secure accommodation.

Available at: <https://www.diigo.com/item/image/cj3t/9jut?size=o>. Accessed on: May 28, 2014.

5. Include your city in the contrast established in activity 4. In pairs, write sentences contrasting the cost of living in your city with the cities mentioned in the text and others from your region.

_____

_____

_____

6. Do you live in a city or in the countryside? Write sentences contrasting life where you live to other places in your region.

_____

_____

_____

Profession spot

› Agronomist

1. Look at these pictures. What are these professionals doing? What do you know about this career?

2. 🔴49 Listen to the recording. What are the speakers talking about?

   _____

3. 🔴49 Listen again. Notice that the text is organized into four parts, as shown in this chart.

A. Definition of agronomy	( ) crop consultant
	( ) study of the environment
	( ) plant science and biotechnology
	( ) study of plants
B. What agronomists focus on	( ) protecting the quality of the environment
	( ) consulting and production
	( ) rangeland manager
C. What careers agronomists work in	( ) sales rep for seed
	( ) study of soils
	( ) soil and environmental science
D. Where agronomists are found	( ) conserving vital soil and water resources
	( ) sustaining the world's food production

4. 🔴49 Now listen one more time and match the information on the right to the corresponding parts on the left in the chart above.

5. What else could you understand from the passage in terms of

   a) possible careers for agronomists? _____

   _____

   b) areas where agronomists are found? _____

   _____

   c) what agronomists do? _____

   _____

6. Talk about these questions with a classmate.

   a) What is the importance of agronomy to the world's sustainability?
   b) Do you know anyone involved in this profession? Would you follow this career?

245

UNIT 18 Going green!

Language in action

- Understand slogans and campaigns
- Learn how to read campaigns and comic strips critically
- Ask questions and check information
- Indicate the location of people and things

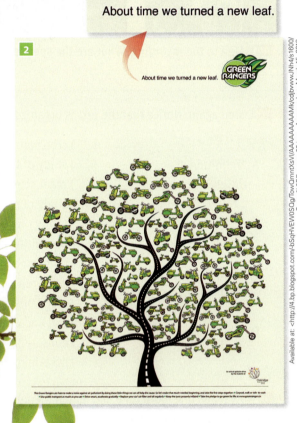

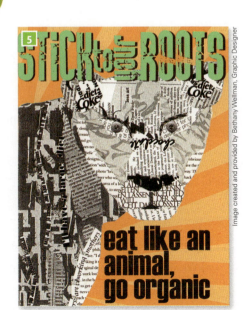

> Lead-in

1. What do you understand by "going green?"

_____

2. Look at the texts on the previous page and answer.

a) They are examples of ( ) campaigns, ( ) cartoons, ( ) commercials,

whose main features are ( ) creativity, ( ) irony,

( ) criticism, ( ) contrasting colors,

( ) catchy slogans, ( ) appealing images,

( ) only verbal language, ( ) verbal and nonverbal language interaction.

b) Where can we normally find this type of text?

_____

c) What's the target public?

_____

d) What's the purpose of these texts specifically?

_____

3. Below are some common features of slogans. Which of these features can you identify in the examples on the previous page? Write the numbers of the texts next to the matching features.

1. At the graphetic level	4. At the syntactic level
1.1 Consistent use of initial capitalization: _____	4.1 Use of short simple sentences: _____
1.2 Sometimes full use of capitalization: _____	4.2 Use of everyday sentences: _____
1.3 Consistent use of small letters: _____	4.3 Use of phrases: _____
2. At the phonological level	4.4 Use of questions: _____
2.1 Use of rhymes: _____	4.5 Use of imperative sentences: _____
2.2 Use of alliteration: _____	4.6 Use of (present) tense: _____
3. At the lexical level	4.7 Creative use of idioms or proverbs: _____
3.1 Common uses of 2nd person addressee _you_, and 1st person addresser _we, us_: _____	4.8 Use of parallel structures: _____
3.2 Use of unqualified comparison: _____	**5. At the semantic level**
3.3 Use of _every, always_, etc.: _____	5.1 Semantic ambiguity: _____
3.4 Use of _no, none_, etc.: _____	5.2 Use of puns: _____
3.5 Use of coined words: _____	

Adapted from: <http://www.translationdirectory.com/article49.htm>. Accessed on: December 6, 2013.

4. Think of initiatives on "going green" in your own house. If there aren't any so far, what do you think you and your family could start doing?

> Let's read!

Before you read...
- Take a look at the campaign poster below. Who is it promoted by?
- What is the subject of this campaign?
- What is its purpose?

Hint
Images can also be "read." When you are asked to read an image, find its "intentions" and observe how its structural elements (the line, the colors, the light, the movements, etc.) are organized to communicate something.

According to their website, Greenpeace is the largest independent direct-action environmental organization in the world. They claim that Greenpeace exists because this fragile planet deserves a voice, needs solutions, needs change, and needs action. This "storytelling" campaign aims to spread awareness of deforestation, making people imagine what future they are creating for their children by the actions they take today.

1. Look more carefully at the text above and answer.

   a) The creator of this campaign uses the image of a classic fairy tale to create another text. What fairy tale is it?

   _____

   b) What is the setting portrayed in the poster?

   _____

   c) How is it different from the setting of the fairy tale which inspired the creator?

   _____

   d) What is the predominant visual element in this campaign? What does it represent?

   _____

   e) Associating the verbal and nonverbal language in this poster, what is the main message?

   _____

   f) Is this campaign addressed to children or adults? How do you know?

   _____

2. We can say that the image used in this poster is very effective for the campaign. Why? Choose two possible reasons from the options below.

( ) Most children like colorful images, as they don't know how to read yet.

( ) The reader's familiarity with the fairy tale makes it easier to understand the message.

( ) The combination of colors is incredibly harmonious.

( ) The image chosen by the author evokes an emotional response from the reader.

3. One of the interpretations of this campaign is that deforestation is a story that

( ) affects children.

( ) can be changed.

( ) will affect other stories.

4. Talk to a classmate about these questions.

a) What do you know about Greenpeace? Is it present in Brazil?

b) This campaign was produced for English-speaking people. Would it be effective in Brazil as well if you translated the sentence into Portuguese and used the same image?

c) Do you belong to an environmental or conservation group? If not, do you know anybody who does?

5. Take a quick look at this comic strip and answer.

a) Who is the main character?

b) What is he doing? Which visual elements confirm that?

6. Read the comic strip on the previous page and answer the questions.

a) What is the topic of the text?

_____

_____

b) What is the main character's attitude towards the topic?

_____

_____

c) What does the rise in water level (panels 3, 4 and 5) represent?

_____

_____

7. Read the comic strip again and decide if the statements below are (T)rue or (F)alse.

( ) The main character denies the existence of global warming.

( ) He considers the phenomenon a media invention.

( ) He pleads guilty about the phenomenon.

( ) He believes that global warming is an important issue.

( ) He ends up being affected by the phenomenon.

8. Focus on the text in the fifth panel of the comic strip and answer.

a) What is the creator of this cartoon criticizing?

_____

_____

_____

b) "Hot air," in this context, means

( ) air that has been heated and tends to rise.

( ) loud, confused, and empty talk.

c) The author uses the idiom "hot air" to create a double interpretation, considering the literal and the figurative meaning. How do you interpret "They have enormous reserves of hot air?"

_____

_____

_____

Beyond the lines...

a) Does the couple in the cartoon on the previous page respond critically to the politician's speech? Why (not)?

b) A proverb says that "people get the government they deserve." What is our role as citizens in relation to the way politicians treat us?

› Let's listen and talk!

1. Look at the picture on the right side and talk about these questions.
   a) Who is this person?
   b) What kind of activism is he involved in?

2. 🔴50 Listen to the man portrayed in this picture speaking to a reporter. Check (✔) the correct options.
   a) His thesis is that
      ( ) extreme weather events are linked to the climate crisis.
      ( ) weather events should be seen as a question for debate.
      ( ) society ignores that many people in the world are suffering.
   b) The natural disasters mentioned in this passage are
      ( ) drought   ( ) wind storms
      ( ) earthquakes   ( ) hurricanes
      ( ) heat waves   ( ) fires
      ( ) flooding   ( ) volcanic eruptions
      ( ) tornados

3. 🔴50 Listen to the recording one more time and complete this statement. During his speech, he uses arguments and statistical data to state that
   _____

4. Consider the place where you live. Can you see the environmental effects of global warming? If so, what are they? Discuss with your classmate.

5. There are many ways to protect the environment. Walk around the class and find someone who recycles paper, takes quick showers, reads online to avoid printing paper, turns the lights off when leaving the room, takes their own bags to the market, etc.

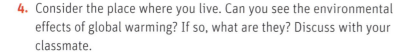

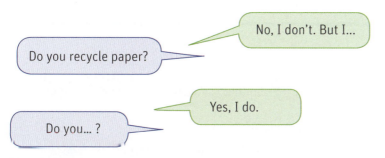

■ Did you know…?

Al Gore is chairman of the Climate Reality Project and former vice-president of the USA. He is famous for his 2006 documentary *An Inconvenient Truth*.

251

❯ Turn on the jukebox!

1. Discuss these questions with a classmate.

a) Which environmental problems are you concerned about? Why?

b) What are the possible solutions for these problems?

2. 🔘**51** Listen to the song and write the missing words.

The 3 R's
by Jack Johnson

_____, it's a magic number
Yes it is, it's a magic _____
Because two times three is six
And three times six is eighteen
And the eighteenth _____ in the alphabet
  is "R"
We've got three R's
We're gonna talk about today
We gotta _____ to
Reduce, Reuse, Recycle (4x)

And if you're going to the _____ to buy
  some juice
You've gotta bring _____ own bags
And you learn to reduce your waste
We've gotta learn to reduce
And if your _____ or your sisters got
  some cool clothes

You can try them on _____ you buy some
  more of those
_____, we've gotta learn to reuse
And if the first two R's don't _____ out
And if you gotta make some trash
Well, don't do it all
_____, we've gotta learn to recycle,
We've gotta learn to
Reduce, Reuse, Recycle (x4)

Because three, it's a magic number
Yes it is, it's a magic number
3, 3, 3
3, 6, 9, 12, 15 ...3... 18, 21, 24, 27...3...
30, 33, 36 ...3... 33, 30, 27 ...3...
24, 21, 18 ...3... 15, 12, 9, 6 and
3 ... it's a magic number

Available at: <http://www.vagalume.com.br/jack-johnson/the-3-rs.html>.
Accessed on: December 6, 2013.

Daniel Ochoa de Olza/AP/Glow Images

3. The speaker gives us some tips on recycling. What are they?
Do you think they are applicable to the people in your community?

_____

_____

Pronunciation spot – /r/

1. 🔘**52** Listen and repeat the words.

replenish	raise	recycle	reuse	reduce	brother	sister	number	your

2. 🔘**53** Listen to the words below. How is the letter **r** pronounced?

hat	rat		hair	rare		height	right		head	red

Notice that **r** is most commonly pronounced in English by raising the tip of your tongue and curving it a little. It never sounds like the letter **h**.

3. 🔘**54** Listen and circle the words you hear.

a) hair / rare   b) role / hole   c) rose / hose   d) home / roam   e) hat / rat

9 ▪ Life on Earth

> Let's focus on language!

1. Read the sentence from the Greenpeace campaign poster again and check (✔) the appropriate options.

"You don't want to tell this story to your children, do you?"

This kind of question at the end of a statement is normally used when we want to

( ) ask another person to agree with us.

( ) express surprise.

( ) check information that we know is true.

( ) make a comment and keep the conversation open.

This kind of question

( ) always expects an answer.

( ) does not necessarily expect an answer.

( ) is more commonly used in informal language.

( ) is used in both formal and informal language.

( ) always comes after a comma (,) in writing.

> Tag questions turn a statement into a question. Usually, if the main clause is negative, the tag question is affirmative, and if the main clause is affirmative, the tag question is negative.

2. Work alone. Decide if these statements about deforestation are (T)rue or (F)alse.

a) ( ) Deforestation is clearing Earth's forests on a massive scale.

b) ( ) The world's rainforests could completely vanish in a hundred years at the current rate of deforestation.

c) ( ) The biggest driver of deforestation isn't agriculture.

d) ( ) Farmers don't cut forests to provide more room for planting crops or grazing livestock.

e) ( ) Deforestation has many negative effects on the environment.

f) ( ) Trees also play a critical role in absorbing the greenhouse gases that fuel global warming.

g) ( ) The quickest solution to deforestation wouldn't be to simply stop cutting down trees.

h) ( ) Deforestation rates haven't slowed a bit in recent years.

Adapted from: <http://environment.nationalgeographic.com/environment/global-warming/deforestation-overview/>. Accessed on: December 6, 2013.

3. Now work in pairs. Confirm your answers by adding an appropriate tag question to each statement above. Attention: if you know that the statement is false, change the verb in the main clause, as in these examples.

> Deforestation ISN'T clearing Earth's forests on a massive scale, is it?

> The biggest driver of deforestation IS agriculture, isn't it?

Pronunciation spot – Intonation in tag questions

1. **○55** Listen to these sentences. What do you think their intended meanings are?

   You don't want to tell this story to your children, **do you**?
   ( ) a real question   ( ) checking information

   Deforestation rates haven't slowed a bit in recent years, **have they**?
   ( ) real question   ( ) checking information

2. Pick sentences from activity 2 (previous page) and choose an intended meaning for each one. Then say these sentences to a classmate with the suitable intonation. Can your classmate guess the intended meaning?

4. Complete the six questions below with the correct auxiliary verb. Then match each question to its corresponding answer. Choose words from the boxes.

AUXILIARY VERBS
does   can   did
were   is   are

ANSWERS
Africa   100 years   18   0.1%
cold-water corals   3%

a) How long _____ it take for carbon dioxide in the atmosphere to disperse?

_____

b) What _____ scientists discover in the waters off Ireland in 2005?

_____

c) What percentage of the world's water _____ freshwater?

_____

d) On what continent _____ grasslands called savannahs?

_____

e) How many different ways _____ marine worm species reproduce?

_____

f) What percentage of the world's oceans _____ closed to fishing in 2007?

_____

Source: <http://environment.nationalgeographic.com/environment/global-warming/quiz-global-warming/> (a); <http://environment.nationalgeographic.com/environment/habitats/quiz-habitat/> (c, d); <http://ocean.nationalgeographic.com/ocean/oceans-quiz/> (b, e, f). (All accessed on: December 6, 2013.)

5. Match the statements to the tag questions in the box. Complete the sentences accordingly.

a) Carbon dioxide takes a long time to disperse in the atmosphere, _____

b) Irish scientists discovered cold-water corals in the waters off Ireland in 2005, _____

c) Only 3% of the world's water is freshwater, _____

d) Grasslands in Africa are called savannahs, _____

e) Marine worm species can reproduce in eighteen ways, _____

f) 0.1% of the world's oceans were closed to fishing in 2007, _____

aren't they?

weren't they?

isn't it?

can't they?

didn't they?

doesn't it?

6. Reread these sentences used in different sections of this unit. Focus on the words in bold and choose the best option.

"By taking the bus you're helping keep our heads **above** water!"

"How do politicians breathe **under** water like that?"

They refer to ( ) duration or place. ( ) place or position. ( ) place or time.

> **Prepositions of place** are commonly used to indicate where people and things are located.

In English, the most common prepositions of place are:

IN   ON   UNDER   NEAR   NEXT TO   IN FRONT OF   BEHIND   BETWEEN   OPPOSITE

Illustrations: Estúdio Mil/ID/BR

7. Take a look at these pictures and complete the sentences with the appropriate prepositions of place.

catetus/iStockphoto.com/ID/BR

a) This is a battery disposal bin. The batteries _____ the bin will be recycled.

Biosphoto/Pierre Huguet/AFP

b) Turtles die when they mistakenly eat the plastic bags they find _____ them.

Giordano Aita/ Shutterstock/ID/BR

c) In this picture, the plastic bin is placed _____ the metal bin and the glass bin.

Smileus/Shutterstock/ID/BR

d) Solar energy panels are generally installed _____ the roof of a house.

Igor Jandric/Shutterstock/ID/BR

e) Water pollution is a serious problem to our planet, especially to the creatures that live _____ water.

8. Complete the slogans and quotes using the following words: **behind**, **in**, **near**, **on** (2x).

a) *Don't let the water run _____ the sink, our life's _____ the brink!*

b) *Earth is not growing _____ trees*

c) *Reuse yesteryear, recycle the current, save the _____ future!*

d) *Humanity is on the march, earth itself is left _____.*

Available at: <http://www.thinkslogans.com/slogans/environmental-slogans/save-water-slogans/> (a); <https://sites.google.com/site/supersonicsindus/who-we-are> (b); <http://gogreenguyz.blogspot.com/2011/09/top-go-green-slogans-and-recycling.html> (c); <http://en.wikiquote.org/wiki/Environment> (d). (All accessed on: December 6, 2013.)

255

Let's act with words!

Write slogans for a "going green" campaign

A slogan is a catchy phrase. It is easily remembered and it attracts attention. It is no longer than a sentence and must please the ear with rhymes or alliterations.

Your mission is to write a slogan to convince people in your community to "go green." Use an image to illustrate and contextualize it.

Suggested themes
- Recycling
- Using eco bags
- Protecting green areas
- Keeping streets clean

Genre: Slogan

Purpose: To motivate people to engage themselves in a campaign

Tone: Informal

Setting: Wall newspaper or Padlet

Writer: You

Audience: Wall newspaper or Padlet readers

Writing Steps

Organizing
- Read other slogans and observe their main elements.
- Choose a theme for your slogan.
- Choose an adequate image.
- Select adequate letter format(s) and color(s).

Preparing the first draft
- Make a first draft.
- Use a dictionary to help you.

Peer editing
- Evaluate and discuss your work with a classmate.
- Make the necessary corrections.

Publishing
- Publish your slogan on a wall newspaper or on Padlet.

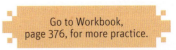

Go to Workbook, page 376, for more practice.

Learning tips

Learning English with the help of *Delicious*

Delicious is a social bookmarking site, that is, an online service for saving and sharing collections of links one can visit in the future. Users can also add comments about the selected links.

Go to the *Delicious* page at <http://delicious.com/> (accessed on: December 6, 2013) and type one or more key words to find resources to learn English. If you type "Learning English," you will see a page like the one below.

Click on the hyperlinks to access the content of each page and find lots of good stuff to develop your English.

Learn more about *Delicious* with a free e-book available at <http://ebookbrowse.com/delicious-tutorial-pdf-d205838964>. You can also watch a video at <http://www.commoncraft.com/video/social-bookmarking> (both accessed on: December 6, 2013).

Create an account and share links with your classmates.

Let's reflect on learning!

You are now invited to assess what you learned and how you learned. Finish the ideas below on an extra sheet of paper and become a more autonomous and reflective learner.

In Part 9

I learned _____

I liked _____

I need to review/learn more _____

My experiences with English outside school were _____
_____

257

Let's study for Enem!

Enem Questions

Gênero
Anúncio publicitário/Cartão-postal

Competência de área 2
H7 - Relacionar um texto em LEM, as estruturas linguísticas, sua função e seu uso social.

O uso do imperativo logo no início sinaliza que o gênero textual em questão pode ser anúncio publicitário. No caso, um anúncio produzido no formato de um cartão-postal.

Como você sabe, cartões-postais não costumam ser publicados na internet e, sim, enviados pelo correio. Portanto, quando o enunciado diz que o texto tem o formato de cartão-postal, já é possível supor que ele está sendo usado com uma função diferente. É importante estar atento a essas informações ao ler as questões da prova.

Os cartões-postais costumam ser utilizados por viajantes que desejam enviar notícias dos lugares que visitam a parentes e amigos. Publicado no *site* do projeto ANDRILL, o texto em formato de cartão-postal tem o propósito de

Ⓐ comunicar o endereço da nova sede do projeto nos Estados Unidos.
Ⓑ convidar colecionadores de cartões-postais a se reunirem em um evento.
Ⓒ anunciar uma nova coleção de selos para angariar fundos para a Antártica.
Ⓓ divulgar às pessoas a possibilidade de receberem um cartão-postal da Antártica.
Ⓔ solicitar que as pessoas visitem o *site* do mencionado projeto com maior frequência.

Tome cuidado para não marcar a primeira alternativa só porque há um endereço no "cartão-postal". Se a função do texto fosse comunicar um novo endereço, isso estaria indicado no texto, e não no local de endereçamento ao destinatário.

Extraído de: Exame Nacional do Ensino Médio, 2010, Caderno 7 – AZUL – Página 3 (questão 95).

Part 9 (Life on Earth)

Typical questions of Enem

1. A mensagem do cartum evidencia que o efeito estufa é
   a) ( ) um fenômeno provocado pelo homem.
   b) ( ) um fenômeno normal da natureza.
   c) ( ) um resultado de altas temperaturas.
   d) ( ) uma causa do aumento do nível do mar.
   e) ( ) um produto da mudança do clima.

2. O cartum evidencia que produtos orgânicos
   a) ( ) chegam mais rápido ao consumidor.
   b) ( ) devem ser transportados em caminhões.
   c) ( ) necessitam de um transporte rápido.
   d) ( ) possuem resistência ao transporte.
   e) ( ) são mais resistentes que os não orgânicos.

3. A mensagem desta campanha publicitária é a prevenção
   a) ( ) de acidentes de ônibus.
   b) ( ) do afogamento de filhotes.
   c) ( ) da redução de carbono.
   d) ( ) da extinção de animais.
   e) ( ) da mudança climática.

Exam Practice Questions (Vestibular)

Test-Taking Tips

Being well informed is the key!

Admission exams often use texts dealing with contemporary issues. For example, Text 1 talks about a sustainable campaign in New York and Text 2 is about climate change. It's good to be well informed about the trending topics in magazines and newspapers. In Part 1, you learned how important it is to be a regular reader: If you are a good reader, you are more likely to pass exams than someone who is a weak reader. Reasons: You can understand the individual sentences and the organizational structure of a text. You can comprehend ideas, follow arguments, and detect implications. You can extract from the passage what is essential for that particular task you are employed in.

▪ TEXT 1 – Question 1
UnB-DF, 2013

Marque, para cada item: o campo designado com o código C, caso julgue o item CERTO; ou o campo designado com o código E, caso julgue o item ERRADO.

New York City's Mayor, Michael Bloomberg, is about to add a whole lot of greenery to the concrete jungle. He just announced a campaign to install green roofs, sidewalks and porous parking lots in order to capture excess rainwater and runoff. The idea comes as part of Bloomberg's PlaNYC goal of making 90% of New York City's waterways suitable for recreation — right now excess sewer and rain runoff is making them unsuited for fun. The proposed green surfaces would eliminate 40% of the existing runoff into the waterways and save taxpayers $ 2.4 billion dollars over the next 20 years.

One of the problems the city must get around is its antiquated water system, which was built 150 years ago when the concept of pollution wasn't at the forefront of engineers' minds. Currently the system works fine, until it rains, when runoff and sewage are spewed into rivers, canals and the harbor. The proposed green roofs, sidewalks, and parking lots would be equipped to soak up at least an inch of rain — sometimes more — and would seriously reduce the need for costly water system infrastructure that is needed to stop the sewage from spewing all over New York City's waterways.

Currently the city's plan is to ramp up the technological infrastructure of the water system and use costly equipment to stop the spewing. This plan would cost $ 6.8 billion; however, Bloomberg's initiative could accomplish the same goal at a fraction of the cost. Not only would the green roofs be less expensive but they'd save taxpayers money by keeping their water bills low — more infrastructure, more cost to the taxpayers. This is all part of Bloomberg's ambitious PlaNYC goals of cutting the city's emissions and cleaning its air and waterways. As with many of the PlaNYC initiatives, Bloomberg has just announced the strategy — details of how many green roofs and where they will be placed will come at a later date.

Brit Liggett. NYC Mayor Bloomberg Announces Green Roof Initiative.
Internet: <www.inhabitat.com>.

1. Judge the following items according to the text above.

	C	E
a) The pollution of rivers is not a concern in New York City if it is not raining.		
b) The green roofs initiative is an attempt to fix an outdated system.		
c) PlaNYC was designed to address different environmental problems.		
d) The first place to benefit from the green roofs initiative will be Manhattan.		
e) Mayor Bloomberg's green roof initiative consists of building more parks in New York City.		
f) Without green roofs, New York City's taxpayers spend US$ 2.4 billion a year.		
g) The word "runoff" is a synonym for **wastewater**.		
h) In New York City, the same system carries both rainwater and wastewater.		
i) The current water system in New York City cannot be fixed to reduce pollution.		

▪ TEXT 2 – Questions 2 to 4
UFPR, 2014

Climate Change: Forecast for 2100 is Floods and Heat ... and It's Man's Fault

By Nick Allen
9:04PM BST 16 Aug 2013

Climate scientists have concluded that temperatures could jump by up to 5°C and sea levels could rise by up to 82 cm by the end of the century, according to a leaked draft of a United Nations (UN) report.

Part 9 (Life on Earth)

The UN Intergovernmental Panel on Climate Change (IPCC) also said there was a 95 per cent likelihood that global warming is caused by human activities. That was the highest assessment so far from the IPCC, which put the figure at 90 per cent in a previous report in 2007, 66 per cent in 2001, and just over 50 per cent in 1995.

Reto Knutti, a professor at the Swiss Federal Institute of Technology in Zurich, said: "We have got quite a bit more certain that climate change is largely man-made. We're less certain than many would hope about the local impacts." The IPCC report, the first of three in 2013 and 2014, will face intense scrutiny particularly after errors in the 2007 study, which wrongly predicted that all Himalayan glaciers could melt by 2035.

Almost 200 governments have agreed to try to limit global warming to below 2°C above pre-industrial times, which is seen as a threshold for dangerous changes including more droughts, extinctions, floods and rising seas that could swamp coastal regions and island nations. Temperatures have already risen by 0.8°C since the Industrial Revolution.

The report will say there is a high risk global temperatures will rise by more than 2°C this century. They could rise anywhere from about 0.6°C to almost 5°C, a wider range at both ends of the scale than predicted in the 2007 report. **It** will also say evidence of rising sea levels is "unequivocal". The report projects seas will rise by between 30 cm and 82 cm by the late 21st century. In 2007 the estimated rise was between 18 cm and 58 cm, but that did not fully account for changes in Antarctica and Greenland.

Scientists say it is harder to predict local impacts. Drew Shindell, a NASA scientist, said: "I talk to people in regional power planning. They ask, 'What's the temperature going to be in this region in the next 20 to 30 years, because that's where our power grid is?' We can't really tell."

(Adapted from <telegraph.co.uk>)

2. Consider the following statements concerning global warming and the leaked draft of the IPCC report:

1. Scientists think it is 95% likely that human activity is causing global warming.
2. Temperatures could be 5°C warmer by the end of the current century.
3. Sea levels are not likely to be higher than today by the end of the century.

4. Scientists are surer now than in 2007 that humans are causing global warming.
5. 50% of the scientists believed humans were the cause of climate change in 1995.

Which of the statements above are TRUE, according to the text?

a) (   ) Only statements 1, 3 and 5.
b) (   ) Only statements 2, 3 and 4.
c) (   ) Only statements 3 and 5.
d) (   ) Only statements 1, 2 and 4.
e) (   ) Only statements 2 and 5.

3. Considering what the text says about the IPCC and its predictions and conclusions on global warming, mark true (T) or false (F) for the following statements:

(   ) The IPCC made a wrong prediction about the Himalayas in the 2007 report.

(   ) Himalayan glaciers will certainly disappear by 2035 because of global warming.

(   ) The IPCC can now be sure of how climate change will impact different locations.

(   ) IPCC's new report will be carefully examined after the errors committed in 2007.

(   ) Global warming will have a huge impact in Switzerland because of its large glaciers.

Mark the alternative which presents the correct sequence, from top to bottom.

a) (   ) T F F T F
b) (   ) F T T F T
c) (   ) T F T F T
d) (   ) F F F T T
e) (   ) T T T T F

4. Mark the correct alternative, according to the text. The word "it," in boldface and italics (paragraph 5), refers to:

a) (   ) global warming.
b) (   ) the greenhouse effect.
c) (   ) rising sea levels.
d) (   ) the 21st century.
e) (   ) the IPCC report.

261

PART

10 Healthy Life

Learning plan

Discussing facts and myths

Talking about events which will probably happen in the future or have a real possibility of happening

Talking about well-being

Contrasting two actions in the past

Talking about unreal or imagined situations related to physical and mental health

Making a poster

Learning English with social bookmarking

What is social bookmarking? It is tagging a website and saving it for later. Instead of saving it to your web browser, you are saving it to the web. And, because your bookmarks are online, you can easily share them with friends.

Available at: <http://webtrends.about.com/od/socialbookmarking101/p/aboutsocialtags.htm>. Accessed on: December 6, 2013.

Some bookmarking tools are **Diigo** (https://www.diigo.com) and **Delicious** (https://delicious.com/). You can visit their websites and see how they work. Find dictionaries, songs, magazines and newspapers in English, comics, videos, etc. Tag and save your findings with the help of one of those tools. Share them with your friends.

Another interesting social bookmarking is **Pinterest** (http://pinterest.com/). You can use this online tool to organize a virtual picture dictionary. Look for images on the web and organize them in tags such as food, arts, animals, flowers, clothes, occupations etc.

(All sites were accessed on: December 6, 2013.)

263

UNIT 19

I am what I eat

Language in action

- Discuss facts and myths
- Talk about diets
- Learn to talk about actions or events which will probably happen in the future or have a real possibility of happening

We like to tell ourselves we're far too busy to cook these days...

Less than forty years ago people had jobs and families to look after, but still managed to prepare and cook meals from scratch every day of the week – without the modern conveniences of supermarkets and fast food; or a fridge, food processor or microwave.

But it is possible to feed your family a healthy, balanced diet (without depriving them of the things they like) even if you work full-time and don't have a lot of money.

This book provides simple, wholesome and nutritious recipes for family meals; quick lunches, tasty puddings and cakes – and you don't have to spend hours slaving over a hot stove, or spend a fortune at the supermarket.

There are menu plans, recipes, shortcuts and dozens of ideas for every meal, together with tried and tested tips to help you save your valuable time and money.

Now everyone can be a yummy mummy or daddy in the kitchen.

GILL HOLCOMBE is passionate about feeding her kids good food. She grew up before the culture of convenience food took hold – and knows how to cook. Having brought up three children on her own for over ten years, she says the proof of the pudding is in the eating, and has three fit, healthy teenagers with loads of energy – and no fillings in their teeth.

Spring Hill
info@springhillbooks.co.uk
www.howtobooks.co.uk

COOKERY
ISBN 978-1-905862-15-3
£9.99

HOLCOMBE, Gill. *How to feed your whole family a healthy, balanced diet*. Oxford: Spring Hill, 2007.

> Lead-in

1. Look at the back cover of a book on the previous page. Where was it published and commercialized? How do you know?

   _____
   _____
   _____

2. What experiences prompted Gill Holcombe to write the book?

   _____
   _____
   _____

3. What does it mean to "prepare and cook meals from scratch?" Does the author encourage or discourage this? Why?

   _____
   _____
   _____

4. Look at one of the illustrations used in Gill Holcombe's book. How is it related to the topic of the book? What does the caption mean?

   _____
   _____
   _____
   _____
   _____

"Don't dig your grave with your own knife and fork."

Old English proverb

5. Would you like to read this book? If you don't, to whom would you recommend it? Why?

   _____
   _____
   _____
   _____
   _____

Beyond the lines...

a) Do you think all this emphasis on eating healthy food is relevant?

b) Is healthy food normally available in supermarkets in your city?

c) If not, how can you improve your diet using the resources you have?

> Let's read!

Before you read...
- Is it OK to go on a diet without consulting a doctor? Why (not)?
- What kind of people normally go on a diet? Do you think diets work?
- What can happen if we regularly cut out some types of food (or skip some meals, like breakfast)?

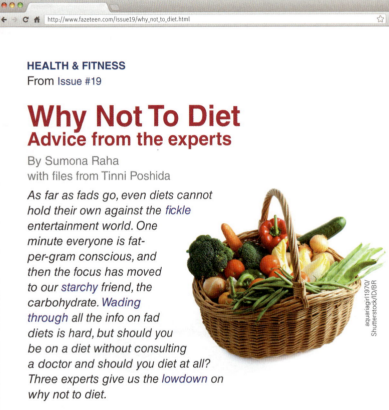

HEALTH & FITNESS
From Issue #19

Why Not To Diet
Advice from the experts

By Sumona Raha
with files from Tinni Poshida

As far as fads go, even diets cannot hold their own against the fickle entertainment world. One minute everyone is fat-per-gram conscious, and then the focus has moved to our starchy friend, the carbohydrate. Wading through all the info on fad diets is hard, but should you be on a diet without consulting a doctor and should you diet at all? Three experts give us the lowdown on why not to diet.

Terri Sonnabend
Registered Dietitian/Nutritionist

Once you start to "diet," there is a preoccupation with food instead of the idea of healthy eating. You need to be more aware of nutrition and proper food options. If you restrict the amount of calories consumed, you don't get the proper nutrients needed for growth and development. Sometimes, you may use dieting to cope with pressures felt from society and peers, which can lead to a food fixation and eating disorders. Healthy weight can be measured by the Body Mass Index, which takes into account both height and weight. Twenty to 25 on BMI is a healthy teen. A lot of teens may appear to be thin or in good shape, but their eating habits are poor, which affects health in later life. So you should not be counting calories, but instead you should be aware of healthy nutrition — brown bread instead of white, high fibre, less sugar, etc. The Canadian Food Guide is a good starting point for making more informed eating choices.

terri@fitnessinstitute.com

Available at: <http://www.fazeteen.com/issue19/why_not_to_diet.html>. Accessed on: December 6, 2013.

Faze is a magazine published for Canadian teenagers. It covers several issues, such as youth culture, music, movies, personal style, current affairs, technology, travel, careers, health, fitness, etc. It is also available at magazine stands across Canada and is in nearly all school libraries in that country. It is written by teens and other young adults.

1. Read the title and subtitle of the text on the previous page. What do they suggest?
   ( ) It is OK to go on diets without the help of an expert.
   ( ) Diets don't work if you are not an expert.
   ( ) Diets can be a problem for your health.

2. Scan the text and find recommendations the expert Terri Sonnabend gives on teens' diets.

   _____
   _____
   _____
   _____

3. Match each of these images to its corresponding excerpt from the text.

   a)

   b)

   c)

   ( ) "A lot of teens may appear to be thin or in good shape, but their eating habits are poor, which affects health in later life."
   ( ) "So you should not be counting calories, but instead you should be aware of healthy nutrition — brown bread instead of white, high fibre, less sugar, etc."
   ( ) "Sometimes, you may use dieting to cope with pressures felt from society and peers, which can lead to a food fixation and eating disorders."

4. Discuss these questions with your classmates.

   a) What are the current fad diets? Can they be dangerous for your health?

   b) What type of pressure does society put on people about their appearance? Is it the same for boys and girls?

   c) *Faze* is a magazine published for young Canadians. Would teenagers in Brazil find the information in this magazine useful as well?

   d) Did you change your opinion about diets after reading Terri Sonnabend's text? Why (not)?

5. Visit the *Faze* magazine link and search for the following information.

   a) Who are the other two experts? What do they do?

   _____

   _____

   b) Which expert talks about the danger of cutting all carbohydrates from our diet?

   _____

Beyond the lines...

a) Does the woman know what the three basic food groups are?
b) What kind of food does she eat?
c) How does the cartoonist represent someone who eats these types of foods?
d) Do you think this cartoon reinforces a stereotype? Explain.

Vocabulary corner

1. Look at the words in the box. Match each term to its corresponding definition in the graphical dictionary.

> Balanced diet   Low-sodium diet   Obesity diet
> Dietary supplement   Vegetarianism

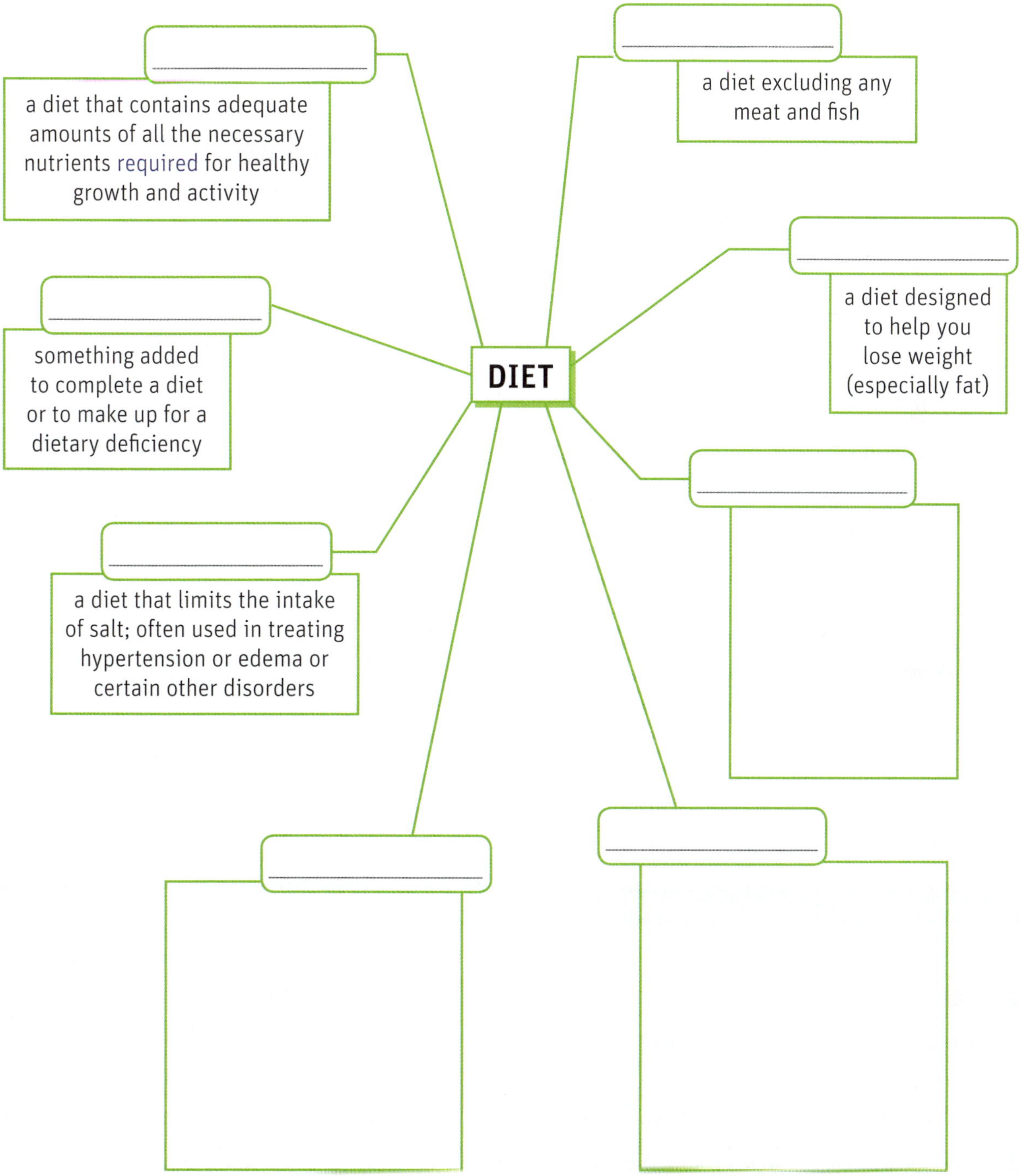

DIET

a diet that contains adequate amounts of all the necessary nutrients required for healthy growth and activity

a diet excluding any meat and fish

something added to complete a diet or to make up for a dietary deficiency

a diet designed to help you lose weight (especially fat)

a diet that limits the intake of salt; often used in treating hypertension or edema or certain other disorders

Adapted from: <http://visuwords.com/>. Accessed on: December 6, 2013.

2. Visit the website <http://visuwords.com/>. Type the word **diet** to see more associations. Then add three more expressions and definitions to the graphic above.

269

⟩ Let's listen and talk!

1. Read some myths related to food and nutrition.

a)

If you eat sugar, you get diabetes.

b)

Your stomach will shrink if you eat less.

c)

If you eat eggs, your cholesterol will go up.

d)

If you eat snacks, you will spoil your appetite.

e)

If you eat later in the evening, you will gain weight.

2. Did you already know any of these myths? Which one(s)? Discuss with your classmates.

3. ⊚56 Now listen to some facts and choose the corresponding myth for each one. Write the letter.

Fact	Myth
I	
II	
III	
IV	
V	

Adapted from: <http://www.eiu.edu/dining/
files/25%20Common%20Food%20Myths.pdf>.
Accessed on: December 6, 2013.

4. Let's play "Myth Buster." In groups, think of other myths and facts related to food and nutrition. Try to remember popular myths of your region. After discussing them in groups, tell the myths to the class and challenge the other groups to find out what the facts are. Use the pattern in activity 1 as a model.

Pronunciation spot – Ending sounds: /s/ and /z/

1. Look at the eleven words listed in activity 2. Two of them are not examples of plural words. Circle them.

2. ⊚57 Listen to these words and write /s/ or /z/ according to their ending sounds.

diets / /   methods / /   groups / /   types / /

eats / /   cakes / /   eggs / /   teenagers / /

raisins / /   nutritious / /   snacks / /

3. Circle the appropriate words below to complete the rules.

a) The –s forming the plural and 3rd person sounds like /s/ when the last sound of the word is **voiced / voiceless**.

b) The –s forming the plural and 3rd person sounds like /z/ when the last sound of the word is **voiced/ voiceless**.

> Let's focus on language!

1. Read the myths introduced in the previous section again and do the activities.

   A. If you eat sugar, you get diabetes.

   B. Your stomach will shrink if you eat less.

   C. If you eat eggs, your cholesterol will go up.

   D. If you eat snacks, you will spoil your appetite.

   E. If you eat later in the evening, you will gain weight.

   Hint
   Comparing predictions A and B, we notice: if we start the sentence with **if**, we need a comma (,) between the two parts of the sentence. If we start the sentence with the prediction or fact, we don't need to use a comma.

   a) What idea does each sentence above convey? Write the corresponding letters.
   - It describes what will probably happen in the future: _____.
   - It describes a logical conclusion: _____.

   b) Underline the parts of the sentences above that describe a condition.

   c) Circle the parts of the sentences that describe a prediction.

   d) Complete the rules in the box below using **Simple Present** and **will + verb**.

   - When we want to give facts, we use **if** + _____ _____ for the condition, and _____ _____ in the other part of the sentence that presents what always happens.

   - When we want to talk about possibilities in the future, we use **if** + _____ in the part of the sentence that describes the condition, and _____ in the other part of the sentence that presents the prediction.

271

2. Read some more opinions about eating and complete the sentences with an appropriate ending.

I. *Excessive consumption of the pigment lycopene, found in such plants as tomatoes, can also cause your skin to turn orange. This is harmless and reversible by simply stopping consuming the lycopene.*

a) If you eat too much lycopene, your skin _____

_____

b) Your skin goes back to its normal color _____

_____

II. *If you want to keep your eyes healthy, eating fresh fruits and leafy vegetables is better than getting your vitamin A from carrots. Leafy vegetables are a source of vitamin A, but they also contain vitamins C and E, which have been shown to prevent cataracts.*

c) If you want to keep your eyes healthy, eat _____

_____

d) If you eat fresh fruits and leafy vegetables, you _____

_____

e) _____ if you

eat leafy vegetables.

f) If you consume vitamins C and E, _____

_____

III. *Another eye related myth is that reading in dim light damages your vision. In fact, this will do nothing to harm your eyesight, other than fatigue your eyes more quickly than normal.*

g) If you read in dim light, you will _____

_____

h) You will fatigue your eyes more quickly than normal if you

_____

_____

Adapted from: <http://www.todayifoundout.com/index.php/2012/02/if-you-eat-an-excessive-amount-of-carrots-your-skin-will-turn-an-orangishyellow-shade/>. Accessed on: December 7, 2013.

3. With a classmate, decide if the opinions in activity 2 are **fact** or **myth**. To make the activity even more interesting, you can have an interdisciplinary project with your science teacher.

Profession spot

> ## Dietitian career

1. Victoria Retelny is a registered, licensed dietitian working in Chicago. She is currently working on a book on nutrition and owns her own private practice. Below are fragments of an interview she gave to a website. What are her quotes about? Classify them using the headings in the box.

> Job Description   Steps for a Successful Career
> Dietitian Routine   University Experiences
>   Job Opportunities

"The internship I went through allowed students to rotate through many different areas of dietetics, such as clinical, foodservice, media/communications, and community [...]. This gives you the chance to work one-on-one with patients, write your own press releases or media pitches, and work in WIC (Women, Infants and Children) clinics to prepare you for real world scenarios."

Victoria Retelny, dietitian

"In my nutrition communications practice, [...] my days vary as I research and write articles, answer media interviews, counsel corporate wellness clients, and speak to groups on current nutrition topics. It runs the nutrition gamut, and that keeps it interesting!"

"In my work, I write, blog, speak publicly, counsel individuals, teach culinary classes and serve as a nutrition expert to the media" [...].

"In order to get the job you want, you have to stand out by marketing your services, providing discounted services at first to get your foot in the door, give public nutrition seminars and charge what you're worth once established" [...].

"You have to be flexible and willing to go with the flow of scientific changes [...]. You also need to be a chameleon by taking roles in the industry that you may never have had, but want to try."

Adapted from: <http://myfootpath.com/career-advice-and-answers/career-interviews/dietitian-career-interview/>. Accessed on: December 7, 2013.

2. In your opinion, what are the most interesting aspects of the life of a dietitian? How are they important for our society? Is this career common in your region?

UNIT 20 Sound body

Language in action
- Talk about well-being
- Learn to contrast two actions in the past
- Learn to talk about unreal or imagined situations

Health is a state of complete physical, mental and social well-being and not merely the absence of disease or infirmity.

Available at: <http://www.who.int/hac/about/definitions/en/>. Accessed on: December 7, 2013.

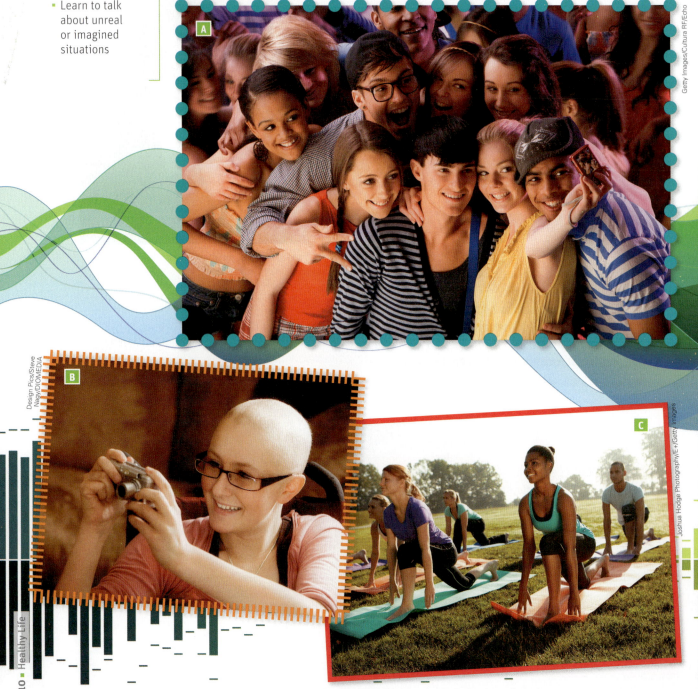

> Lead-in

1. What do the three pictures on the previous page represent? How are they related to the title of this unit?

   _____
   _____

2. What does the expression "Sound mind, sound body" mean? What is the equivalent expression in Portuguese?

   _____
   _____

Beyond the lines...
a) How can the environment affect bodies and minds?
b) Do you think that the idea of "sound mind, sound body" applies to everybody?

3. According to the World Health Organization (WHO), health "is a state of complete physical, mental and social well-being and not merely the absence of disease or infirmity." Do you agree with this statement? Explain.

   _____
   _____

4. What can people do in order to have a sound mind and a sound body? Work with a classmate and list as many things as you can.

   SOUND MIND   **SOUND BODY**

   _____   _____
   _____   _____
   _____   _____
   _____   _____

Did you know...?

Selfie: a photo that people have taken of themselves, typically with a smartphone or webcam and uploaded to a social media website.

Adapted from: <http://www.oxforddictionaries.com/us/definition/american_english/selfie?q=selfie>. Accessed on: February 20, 2014.

Let's read!

Before you read...

- Why do people want to be healthy? Share your reasons with a classmate.
- What are the characteristics of a healthy person? Write a list in your notebook.
- Is every thin person you know healthy? Is every fat person you know unhealthy?

According to its owners, *Livestrong.com* is a service which offers authoritative expert content in the diet, nutrition, fitness, wellness, and lifestyle categories that informs and empowers. They believe that eating well and staying active are critical components in preventing cancer and fighting other illnesses.

WHY YOU WANT TO BE HEALTHY

Jan 27, 2011 | By Diana Gamble

A healthy person is free of illness and disease, at a normal weight for his height and naturally *energetic*. In 2009, the Centers for Disease Control and Prevention, or CDC, said poor diets lead to obesity, type 2 diabetes, high blood pressure, heart disease, arthritis and poor health *overall*. Some schools have health and nutrition programs to teach children about the value of healthy eating. Along with healthful eating, perform regular exercise, which is just as important for a healthy body.

Eat Healthy Diet – The desire to live a long, pain-free life is the goal of most people, and a healthy diet can have one of the greatest impacts in your current and future health. However, many foods today are made with chemical ingredients, unhealthy fats and pesticides. Healthy food provides you with minerals, vitamins, antioxidants, fiber and other nutrients that help build up your immune system to *ward off* illness. The most effective way to absorb these nutrients is with foods as opposed to supplements.

Lose Weight – Those who are overweight or obese have a higher risk of developing illnesses such as heart disease, type 2 diabetes and cancer, and children who are obese will most likely grow up to become obese adults and contract these illnesses earlier in their lives. Eating low-calorie food free of saturated and trans fats can help reduce weight and prevent illnesses – especially if those foods are nutrient-rich.

Increase Energy – Many people who eat healthy enjoy the benefits of an abundance of natural energy. If you eat a diet that focuses on raw fruits, vegetables, whole grains, legumes, nuts and seeds, your body will start to respond to these quality sources of "fuel," start to work more effectively and efficiently, and provide you with natural vitality.

Enjoy Beauty – Healthy people enjoy the positive aesthetic side effects of health, such as attractive skin, hair and teeth, because they are giving their bodies antioxidants and nutrients such as vitamins A, C and E and biotin, which it needs to support these physical features.

Available at: <http://www.livestrong.com/article/367568-why-you-want-to-be-healthy/>. Accessed on: October 3, 2012.

1. Read the text on the previous page quickly and check if it mentions any of your answers in the *Before you read* part.

2. Read the text more carefully now and find out the following information.

   a) The definition of a healthy person: _____

   _____

   b) Nutrients found in healthy foods: _____

   _____

   c) Diseases related to obesity: _____

   d) Foods that help people lose weight: _____

   e) Sources of "fuel" for our bodies: _____

   _____

   f) Aesthetic side effects of being healthy: _____

   g) Substances that help people look healthier: _____

> Diana Gamble's health-oriented articles have been published in magazines such as *The Natural Journal* since 2007. She earned certifications for massage therapy and nutritional consulting from the North Carolina School of Holistic Medicine. She graduated from the University of North Carolina-Asheville with a Bachelor of Arts in literature.
>
> Available at: <http://www.livestrong.com/article/367568-why-you-want-to-be-healthy/>. Accessed on: October 3, 2012.

3. When you read an article, do you normally search for information about its author? Above is some biodata about Diana Gamble, author of the text on the previous page. Read the information and answer the questions below.

   a) What kind of articles does she write? _____

   b) What kinds of courses did she take? _____

   c) Do you think she is qualified to write this kind of article? _____

4. While some people do their best to be healthy, others experience the effects of bad habits, like *substance abuse*. Do you know what it is? Check its possible consequences.

   (   ) strong need of a type of drug   (   ) physical symptoms when not taking it

   (   ) increased tolerance to a type of drug   (   ) better socialization skills

   (   ) ability to control its use   (   ) desire to stop using after harmful results

Did you know...?

> According to the World Health Organization, "at least 20% of young people will experience some form of mental illness – such as depression, mood disturbances, substance abuse, suicidal behaviours or eating disorders."
>
> Excerpt from: <http://www.who.int/features/factfiles/adolescent_health/facts/en/index4.html>. Accessed on: December 7, 2013.

Hint
Look quickly at what each exercise asks you to do and find key words, that is, significant words. Then check if these key words appear in the text. When you find them, read this part of the text carefully until you feel safe to write the answer.

5. Now read the text below and check your answers in activity 4.

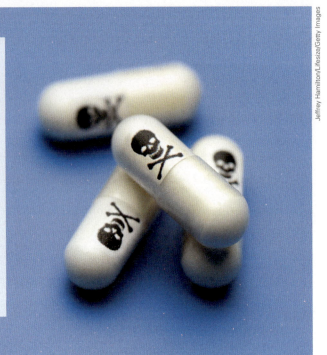

> **Substance abuse** refers to the harmful or hazardous use of psychoactive substances, including alcohol and illicit drugs. Psychoactive substance use can lead to dependence syndrome – a cluster of behavioural, cognitive, and physiological phenomena that develop after repeated substance use and that typically include a strong desire to take the drug, difficulties in controlling its use, persisting in its use despite harmful consequences, a higher priority given to drug use than to other activities and obligations, increased tolerance, and sometimes a physical withdrawal state.
>
> Available at: <http://www.who.int/topics/substance_abuse/en/>.
> Accessed on: December 7, 2013.

Vocabulary corner

1. Notice how the noun **illness** (a disease) is formed.

> **ill** (adjective = being sick) + **ness** (suffix)

- What other nouns formed with an adjective + the suffix -**ness** do you know? Use a dictionary to help you.

_____

2. Notice how the adjective **hopeless** is formed.

> **hope** (noun = something good you want to happen in the future) + **less** (suffix)

- What other adjectives formed with a noun + the suffix -**less** do you know? Use a dictionary to help you.

_____

3. Now match the words on the left to their definitions on the right.

a) speechless   ( ) quality or state of being shy
b) fitness   ( ) the state of being healthy
c) painless   ( ) quality of being generous, friendly
d) shyness   ( ) unable to speak
e) kindness   ( ) causing no physical pain
f) wellness   ( ) condition of being physically fit and healthy

4. To sum up, the suffix -**ness** forms _____ and the suffix -**less** forms _____.

> To add the suffix -**ness** when a word ends with **y** (that sounds like "ee"), you need to change the **y** to an **i**, as in "happ**y**"(happ**i**ness), "ugl**y**" (ugl**i**ness), "lonel**y**" (lonel**i**ness), "laz**y**" (laz**i**ness).
> **Attention**: _Shyness_ is an exception to this rule!

Let's listen and talk!

Before you listen...
- What do you know about yoga?
- Can you think of some benefits of this practice?

1. ⦿58 Listen to a person talking about yoga and check (√) the appropriate options.

   a) The speaker is probably
   - ( ) a reporter.
   - ( ) a person who does yoga.
   - ( ) an expert in yoga.

   b) The main idea of this oral text is
   - ( ) to talk about the benefits of yoga.
   - ( ) to teach some yoga exercises.

2. According to the speaker, the number one advantage of doing yoga is
   - ( ) you realize your full potential.
   - ( ) you allow for greater circulation.
   - ( ) you get physically stronger.

3. The text also emphasizes that becoming happy involves
   - ( ) an attitude regarding compassion.
   - ( ) a desire for connection and fulfillment.
   - ( ) a process of getting physically stronger.

4. Work in pairs. Talk about other activities and how they can be beneficial to our mental and physical health.

   Useful language

   One possibility is to… because…
   Another activity is… It can help us…

   … practice sports   … make some art craft
   … practice yoga   … do gardening
   … walk / run   … create a blog
   … listen to music   … do some volunteer work

Pronunciation spot – Initial sound /p/

A stressed /p/ at the beginning of words must be produced with strong aspiration.

1. ⦿59 Listen to the words and repeat. Practice saying the /p/ by loosely holding a tissue in front of your lips. If you aspirate /p/ correctly, releasing a puff of air, the tissue will flutter.

   | people | person | past |
   | perform | practice | publish |

2. Make a list of words beginning with /p/ and practice pronouncing this aspirated sound.

❯ Let's focus on language!

1. Read the text and answer these questions.

   a) Do you know anyone who has been in a situation that is similar to Christina's? What happened?

   b) What do you think about her attitude of writing about it on the Internet? Do you think it can be helpful to other teenagers with cancer? Why (not)?

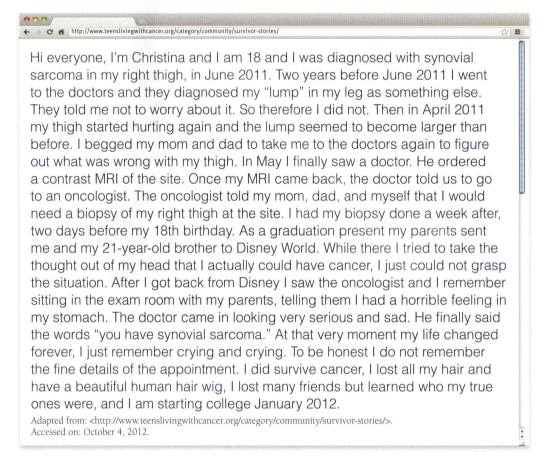

Hi everyone, I'm Christina and I am 18 and I was diagnosed with synovial sarcoma in my right thigh, in June 2011. Two years before June 2011 I went to the doctors and they diagnosed my "lump" in my leg as something else. They told me not to worry about it. So therefore I did not. Then in April 2011 my thigh started hurting again and the lump seemed to become larger than before. I begged my mom and dad to take me to the doctors again to figure out what was wrong with my thigh. In May I finally saw a doctor. He ordered a contrast MRI of the site. Once my MRI came back, the doctor told us to go to an oncologist. The oncologist told my mom, dad, and myself that I would need a biopsy of my right thigh at the site. I had my biopsy done a week after, two days before my 18th birthday. As a graduation present my parents sent me and my 21-year-old brother to Disney World. While there I tried to take the thought out of my head that I actually could have cancer, I just could not grasp the situation. After I got back from Disney I saw the oncologist and I remember sitting in the exam room with my parents, telling them I had a horrible feeling in my stomach. The doctor came in looking very serious and sad. He finally said the words "you have synovial sarcoma." At that very moment my life changed forever, I just remember crying and crying. To be honest I do not remember the fine details of the appointment. I did survive cancer, I lost all my hair and have a beautiful human hair wig, I lost many friends but learned who my true ones were, and I am starting college January 2012.

Adapted from: <http://www.teenslivingwithcancer.org/category/community/survivor-stories/>. Accessed on: October 4, 2012.

2. Read the first three sentences of the text above. What happened first? Choose the correct answer.

   ( ) Christina was diagnosed with synovial sarcoma in her right thigh.

   ( ) The doctors told Christina not to worry about the "lump" in her leg.

> To talk about two events in the past, we use the Past Perfect (**had** + **Past Participle**) to show which event happened first. For example: *Doctors* **had told** *Christina not to worry about the lump in her leg when she was diagnosed with synovial sarcoma.* For negatives, we use **hadn't** (**had not**).

Beyond the lines...

   a) How long does it take for a patient in your region to be examined by a doctor in the public health system?

   b) Can patients in the public health system have a Magnetic Resonance Imaging (MRI) exam easily in your region?

3. Read the text about Christina again and complete the sentences below using the appropriate endings. Use the options in the two boxes.

had lost	all her hair
had seen	college
saw	diagnosed with synovial sarcoma
had	her MRI
started	the oncologist again
was	her biopsy done

a) Doctors had told Christina not to worry about the problem in her leg when _____

_____

b) Christina survived cancer after she _____

c) The doctor told Christina she would need a biopsy after he _____

d) Christina had lost many friends before she _____

e) Christina had returned from Disney when she _____

f) She hadn't celebrated her 18th birthday yet when she _____

4. Read these quotes about illness and health and answer the four questions.

If I had my way **I'd make** health catching instead of disease.
(Robert Ingersoll)
Available at: <http://www.quotegarden.com/health.html>. Accessed on: December 7, 2013.

A lot of people don't realize that depression is an illness. I don't wish it on anyone, but **if** they **knew** how it feels, I swear they **would think** twice before they just shrug it.
(Jonathan Davis)
Available at: <http://www.brainyquote.com/quotes/keywords/illness.html#Q9sfTwTbsrB0oQJv.99>. Accessed on: December 7, 2013.

Jag_cz/Shutterstock.com/ID/BR

a) Are the conditions presented in the quotes above real or imaginary? _____

b) Is there a real possibility that these conditions will happen? _____

c) Which verb tense is used after **if**? _____

d) What word is abbreviated as "d" (in I'd)? _____

5. Read the quotes again, paying attention to the words in bold. Then complete this grammar rule by writing *Past Tense* and *would* in the appropriate spaces.

The Second Conditional is used to imagine situations that are not true. The main clause is formed by _____ **+ verb**, and the if-clause is formed by _____ or **could + verb**.

281

6. Look at these posters. Then complete the sentences accordingly. Follow the examples.

Poster 1 How different would the boy's life be if he didn't abuse prescription drugs?

If he didn't abuse prescription drugs,

a) he _____would go to_____ football games.

b) he _____ sports.

c) he _____ with friends.

d) he _____ crazy family vacations.

e) he _____ healthy.

Poster 2 What would happen to me if I abused drugs?

If you abused drugs,

a) you _____could get_____ fired.

b) you _____ to rehab.

c) you _____ busted.

d) you _____ tests.

Did you know…?

Rx = a medical prescription.

7. Look at poster 2 again. Write at least three more sentences in the Second Conditional using the ideas that were not covered in the second part of activity 6. Look at the example.

a) If you abused drugs, you would be unhealthy.

b) _____

c) _____

d) _____

Profession spot

> Health careers

1. The Holland Inventory is a tool used to map different personality types in suit with prospective careers. This model is tailored to the field of public health. In the chart below, relate the categories to their descriptions. Write the words.

Category	Description
	People who have athletic or mechanical ability prefer to work with objects, machines, tools, plants or animals, or to be outdoors. Careers: _____
	People who like to analyze, evaluate or solve problems. Careers: _____
	People who have artistic, innovating or intuitional abilities. Careers: _____
	People who like to work with people to enlighten, inform, train, or cure them, or are skilled with words. Careers: _____
	People who like to work with people, leading or managing. Careers: _____
	People who like to work with data, have clerical or numerical ability, carry out tasks in detail or follow through on others' instructions. Careers: _____

Available at: <http://www.roguecc.edu/Counseling/HollandCodes/>. Accessed on: October 5, 2012.

2. Match the professions in this box to the most appropriate description in the chart above. Write the words.

> biochemist   biologist   biostatistician   dental technician   dentist   dietitian   epidemiologist
> health educator   medical assistant   medical record technician   policymaker
> public health planner   science teacher   communication specialist   veterinarian

3. If you had to choose a career in the health area, which personality type would you fit into?
   Which profession would you choose? _____

283

Let's act with words!

Making a poster

A poster is a large print or a digital file to make announcements or to persuade people to change behavior. You can find posters on the walls, billboards, or on the Internet.

Your task here is to make a poster to try to convince people to eat healthily or to avoid bad habits. You and your classmates can engage in a campaign to reduce bad habits in your community.

Did you know...?

Drag down means to make someone feel down or depressed.

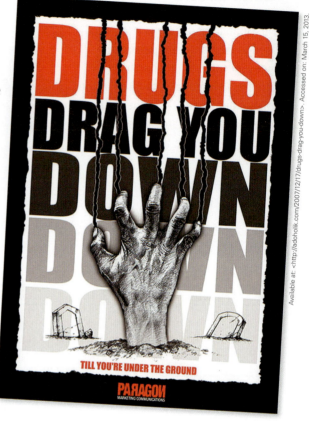

Suggested themes
- Anti-fast food campaign
- Anti-sedentarism campaign
- Anti-drug campaign
- Anti-alcohol campaign
- Anti-smoking campaign

Writing Steps
Organizing
- Look at other posters and observe their main elements.
- Choose a theme for your poster.
- Find a picture which creates impact.
- Write a creative message.
- Select adequate letter format(s) and color(s) for the multimodal composition.

Preparing the first draft
- Make a first draft.
- Use a dictionary to help you.

Peer editing
- Evaluate and discuss your text with a classmate.
- Make the necessary corrections.

Publishing
- Publish your poster on a wall newspaper or on Padlet.
- You can also make a digital poster using PowerPoint or Glogster, at <http://www.glogster.com/> (accessed on: May 28, 2014).
- Read more about posters at <http://www.wikihow.com/Make-a-Poster> (accessed on: May 28, 2014).

Go to Workbook, page 379, for more practice.

Genre: Poster

Purpose: To motivate people to have good habits

Tone: Informal (or Formal)

Setting: Wall newspaper or Padlet

Writer: You

Audience: Wall newspaper or Padlet readers

Learning tips

Chunking

It is easier to memorize information when you break it up into small chunks. This process of breaking up information into small significant amounts is called "chunking." You may not notice it, but you use "chunking" in many situations, for example, when you memorize your friend's cell phone number. It is easier to remember long numbers when you "chunk" them into groups of threes, fours, and fives. That's because most people can only remember about three, four, or five bits of information at a time.

Here are suggestions on how you can use "chunking" to remember information:
- Chunk vocabulary words by grouping them into parts of speech or other attributes.
- Chunk history by time periods or events.
- Chunk foreign language by grouping words into categories like clothes or occupations.
- If there is no pattern to the information you need to study, just group the items into three, four or five at a time, and that will help a lot.

Association

Another learning strategy is to associate each word or event with a person, place, thing, situation, etc. For example, you may connect what you are trying to learn with someone you know or with a movie character. When you have to learn vocabulary words, just write the new words with the definitions next to them, and then think of a person, thing, movie, or any strong association to help you remember the meaning of each word. For instance, "Jim Carrey is really **funny**." (**Funny** means amusing, hilarious, entertaining...)

Adapted from: "Top 12 Memory Strategies for Better Grades", by Linda Bress Silbert and Alvin J. Silbert.
Available at: <http://www.teachhub.com/top-12-memory-strategies-better-grades>. Accessed on: May 29, 2014.

Morgan Creek International/The Kobal Collection/The Picture Desk/AFP

Let's reflect on learning!

You are now invited to assess what you learned and how you learned. Finish the ideas below on an extra sheet of paper and become a more autonomous and reflective learner.

In Part 10

I learned _____

I liked _____

I need to review/learn more _____

My experiences with English outside school were _____

285

Let's study for Enem!

Enem Questions

Gênero

Letra de música

Competência de área 2

H7 – Relacionar um texto em LEM, as estruturas linguísticas, sua função e seu uso social.

War

Until the philosophy which holds one race superior
And another inferior
Is finally and permanently discredited and abandoned,
Everywhere is war – Me say war.

That until there is no longer
First class and second class citizens of any nation,
Until the color of a man's skin
Is of no more significance than the color of his eyes –
Me say war.
[…]

And until the ignoble and unhappy regimes
that hold our brothers in Angola, in Mozambique,
South Africa, sub-human bondage have been toppled,
Utterly destroyed –
Well, everywhere is war – Me say war.

War in the east, war in the west,
War up north, war down south –
War – war – Rumors of war.
And until that day, the African continent will not know peace.
We, Africans, will fight – we find it necessary –
And we know we shall win
As we are confident in the victory.
[…]

MARLEY, B. Disponível em: <http://www.sing365.com>. Acesso em: 30 jun. 2011. Fragmento.

> Preste a atenção ao título e à repetição de palavras para identificar o tema. Entretanto, às vezes, é preciso ir além da identificação do tema geral para responder a uma questão. No caso de "War", por exemplo, precisamos perceber que o tema geral (guerra) é delimitado pela noção de "persistência" por meio de expressões como *until*, *that until* e *and until* e de ideias associadas a diferenças raciais e sociais.

> O enunciado traz o verbo "alertar", e isso indica que vamos encontrar na letra referência(s) a algo negativo. Faça uma leitura detalhada (*scanning*) para localizar palavras ou expressões que o autor teria usado para nos "alertar" sobre algo ruim.

Bob Marley foi um artista popular e atraiu muitos fãs com suas canções. Ciente de sua influência social, na música *War*, o cantor se utiliza de sua arte para alertar sobre

A a inércia do continente africano diante das injustiças sociais.

B a persistência da guerra enquanto houver diferenças raciais e sociais.

C as acentuadas diferenças culturais entre os países africanos.

D as discrepâncias sociais entre moçambicanos e angolanos como causa de conflitos.

E a fragilidade das diferenças raciais e sociais como justificativas para o início de uma guerra.

Extraído de: Exame Nacional do Ensino Médio, 2011, Caderno 7 – AZUL – Página 3 (questão 94).

10 ■ Healthy Life

286

Part 10 (Healthy Life)

Typical questions of Enem

1. A imagem ao lado é a capa de um livro de receitas culinárias escrito por Gill Holcombe. A capa, além de trazer o título do livro e o nome do autor, tenta convencer o leitor a comprar a obra, afirmando que o livro contém receitas que

    a) ( ) demandam apenas três tipos de panelas encontradas em todas as cozinhas.

    b) ( ) estão dentro do orçamento de famílias que precisam de uma dieta balanceada.

    c) ( ) podem ser feitas por pessoas pobres que moram em apartamentos pequenos.

    d) ( ) são econômicas, rápidas e não demandam espaço ou utensílios sofisticados.

    e) ( ) têm como característica o uso de ingredientes simples e dietéticos.

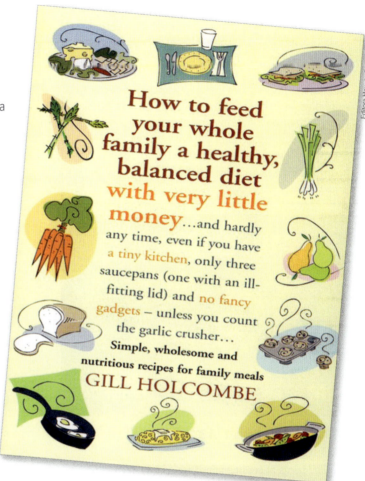

2. O *Holland Inventory* é uma ferramenta usada para mapear diferentes tipos de personalidade adequados a carreiras potenciais. A imagem ao lado reúne carreiras no campo da

    ( ) administração.
    ( ) comunicação.
    ( ) educação.
    ( ) estatística.
    ( ) saúde.

Exam Practice Questions (Vestibular)

Test-Taking Tips

Associate bits of information!

Reading science news may help you familiarize yourself with the language of this text genre. Try to associate bits of information, integrating verbal and non-verbal information whenever possible. Pay attention to the major concepts, definitions, causes, effects and arguments that the text may present. When the author makes comparisons and gives examples, as in the second paragraph of **Text 1**, link them to their descriptions and explanations. You can find more science news in the links below:
- <https://www.sciencenews.org/>
- <http://www.livescience.com/>

(both accessed on: January 18, 2014)

- **TEXT 1 – Questions 1 to 3**
Fuvest-SP, 2011

The perils of counterfeit drugs go way beyond being ripped off by dubious online pill-pushers. The World Health Organization (WHO) estimates that 50 per cent of all medicines sold online are worthless counterfeits. In developing nations fake pills may account for as much as 30 per cent of all drugs on the market. Even in the developed world, 1 per cent of medicines bought over the counter are fakes.

Some key events illustrate the risk these pose. In Nigeria, 2500 children died in 1995 after receiving fake meningitis vaccines. In Haiti, Bangladesh and Nigeria, around 400 people died in 1998 after being given paracetamol that had been prepared with diethylene glycol – a solvent used in wallpaper stripper. The fakers are nothing if not market-aware: in the face of an outbreak of H5N1 bird flu in 2005, they began offering fake Tamiflu.

What can be done? The WHO coordinates an umbrella body called the International Medical Products Anti-Counterfeiting Taskforce (IMPACT), an industry initiative that issues alerts when it finds anomalies in the medicine supply chain. Such events include sudden drops in wholesale prices, hinting at fakes coming onto the market, or the mimicking of anti-counterfeiting features on packaging, such as holograms or barcodes, says Nimo Ahmed, head of intelligence at the UK's Medicine and Healthcare Products Regulatory Agency.

New Scientist, 10 July 2010, p. 18. Adaptado.

1. De acordo com o texto, medicamentos falsificados, em geral,
   a) ( ) são consumidos apenas em países pobres e de pouco acesso à internet.
   b) ( ) encontram dificuldade de comercialização com o aparecimento de novas doenças.
   c) ( ) são ineficazes e contêm elementos danosos à saúde em sua composição.
   d) ( ) possuem embalagens atraentes que ludibriam o consumidor.
   e) ( ) vêm sendo criteriosamente apreendidos pela Organização Mundial da Saúde.

2. O texto informa que os falsificadores
   a) ( ) atuam na venda de remédios no mercado atacadista.
   b) ( ) roubam o selo de qualidade da Organização Mundial da Saúde.
   c) ( ) utilizam placebo nos medicamentos.
   d) ( ) apresentam-se como representantes oficiais da indústria farmacêutica.
   e) ( ) estão sempre alertas à demanda do mercado.

3. Segundo o texto, para conter a venda de medicamentos falsificados, a Organização Mundial da Saúde
   a) ( ) estimula a venda promocional de medicamentos importantes sempre que necessário.
   b) ( ) coordena o trabalho de uma organização que acompanha o fornecimento de remédios no mercado farmacêutico, alertando para possíveis irregularidades.
   c) ( ) exige que todos os medicamentos exibam o holograma da organização e o código de barras.
   d) ( ) controla o lançamento de novos medicamentos no mercado, a exemplo do Tamiflu.
   e) ( ) autoriza apenas a comercialização de medicamentos que passaram pelo crivo das agências sanitárias internacionais.

Part 10 (Healthy Life)

- **TEXT 2 – Questions 4 and 5**
PUC-PR, 2012

Watch Out for Fruit Juice!

There's a big difference between a "fruit juice" and a "fruit drink."

If it says "fruit juice", it must contain undiluted fruit juice. This can have up to 4% added sugar.

If it says "fruit drink", it must contain at least 5% fruit juice. It can contain a lot more than that.

The pictures on the pack can easily be misinterpreted by a harried shopper. Even if you can't do it in-store, stop and have a read of the packaging when you're at home: the only way to know what you're getting with fruit juices and fruit drinks is to read the label properly.

What the labels mean

Many fruit juices are made from concentrated fruit juice.

The juice has been concentrated by removing some of the water, which makes it a lot cheaper to transport. It is then reconstituted by adding water back.

These juices sometimes have vitamins added back in as well, as some of the water soluble vitamins will be lost in the concentration process.

For juices made from concentrate, you'll see one of these on the pack:

"Made from concentrate"

"Reconstituted" (from concentrate)

For juices NOT made from concentrate, you'll see one of these on the pack:

"Not from concentrate"

"Pure" (not from concentrate and contains no additives)

"Fresh" (not from concentrate and contains no additives)

<http://www.healthyfood.co.nz/articles/2007/september/fruit-juice-orfruit-drink_September, 2012>

4. Choose the alternative that is TRUE according to the text.
   a) (   ) "Fruit juice" must contain diluted fruit juice and up to 4% sugar added.
   b) (   ) "Fruit drink" must contain at least 5% fruit juice or a lot less than that.
   c) (   ) Fruit juices made from concentrate have the word "fresh" on the pack.
   d) (   ) In order to make transportation cheaper, the juice is concentrated by removing some of the water.
   e) (   ) Fruit juices not made from concentrate are also called "reconstituted."

5. Read the following sentence from the text:
   "For juices made from concentrate, you'll see one of these on the pack."

   The contraction **'ll** is a short form for **will** and it stands for the future tense. There are other ways of referring to the future.

   Select the alternatives that are in the future tense:
   I. Vitamins are going to be added to the fruit juices.
   II. Supermarkets are selling both kinds of juices.
   III. Sugar and water'll be reduced to make juices healthier.
   IV. The juice ingredient is going to be changed.

   a) (   ) Alternatives III and IV are correct.
   b) (   ) Alternatives I and III are correct.
   c) (   ) Alternatives II and IV are correct.
   d) (   ) Alternatives II and III are correct.
   e) (   ) Alternatives I, III and IV are correct.

- **TEXT 3 – Questions 6 and 7**
IFG, 2014

Available at: <http://www.azcentral.com/thingstodo/comics/kingcomics.html?feature_id=Hagar_The_Horrible&feature_date=2013-11-02>. Access on: 3 Nov. 2013.

6. By reading the comic strip, it is correct to affirm that Hagar has
   a) (   ) thought the doctor was kidding him.
   b) (   ) mistaken the doctor's prescriptions.
   c) (   ) misunderstood what the doctor said.
   d) (   ) preferred to consider the doctor's advice.
   e) (   ) believed the doctor won't call him back.

7. The verb *get out*, in the sentence "He's thinking of getting out of the medical profession", can be replaced, without changing the meaning, by:
   a) (   ) go into.
   b) (   ) search for.
   c) (   ) find out.
   d) (   ) start over.
   e) (   ) give up.

PART

11 Yes, We Can

Learning plan

Learning how to talk about abilities

Learning how to read concept maps

Expressing and justifying opinion about multiple intelligences and careers

Understanding and taking surveys

Discussing affirmative action programs

Learning how to report what someone has said or written

Learning how to write a testimonial

CONCEPT MAPS
What are they?

They are graphical tools for organizing and representing knowledge. They include concepts, usually enclosed in circles or boxes of some type, and relationships between concepts indicated by a connecting line linking two concepts. Words on the line, referred to as *linking words* or *linking phrases*, specify the relationship between the two concepts. [...]

Available at: <http://cmap.ihmc.us/docs/conceptmap.html>. Accessed on: December 9, 2013.

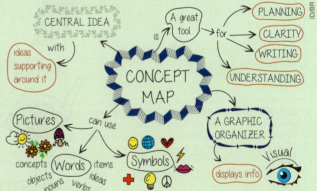

You can create concept maps (also called *mind maps*) with paper and pencil, or you can use some free tools on the Web. One of them is **Bubbl.us**, available at <https://bubbl.us/> (accessed on: December 9, 2013).

To begin your Bubbl.us concept map, you type the main idea in the first bubble. Then you can click on this bubble and add other new bubbles with more information. You can change colors, move the bubbles, and add arrows. If you are interested in using this tool, you can watch a tutorial video at <http://www.multimediatrainingvideos.com/mind/> (accessed on: December 9, 2013).

UNIT 21 Intelligences and abilities

Language in action

- Learn how to talk about abilities
- Learn how to read concept maps
- Express and justify opinion about multiple intelligences and careers
- Learn how to give additional information about people, things or places

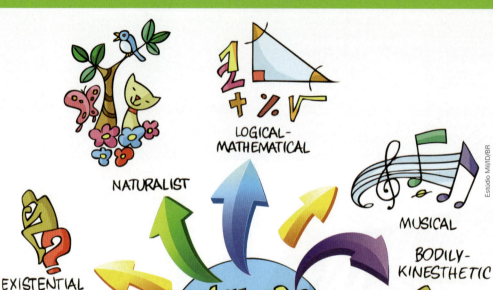

Intelligence types
Logical-Mathematical: An ability to develop equations and proofs, make calculations, and solve abstract problems.
Musical: An ability to produce, remember, and make meaning of different patterns of sound.
Bodily-Kinesthetic: An ability to use one's own body to create products or solve problems.
Intrapersonal: An ability to recognize and understand one's own moods, desires, motivations, and intentions.
Spatial: An ability to recognize and manipulate large-scale and fine-grained spatial images.
Interpersonal: An ability to recognize and understand other people's moods, desires, motivations, and intentions.
Linguistic: An ability to analyze information and create products involving oral and written language such as speeches, books, and memos.
Existential: An ability to consider "big questions" about life, death, love, and being.
Naturalist: An ability to identify and distinguish among different types of plants, animals, and weather formations that are found in the natural world.

Source: <http://howardgardner01.files.wordpress.com/2012/06/443-davis-christodoulou-seider-mi-article.pdf>. Accessed on: December 9, 2013.

Howard Gardner, 2011.

"An intelligence is the ability to solve problems, or to create products, that are valued within one or more cultural settings."

GARDNER, H. *Frames of Mind: The Theory of Multiple Intelligences.* New York: Basic Books, 2011. p. xxviii.

› Lead-in

1. Based on the diagram on the left page, what do you understand by "multiple intelligences," proposed by Howard Gardner?

2. Read this **can do** list and check (✔) the things that have to do with you. Then share your answers with a classmate.

I can

1. use different words to express myself. ◯
2. work well on my own. ◯
3. sense the moods and feelings of other people. ◯
4. work with my hands. ◯
5. work with plants and animals. ◯
6. understand color combinations. ◯
7. quickly grasp cause and effect relationships. ◯
8. get actively involved with social causes. ◯
9. participate in active sports. ◯
10. pick out different instruments when I listen to a piece of music. ◯
11. understand my feelings and how I will react to situations. ◯
12. notice similarities and differences in plants and other things in nature. ◯
13. sort out arguments between friends. ◯
14. remember pieces of music easily. ◯
15. easily use words to defend my point of view. ◯
16. easily read charts, maps, and floor plans. ◯
17. play brainteasers and logic puzzles. ◯
18. see how something relates to the "big picture." ◯

Sources: <http://www.collegesuccess1.com/InstructorManual4thEd/Learning%20Style/MI_quiz.pdf> and <http://surfaquarium.com/MI/profiles/index.htm>. Accessed on: December 9, 2013.

3. In pairs, identify the multiple intelligences in activity 2. Then write the number of each sentence next to its appropriate type of intelligence below.

Intrapersonal: _____ Spatial: _____ Musical: _____

Interpersonal: _____ Naturalist: _____ Bodily-Kinesthetic: _____

Linguistic: _____ Existential: _____ Logical-Mathematical: _____

4. Many experts believe that understanding the Multiple Intelligences (MI) theory can help students improve their learning. From these options choose possible ways you think this could happen.

( ) I can select the resources that are more appropriate for the "intelligences" I identify myself with.

( ) I can stop torturing myself trying to understand what is impossible for me to dominate.

( ) I can be more helpful in group work if I know what my strongest intelligences are.

( ) I can explore more effectively my intellectual capacities and abilities.

( ) I can put forth more effort to develop and stimulate intelligences I am not so good at.

( ) I can trust in my natural abilities and depend exclusively on them in every learning situation.

> Let's read!

Before you read…
- What makes a good leader? In pairs, list some major qualities of a successful leader.
- Think of leaders in your community and in the world. Do they have the qualities you listed above?

Hint
Reading the text quickly without focusing on details can help grasp the general idea.

1. Read the article below quickly and answer the two questions.

a) Does it mention the names of any great leader? _____

b) Does it mention any qualities of a good leader? If so, which one(s)? _____

Successful Leaders Need Multiple Intelligences
Published on May 7, 2009 by Ray Williams in Wired for Success

Do smarter people make better leaders? The answer is no... and... yes.

If you mean by smart, only IQ, then the answer is no. There is no evidence to support the link between IQ and great leadership. In fact, there is a lot of evidence to the reverse. If you mean by smart, emotional intelligence or EQ, as described by Daniel Goleman and others, who describe it as the ability to communicate positively with others at an emotional level, then the answer is yes. In addition, research by Goleman suggests that social intelligence or SQ, which requires the individual to understand social situations, can also influence others positively, as well as ecological intelligence or ECQ, which talks about our awareness of our place in the planetary ecological system.

Howard Gardner, one of the foremost experts on human intelligence, proposes that people use at least seven relatively autonomous intelligences, including linguistic, musical, logical-mathematical, spatial, bodily-kinesthetic, interpersonal and intrapersonal, and while they are not necessarily dependent on each other, they often act collaboratively.

[…]

We can add to these intelligences Success IQ, or SIQ, which is the street smarts version of intelligence and almost never taught in school. Success IQ is the ability to understand and apply the principles and systems on how to be successful in multiple contexts of life and work. There is evidence to show that the most successful people, in most realms of life and work, were never the ones at the top of their class, nor deemed to have been chosen "most likely to succeed." And while it may be argued that success is defined differently by people, most people accept some general measures of wealth, achievement, happiness, contribution to others and fulfillment as being valid measures.

It's clear from research evidence of failed and unsuccessful leaders in recent years that academic learning and training or natural intellectual ability alone is insufficient to prepare for and execute good leadership.

The good news is that emotional intelligence, social intelligence and success intelligence can all be taught and learned, providing individuals with the tools to become successful leaders. A greater focus particularly on success IQ by our education system, organizations and individuals would have a significant impact on greater numbers of individuals experiencing success in our society.

Adapted from: <http://www.psychologytoday.com/blog/wired-success/200905/successful-leaders-need-multiple-intelligences>. Accessed on: May 29, 2014.

Ray Williams is a columnist of *PsychologyToday.com*, a magazine which gathers academics, psychiatrists, psychologists, and other experts.

2. The article you have just read was published on a website devoted to

( ) entertainment.

( ) culture.

( ) psychology.

( ) the multiple intelligences theory.

3. Who wrote it?

_____

4. When was this article published?

_____

5. Based on the author's ideas, what is the key to success?

_____
_____
_____

6. According to the author, what would increase the number of individuals experiencing success in our society? _____

_____
_____

> **Did you know…?**
>
> The abbreviation IQ stands for **intelligence quotient** and is a measure of a person's intelligence.

7. Discuss these questions with your classmates.

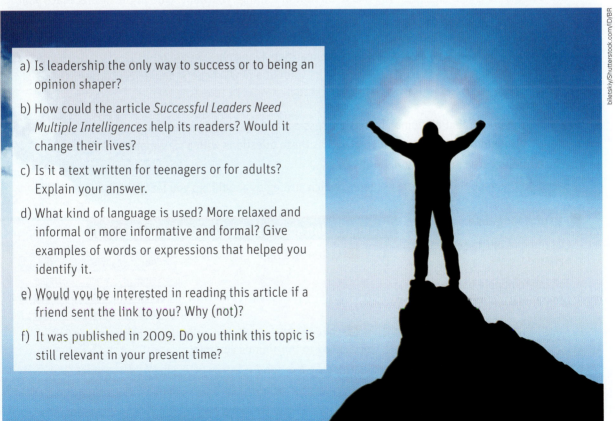

a) Is leadership the only way to success or to being an opinion shaper?

b) How could the article *Successful Leaders Need Multiple Intelligences* help its readers? Would it change their lives?

c) Is it a text written for teenagers or for adults? Explain your answer.

d) What kind of language is used? More relaxed and informal or more informative and formal? Give examples of words or expressions that helped you identify it.

e) Would you be interested in reading this article if a friend sent the link to you? Why (not)?

f) It was published in 2009. Do you think this topic is still relevant in your present time?

> Let's listen and talk!

1. Look at the text in activity 2 and answer these questions.

a) What is the topic? _____

b) Which words in this text are similar in Portuguese? Find at least seven.

_____

_____

2. ⊚**60** Listen to a text about multiple intelligences and fill in the blanks with the missing words. You can also try to write them down before listening to the audio, based on the hints given by the text.

> Visual or spatial learners think in terms of visual space. If you enjoy _____, puzzles, _____ maps or daydreaming you may be a spatial or visual learner. If this is you, here are _____ ways you can study a language that may help.
>
> 1. **Flashcards**: Create flashcards _____ pictures and visual imagery instead of words. This will help you remember new vocabulary.
> 2. _____ **notes**: When taking notes use _____ colors and organize verb tenses into charts.
> 3. **Visual stories**: Draw or take pictures and label what is in _____ or what people are _____. You can even create a story about _____ using photographs.
> 4. **Verb posters**: To remember how different verb tenses are used, create posters with pictures of things you used to do, what you did on your last _____ or birthday, _____ you like to do now and things you want to do in the future. Place your posters around your _____ to help you remember how to talk about different events.
>
> *Remember*! No matter what you decide to do, learning a language should be _____, so be creative and enjoy _____ about a new language and a new culture.
>
> Transcribed from: <http://www.youtube.com/watch?v=pAfeOQR1HG0>. Accessed on: December 9, 2013.

3. Howard Gardner says that **all** human beings possess each of the intelligences, but each of us is more attuned to some than to others. Discuss these questions with a classmate.

a) Which intelligence comes most naturally to you?

b) Based on the multiple intelligences theory, which strategies could help you learn English?

■ Useful language

Listening to music can help me...

Talking to people online can be interesting because...

Making concept maps could help me...

Pronunciation spot – Ending sounds: /m/, /n/, /ŋ/

1. ⊚**61** Listen and repeat the words.

/m/	/n/	/ŋ/
so**me**	whe**n**	thi**ng**
roo**m**	fu**n**	do**ing**
drea**m**	ca**n**	u**sing**

2. ⊚**62** Listen to the words and write the symbols /m/, /n/ or /ŋ/ according to the sounds you hear.

learning / /   son / /   sing / /   roam / /

song / /   win / /   him / /   situation / /

thing / /   networking / /   run / /   system / /

> Let's focus on language!

> **Let's remember!**
> We use **can + verb** to express an ability that we have: *I can work with plants and animals.*
> To form the negative, we use **cannot** (formal) or **can't** (informal conversation or writing): *I **can't** work with plants or animals.*
> To make a question, put **can** before the subject: *Can you play brainteasers and puzzles?*

1. Read these two statements from the **can do** list in the *Lead-in* section. Then check (✓) the correct option.

   > I can play brainteasers and logic puzzles.
   > I can work with plants and animals.

   In both statements, you are saying that
   ( ) you have the ability to do it.
   ( ) you need skills to do it.

2. Look at the information about linguistic intelligence in this concept map and complete the sentences below accordingly.

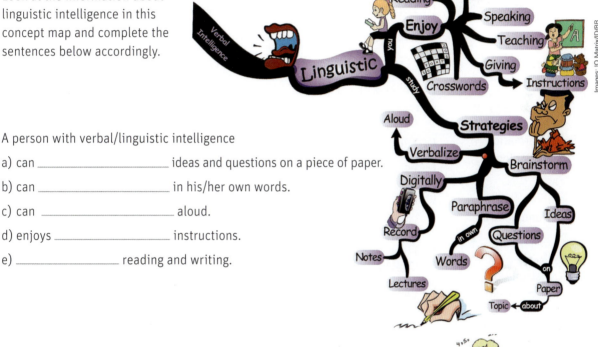

   A person with verbal/linguistic intelligence
   a) can _____ ideas and questions on a piece of paper.
   b) can _____ in his/her own words.
   c) can _____ aloud.
   d) enjoys _____ instructions.
   e) _____ reading and writing.

3. Look at the information about logical intelligence in this other concept map. List five things people with primary logical intelligence can easily do.

   _____
   _____
   _____
   _____
   _____

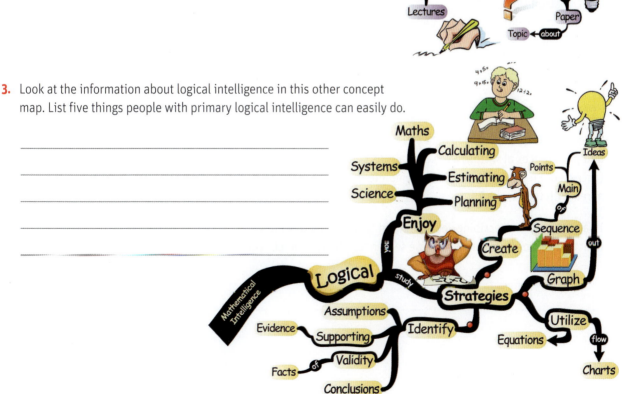

297

4. Use the information in the concept maps on the previous page to write about things that you **can** and **can't** do. Use your notebook. Share your work with a partner.

5. Look at the six career options in the left column below. Then read some of the abilities required to pursue these careers. Match the columns. Remember: there are three abilities for each career option.

A. Agriculture, Food & Natural Resources

( ) Work with numbers and detailed information.

( ) Reason clearly and logically to solve complex problems.

( ) Visualize objects in three dimensions from flat drawings.

( ) Make the best use of the earth's natural resources.

B. Business, Management & Administration

( ) Drive or ride.

( ) Operate machines and keep them in good repair.

( ) Communicate easily, tactfully, and courteously.

C. Hospitality & Tourism

( ) Create reports and communicate ideas.

( ) Work with computers.

( ) Design efficient processes.

D. Information Technology

( ) Protect the environment.

( ) Solve mechanical problems.

( ) Work with one's hands and learn that way.

E. Manufacturing

( ) Work with all ages and types of people.

( ) Use hand and power tools and operate equipment/ machinery.

F. Distribution, Transportation & Logistics

( ) Make business contact with people.

( ) Play video games and figure out how they work.

( ) Organize activities in which people enjoy themselves.

Adapted from: <http://www.careertech.org/file_download/9c847753-a889-4b50-ae56-25ffef6e6118>. Accessed on: December 9, 2013.

6. Take an online career test to help you identify areas of study that may suit your abilities and preferences at <http://www.educations.com/educationtest/starttest?testid=18> (accessed on: December 9, 2013). Complete their personality quiz and decide: Do you agree with the results?

7. Imagine you are describing your potential to a prospective employer. Which of the abilities in activity 5 do you have? Write true sentences about yourself using *I can...*

_____

_____

_____

_____

8. Which abilities in activity 5 are more challenging for you and would require more effort? Write true sentences about yourself using *I can't/cannot...*

_____

_____

_____

_____

9. Work in pairs. Interview each other using the **can do** list in the *Lead-in* section as well as the abilities in activity 5. Look at the examples in the speech bubbles.

> Can you work well on your own?

> Can you work with all ages and types of people?

> Yes, I can.

> No, I can't.

10. Based on the answers in activity 9, talk to your classmate and come to a consensus about his or her primary intelligence.

> ### Useful language
>
> I believe your primary intelligence is...
> Your primary intelligence is associated with...
> I find your abilities related to...
> It seems you'll be successful in... because...
> Your abilities seem to be associated with... because...

11. Look at these excerpts from the article *Successful Leaders Need Multiple Intelligences*. Then answer the questions.

"If you mean by smart, emotional intelligence or EQ, as described by Daniel Goleman and others, **who describe it as the ability to communicate positively with others at an emotional level**, then the answer is yes."

"We can add to these intelligences Success IQ, or SIQ, **which is the street smarts version of intelligence and almost never taught in school**."

a) Is the information in bold essential to understand the meaning of the excerpt, or is it extra information?

_____

b) Which piece of information does **who** refer to?

_____

c) Which piece of information does **which** refer to?

_____

> The phrases in bold are called non-defining relative clauses. We use them to give additional information about people (**who**) and things (**which**).

12. Complete the blanks with **who** or **which**.

> ### Emotional Intelligence Predicts Job Performance
> *ScienceDaily* (Oct. 27, 2010)
>
> Emotional intelligence is a strong predictor of job performance, according to a new study conducted at Virginia Commonwealth University that helps settle the ongoing debate in a much-disputed area of research.
>
> "The Relation Between Emotional Intelligence and Job Performance: A Meta-Analysis," _____ has been published online by the *Journal of Organizational Behavior* and will appear in a future issue of the journal, builds upon years of existing studies in the area of emotional intelligence, _____ is a measure of someone's ability to understand the emotions of themselves and others.
>
> [...]
>
> The study was conducted at the VCU School of Business by Ernest H. O'Boyle Jr., _____ received his Ph.D. in management at VCU and is now an assistant professor of management at Longwood University; Ronald H. Humphrey, professor of management at VCU; Jeffrey M. Pollack, _____ received his Ph.D. in management at VCU and is now an assistant professor of management at the University of Richmond; Thomas H. Hawver, a Ph.D. candidate in management at VCU; and Paul A. Story, _____ received his Ph.D. in psychology at VCU and is now a visiting professor of psychology at the College of William & Mary.
>
> Available at: <http://www.sciencedaily.com/releases/2010/10/101027153041.htm>. Accessed on: December 9, 2013.

13. Read some information about Albert Einstein's life. Join the two statements, as in the example.

a) Albert worried about his mother. She was getting older and frail.

   Albert worried about his mother, who was getting older and frail.

b) In 1905, Einstein published five of the most important papers in the history of science. The papers were written in his "spare time."

   _____

   _____

Albert Einstein in 1947.

c) Einstein published five papers in a single year. He had been thinking about physics since childhood.

   _____

   _____

d) He argued that light came in little bits. This laid the foundation for quantum mechanics.

   _____

   _____

e) In his theory of special relativity, space and time were threads in a common fabric. This common fabric could be bent, stretched, and twisted.

   _____

   _____

Adapted from: <http://science.nasa.gov/science-news/science-at-nasa/2005/23mar_spacealien/>. Accessed on: December 10, 2013.

Profession spot

> ## Arts and humanities

1. Look at these professions. Which one goes with each picture? After you have matched the words to the images, tell a classmate what you know about these careers.

A) Craft Artists
B) **Museum Technicians**
C) *Musicians*
D) Public Relation (PR) Specialists
E) Actors
F) *Interpreters and Translators*
G) **GRAPHIC DESIGNERS**
H) **Interior Designers**

2. Read these job descriptions and find the corresponding words in the previous activity. Write the professions.

	play parts in stage, television, or motion picture productions. Interpret roles to entertain or inform an audience.
	create or reproduce hand-made objects for sale and exhibition.
	design or create graphics to meet specific commercial or promotional needs.
	translate or interpret written, oral, or sign language text into another language for others.
	play one or more musical instruments in recital, in accompaniment, or as members of a musical group.
	prepare specimens for museum collection and exhibits.
	plan, design, and furnish interiors of residential, commercial, or industrial buildings.
	engage in promoting or creating good will for individuals, groups, or organizations.

Adapted from: <https://careerzone.ny.gov/views/careerzone/search/search.jsf>. Accessed on: December 10, 2013.

3. Talk to a classmate about these questions.

a) Which of these humanities professions are you most and least inclined to choose?

b) Which ones do you think are more appropriate for your brother/sister/best friend? Why?

UNIT

22 Affirmative action

Language in action

- Understand and do surveys
- Discuss affirmative action programs
- Learn how to report what someone has said or written

Survey Results Suggesting Majority Support for Affirmative Action		
Item	**Source[a]**	**Responses in %**
Do you favor or oppose affirmative action programs for minorities and women for job hiring in the workplace?	Gallup[b] Date: 8/2001 Size: 1,523	Favor: 58 Oppose: 36 Don't know/Refused: 5
Do you favor or oppose affirmative action programs for minorities and women for admission to colleges and universities?	Gallup[c] Date: 8/2001 Size: 1,523	Favor: 56 Oppose: 39 Don't know/Refused: 6
[...] Do you think we need to increase, keep the same, or decrease affirmative action programs in this country?	Gallup[d] Date: 4/2003 Size: 1,044	Increase: 28 Keep the same: 37 Decrease: 26 Don't know/Refused: 10
Do you generally favor or oppose affirmative action programs for women and minorities?	CNN/USA Today[e] Date: 1/2000 Size: 1,027	Favor: 58 Oppose: 33 Not sure: 9
What's the best thing to do with affirmative action programs giving preference to some minorities – leave the programs as they are, change the programs, or do away with the programs entirely?	CBS/NY Times[f] Date: 12/1997 Size: 1,258	Leave as are: 24 Keep but change: 43 Do away with: 25 Not sure: 8
[...] Do you favor affirmative action programs with quotas, or do you favor affirmative action programs only without quotas, or do you oppose all affirmative action programs?	Associated Press[g] Date: 7/1995 Size: 1,006	Favor with quotas: 16 Favor without quotas: 47 Oppose all: 28 Don't know: 9

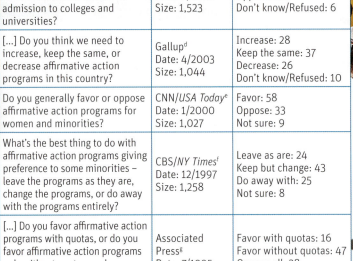

[a]All polls are from the Roper Center for Public Opinion (RCPO) or Gallup. [b]RCPO (2001a). [c]RCPO (2001b). [d]Ludwig (2003). [e]RCPO (2000). [f]RCPO (1997). [g]RCPO (1995b).

Available at: <http://www.understandingprejudice.org/readroom/articles/affirm.htm>. Accessed on: December 11, 2013.

› Lead-in

1. Based on your knowledge and on the text and images on the previous page, what are affirmative action programs?

   _____

2. What types of affirmative action programs are being represented in these images?

   _____

   _____

3. The chart on the previous page presents data retrieved from

   ( ) opinion articles.　　　( ) surveys.　　　( ) books.

4. The data presented in the chart reflect

   ( ) personal opinions.　　( ) laws and rights.　　( ) governmental policies.

5. Do you know any affirmative action programs in Brazil? Search the Web or any other sources and name programs involving the "minorities" and women.

   a) Public school students: _____

   b) Race: _____

   c) Low-income communities: _____

   d) Disabled: _____

   e) Women: _____

6. Refer back to the chart on the previous page and find out some of the characteristics of a survey. Use the ideas below to prompt your analysis.

   a) Type of questions: _____

   b) Expected answers: _____

   c) Presentation of results: _____

   d) Format: _____

   e) Information about the survey: _____

   f) Source: _____

7. Study the nonverbal information in some of the pictures. How do the following elements help build meaning?

   a) Color: _____

   b) Font face: _____

   c) Picture D: _____

   _____

   d) Picture F: _____

   _____

303

> Let's read!

Before you read...

- We can commonly find reports on what another person said in
  ( ) profiles.   ( ) testimonials.   ( ) biographies.   ( ) recipes.
  ( ) gossip columns.   ( ) straplines.   ( ) headlines.   ( ) articles.

- The three texts (A, B and C) in activity 1 are examples of _____

Hint
Remember that we don't need to know **all the words** to understand a text.

1. Now read the texts below and answer the questions on the next page.

A

Eva Jefferson Paterson - *Executive Director of the Lawyers Committee for Civil Rights, one of California's most brilliant attorneys.* She is an African American and a beneficiary of affirmative action.

"I got into Boalt Law School (U. C. Berkeley) through an affirmative action program, a program that gave me the opportunity to study law. Affirmative action gave me an opportunity, but I cracked the books, did the work, and passed the tests."

"Never apologize for affirmative action," she tells the crowd, "I am proud of affirmative action because I am qualified."

B

Albert Vetere Lannon - Affirmative action programs are not unique to women and African Americans. White males are beneficiaries of many types of special programs, including programs that make exceptions to strict meritocracy. Albert Vetere Lannon lives in San Francisco. He writes: "The fact is that we older white men are beneficiaries of affirmative action. I'm a tenured teacher now, but seven years ago, I was a high school dropout. I entered San Francisco State University at age 50 through the re-entry program, a form of affirmative action. I graduated with honors and am working on a master's degree in history."

"Affirmative action benefited me directly, and I am now able to give something back to the society that gave me a hand."

Both texts adapted from: <http://www.inmotionmagazine.com/rocktr.html>. Accessed on: December 11, 2013.

C

Affirmative Action Tops NAACP List

By Michael A. Fletcher Washington Post Staff Writer Tuesday, July 14, 1998; Page A03

ATLANTA, July, 13—Declaring that "race and skin color" still dominate every aspect of American life, NAACP President Kweisi Mfume said today that protecting the nation's embattled affirmative action programs must remain at the top of the civil rights group's agenda.

Available at: <http://www.washingtonpost.com/wp-srv/politics/special/affirm/stories/naacp071498.htm>. Accessed on: December 11, 2013.

a) What is the common subject of the three texts? _____

b) Who wrote each text? _____

c) Is it correct to say that the three writers are beneficiaries of affirmative action programs?

_____

d) Based on your answer in **c**, can we say that the purpose of the three texts is to write about personal experiences?

_____

2. Read the texts on the previous page again and check (✓) the appropriate boxes.

a) This text reports facts indirectly, that is, someone reporting what another person said:

(　) Text A　　　　　　(　) Text B　　　　　　(　) Text C

b) These texts report facts directly, that is, they bring the exact words the person used:

(　) Text A　　　　　　(　) Text B　　　　　　(　) Text C

3. Circle the part of the text on the previous page which shows that the writer is reporting facts indirectly.

4. Underline the parts of the text on the previous page which show that the writer is reporting facts directly.

5. What opposing opinion about affirmative action programs can we infer from Eva's statements?

(　) Many people believe affirmative action programs make beneficiaries work harder.

(　) Some people believe beneficiaries of these programs don't have to work hard.

(　) Many people consider affirmative action programs totally useless.

6. Study this excerpt of text C carefully. Pay attention to the highlighted words.

a) "Declaring that 'race and skin color' still dominate every aspect of American life, NAACP President Kweisi Mfume said today that protecting the nation's embattled affirmative action programs must remain at the top of the civil rights group's agenda."

Now look at these other possible versions of the excerpt above.

b) "Declaring that 'race and skin color' still dominate every aspect of American life, NAACP President Kweisi Mfume explained today that protecting the nation's embattled affirmative action programs must remain at the top of the civil rights group's agenda."

c) "Declaring that 'race and skin color' still dominate every aspect of American life, NAACP President Kweisi Mfume insisted today that protecting the nation's embattled affirmative action programs must remain at the top of the civil rights group's agenda."

Work with a classmate. Discuss what changes in each situation above (**a**, **b**, and **c**) depending on the verb the writer uses to report what others have said.

> **Did you know...?**
>
> **NAACP** stands for National Association for the Advancement of Colored People, a civil rights organization founded in 1909. The expression "colored people" is considered offensive today.

Beyond the lines...

a) Would an elderly person in Brazil have to resort to an inclusion program in order to get higher education?

b) Do you think that the existence of associations helps minority groups to become more visible and respected in a society?

305

› **Let's listen and talk!**

Before you listen...

- What is a testimonial? Have you ever listened to one?
- What words do you expect to find in testimonials about affirmative action programs? Write your predictions in this chart.

Verbs	Nouns	Adjectives

> **Hint**
> Be prepared to pay attention to everything, but **avoid focusing on one thing in particular**.

1. ◎**63** Listen to a street survey by Lori Harfenist, the Resident's reporter. What does she want to know?

_____

2. ◎**63** Listen to the recording again and answer these questions about the second interviewee's answers.

a) Does she believe in affirmative action as a policy?

_____

b) The issue discussed in this part of the survey is related to

( ) racism.   ( ) sexism.   ( ) sexual orientation.

Pronunciation spot – Letter *y* in word final position

1. ◎**64** Listen to the words and pay attention to how the letter **y** is pronounced.

| opportunity | diversity | society |
| historically | minority | policy |

2. ◎**65** Listen to the words and discuss with a classmate why it is important to pronounce the letter **y** in word final position.

men	many	blood	bloody
stud	study	sit	city
occasional	occasionally	noise	noisy

11 ■ Yes, We Can

3. Take a class survey to find out what actions your classmates consider "sexist." In pairs, walk around the class and interview seven students. Use tally marks (𝍬) and the chart below. Make graphs and report your findings using ideas from the box *Useful language*.

	Yes	No	%
a) Is it sexist for a man to open a door for a woman?			
b) Is it sexist for a woman to use her husband's last name after marriage?			
c) Is it sexist to refer to a ship (or any inanimate object) as "she" or "her"?			
d) Is it sexist for a man to want to "show off" his wife or girlfriend?			
e) Is it sexist to think that women are different from men?			
Free question:			

Adapted from: <http://www.gather.com/viewArticle.action?articleId=281474977359922>. Accessed on: December 11, 2013.

4. Have you ever heard a testimonial on experiences lived by minorities in your school/city? In pairs, list some possible actions that can be taken in your school/city regarding one or more of the following topics.

Bullying: _____
_____

Sexism: _____
_____

Racism: _____
_____

Homophobia: _____
_____

Useful language

Activity 3
The survey investigates/is about…
Participants include…
Results indicate/suggest that…
(number) % of the participants said that…

Activity 4
The testimonial is about…
She/He is a/an… (profession/ ethnic group)
She/He said that…
She/He also says/claims/ recognizes that…
She/He concludes that…

5. Based on your notes in activity 4, report to your classmates and your teacher the experience and your suggestions for action. Use the language in the box *Useful language* to help you.

> Let's focus on language!

1. In our daily conversations, we often tell people what others have told us. Study this example.

> *ATLANTA, July, 13 - Declaring that "race and skin color" still dominate every aspect of American life, NAACP President Kweisi Mfume said today that protecting the nation's embattled affirmative action programs must remain at the top of the civil rights group's agenda.*
>
> Available at: <http://www.washingtonpost.com/wp-srv/politics/special/affirm/stories/naacp071498.htm>. Accessed on: February 21, 2014.

a) Which verb in the example above indicates that what we read corresponds to what another person has said?

_____

b) Who is responsible for the opinion in the example above: the author of the text or the person mentioned in it?

_____

c) The structure which appears in the example above is normally used

( ) in reports by the media.

( ) to tell someone what we have heard or read in a speech, TV program, interview, etc.

( ) to directly quote what someone said or wrote.

2. Complete this grammar rule by underlining the appropriate option in the last sentence.

> We can report what someone has said in two ways. We use **direct speech** to quote the exact words that someone said (in written text we indicate it with quotations marks: " "). We use **indirect speech** to give the meaning of the words, but not necessarily using the same words. The excerpt in activity 1 is a case of **direct speech** / **indirect speech**.

3. Look at these pieces of news. Underline the verbs used to report what someone has said.

a) "(...) a book by two political scientists suggests that people do not always say what they really think about race (...)"

b) "University of Texas officials agree that the scarcity of minority students is a direct result of new prohibitions on racial preferences (...)"

c) "The University of California's two premier campuses are reporting that their first undergraduate classes chosen without the use of affirmative action will have an extraordinarily low number of black and Hispanic students."

d) "The Clinton administration's five-month review of government affirmative action programs concludes that the vast majority of them should continue (...)"

Available at: <http://www.washingtonpost.com/wp-srv/politics/special/affirm/keystories.htm>. Accessed on: December 11, 2013.

Vocabulary corner

Match the reporting verbs on the left to their definitions on the right.

a) explain   ( ) to have the same opinion

b) say   ( ) to announce something officially or publicly

c) agree   ( ) to make something clear by giving information about it

d) suggest   ( ) to give information about something to someone

e) declare   ( ) to express a thought, opinion, or suggestion, or to state a fact or instruction

f) report   ( ) to mention an idea, plan, or action for other people to consider

> One of the most common verbs used to report statements is **said**, but there are other reporting verbs that can be used in many different situations. For example: *announced, argued, asked, begged, believed, complained, cried, declared, defended, demanded, denied, claimed, recognized, requested, stated, warned, whispered,* etc.

4. Read these two excerpts and decide if the sentences are in direct (**D**) or indirect (**I**) speech. Write **D** or **I** in the boxes accordingly.

a) "Do you think African-Americans still need affirmative action?" I asked ☐. "No," he said ☐. The average black American child would meet racism in his lifetime, Obama said, but not the pervasive hatred faced by earlier generations, and not of a kind that could not be overcome by energy and initiative ☐. [...] Obama said much the same thing during last year's presidential campaign when ABC's George Stephanopoulos asked him if daughters Sasha and Malia should get preferred treatment ☐. "I think that my daughters should probably be treated by any admissions officer as folks who are pretty advantaged," Obama said ☐.

Available at: <http://www.usnews.com/opinion/articles/2009/06/10/obamas-election-shows-that-affirmative-actions-day-has-passed>. Accessed on: December 11, 2013.

b) Relatively few people, white or black, report having real life experiences with affirmative action: only 16% overall have been helped or hurt ☐. Among those who've been affected, whites generally say they were hurt while blacks say they have been helped ☐.

Available at: <http://www.intellectualtakeout.org/library/chart-graph/personally-affected-affirmative-action>.
Accessed on: December 11, 2013.

Helder Almeida/Shutterstock.com/

309

5. Imagine you were present when all the protests represented in these pictures took place. Report each situation to a friend. Use different reporting verbs. The first one is done for you as an example, but you can recreate it as well.

a) They defended that women must be treated with justice.

b) _____

c) _____

d) _____

6. To report what others have said, we usually change the verb of the sentence that we are reporting. Study these examples and answer the questions.

> I am proud of affirmative action.

Eva Jefferson Paterson

> I graduated with honors and am working on a master's degree in history.

Albert Vetere Lannon

Eva said that she **was** proud of affirmative action.

Albert said that he **had graduated** and **was working** on a master's degree in history.

a) What changed in the verbs used by Eva and Albert when the two sentences turned into reported speech?

_____

_____

b) What is the rule for changing sentences from direct into indirect speech?

( ) Change the verb to its past form.   ( ) Keep the verb in the same form.

c) How did the pronoun **I** change in the reported speech examples?

_____

_____

7. If you heard what the people below said, how would you report it to a friend? Turn these sentences into reported speech. Use the verbs in parentheses to write more precise sentences.

a) "I got into Boalt Law School (U. C. Berkeley) through an affirmative action program, a program that gave me the opportunity to study law." (**state**)

Eva Jefferson Paterson _____

_____

_____

b) "The fact is that we older white men are beneficiaries of affirmative action." (**recognize**)

Albert Vetere Lannon _____

_____

c) "I entered San Francisco State University at age 50 through the re-entry program, a form of affirmative action." (**point out**)

Albert _____

_____

d) "Affirmative action benefited me directly, and I am now able to give something back to the society that gave me a hand." (**claim**)

He _____

_____

311

Let's act with words!

Write a testimonial

We write a testimonial to show our admiration or gratitude to someone or for something.

Brazil tackles poverty with some social programs. Can you give your testimonial about one of the following programs?

- Quotas for Afro-Brazilian students in institutions of higher education

- Quotas for public school students in institutions of higher education

- The family grant program

- Popular pharmacy program

Some possible aspects you can include in your testimonial
- the benefits
- facts and experiences
- arguments highlighting one or more positive aspects
- impressions from a beneficiary in the form of a quotation
- expression of gratitude

Writing Steps

Organizing
- Choose a theme to develop your testimonial.
- Take notes of your arguments.
- Choose a title for your testimonial.

Preparing the first draft
- Make a first draft.
- Look at the two examples of testimonials in the *Let's read!* section: texts A and B.
- Use a dictionary to help you.

Peer editing
- Evaluate and discuss the draft with a classmate.
- Make the necessary corrections.

Publishing
- Publish your testimonial on a wall newspaper or on Padlet.
- You can also record your testimonial as a podcast or a video.

Genre: Testimonial

Purpose: To make a statement about something presenting facts, proof, or reasonable arguments

Tone: Formal

Setting: Wall newspaper or Padlet

Writer: You

Audience: Wall newspaper or Padlet readers

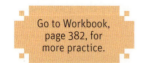

Go to Workbook, page 382, for more practice.

Learning tips

Using graphic organizers to enhance learning

Graphic organizers help us organize ideas and communicate more effectively. They can also be a good learning strategy because they facilitate comprehension and memorization of new information. Look at these two examples.

Venn diagram - consists of two or more partially overlapping circles. It can be used to make comparisons and to identify similarities and differences between two topics. In the example below the main topic is "vocabulary" and the comparison is between words used in American and British English for the same objects.

Fishbone diagram - can be used to synthesize ideas. As a task, complete the fishbone diagram below making a comparison between life in a big city and life in the country.

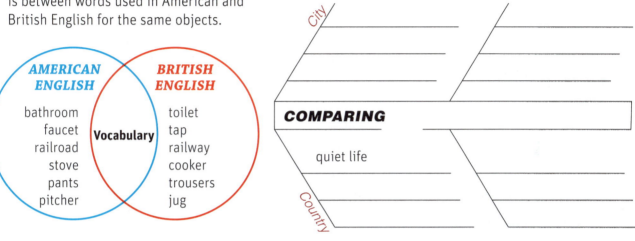

You can find free templates for diagrams at <http://www.worksheetworks.com/miscellanea/graphic-organizers.html> (accessed on: December 11, 2013).

Let's reflect on learning!

You are now invited to assess what you learned and how you learned. Finish the ideas below on an extra sheet of paper and become a more autonomous and reflective learner.

In Part 11

I learned _____

I liked _____

I need to review/learn more _____

My experiences with English outside school were _____

_____

Let's study for Enem!

Enem Questions

REPORTS
DUE TODAY!

"My report is about how important it is to save
paper, electricity, and other resources.
I'll send it to you telepathically."

GLASBERGEN, R. Today's cartoon. Disponível em: <http://www.glasbergen.com>.
Acesso em: 23 jul. 2010.

Gênero

Charge

Competência de área 2

H7 – Relacionar um texto em LEM, as estruturas linguísticas, sua função e seu uso social.

A imagem, destacando-se a anotação no quadro de giz nesta charge, é essencial para o entendimento do texto, pois estabelece o contexto da cena. Note que a aluna está com as mãos no bolso; logo, não levou o trabalho escolar escrito cuja entrega é hoje.

Nunca ignore o papel comunicativo das imagens e seus detalhes, principalmente no caso de gêneros como a charge e a tira. A escolha dos elementos pelo autor é sempre intencional.

Na parte verbal da charge há várias palavras cognatas que ajudam na compreensão. Observe também o tempo verbal em *I'll send*, pois ele indica se o trabalho foi entregue ou não.

Na fase escolar, é prática comum que os professores passem atividades extraclasse e marquem uma data para que as mesmas sejam entregues para correção. No caso da cena da charge, a professora ouve uma estudante apresentando argumentos para

A discutir sobre o conteúdo do seu trabalho já entregue.

B elogiar o tema proposto para o relatório solicitado.

C sugerir temas para novas pesquisas e relatórios.

D reclamar do curto prazo para entrega do trabalho.

E convencer de que fez o relatório solicitado.

Extraído de: Exame Nacional do Ensino Médio, 2011, Caderno 7 – AZUL – Página 2 (questão 92).

Part 11 (Yes, We Can)

Typical questions of Enem

1. O cartaz exibido por este veterano de guerra demonstra que ele:

a) ( ) apoia os imigrantes.

b) ( ) condena os imigrantes.

c) ( ) convive com imigrantes.

d) ( ) é um imigrante.

e) ( ) luta contra imigrantes.

2.

> **Eva Jefferson Paterson** – Executive Director of the Lawyers Committee for Civil Rights, one of California's most brilliant attorneys. She is an African-American and a beneficiary of affirmative action.
>
> "I got into Boalt Law School (UC Berkeley) through an affirmative action program, a program that gave me the opportunity to study law. Affirmative action gave me an opportunity, but I cracked the books, did the work, and passed the tests."
>
> "Never apologize for affirmative action," she tells the crowd, "I am proud of affirmative action because I am qualified."
>
> Adapted from: <http://www.inmotionmagazine.com/rocktr.html>. Accessed on: December 11, 2013.

O depoimento de Eva Jefferson Paterson sobre ações afirmativas demonstra que

a) ( ) ela acredita que as pessoas contrárias às ações afirmativas não devem pedir desculpas.

b) ( ) ela é a advogada africana mais brilhante do comitê de direitos civis no estado da Califórnia.

c) ( ) ela é beneficiária de ações afirmativas em uma escola de Direito para afrodescendentes.

d) ( ) ela se tornou uma advogada brilhante porque estudou muito e foi aprovada nos exames.

e) ( ) ela teve oportunidade de estudar Direito, mas teve dificuldade em comprar os livros.

3. Esta charge mostra uma cena em uma universidade americana, onde uma aluna é informada de que

a) ( ) a escolha da carreira pode afetar a sua independência.

b) ( ) a volta para casa mais cedo depende das notas das provas.

c) ( ) ela tem chance de ser mais rica do que seus parentes.

d) ( ) retornar à casa dos pais é normal entre os formandos.

e) ( ) tem muita chance de se mudar com a família após a formatura.

"Students who major in these subjects have a 7% less chance of moving back in with their parents after graduation."

Exam Practice Questions (Vestibular)

Test-Taking Tips

First, understand the question well!

Read the question carefully before you try to answer it. Focus on what is being asked: What piece of information do you need to find? For example, in question 1, you need to find where texts were stored, so look for a "place" or "spot." Question 4 demands a careful study of the context in which those words are used in the text. In question 9 you need to find the option which is "correct," so a lot of attention is necessary as far as instructions are concerned. But let's imagine you have done your best and you are still not sure enough in a multiple-choice task. The best thing to do is to eliminate as many incorrect answers as you can and then make an educated "guess" among those remaining.

- **TEXT 1 – Questions 1 to 5**
UEPB, 2013

The Art of Memory

1   In the age before books and tablets, orators stored texts in less reliable devices: their minds. To boost his memory capacity, Roman philosopher Cicero used tricks called mnemonics to bind his words to vivid
5   mental images, "as if inscribing letters into wax."

    Such ancient techniques may no longer be needed, but this month they'll take center stage when 50 "mental athletes" go head-to-head in the 15th USA Memory Championship in New York City. Their minds
10   aren't photographic, even memory experts need a coding system to remember strings of words, numbers, names, or playing cards. The key is training – hundreds of hours of it. And speed. Linking items to celebrities is common practice because they're easy to visualize.
15   However, "an emotional tie makes the image louder" says last year's champ, Nelson Dellis. When creating his mnemonic code for cards, he passed on a popular heartthrob for the king of hearts. "Brad Pitt I had to think about. But my dad – I can picture him in an
20   instant".

Oliver Uberti, *National Geographic*, March 2012.

1. According to the text, texts were first stored in
   a) ( ) devices.
   b) ( ) tablets.
   c) ( ) books.
   d) ( ) orators.
   e) ( ) minds.

2. The text states that the process of memorizing requires
   a) ( ) a set of playing cards.
   b) ( ) groups of words.
   c) ( ) strings of numbers.
   d) ( ) a coding system.
   e) ( ) a list of names.

3. The text asserts that items are linked to celebrities because
   a) ( ) it is easy to visualize them.
   b) ( ) they are heartthrobs.
   c) ( ) they are the key to memory.
   d) ( ) they resemble the King of Hearts.
   e) ( ) they are found on memory cards.

4. The group of words from the text which is made up of the words *inscribing* (line 5), *coding* (line 11), *playing* (line 12), *training* (line 12) and *linking* (line 13) includes
   a) ( ) only nouns and present participles.
   b) ( ) only present and past participles.
   c) ( ) only present participles, adjectives and a noun.
   d) ( ) only adjectives and present participles.
   e) ( ) only past and present participles and an adjective.

5. Which of the following groups of words from the text is related only to time?
   a) ( ) boost, hours, year's, instant, ancient
   b) ( ) month, hours, year's, instant, ancient
   c) ( ) mnemonics, year's, month, instant, ancient
   d) ( ) hours, month, year's, ancient, stage
   e) ( ) speed, month, hours, year's, instant

- **TEXT 2 – Questions 6 to 9**
IFMT, 2014

Favela in Rio de Janeiro, Brazil

Social Inclusion in Brazil

1   Citizenship restricted to the few, poverty, lack of a culture of respect for human rights, racial discrimination and racism, lack of access to justice, chauvinism and inappropriate public security practices,
5   all lead to extremely high rates of violence.

Part 11 (Yes, We Can)

Brazil has been historically marked by social, economic
and cultural inequalities. Both society and government
are increasingly aware of the need for changing that
scenario by creating mechanisms of social participation
10 and control, programmes, projects, and actions that
represent a movement towards positive changes.

Although it has a large number of poor people
Brazil is not a poor country, but still has to overcome
social injustice and inequality. The social injustices are
15 reflected in a medium rank in the Human Development
Index (HDI), which means that difficulties are still to be
overcome in education, health, income distribution and
employment conditions.

It is worth mentioning that despite the positive
20 changes reflected in the figures above, in absolute
terms, the improvements are insufficient to promote
the great leap that Brazil needs to make. Another
aspect to be considered is that the study defines as
indigent only those people with per capita earnings
25 of less than one fourth of the minimum wage and
classifies as poor, those with earnings in the range of
a minimum wage – and those are very low amounts.
(Source: IPEA – Ipeadata).

Poverty reduction and fight against social
30 inequalities are key priorities for the Social and
Human Sciences Programme in Brazil. UNESCO puts
in place an upstream and strategic approach rooted in
social sciences information, knowledge and research
in order to influence policy-making and strengthen
35 capacity building.

Social inclusion initiatives, in close cooperation
with NGOs and civil society, receive close attention.
UNESCO technical cooperation is present in all stages,
from the planning to the implementation of projects
40 and in innovative activities.

UNESCO in Brazil intends to focus its messages,
practices, perspectives, and resource to provide tools
to education, cultures, science, and communication
and information in order to reduce poverty and raise
45 human development rates of Brazilian population by:

• serving as a forum to exchange ideas on
international social policies,

• exchanging, promoting, and disseminating successful
experiences in the field of poverty reduction in Brazil.

(Disponível em <http://www.unesco.org/new/en/brasilia/social-and-human-sciences/social-inclusion/>).

6. Marque a alternativa que apresenta o gênero, em
inglês, a que o texto pertence.
a) (   ) advertisement
b) (   ) abstract
c) (   ) biography
d) (   ) chronicle
e) (   ) opinion article

7. Pode se dizer que o autor argumenta a favor
a) (   ) do capitalismo.
b) (   ) do neologismo.
c) (   ) da extinção das ações não governamentais.
d) (   ) da atuação da UNESCO no sentido de elevar
o índice de desenvolvimento humano (IDH),
através de projetos sociais direcionados às
classes menos favorecidas.
e) (   ) da expansão das áreas periféricas e a
verticalização das favelas do Rio de Janeiro
como marca de pleno desenvolvimento social.

8. O objetivo do texto é:
a) (   ) Refletir sobre os argumentos contraditórios,
referentes a políticas de ações afirmativas.
b) (   ) Questionar a responsabilidade e os
critérios da UNESCO referentes às normas
estabelecidas para a elaboração e execução
de projetos educacionais.
c) (   ) Refletir sobre as desigualdades sociais
resultantes de fatores habitacionais,
econômicos, educacionais e culturais; e
também sobre a atuação da UNESCO na
contribuição para a paz e segurança no
mundo.
d) (   ) Analisar a política de autonomia e controle
dos órgãos não governamentais que definem
os investimentos na área de cooperação
técnica, destinados às classes menos
favorecidas no Brasil.
e) (   ) Relatar a omissão da UNESCO com relação
à política desenvolvida em termos de
comunicação e informação, direcionados
para os jovens da periferia do Rio de Janeiro.

9. Em referência ao uso da linguagem utilizada no
texto, é correto afirmar que
a) (   ) a expressão "less than" (linha 25) está no
grau comparativo de igualdade.
b) (   ) o vocabulário "both" (linha 7) é referente à
sociedade e ao governo.
c) (   ) a palavra "inappropriate" (linha 4) é
formada pelo acréscimo de um sufixo que
nega o sentido original do vocábulo.
d) (   ) a palavra "still" (linha 13) pode ser
substituída por "since" sem prejuízo de
sentido.
e) (   ) "although" (linha 12) é uma conjunção que
expressa ideia de alternância.

PART 12
Modern Accomplishments

•Xerography
1939

Learning plan

Discussing monuments around the world

Learning how to predict the connotation of some words in a text

Identifying cognate and false cognate words

Learning how to talk about processes in an impersonal way

Learning how to present arguments, to agree or disagree politely, and to clarify ideas

Learning how to create concept maps and a multimodal timeline

1960
•Laser

1961
•Optical disc

1963
•Computer mouse
•Smiley face

1964
•Coronary artery bypass
•Supercomputer

1967
•First heart transplant

1968
•Video game console

1969
•ARPANET

1971
•First e-mail
•Liquid crystal display
•Floppy disk
•Pocket calculator
•eBook

1973
•Personal computer

1977
•DNA sequencing

1983
•Camcorder

1990
•World Wide Web

1997
•Google

2001
•Digital satellite radio
•iPod
•Wikipedia
•Segway HT

2005
•Superjumbo Airbus A380

2010
•iPad

| 1960 | 1970 | 1980 | 1990 | 2000 |

Images: ID/BR

TIMELINES
How to create and share them on the web

Some free online tools to create timelines include Dipity, Timetoast, and Preceden. Choose one of them.

Dipity

It is a free digital timeline website. Read more at <http://www.dipity.com/> (accessed on: May 30, 2014).

Timetoast

It is another tool that enables you to create a timeline... Read more at <http://www.timetoast.com/> (accessed on: May 30, 2014).

Preceden

It is a free web 2.0 timeline visualization tool. See more at <http://www.preceden.com/> (accessed on: May 30, 2014).

Beyond the lines...

a) Why does the information about the same invention vary so much depending on the source we choose?

b) Do you know any controversy involving famous inventions?

c) What other inventions would you add to the timeline above and why?

UNIT

23 Man-made wonders

Language in action

- Discuss monuments around the world
- Learn how to predict the connotation of some words in a text
- Identify cognate and false cognate words

> **Lead-in**

1. Which of these statements express what is implicit in the title of this unit? Check (✔) the options.

   ( ) There are many wonders on Earth that humans did not create.

   ( ) The things that humans create are less beautiful than the natural wonders.

   ( ) Humans have the capacity to interfere with nature and create wonderful things.

2. Test your knowledge of famous monuments around the world. Read the descriptions and check which monuments on the left page they refer to. Write the letters.

   ( ) **Leaning Tower of Pisa**, medieval structure in Pisa, Italy, that is famous for the settling of its foundations, which caused it to lean 5.5 degrees (about 4.5 meters) from the perpendicular in the late 20th century.

   ( ) **Hagia Sophia**, cathedral built at Constantinople (now Istanbul, Turkey) in the 6th century CE (532-537) under the direction of the Byzantine emperor Justinian I. The building was secularized in 1934, and in 1935 it was made into a museum.

   ( ) **Borobudur**, massive Buddhist monument in central Java, Indonesia. The monument was designated a UNESCO World Heritage site in 1991. It was constructed between about 778 and 850 CE, under the Shailendra dynasty.

   ( ) **Easter Island**, Chilean dependency in the eastern Pacific Ocean. It is famous for its giant stone statues (Moai figures). To its original inhabitants the island is known as Rapa Nui ("Great Rapa") or Te Pito te Henua ("Navel of the World").

   ( ) **Christ the Redeemer**, colossal statue at the summit of Mount Corcovado, Rio de Janeiro, Brazil. It was completed in 1931 and stands 30 meters tall, its horizontally outstretched arms spanning 28 meters.

   ( ) **Angkor Wat**, a temple complex built in the 12th century by King Suryavarman II (reigned 1113-c. 1150) in what is now northwestern Cambodia. It is still the largest religious structure in the world and one of the most beautiful.

   Source: <http://www.britannica.com/>. Accessed on: December 12, 2013.

3. Look at the images of monuments again and discuss these questions with a classmate.

   a) Which of the monuments introduced here had you never seen?

   b) Most of these monuments are associated with religion. Do you think they are representative of the faith of most people who live in these countries?

   c) What architectural elements in some of these monuments impressed you? Can you see similar sites in your country?

   d) Why do you think emperors and kings built such colossal monuments as Angkor Wat and Borobudur?

4. What are the sites that are truly all-time marvels of architecture in your region? Are they famous in other parts of the country as well?

> **Did you know...?**

To quickly find images in search engines like Google, Bing, or Yahoo, just type a word or phrase. For example: **Angkor Wat Temples**. Then, click on the icon Images. You will be surprised to see all the pictures of this monument. You can also see the number of results.

321

Let's read!

Before you read...

- What is the name of the blog where the text below was posted?
- What phrase is used as their motto?
- Based on this motto, which words do you think the writer has used in the article?

( ) amazing
( ) the most beautiful
( ) best-known
( ) like no other
( ) the most depressing
( ) enormous
( ) famous
( ) breath-taking beauty
( ) decadent
( ) imagination
( ) shocking
( ) greatness
( ) talent
( ) refinements
( ) tedious
( ) vibrant
( ) paradise
( ) weird
( ) lovingly built
( ) well preserved

Hint
When you know what the objective of a text is, you can predict, for example, if the connotation of some words used is positive or negative. You become less dependent on the dictionary.

1. Read the text quickly and check if your predictions in the previous activity were correct. Circle the words in the list above that the author has used here.

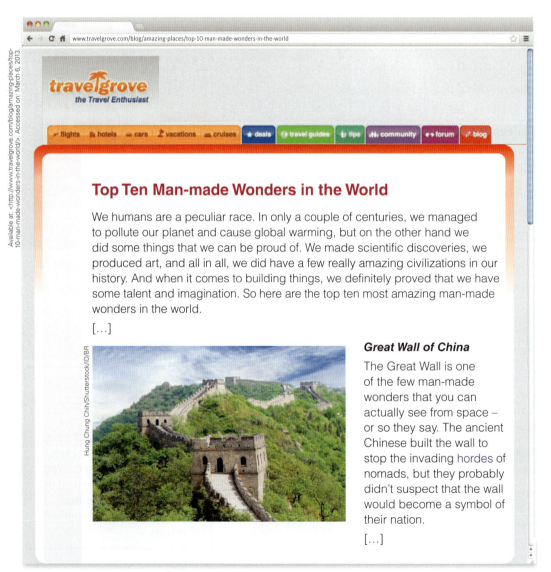

Top Ten Man-made Wonders in the World

We humans are a peculiar race. In only a couple of centuries, we managed to pollute our planet and cause global warming, but on the other hand we did some things that we can be proud of. We made scientific discoveries, we produced art, and all in all, we did have a few really amazing civilizations in our history. And when it comes to building things, we definitely proved that we have some talent and imagination. So here are the top ten most amazing man-made wonders in the world.

[...]

Great Wall of China

The Great Wall is one of the few man-made wonders that you can actually see from space – or so they say. The ancient Chinese built the wall to stop the invading hordes of nomads, but they probably didn't suspect that the wall would become a symbol of their nation.

[...]

Machu Picchu

The Inca rulers used the city of Machu Picchu as their residence for only about one century (they would have probably stayed for longer if the Spanish hadn't come), and the outside world didn't find out about its existence until the early 20th century. One of the most beautiful examples of classical Inca architecture ever.

[...]

Karnak Temple

Ramses II was a bit of a megalomaniac, and thank heaven for that, because otherwise he probably wouldn't have begun building the Karnak temple complex. The temples were built in celebration of the Theban Triad of gods, Amun, Mut, and Khonsu. The Precinct of Amun-Re is probably the most famous part of the complex.

Teotihuacan

Teotihuacan is probably the best-known archaeological site in Mexico, and for good reason. The enormous city is very well preserved, and even today you can see the vibrant colors of the murals that decorate many of the buildings.

Available at: <http://www.travelgrove.com/blog/amazing-places/top-10-man-made-wonders-in-the-world/>. Accessed on: December 12, 2013.

2. Read the text again quickly and underline all the cognate words you find. Compare your answers to a classmate's.

3. Did you find any false cognate words? What are they and what do they mean?

_____
_____

4. We can say that this article was written in an informal style. Find words or groups of words in the text that justify this.

_____
_____
_____
_____

5. What kind of service does this blog offer?

( ) Only articles and images related to wonderful places around the world.

( ) Articles and also support for people to plan their trips and get new ideas of where to go.

323

6. What elements in the text helped you answer question 5?

_____
_____
_____

7. Read the text more carefully now and answer: Which wonder

a) still has some of its original beauty? _____

b) had a military application? _____

c) is a product of an eccentric ruler? _____

d) was abandoned because of an invasion? _____

8. According to the author, what have humans done that compensates for the bad things they have done to the environment? Do you agree?

_____
_____
_____

9. All the "positive" words in the *Before you read...* box that you didn't find in the text were used to refer to the other monuments that complete the "top 10 list." Visit the *Travelgrove* website and search for them. Select two or three fragments and copy them here or in your notebook.

_____
_____
_____
_____
_____

▎**Did you know...?**

Cognate words are pairs of words from different languages that are similar in meaning and form, as in the pair "passport - *passaporte.*" **False cognate words** are similar in form but different in meaning.

❯ Let's listen and talk!

❯ Ben Kacyra: Ancient wonders captured in 3D

"Ancient monuments give us clues to astonishing past civilizations – but they're under threat from pollution, war, neglect. Ben Kacyra, who invented a groundbreaking 3D scanning system, is using his invention to scan and preserve the world's heritage in archival detail."

Available at: <http://www.ted.com/talks/ben_kacyra_ancient_wonders_captured_in_3d.html>. Accessed on: December 12, 2013.

Before you listen...

- Have you ever read about monuments which were destroyed by humans?
- Do you know any famous monument which is threatened by pollution?
- Which words do you think are likely to appear in Ben Kacyra's speech?

1. ◎**66** Listen to some excerpts from Ben Kacyra's talk at TED and do the following activities. Remember that the cognate words can help you!

a) Who are the founders of CyArk or Cyber Archive? _____

b) Check (✔) the monument which motivated them to create their foundation.

    (   ) Bamiyan Buddhas   (   ) Royal Kasubi Tombs

c) In which countries were these monuments found?

_____

d) What natural phenomena are mentioned in the talk?

_____

_____

e) What kind of technology do they use?

_____

f) What happened to the Royal Kasubi Tombs?

    (   ) They were blown up by a terrorist attack.

    (   ) They were destroyed by suspected arson (criminal fire).

    (   ) They were damaged by human pollution.

    (   ) They were demolished during a war.

2. Follow these steps to have a conversation with a classmate.

- Sit with a classmate. Make a list of five man-made wonders in your country or abroad which you think should be protected by CyArk.

- Listen to your partner's choice and try to persuade him/her to change his/her choices if you do not agree with them.

- Choose two of the five which you consider to be priorities. Try to convince your partner of your priorities. Remember to be polite!

▪ Useful language

Why don't we...
I think we should...
I'm sure we ought to...
If I were you, I'd...
We'd better...
Don't you think it would be better to...
Yes, but don't you think that...?
But what about...?
I don't think I'd say that.
I see your point; however...
Yes, but on the other hand...
It's important to remember that...
Don't forget that...
We should bear in mind that...
That's an interesting point, but...
You seem to have forgotten...
I'm convinced that...
I'm sure that...
As I see it, ...
I really do think that...

▶ Let's focus on language!

1. Compare the use of **did** in these excerpts from the article "Top Ten Man-made Wonders in the World." Then answer the questions.

    I. "[...] we **did have** a few really amazing civilizations in our history."

    II. "[...] we **did** some things that we can be proud of."

    III. "[...] the outside world **didn't find out** about its existence [...]"

   a) Does **did** have the same function in the three examples? _____

   b) In which example is **did**...   ... the main verb in the Simple Past? _____

   ... the auxiliary in a negative sentence? _____

   ... the indication of emphasis on the verb? _____

   c) Is the sentence with the emphatic statement in the affirmative, negative, or interrogative form? _____

   > - The auxiliaries **do**, **does**, and **did** can be used in affirmative sentences to emphasize the main verb of the sentence.
   > - The emphatic forms are used in only two tenses, the Simple Present and the Simple Past.

2. Read these scenarios and complete the spaces accordingly. Your goal is to give emphasis to the verbs in parentheses in order to show certainty.

   a) You want to convince a member of UNESCO that a monument in Brazil should be included on the World Heritage List.

   _____ _____ (**represent**) a masterpiece of human creative genius. It _____ _____ (**illustrate**) a significant stage in human history.

   b) You want to convince a member of UNESCO that two natural sites in Brazil (forests, waterfalls, parks, etc.) should be included on the World Heritage List.

   _____ _____ (**contain**) areas of exceptional natural beauty and aesthetic importance. I _____ (**believe**) they should be included on the list.

   Both exercises based on information available at: <http://whc.unesco.org/en/criteria>. Accessed on: December 12, 2013.

Serra da Canastra, MG, 2011

Tiradentes, MG, 2010

Monte Negro Canyon, RS, 2010

Rio de Janeiro, RJ, 2011

Guaramiranga, CE, 2008

3. Read another excerpt from the article "Top Ten Man-made Wonders in the World."
Does it refer to a hypothetical or a real situation? _____
situation.

> "They **would have** probably **stayed** for longer **if** the Spanish **hadn't come**."

Sometimes, the **if**-clause is implicit. Study this other sentence taken from the article in *Let's read!*

> "Ramses II was a bit of a megalomaniac, and thank heaven for that, because otherwise
> he probably **wouldn't have begun** building the Karnak temple complex."

An equivalent sentence would be:

> If Ramses II **hadn't been** a bit of a megalomaniac, he probably **wouldn't have begun**
> building the Karnak temple complex.

Pay attention to the highlighted parts in the previous sentence. Complete this rule with **Past Perfect** and **would have** accordingly.

> To talk about an imaginary situation in the past, we use the structure
>
> **If** + _____ and_____ + Past Participle.

Notice that the punctuation changes depending on the position of the **if**-clause. Study the examples and complete the rule by circling the right option.

> When the sentence starts / **ends** with the **if-clause**, we add a comma (,) after it.

4. Look back at the history of some man-made art and say what would have happened had things been different. The first one is done for you.

a) Lúcio Costa and Oscar Niemeyer planned Brasília in an innovative style. / UNESCO has recognized it as a World Heritage Site.

> If Lúcio Costa and Oscar Niemeyer had not planned Brasília in an innovative style,
>
> UNESCO would not have recognized it as a World Heritage Site.

b) Scientists and engineers have decided to remove sandy soil and marine clay. They have reduced the lean of the Tower of Pisa by 20 inches (50 centimeters).

Source: <http://construction.about.com/od/Benchmark-Projects/a/The-Tower-Of-Pisa-What-We-Learned.htm>.
Accessed on: December 12, 2013.

_____

_____

c) Shah Jahan's wife, Mumtaz Mahal, died in 1631. Shah Jahan built the Taj Mahal as a tribute to her.

_____

_____

d) The Chinese feared invasions. The Chinese built the Great Wall of China.

_____

5. Read a blog entry about a man-made disaster. Complete the text using **would have continued**, **would have represented**, **would not have run out**, and **may have been triggered**.

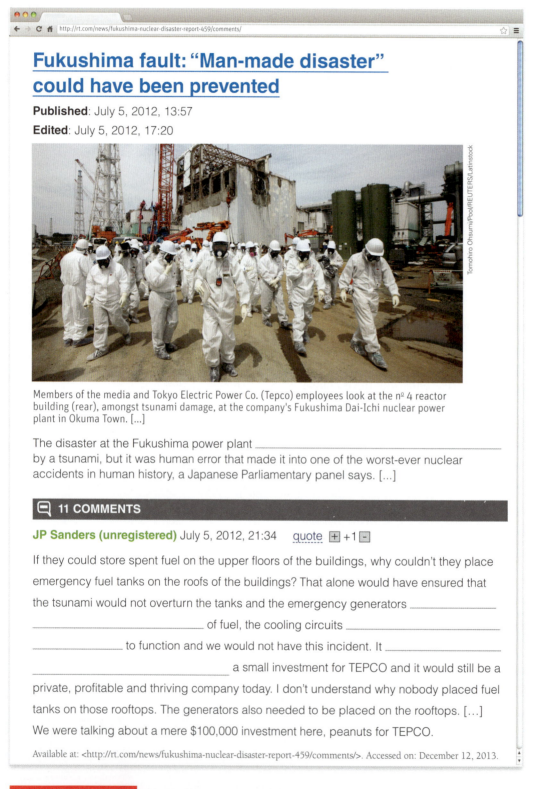

Fukushima fault: "Man-made disaster" could have been prevented

Published: July 5, 2012, 13:57

Edited: July 5, 2012, 17:20

Members of the media and Tokyo Electric Power Co. (Tepco) employees look at the nº 4 reactor building (rear), amongst tsunami damage, at the company's Fukushima Dai-Ichi nuclear power plant in Okuma Town. [...]

The disaster at the Fukushima power plant _____ by a tsunami, but it was human error that made it into one of the worst-ever nuclear accidents in human history, a Japanese Parliamentary panel says. [...]

11 COMMENTS

JP Sanders (unregistered) July 5, 2012, 21:34   quote +1

If they could store spent fuel on the upper floors of the buildings, why couldn't they place emergency fuel tanks on the roofs of the buildings? That alone would have ensured that the tsunami would not overturn the tanks and the emergency generators _____ _____ of fuel, the cooling circuits _____ _____ to function and we would not have this incident. It _____ _____ a small investment for TEPCO and it would still be a private, profitable and thriving company today. I don't understand why nobody placed fuel tanks on those rooftops. The generators also needed to be placed on the rooftops. [...] We were talking about a mere $100,000 investment here, peanuts for TEPCO.

Available at: <http://rt.com/news/fukushima-nuclear-disaster-report-459/comments/>. Accessed on: December 12, 2013.

Beyond the lines...

a) Are there more man-made wonders or more man-made disasters?
b) How do man-made wonders interfere in nature?

Profession spot

› Hospitality industry

1. Are there any "man-made wonders" attracting tourists in your region? Are there good hotels to accommodate them?

2. The hospitality industry offers many job opportunities for people of different educational backgrounds. Match the jobs below to their responsibilities and training requirements.

1. bellhop
2. concierge
3. chef
4. hotel clerk
5. general manager
6. housekeeping manager
7. maitre or head waiter
8. convention planner
9. reservation ticket agent

Illustrations: Estudio MI/ID/BR

( ) Directs the operation and financial result of the property; creates standards for personnel, room rates, publicity, and food selection. *Training*: 2 years of training and/or experience.

( ) Performs services for hotel guests, such as guest check-in and check-out, assigning rooms, and answering inquiries to hotel services. *Training*: 3 to 6 months of training and/or experience.

( ) Escorts incoming hotel guests to rooms; assists with luggage; offers information on services, facilities, and entertainment attractions. *Training*: Short-term on-the-job training.

( ) Plans meetings and special events of various sizes. Coordinates such logistics as budgets, equipment, logistical requirements, food, etc. *Training*: 6 to 12 months of training and/or experience.

( ) Assists guests with restaurant reservations, tickets to special events, travel arrangements, and tours of interesting places to visit. *Training*: Short-term on-the-job training.

( ) Assigns customers to tables; makes advance reservations; oversees waiters and all aspects of the dining room. *Training*: College courses in hotel and restaurant management or business administration.

( ) Oversees all kitchen activity; tracks popularity of dishes; estimates customer food consumption; tests cooked foods; creates special dishes and recipes. *Training*: 4 years of training and/or experience.

( ) Offers information about travel; quotes fares and room rates; books transportation and hotel reservations. *Training*: A high school diploma or college coursework in management or business.

( ) Performs such light cleaning duties as making beds, replenishing linens, cleaning rooms and halls, vacuuming, emptying wastebaskets, and restocking bathroom supplies. *Training*: Short-term on-the-job training.

Adapted from: <http://www.careerbuilder.com/Article/CB-775-Who-is-Hiring-Top-10-Jobs-in-Hospitality/>. Accessed on: December 12, 2013.

3. Think about your abilities. What job do you think would suit you? Why? Share your ideas with your classmates.

329

UNIT 24
Technology advances

Language in action

- Talk about technology
- Learn how to talk about processes in an impersonal way
- Learn how to present arguments, to agree or disagree politely, and to clarify ideas
- Learn how to create words with suffixes
- Learn how to create concept maps

Ryad Sallem, member of the French wheelchair basketball team.

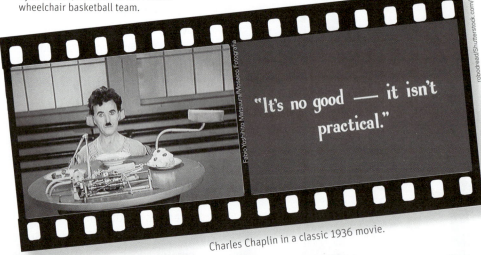

"It's no good — it isn't practical."

Charles Chaplin in a classic 1936 movie.

Desalination plant in the coastal city of Hadera, Israel.

The Bicentennial Man (1999).

› Lead-in

1. How do you think technology has changed our lives? Make a list of some advances in technology and their consequences for people and/or animals. Look at the example.

   Desalination plants: They have made it possible to turn salty water into fresh water.

   _____

   _____

   _____

2. The black and white image shows a fictitious technology advance. Answer the questions about it.

   a) The picture was taken from a movie called

   ( ) Metropolis   ( ) Modern Times

   ( ) Matrix   ( ) The Great Dictator

   ( ) Blade Runner   ( ) Back to the Future

   b) What type of invention is represented in this picture? _____

   c) Do you think this invention would be useful? Explain your answer. _____

   _____

3. What are some of the things that are not possible now but may be possible in the future because of technology advances? _____

4. The text below is related to one of the pictures on the previous page. What is it?

   _____

   _____

"As a robot... I could have lived forever... But I tell you all today, that I would rather die a man, than live for all eternity as a machine. [...] To be acknowledged... for who, and what I am... no more, no less... not for acclaim, not for approval... but the simple truth of that recognition... This has been the elemental drive of my existence... and it must be achieved, if I am to live, or die, with dignity."

Beyond the lines...

a) All advances in technology carry consequences that can be dangerous for society. Do you agree?

b) Companies rarely warn consumers about the risks of certain products. Why do you think this happens?

331

❯ Let's read!

Before you read...
- Read the title and subtitles of the text below. What do you think are the possible uses of the technological advances described in the text?
- Based on the title and subtitles of this text, which words do you expect to find in it?

1. Read the text and check if your predictions in the previous part were correct.

10 Big Science and Technology Advances to Watch

With so many remarkable things happening in the science and tech worlds, it's hard to choose which to talk about. Here are a few ongoing developments worth keeping your eyes on.

Medicine

A **Stem Cell Heart Generation** – For the first time, a human heart has been created using stem cells, a major step forward in organ generation. A couple years ago scientists rebuilt the heart of a rat using stem cells; the same team is behind the latest breakthrough. If all goes as planned, the heart will continue to grow and eventually begin beating automatically. The implications of this development are huge, including overcoming the problems of transplanting donated hearts. More info
[...]

B **Nano Batteries** – Scientists have created the equivalent of a rechargeable lithium-ion battery the size of a nanowire, thousands of times smaller than a human hair. But unlike previous nanobatteries, this one is actually built right into a nanowire. This infinitesimal power source could provide nanomachines with the continuous power needed to accomplish whatever uses they're designed for, such as exploring the cardiovascular system of a heart disease patient. More info
[...]

C **Plasma Arc Waste Disposal** – Imagine harnessing the power of lightning to turn garbage into glass, or into a gas that can be used as an energy source. This technology is gaining momentum in the waste disposal industry and is even in use at some solid waste facilities. The advantages include less garbage in landfills, less carbon from incineration, and creating a natural gas power resource. The problem: it's expensive technology, and in these days of economic woes few public entities can afford it. More info
[...]

D **DNA Neural Networks** – Researchers at the California Institute of Technology say they have created the first DNA neural network that "thinks." They used DNA molecules to build four neurons made up of 112 distinct DNA strands. The amazing part is that the network can be trained to play memory games and come up with correct answers. If this all sounds a little strange, that's because it is... but it's also incredibly cool. More info

Available at: <http://www.forbes.com/sites/daviddisalvo/2011/07/29/10-big-science-and-technology-advances-to-watch/>.
Accessed on: December 12, 2013.

Forbes.com is a website that offers different channels, such as "Technology," in which the text "10 Big Science and Technology Advances to Watch", written by David DiSalvo, was published.

2. From what source was this text taken? _____

_____

_____

3. The advances mentioned in the text belong to the five different areas in the box below. Write them in the appropriate space in the text.

| ~~Medicine~~   Environmental   Neuroscience   Applied Sciences & Engineering |

4. This text is mostly written in a formal style, but there is one sentence that breaks this norm. Find this informal sentence in the text and copy it here. Why do you think the writer decided to use it?

_____

_____

_____

5. Match each of these pictures to its corresponding block in the text "10 Big Science and Technology Advances to Watch." Write down the letter.

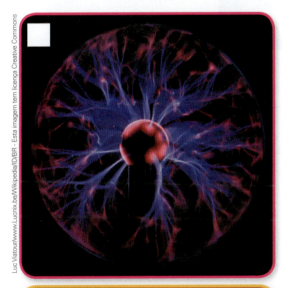

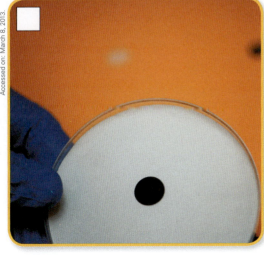

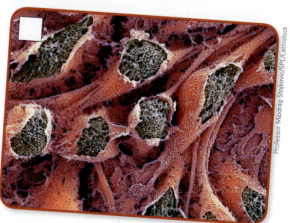

6. Summarize the main ideas of each area in the text "Ten Big Science and Technology Advances to Watch" by creating conceptual maps in your notebook. Use the one below as a reference.

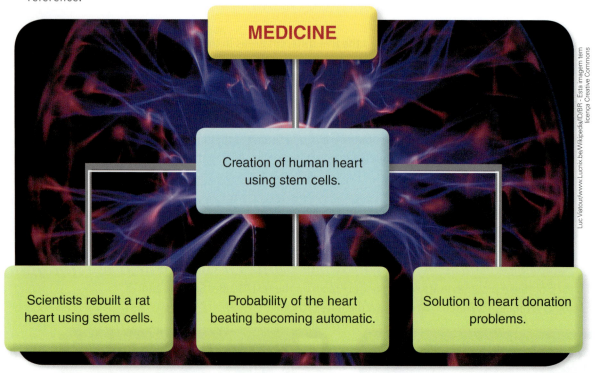

7. With a classmate, discuss these questions about the text in activity 1.
   a) Considering the items presented in the text, which is the most important technology advance? Why?
   b) Are any of these technology advances available in your country/region/city/etc.?
   c) How can technology help our lives? Think about ways in which it can improve our quality of life.
   d) Now, think of some problems technology advances have created or could create. How can we solve them?
   e) What other areas do you think are worth researching? Think about problems that could be solved with science or technology.

8. In your opinion, what are the other six technology advances that were cut from the text in activity 1? Choose from the options below. Then visit the website and check.
   ( ) Paperless Paper
   ( ) Using Nitrogen in Car Tires
   ( ) Transparent Batteries
   ( ) Mimicking Porosity in Nature
   ( ) Underwater Digital Cameras
   ( ) Hybrid MRI / PET Imaging
   ( ) Best iPod FM Transmitter
   ( ) Using EEG to Put the Brakes On
   ( ) Ocean Desalination

› Let's focus on language!

1. Read these statements taken from the text "10 Big Science and Technology Advances to Watch." Pay attention to the highlighted parts and answer the questions.

> "For the first time, a human heart **has been created** using stem cells […]."

> "[…] turn garbage into glass, or into a gas that **can be used** as an energy source."

a) Do we know who created this human heart or who can use this gas as an energy source?

_____

_____

b) Compare the two statements above with the ones below. What has changed?

> Someone **has created** a human heart using stem cells.

> People **can use** a gas derived from garbage as an energy source.

_____

_____

_____

> We form the passive voice with the auxiliary **be + Past Participle** of the main verb.

c) Complete these rules writing the words **action**, **processes** and **impersonal** in the appropriate spaces.

> We use the passive voice to talk about _____, such as scientific or historical processes.
>
> The passive voice is often used in writing to make the text sound more _____, that is, to reduce the importance of the agent of an _____.

Notice that we use **by + agent** when the agent of the passive voice is relevant. This occurs in this example based on a sentence in the text "10 Big Science and Technology Advances to Watch."

> The first DNA neural network that "thinks" has been created **by researchers at the California Institute of Technology**.

2. Match the passive voice forms to their equivalent active voice forms and verb tenses.

a) "is/are built" ( ) planned ( ) Simple Present

b) "has/have been created" ( ) builds ( ) Present Perfect

c) "was/were planned" ( ) will develop ( ) Simple Future

d) "will be developed" ( ) has/have created ( ) Simple Past

> The Irregular Verbs list may be helpful to identify past forms of some verbs.

335

3. Circle the best form to complete these excerpts from the text "Top 10 'Inventions' that Changed the World."

a) **GPS Technology** – Originally developed as a navigation system by the United States military, the Global Positioning System **uses / is used** a network of satellites around the Earth to pinpoint the exact position of a receiver anywhere on the planet. Since its development in 1978, it **now uses / is now used** in cars, aircraft, and boats. Geologists **use / are used** it to track the movements of continental plate tectonics and glaciers while conservation scientists **have tagged / have been tagged** turtles with GPS receivers to follow their epic migrations.

b) **TV Dinners** – Food on the go has been around since the time of Ancient Greece, but convenience food really took off in the 1970s and **transformed / was transformed** the way families ate meals, the high-street, the countryside and national health. Traditional family dinners around the table disappeared and pre-packaged "ready meals" eaten on the sofa became the norm. Due to hectic lifestyles, the products, which were often frozen, **designed / were designed** to make life easier for time-pressed consumers.

Available at: <http://www.telegraph.co.uk/science/4981964/Top-10-inventions-that-changed-the-world.html>. Accessed on: December 12, 2013.

4. Look at some important developments in science and technology from the past. Complete the seven statements with information from this timeline and the verbs from the box in the appropriate form. Two verbs will be left out!

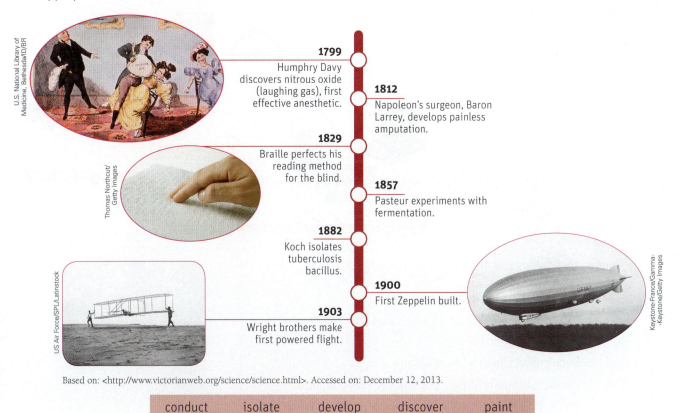

Based on: <http://www.victorianweb.org/science/science.html>. Accessed on: December 12, 2013.

| conduct | isolate | develop | discover | paint |
| make | design | consider | build | perfect |

a) Nitrous oxide _____ by _____ in 1799. The gas _____ the _____.
b) Painless amputation _____ by _____.
c) Braille's reading method for the blind _____ in 1829.
d) Experiments with fermentation _____ by Pasteur in _____.
e) The tuberculosis bacillus _____ by _____ in 1882.
f) The first Zeppelin _____ in 1900.
g) The first powered flight _____ by _____ in 1903.

Pronunciation spot – Sounds of *be*

1. How do you pronounce these different forms of **be**? Use the transcriptions as a guide.

is	/ʊr/
are	/wʌz/
were	/bɪn/
was	/ɪz/
been	/wɜr/

2. ⊙67 Now listen to the recording and check.

❯ Let's listen and talk!

Before you listen...
- Look back at the timeline on the opening page. Which of those inventions are part of your everyday life?
- What are the most important features of a timeline? What do timelines show?

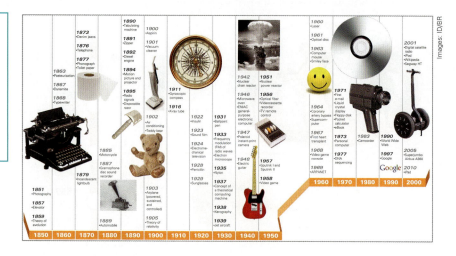

1. Number these steps to make a guide for creating a timeline.

   Plot History on a Line

   ( ) Calculate the number of segments that your timeline will have.

   ( ) Decide what the timeline will show.

   ( ) Decide what units of time you will use (days, months, years, decades, centuries, etc.) to divide your timeline into segments.

   ( ) Draw a line and divide it into the number of equal segments that you figure you will need.

   ( ) List the events in a chronology, a sequence of earliest to latest.

   ( ) Make a list of events that you wish to put on your timeline.

   ( ) Research and note the specific dates when the events that you wish to include occurred. It is a good idea to note your source(s), too, so that you can return later and verify the dates, if necessary.

   Available at: <http://dohistory.org/on_your_own/toolkit/timeline.html>. Accessed on: December 12, 2013.

2. 🔴68 Now listen to the steps and check your answers.

3. Follow these guidelines to have a discussion in class.
   - Arrange yourselves in groups. The goal is to discuss whether technology has a positive or negative influence on our planet.
   - Split the group into two. Each half of the group should create at least three arguments to make their point and present them to the whole group.
   - Take turns to present your arguments, to agree or disagree politely, and to clarify ideas.

Useful language

Supporting opinion with arguments
The way I see it...
If you want my honest opinion...
... because...
If you ask me...
As far as I'm concerned...
... since...

Agreeing
I couldn't agree with you more!
I agree entirely.
Absolutely.
You have a point here.

Disagreeing politely
Yes, that's quite true, but...
I see what you mean, but...
Well, you have a point there, but...

Clarifying ideas
That's not quite what I meant...
Let me put it another way...
Sorry, let me explain...

Profession spot

> Game programmer

1. Have you ever considered working in the video game industry? Why (not)?
   _____

2. Do you think this is a competitive market? Why (not)?
   _____

3. In your opinion, is it necessary to have college degree to be a game programmer?
   _____

4. Do you think there are many girls pursuing this career?
   _____

5. 🔴69 Listen to some tips on how to get a job in the video game industry. Complete the spaces with the missing captions. Use words from the box.

   | Get Lucky | Get in There | Get Passionate | Get Literate | Get Technical |

   ### How To Get A Job In The Video Game Industry

   Step 1: _____
   The video game industry is, obviously, full of gamers… and while you may not want to sound like a gushing fan boy when you go in for an interview, it's a good idea to let those in charge know that you truly love games.

   Step 2: _____
   Starting out in a lower level position may not fulfill your dreams, but it is a foot in the door. It's a good idea to keep one eye on the gaming companies' websites for any and all openings. If you can't design giant robots right away, getting in there is a big step.

   Step 3: _____
   It will come as a surprise to no one that video game companies like people who are familiar with software and hardware. So, it couldn't hurt to take some computer science classes.

   Step 4: _____
   Video games are becoming more and more cinematic. And while game-play and graphics are important, a compelling plot keeps players hooked. So, like most storytellers, aspiring game designers are aided by an appetite for books and a powerful imagination.

   Step 5: _____
   Being in the right place at the right time never hurts anyone.

   Adapted from: <http://www.videojug.com/film/how-to-get-a-job-in-the-video-game-industry>. Accessed on: December 12, 2013.

   ### Did you know…?

   Game programmers basically write the code that makes things happen in a video game. This includes "mapping" the player input from the control pad to the action that is happening on the screen. It also includes all the action of NPCs (non-player characters). So, when you see NPCs wandering the terrain of a video game, it is the programmers who gave the characters the artificial intelligence to roam where they do.

   Adapted from: <http://www.gamecareerguide.com/features/412/game_programming_an_introduction.php>. Accessed on: December 12, 2013.

6. Based on the information in activity 5 and in the *Did you know…?* box, do you think this career would suit you? If not, who do you think it might suit and why?

Let's act with words!

Make a multimodal timeline

A multimodal timeline is a linear representation of important events, using figures, texts, and pictures or photographs, as in this simple example.

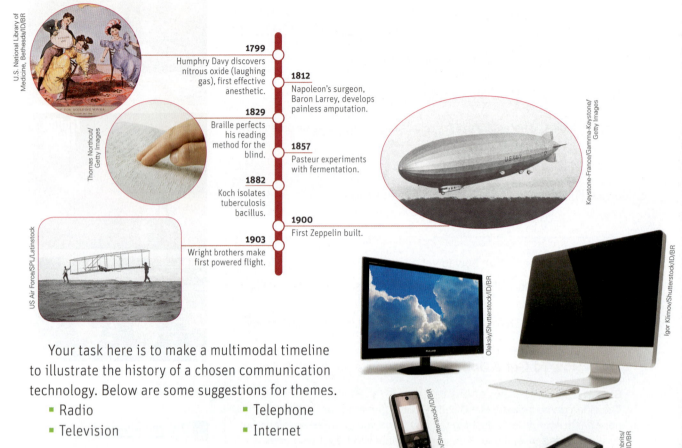

1799 Humphry Davy discovers nitrous oxide (laughing gas), first effective anesthetic.

1812 Napoleon's surgeon, Baron Larrey, develops painless amputation.

1829 Braille perfects his reading method for the blind.

1857 Pasteur experiments with fermentation.

1882 Koch isolates tuberculosis bacillus.

1900 First Zeppelin built.

1903 Wright brothers make first powered flight.

Your task here is to make a multimodal timeline to illustrate the history of a chosen communication technology. Below are some suggestions for themes.

- Radio
- Television
- Telephone
- Internet

Writing Steps

Organizing
- Select a topic for your timeline.
- Read about the history of the chosen technology.
- Find images to illustrate your timeline.
- Follow the steps listed in the *Let's listen and talk!* section.

Preparing the first draft
- Make a first draft.

Peer editing
- Evaluate and discuss your first draft with a classmate.
- Make the necessary corrections.

Publishing
- Publish your timeline on a wall newspaper or on Padlet.
- You can also make a digital timeline. See examples of timeline tools on the opening page of Part 12. Read more about timelines at <http://dohistory.org/on_your_own/toolkit/timeline.html> (Accessed on: December 12, 2013).

Genre: Multimodal timeline

Purpose: To show the passage of time with images, short information, and dates.

Tone: Formal

Setting: Wall newspaper or Padlet

Writer: You

Audience: Wall newspaper or Padlet readers

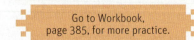

Go to Workbook, page 385, for more practice.

Learning tips

Improve your listening skills with TED

According to its website, TED started out in 1984 as a conference bringing together people from three worlds: Technology, Entertainment, Design.

Visit TED and watch interesting talks in English. You can choose the length of the videos: from three to eighteen minutes. You can also choose if you want subtitles in English or in Portuguese.

> TED is available at <http://www.ted.com/pages/about> (accessed on: June 2, 2014). Once you are there, click on the option "Talks."

Available at: <http://www.ted.com/>. Accessed on: March 10, 2013.

Some tips

1. Choose a talk that interests you.
2. Watch the talk without subtitles.
3. Watch it again and take notes.
4. Watch it once more with the transcript in English and compare it with your notes.
5. Take notes of the unknown words and look them up in a dictionary.
6. If you find it difficult to understand the talk, read the transcript in Portuguese and watch it again. Then go back to the transcript in English.
7. Choose some sentences to practice speaking. You can listen to them over and over and repeat, trying to reproduce the pronunciation and the intonation. This will help you develop or improve your oral skills.

Let's reflect on learning!

You are now invited to assess what you learned and how you learned. Finish the ideas below on an extra sheet of paper and become a more autonomous and reflective learner.

In Part 12

I learned _____

I liked _____

I need to review/learn more _____

My experiences with English outside school were _____

Let's study for Enem!

Enem Questions

Gênero
Reportagem

Competência de área 2
H6 - Utilizar os conhecimentos da LEM e de seus mecanismos como meio de ampliar as possibilidades de acesso a informações, tecnologias e culturas.

Steve Jobs: A Life Remembered 1955-2011

Readersdigest.ca takes a look back at Steve Jobs, and his contribution to our digital world.

CEO. Tech-Guru. Artist. There are few corporate figures as famous and well-regarded as former-Apple CEO Steve Jobs. His list of achievements is staggering, and his contribution to modern technology, digital media, and indeed the world as a whole, cannot be downplayed.

With his passing on October 5, 2011, readersdigest.ca looks back at some of his greatest achievements, and pays our respects to a digital pioneer who helped pave the way for a generation of technology, and possibilities, few could have imagined.

Disponível em: www.readersdigest.ca. Acesso em: 25 fev. 2012.

Alguns textos em revistas e jornais, sejam eles impressos ou eletrônicos, são precedidos de um *lead* (ou lide). Trata-se de um pequeno texto que indica ao leitor o que vem pela frente. Para responder a esta questão do Enem, leia com atenção o *lead* do texto e recorra sempre às palavras cognatas.

É importante levar em conta o seu conhecimento prévio sobre Steve Jobs como recurso para responder a esta questão. Entretanto, tenha em mente que você não pode depender apenas desse conhecimento. Observe que se você tivesse que depender somente de seu conhecimento, uma única alternativa poderia ser eliminada.

Informações sobre pessoas famosas são recorrentes na mídia, divulgadas de forma impressa ou virtualmente. Em relação a Steve Jobs, esse texto propõe

Ⓐ expor as maiores conquistas da sua empresa.

Ⓑ descrever suas criações na área da tecnologia.

Ⓒ enaltecer sua contribuição para o mundo digital.

Ⓓ lamentar sua ausência na criação de novas tecnologias.

Ⓔ discutir o impacto de seu trabalho para a geração digital.

Extraído de: Exame Nacional do Ensino Médio, 2013, Caderno 6 – CINZA – Página 3 (questão 93).

Part 12 (Modern Accomplishments)

Typical questions of Enem

"As a robot... I could have lived forever... But I tell you all today, that I would rather die a man, than live for all eternity as a machine. To be acknowledged... for who, and what I am... no more, no less... not for acclaim, not for approval... but the simple truth of that recognition... This has been the elemental drive of my existence... and it must be achieved, if I am to live, or die, with dignity."

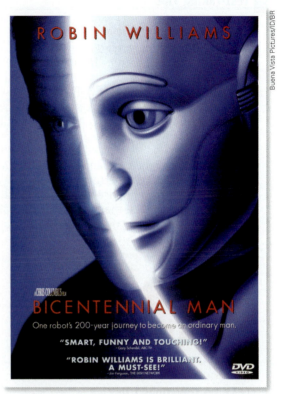

Pôster do filme *Bicentennial Man*

1. Os cientistas no campo da robótica estão sempre em busca de criar robôs que possam substituir os humanos. O texto reproduz a fala do robô Andrew, personagem do filme *Bicentennial Man*. Nessa fala o robô reflete sobre

a) ( ) a consciência de ter sido uma pessoa digna.
b) ( ) a morte como uma dádiva da humanidade.
c) ( ) o desejo da máquina de viver para sempre.
d) ( ) o fato de não ter sido reconhecido em vida.
e) ( ) o sofrimento por ser uma máquina humana.

Top 10 Man-made Wonders in the World

We humans are a peculiar race. In only a couple of centuries, we managed to pollute our planet and cause global warming, but on the other hand we did some things that we can be proud of. We made scientific discoveries, we produced art, and all in all, we did have a few really amazing civilizations in our history. And when it comes to building things, we definitely proved that we have some talent and imagination. So here are the top ten most amazing man-made wonders in the world.

2. O texto acima fala das ações humanas na natureza. O autor defende a ideia de que a raça humana é peculiar porque é capaz de destruir o ambiente e, ao mesmo tempo, de produzir ciência e arte. O propósito desse texto é fazer uma

a) ( ) avaliação da conservação das dez obras mais importantes feitas pelo homem.
b) ( ) comparação entre as construções importantes e o desenvolvimento científico.
c) ( ) crítica ao aquecimento global e à falta de conservação das construções históricas.
d) ( ) denúncia sobre a poluição ao redor de grandes obras arquitetônicas no mundo.
e) ( ) introdução para apresentar as maiores maravilhas produzidas pelo homem.

343

Exam Practice Questions (Vestibular)

Test-Taking Tips

Find some time to review!

You are finishing high school, and we recommend that you become familiar with the type(s) of exam you will be taking. Commit yourself to do past tests in order to be well-acquainted with the institution's style. The web offers lots of good material, including advisable comments! Practicing before will definitely make a big difference when test day arrives. And when the day comes, don't be tempted to finish your exam and leave. Reviewing helps you correct careless errors. Read all your answers carefully and be sure they are the best ones. Finally, we suggest that you also review all the tips you have learned in this book.

- **TEXT 1 – Questions 1 to 7**
FGV, 2013

Timbuktu

By Blake Gopnik

1. From the moment the followers of Muhammad came roaring out of Arabia, in A.D. 633, they've cherished beautiful things. An exhibition that just closed at the Metropolitan Museum in New York showed how the first Muslims were inspired by glorious works from the Greek-speaking world, and their descendants never stopped being art-friendly.

2. That's why it has been such a shock to see the artistic heritage of Timbuktu, one of the great seats of Africa's Islamic culture, fall prey to Muslim puritans. As recently as July 10, members of a group called Ansar Dine, which has been linked to al Qaeda, stormed the 14th-century Djingareyber mosque and destroyed two ancient shrines they found there, according to Reuters and Agence France-Presse. In late March, in the chaos of Mali's civil war, a small number of these fighters gained control of the city and have since been attacking its heritage. At the start of July, we got word of several shrines they had destroyed. They had also broken open a sealed door on the 15th-century Sidi Yahya mosque, which local tradition says ought to stay closed until Judgment Day. "Building on graves is contrary to Islam. We are destroying the mausoleums because it is ordained by our religion," Ansar Dine has insisted, claiming that local followers of the Sufi strain of Islam are guilty of idolatry each time they visit the tombs of their movement's sages.

3. But Shamil Jeppie, director of the Tombouctou Manuscripts Project at the University of Cape Town, rejects the idea that this is about the kind of consistent ideology found in other groups we call Islamist. "These guys, you can't give them such credit," says Jeppie. "It's just hooliganism." He says the locals had been resisting the fighters' authority, and he feels that the attacks on the shrines are a form of punishment. (Jeppie also reports that, so far, Timbuktu's great collections of Islamic manuscripts, which he studies, seem not to have been threatened.) The puritanical religious views that Ansar Dine claims to espouse, Jeppie says, derive from the relatively recent Wahhabi movement, "born in Arabia in the 18th century," and have been taught to today's fighters by patrons from Saudi Arabia.

4. Ansar Dine claims that its attacks on the shrines reflect the pure form of Islam practiced by Muhammad's first followers, but Jeppie and other experts, both Western and Muslim, say that misinterprets the historical evidence. There was always debate about showy entombment in shrines and mosques, but the practice was established from early on and has never been definitively rejected in Islamic law. "All you have to do is look at the Taj Mahal," says Sheila Canby, head of the Metropolitan's Islamic department, to see that "the attitude toward tombs has varied." She calls Ansar Dine's violent rejection "a very, very extreme view."

5. Even with the most recent destruction, however, the particular artistic culture of Mali gives a glimmer of hope. Thomas Schuler, chair of the Disaster Relief Task Force of the International Council of Museums, has been denouncing the damage. But he points out that locals have a more flexible view of their shrines' destruction. "The people in Timbuktu say, 'Let them destroy them. We will rebuild them.' That's why people don't defend [the shrines] to the death." Art historians have started to talk about this as a "substitution" principle, found in many cultures, whereby something new can stand in for something old that has been lost. It's not always the physical substance of an artwork that matters, but its shape or location and the traditions those point to. (Timbuktu's shrines are made of mud brick and so have always required rebuilding.)

Adapted from *Newsweek*, July 23 & 30, 2012.

1. Which of the following is most supported by the information in the article?

a) ( ) Only a small percentage of Muslims understand or appreciate great art.

b) ( ) Contrary to what some people believe, art is forbidden by the Koran.

c) ( ) Contemporary art in Muslim countries still borrows heavily from ancient Greek art.

d) ( ) Despite the beliefs of some Muslim extremists, art has always been a valued part of Islamic culture.

e) ( ) Art is permitted in the Islamic world only if it serves a religious purpose.

Part 12 (Modern Accomplishments)

2. Which of the following best describes what happened on July 10?

   a) ( ) A group of masked gunmen executed Muslim pilgrims in Timbuktu's Ansar Dine mosque.

   b) ( ) A radical Muslim named Ansar Dine decreed that certain Islamic monuments in Timbuktu had to be destroyed.

   c) ( ) A radical Muslim group entered an ancient mosque in Timbuktu and wrecked a couple of religious artifacts.

   d) ( ) A fight between al Qaeda and Ansar Dine resulted in the destruction of a mosque in Timbuktu.

   e) ( ) After a destructive battle, Mali's government expelled a radical Muslim group from Timbuktu.

3. With respect to the Muslim puritans, which of the following is most supported by the information in the article?

   a) ( ) They were the main factor that caused Mali's civil war.

   b ( ) Though they have launched many destructive attacks, they have not succeeded in conquering Timbuktu.

   c) ( ) Because they are Muslims, their religion requires that they protect all Muslim shrines.

   d) ( ) They have declared that their religion prohibits certain kinds of structures.

   e) ( ) Their leader believes that members of the Sufi sect should be expelled from the Muslim religion.

4. In paragraph 3, Shamil Jeppie's statement, "...you can't give them such credit," most likely means which of the following?

   a) ( ) The Muslim puritans in Timbuktu should not be considered members of a serious, coherent religious organization.

   b) ( ) Muslims that destroy religious shrines should not receive financial support from international Islamic organizations.

   c) ( ) Unless they can form an alliance with the local inhabitants of Timbuktu, Muslim puritan groups will never gain control of that city.

   d) ( ) It is wrong to accuse local radicals of destroying Timbuktu's Islamic shrines.

   e ( ) The damage that Muslim puritans have done in Timbuktu is not as serious as many people believe.

5. Which of the following is most supported by the information in the article?

   a) ( ) The destruction of the shrines in Timbuktu was motivated by unquestionable principles of pure, well-founded religious idealism.

   b) ( ) As a punishment, some local inhabitants of Timbuktu have been forced to take part in destroying Islamic shrines.

   c) ( ) If the Muslim puritans in Timbuktu are not stopped immediately, no religious artifact in that city will be left intact.

   d) ( ) The Muslim puritans in Timbuktu belong to a sect that does not accept influence from foreign countries.

   e) ( ) The Muslim puritans in Timbuktu could be mistaken when they declare that their religious principles come from the earliest teachings of Islam.

6. In paragraph 4, Sheila Canby most likely mentions the Taj Mahal in order to

   a) ( ) give an example of another Islamic burial structure that is in danger of being attacked.

   b) ( ) show that magnificent burial architecture can be accepted in the Muslim world.

   c) ( ) point out that both Muslims and non-Muslims appreciate the beauty of great tombs.

   d) ( ) argue that the destruction of certain Muslim religious shrines is not a great loss.

   e) ( ) support her belief that Ansar Dine's ideas have nothing to do with the Muslim religion.

7. As mentioned in the last paragraph, Thomas Schuler most likely believes that if well-armed Muslim extremists announced their intention to destroy more of Timbuktu's religious shrines, the local inhabitants of Timbuktu would

   a) ( ) fight to the death to protect their precious religious architecture.

   b) ( ) try to kill as many of the Muslim extremists as possible.

   c) ( ) allow the destruction to happen.

   d) ( ) move to safer regions of Mali.

   e) ( ) ask for international military help to stop the destruction.

345

Irregular Verbs

Base Form	Simple Past	Past Participle	Translation
arise /əˈraɪz/	arose /əˈroʊz/	arisen /əˈrɪz ən/	levantar(-se); surgir; originar(-se)
be /bi/	was /wʌz/, were /wɜr/	been /bɪn/	ser, estar
bear /bɛər/	bore /bɔr/	born, borne /bɔrn/	carregar; espalhar; exibir, ostentar
beat /bit/	beat /bit/	beaten /ˈbit n/	bater
become /bɪˈkʌm/	became /bɪˈkeɪm/	become /bɪˈkʌm/	tornar-se
begin /bɪˈgɪn/	began /bɪˈgæn/	begun /bɪˈgʌn/	começar
bend /bɛnd/	bent /bɛnt/	bent /bɛnt/	inclinar-se, curvar-se
bet / bɛt/	bet /bɛt/	bet /bɛt/	apostar
bid /bɪd/	bid /bɪd/, bade /bæd/	bid /bɪd/, bidden /ˈbɪd n/	mandar; declarar; fazer um lance
bind /baɪnd/	bound /baʊnd/	bound /baʊnd/	ligar, unir
bite /baɪt/	bit /bɪt/	bitten /ˈbɪt n/	picar, morder
blow /bloʊ/	blew /blu/	blown /bloʊn/	soprar; florescer; espalhar
break /breɪk/	broke /broʊk/	broken /ˈbroʊ kən/	quebrar, partir, romper
breed /brid/	bred /brɛd/	bred /brɛd/	produzir; dar cria, procriar
bring /brɪŋ/	brought /brɔt/	brought /brɔt/	trazer; produzir; levar
broadcast /ˈbrɔdˌkæst/	broadcast /ˈbrɔdˌkæst/	broadcast /ˈbrɔdˌkæst/	transmitir por rádio ou TV; espalhar
build /bɪld/	built /bɪlt/	built /bɪlt/	construir; montar
burst /bɜrst/	burst /bɜrst/	burst /bɜrst/	rebentar, estourar
buy /baɪ/	bought /bɔt/	bought /bɔt/	comprar
cast /kæst/	cast /kæst/	cast /kæst/	lançar, arremessar; emitir
catch /kætʃ/	caught /kɔt/	caught /kɔt/	pegar; capturar
choose /tʃuz/	chose /tʃoʊz/	chosen /ˈtʃoʊ zən/	escolher, selecionar
come /kʌm/	came /keɪm/	come /kʌm/	vir
cost /kɔst/	cost /kɔst/	cost /kɔst/	custar
cut /kʌt/	cut /kʌt/	cut /kʌt/	cortar

Irregular Verbs

Base Form	Simple Past	Past Participle	Translation
deal /dil/	dealt /dɛlt/	dealt /dɛlt/	lidar
dig /dɪg/	dug /dʌg/	dug /dʌg/	cavar, furar; indagar
do /du/	did /dɪd/	done /dʌn/	fazer
draw /drɔ/	drew /dru/	drawn /drɔn/	desenhar; puxar; traçar
drink /drɪŋk/	drank /dræŋk/	drunk /drʌŋk/	beber, tomar
drive /draɪv/	drove /droʊv/	driven /'drɪv ən/	dirigir, conduzir, levar a; pôr em movimento
eat /it/	ate /eɪt/	eaten /'it n/	comer
fall /fɔl/	fell /fɛl/	fallen /'fɔ lən/	cair
feed /fid/	fed /fɛd/	fed /fɛd/	alimentar
feel /fil/	felt /fɛlt/	felt /fɛlt/	sentir
fight /faɪt/	fought /fɔt/	fought /fɔt/	brigar, lutar; combater
find /faɪnd/	found /faʊnd/	found /faʊnd/	achar; julgar; encontrar; procurar
fit /fɪt/	fit /fɪt/	fit /fɪt/	encaixar, ajustar
flee /fli/	fled /flɛd/	fled /flɛd/	fugir
fly /flaɪ/	flew /flu/	flown /floʊn/	voar
forecast /'fɔr‚kæst/	forecast /'fɔr‚kæst/	forecast /'fɔr‚kæst/	prever; projetar
forget /fər'gɛt/	forgot /fər'gɒt/	forgot, forgotten /fər'gɒt n/	esquecer
forgive /fər'gɪv/	forgave /fər'geɪv/	forgiven /fər'gɪv ən/	perdoar
freeze /friz/	froze /froʊz/	frozen /'froʊ zən/	congelar
get /gɛt/	got /gɒt/	got, gotten /'gɒt n/	conseguir; receber; entender; ficar; pegar, contrair
give /gɪv/	gave /geɪv/	given /'gɪ vən/	dar
go /goʊ/	went /wɛnt/	gone /gɒn/	ir
grow /groʊ/	grew /gru/	grown /groʊn/	crescer; criar; cultivar
hang /hæŋ/	hung /hʌŋ/	hung /hʌŋ/	dependurar; ficar
have /hæv/	had /hæd/	had /hæd/	ter, possuir

Irregular Verbs

Base Form	Simple Past	Past Participle	Translation
hear /hɪər/	heard /hɜrd/	heard /hɜrd/	ouvir, escutar
hide /haɪd/	hid /hɪd/	hidden /'hɪd n/	esconder
hit /hɪt/	hit /hɪt/	hit /hɪt/	atingir; chegar a; chocar(-se) com; bater
hold /hoʊld/	held /hɛld/	held /hɛld/	segurar, agarrar; sediar
hurt /hɜrt/	hurt /hɜrt/	hurt /hɜrt/	machucar, ferir; magoar; causar prejuízo; doer
keep /kip/	kept /kɛpt/	kept /kɛpt/	manter; permanecer
know /noʊ/	knew /nyu/	known /noʊn/	conhecer; saber
lay /leɪ/	laid /leɪd/	laid /leɪd/	pôr; estender
lead /lid/	led /lɛd/	led /lɛd/	conduzir a; levar a
learn /lɜrn/	learnt /lɜrnt/ *	learnt /lɜrnt/ *	aprender; ficar sabendo, descobrir
leave /liv/	left /lɛft/	left /lɛft/	partir; sair; sobrar
lend /lɛnd/	lent /lɛnt/	lent /lɛnt/	emprestar algo a alguém
let /lɛt/	let /lɛt/	let /lɛt/	fazer com que; deixar; alugar (para alguém)
lie /laɪ/	lay /leɪ/	lain / leɪn/	jazer, estar deitado(a)
light /laɪt/	lit /lɪt/	lit /lɪt/	iluminar; acender
lose /luz/	lost /lɔst/	lost /lɔst/	perder
make /meɪk/	made /meɪd/	made /meɪd/	fazer
mean /min/	meant /mɛnt/	meant /mɛnt/	querer dizer; significar
meet /mit/	met /mɛt/	met /mɛt/	encontrar alguém
overcome /ˌoʊvərˈkʌm/	overcame /ˌoʊvərˈkeɪm/	overcome /ˌoʊvərˈkʌm/	superar
pay /peɪ/	paid /peɪd/	paid /peɪd/	pagar
put /pʊt/	put /pʊt/	put /pʊt/	pôr, colocar
quit /kwɪt/	quit /kwɪt/	quit /kwɪt/	renunciar, abandonar, desistir, deixar
read /rid/	read /rɛd/	read /rɛd/	ler
rid /rɪd/	rid /rɪd/	rid /rɪd/	livrar(-se) de

* A forma irregular do verbo *learn* é mais comum na variante britânica. Na variante estadunidense, usa-se *learned* tanto para o passado quanto para o particípio. Outros verbos desse tipo em inglês incluem *burn*, *dream*, *kneel*, *lean*, *leap*, *spell*, *spill* e *spoil*.

Irregular Verbs

Base Form	Simple Past	Past Participle	Translation
ride /raɪd/	rode /roʊd/	ridden /'rɪd n/	cavalgar; andar de
ring /rɪŋ/	rang /ræŋ/	rung /rʌŋ/	tocar (campainha, telefone, sino)
rise /raɪz/	rose /roʊz/	risen /'rɪz ən/	levantar, sair da cama; subir; tornar-se audível
run /rʌn/	ran /ræn/	run /rʌn/	correr; dirigir, administrar; ter a duração de; executar (programa de computador)
say /seɪ/	said /sɛd/	said /sɛd/	dizer
see /si/	saw /sɔ/	seen /sin/	ver; enxergar
seek /sik/	sought /sɔt/	sought /sɔt/	procurar obter, buscar; aspirar; empenhar(-se)
sell /sɛl/	sold /soʊld/	sold /soʊld/	vender
send /sɛnd/	sent /sɛnt/	sent /sɛnt/	enviar
set /sɛt/	set /sɛt/	set /sɛt/	estabelecer; passar(-se); ter lugar (em)
sew /soʊ/	sewed /soʊd/	sewn /soʊn/, sewed	costurar
shake /ʃeɪk/	shook /ʃʊk/	shaken /'ʃeɪkən/	sacudir, agitar
shine /ʃaɪn/	shone /ʃoʊn/	shone /ʃoʊn/	brilhar; refletir luz
shoot /ʃut/	shot /ʃɒt/	shot /ʃɒt/	filmar; atirar; percorrer em grande velocidade; dizer logo
show /ʃoʊ/	showed /ʃoʊd/	shown /ʃoʊn/	mostrar, apresentar; exibir
shut /ʃʌt/	shut /ʃʌt/	shut /ʃʌt/	fechar
sing /sɪŋ/	sang /sæŋ/	sung /sʌŋ/	cantar
sink /sɪŋk/	sank /sæŋk/, sunk /sʌŋk/	sunk /sʌŋk/	descer; afundar; decair
sit /sɪt/	sat /sæt/	sat /sæt/	sentar(-se); deixar por um tempo
sleep /slip/	slept /slɛpt/	slept /slɛpt/	dormir
slide /slaɪd/	slid /slɪd/	slid, slidden /'slɪd n/	deslizar
speak /spik/	spoke /spoʊk/	spoken /'spoʊ kən/	falar
spend /spɛnd/	spent /spɛnt/	spent /spɛnt/	passar (tempo); gastar
spill /spɪl/	spilt /spɪlt/ *	spilt /spɪlt/	derramar; entornar
spin /spɪn/	spun /spʌn/	spun /spʌn/	girar; torcer

* Ver nota de rodapé na página anterior.

Irregular Verbs

Base Form	Simple Past	Past Participle	Translation
split /splɪt/	split /splɪt/	split /splɪt/	rachar; separar(-se); dividir
spread /sprɛd/	spread /sprɛd/	spread /sprɛd/	espalhar; estender
spring /sprɪŋ/	sprang /spræŋ/	sprung /sprʌŋ/	surgir
stand /stænd/	stood /stʊd/	stood /stʊd/	aturar, suportar; estar de pé; ocupar certo lugar
steal /stil/	stole /stoʊl/	stolen /ˈstoʊ lən/	roubar; furtar
stick /stɪk/	stuck /stʌk/	stuck /stʌk/	grudar
sting /stɪŋ/	stung /stʌŋ/	stung /stʌŋ/	picar, ferroar; doer; ferir
strike /straɪk/	struck /strʌk/	struck /strʌk/	impressionar; abater; chocar(-se) com
swear /swɛər/	swore /swɔr/	sworn /swɔrn/	jurar, prometer; xingar, praguejar
sweep /swip/	swept /swɛpt/	swept /swɛpt/	varrer; passar rapidamente
swim /swɪm/	swam /swæm/	swum /swʌm/	nadar
swing /swɪŋ/	swung /swʌŋ/	swung /swʌŋ/	balançar
take /teɪk/	took /tʊk/	taken /ˈteɪ kən/	pegar; agarrar; levar; fazer (aula); tomar, assumir
teach /titʃ/	taught /tɔt/	taught /tɔt/	ensinar, lecionar
tear /tɛər/	tore /tɔr/	torn /tɔrn/	rasgar; dividir
tell /tɛl/	told /toʊld/	told /toʊld/	contar; dizer
think /θɪŋk/	thought /θɔt/	thought /θɔt/	pensar; achar
throw /θroʊ/	threw /θru/	thrown /θroʊn/	atirar, jogar; arremessar
understand /ˌʌn dərˈstænd/	understood /ˌʌn dərˈstʊd/	understood /ˌʌn dərˈstʊd/	entender
upset /ʌpˈsɛt/	upset /ʌpˈsɛt/	upset /ʌpˈsɛt/	perturbar; desarranjar; impedir
wake /weɪk/	woke /woʊk/	woken /ˈwoʊ kən/	acordar; despertar
wear /wɛər/	wore /wɔr/	worn /wɔrn/	usar; vestir; gastar (pelo uso)
win /wɪn/	won /wʌn/	won /wʌn/	ganhar, vencer
wind /waɪnd/	wound /waʊnd/	wound /waʊnd/	enrolar; serpentear; girar
withdraw /wɪðˈdrɔ/	withdrew /wɪðˈdru/	withdrawn /wɪðˈdrɔn/	retirar(-se); afastar(-se); sacar dinheiro
write /raɪt/	wrote /roʊt/	written /ˈrɪt n/	escrever

Workbook

Contents

Part 1 Units 1 & 2 352

Part 2 Units 3 & 4 355

Part 3 Units 5 & 6 358

Part 4 Units 7 & 8 361

Part 5 Units 9 & 10 364

Part 6 Units 11 & 12 367

Part 7 Units 13 & 14 370

Part 8 Units 15 & 16 373

Part 9 Units 17 & 18 376

Part 10 Units 19 & 20 379

Part 11 Units 21 & 22 382

Part 12 Units 23 & 24 385

This section gives you the opportunity to revise, broaden and deepen the contents presented in each of the 24 Units that make up this book. Each item of the Workbook has been organized into three parts: **Reading / Grammar / Vocabulary.**

Workbook

A. READING

1. Read this text and check (✔) the appropriate options.

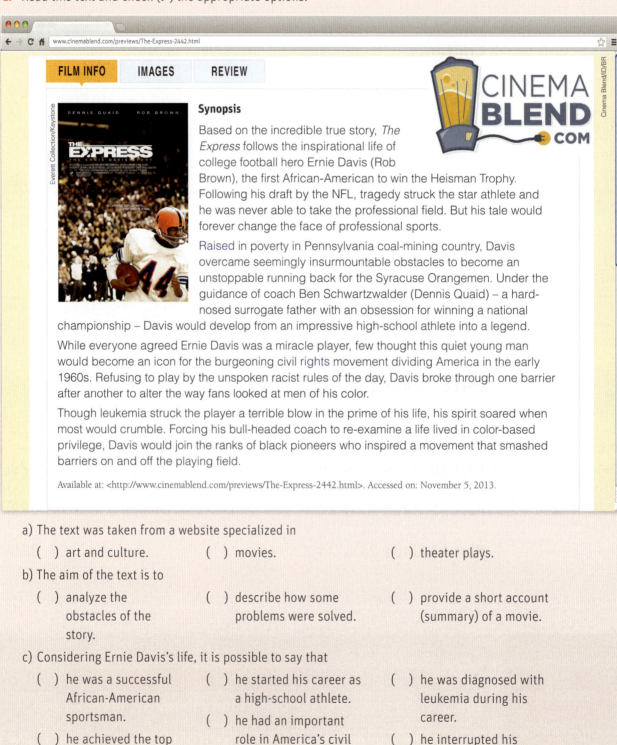

a) The text was taken from a website specialized in

( ) art and culture.   ( ) movies.   ( ) theater plays.

b) The aim of the text is to

( ) analyze the obstacles of the story.
( ) describe how some problems were solved.
( ) provide a short account (summary) of a movie.

c) Considering Ernie Davis's life, it is possible to say that

( ) he was a successful African-American sportsman.
( ) he started his career as a high-school athlete.
( ) he was diagnosed with leukemia during his career.
( ) he achieved the top when he started running.
( ) he had an important role in America's civil rights.
( ) he interrupted his career because of his racist coach.

2. Do you know any stories similar to Ernie Davis's? Answer in your notebook.

Part 1 (Units 1 & 2)

B. GRAMMAR

1. Read and match the two halves of these sentences about street art.

a) "The laws on public property are very strict and anyone caught doing graffiti can	( ) legally paint on', said Joey Mac, 22, a TMK1 writer from Beaverton."
b) "Street art can	( ) therefore be considered as an atypical exhibition, which can amaze and amuse."
c) "'The M&M Marketplace is the only wall in the Portland Metro area that graffiti artists can	( ) be found around the world and street artists often travel to other countries foreign to them so they can spread their designs."
d) "Cow Parade can	( ) be arrested and prosecuted under the Criminal Damage Act 1971."

Sources: <http://www.thesite.org/homelawandmoney/law/yourrights/graffitiandthelaw> (a); <http://en.wikipedia.org/wiki/Street_art> (b); <http://www.oregonlive.com/hillsboro/index.ssf/2012/07/graffiti_artists_paint_legally.html> (c); <http://www.articledashboard.com/Article/Open-Air-Art-Exhibition-Cow-Parade-in-Madrid/715153> (d). Accessed on: November 5, 2013.

Hint
Read all of the possibilities first and try to find the contextual link between the parts.

2. Read the text below and complete the statement saying what street artists are allowed to do and what they are prohibited to do.

The Legalization of Street Art in Rio de Janeiro, Brazil

Posted In Art, Culture, Rio de Janeiro, Street Art

by: Michelle Young

"Brazilian graffiti art is considered among the most significant strand[s] of a global urban art movement, and its diversity defies the increasing homogeneity of world graffiti." — Design Week

Graffiti on a wall in Rio de Janeiro.

In March 2009, the Brazilian government passed law 706/07 which decriminalizes street art. In an amendment to a federal law that punishes the defacing of urban buildings or monuments, street art was made legal if done with the consent of the owners. As progressive of a policy as this may sound, the legislation is actually a reflection of the evolving landscape in Brazilian street art, an emerging and divergent movement in the global street art landscape. In Brazil, there is a distinction made between tagging, known as *pichação*, and *grafite*, a street art style distinctive to Brazil.

Available at: <http://untappedcities.com/2012/02/13/the-legalization-of-street-art-in-rio-de-janeiro-brazil/>. Accessed on: November 5, 2013.

Street artists in Brazil can _____,
but they can't _____

353

Workbook

C. VOCABULARY

1. Look at the greetings below and answer the questions.

Hey! How's life? How are you?
Are you fine?
What's up! How's it going? How do you do?
Hello! Good to see you! Good morning!

a) Which ones would you use to greet a classmate (informal)?

_____

b) Which ones would you use to greet the school principal (formal)?

_____

2. Complete this encrypted sentence and learn the names of some other forms of street art.

A	B	C	D	E	F	G	H	I	J	K	L	M	N	O	P	Q	R	S	T	U	V	W	X	Y	Z
8				7				9						19			22	12	20	6					

S T R E E T   A R T   _ O R _   S I _ _ _ U E
12 20 22 7 7 20   8 22 20   5 19 22 1 12   9 13 18 16 6 26 7

_ R A _ _ I T I , S T E _ C I _ , S T I _ _ E R ,
10 22 8 5 5 9 20 9   12 20 7 13 18 9 16   12 20 9 18 _ 4 7 22

_ O S A I _ , _ I _ E O   _ R O _ E _ T I O _ ,
1 19 12 8 9 18   3 9 26 7 19   17 22 19 25 7 18 20 9 19 13

S T R E E T   I _ S T A _ _ A T I O _ ,
12 20 22 7 7 20   9 13 12 20 8 16 16 8 20 9 19 13

_ O O _   _ _ O _ I _ , _ A S _ _ O _ I _ _ ,
23 19 19 26   15 16 19 18 4 9 13 10   5 16 8 12 24   1 19 15 15 9 13 10

A _ _   A R _   O _ I _ _ .
8 13 26   11 8 22 13   15 19 1 15 9 13 10

Part 2 (Units 3 & 4)

A. READING

1. Aled Davies is a British Paralympic athlete. Read his factfile and answer the questions.

Factfile:
Hometown: Bridgend
Born: 24 May 1991
Events: discus & shot put
Class: F42
Disability: born with hemimelia of right leg
Medals won: (Gold, Bronze) Men's Discus Throw F42; Men's F42/44 Shot Put

Aled Davies of Great Britain wins gold in the Men's Discus Throw at the London 2012 Paralympic Games.

a) Where is he from? _____
b) How old is he now? _____

2. Now insert the questions of an interview with Davies back into their correct places.

Questions
Apart from athletics, what is your favourite sport?
What is the greatest moment in your career so far?
Who is your sporting idol?
Do you have a party trick?
Do you have any superstitions?

Aled Davies profile

_____
"It has to be winning the bronze medal at the World Championships in New Zealand."

_____
"I always wear the same pair of socks when I throw."

_____
"I'm a big rugby fan, which is no surprise considering I'm from Wales. I also like ultimate cage fighting."

_____
"I have two. The first is Dan Greaves, who throws discus in the class above me and the second is the runner Richard Whitehead, who's a good friend and the original Mr Motivator."

_____
"I can dance. Growing up, I trained as a salsa dancer."

Adapted from: <http://paralympics.channel4.com/the-athletes/athleteid=96/qa.html> (interview) and <http://paralympics.channel4.com/the-sports/athletics/gevent=shot/index.html> (fact file). Accessed on: January 26, 2013.

Workbook

B. GRAMMAR

1. Take a look at the diver Tom Daley's usual day and complete the text about his daily routine. Use the verbs from the box in the appropriate form. You can use them more than once.

British Olympic diver Tom Daley

go	have	eat

7:30am	Wake up and shower
8am	Breakfast
9am	School for two lessons
10:15am-12:15pm	Morning training session
1pm	Jacket potato and chicken to replenish protein levels
2pm	Back to school for another couple of lessons
4:30pm	Dinner
5:30pm	Afternoon training session
10:30pm	Lights out

Adapted from: <http://www.menshealth.co.uk/blogs/train-like-an-olympian/train-like-an-olympian-tom-daley>. Accessed on: November 5, 2013.

Tom Daley has a very disciplined routine. In the morning, the diver <u>wakes up and takes a shower</u> at 7:30.
Afterwards, he _____ and _____
Then, from 10:15am to 12:15pm, he _____
In the afternoon, he _____
at 1 o'clock and _____
at 2. Next, at 4:30pm, he _____ and, at 5:30pm, he _____
_____
In the evening, he _____ to bed at 10:30.

2. Imagine you are a reporter and you have to make a profile of a music idol. What questions would you ask him or her to get the following pieces of information?

a) full/real name: _____
b) age: _____
c) place of birth: _____
d) occupation: _____

3. Now, use the questions you created in activity 2 to simulate an interview with a music idol. Search his/her profile on the Internet and answer the questions.

YOU: _____
idol: _____
YOU: _____
idol: _____
YOU: _____
idol: _____
YOU: _____
idol: _____

Part 2 (Units 3 & 4)

C. VOCABULARY

Test your knowledge of the parts of the body in English. Read the instructions for the following exercise routine and complete them with the appropriate words from the boxes.

Judo Pushup

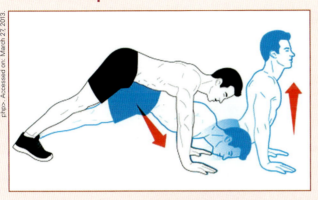

| shoulders | feet | chin | head | hips |

Begin in a pushup position but move your _____ hip-width apart and forward, and raise your _____ so your body almost forms an upside-down V. Lower the front of your body until your _____ nears the floor. Then lower your hips as you raise your _____ and _____ toward the ceiling. Now reverse the movement and return to the starting position.

Available at: <http://www.menshealth.com/mhlists/quick-full-body-workout/judo-pushup.php>. Accessed on: November 5, 2013.

Body-Weight Squat

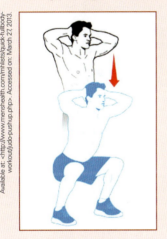

| knees | feet | thighs | hips |

Stand with your _____ shoulder-width apart. Lower your body as far as you can by pushing your _____ back and bending your _____ until your _____ are parallel to the floor. Pause, and slowly stand back up.

Available at: <http://www.menshealth.com/mhlists/quick-full-body-workout/body-weight-squat.php>. Accessed on: November 5, 2013.

Sprinter Situp

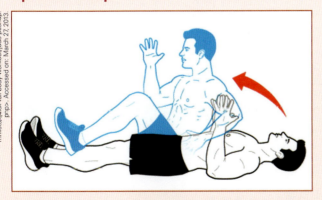

| elbow | knee | back | arms | legs |

Lie on your _____ with your _____ straight and _____ at your sides, keeping your elbows bent at 90 degrees. As you sit up, twist your upper body to the left and bring your left _____ toward your right _____ while you swing your left arm back. Lower your body to the starting position, and repeat to your right. That's 1 rep.

Available at: <http://www.menshealth.com/mhlists/quick-full-body-workout/sprinter-situp.php>. Accessed on: November 5, 2013.

357

Workbook

A. READING

1. Read the text below. What kind of text is it?

   _____

Print ad for a mall in Dubai, United Arab Emirates.

2. Now, answer the questions about the text above.

   a) Where is Burjuman Shopping Mall located?

   _____
   _____

   b) What is the woman in the campaign wearing?

   _____
   _____

   c) Which idea does the text want to sell?

   _____
   _____

   d) Why do you think people buy brand-name clothes?

   _____
   _____

   e) Do young people feel pressured to wear certain brands and fashionable accessories in your country? How do you feel about it?

   _____
   _____

   f) Do you think you are judged on what you wear or have?

   _____

Part 3 (Units 5 & 6)

B. GRAMMAR

1. The fashion industry is strongly criticized for many reasons in protests around the world. Look at these pictures and say what the people are doing. Use the verbs from the box to write your sentences.

protest	condemn	complain	criticize

a) _____

_____

b) _____

_____

c) _____

_____

d) _____

_____

2. The Week of Modern Art of 1922 was an artistic festival which inaugurated Modernism in Brazil – a cultural movement marked by a strong focus on Brazilian cultural elements and freedom of style. Read the text below and fill in the gaps with the appropriate forms of the verbs in the box.

define	occur (2x)	be	celebrate	take	give	include

The art festival that _____ place in Sao Paulo, Brazil, from February 11 to 18, 1922, is known as the Week of Modern Art. In Portuguese, it is called the "Semana de Arte Moderna." Because of historical evidence, it is clear that this week _____ Brazilian Modern Art and Brazilian Modernism. Before this festival _____, a group of Brazilian artists had started rethinking their works. The Modernist movement in Brazil was marked by blending and _____ itself particularly in the context of Brazilian society. This festival _____ important for Brazil as it _____ international exposure to Modern Art. The week's events _____ in Sao Paulo's Municipal Theater, and they _____ lectures, concerts, poetry recitations, and exposition of plastic arts.

Adapted from: <http://whysocurious.net/modern-art-week/>. Accessed on: November 6, 2013.

359

Workbook

C. VOCABULARY

1. Test your artistic knowledge by answering this quiz.

    I. What tool is normally used by designers to do their pieces of art?

    A. a brush   B. a digital pen   C. a pen

    II. What artistic expression depends strongly on advanced technology?

    A. 3D filmmaking   B. painting   C. printmaking

    III. What material is commonly used in sculptures?

    A. chalk   B. marble   C. paint

    IV. What cannot be used for illustrating?

    A. a crayon   B. a pen   C. a stone

    V. What artistic expression is not made using cameras?

    A. filmmaking   B. photography   C. printmaking

    VI. What material is not found ready in the environment?

    A. glass   B. marble   C. stone

2. Look at this store window. What clothing items and accessories does it display?

A	B	C	D

360

Part 4 (Units 7 & 8)

A. READING

1. Do you think sustainability and art have anything in common?
_____

2. Do you know any projects that link both areas?
_____

AMOR-PEIXE PROJECT CONSOLIDATED AS AN EXAMPLE OF SUSTAINABLE HANDICRAFT PRODUCTION
10 Novembro 2010 | 0 *Comments*
By *Geralda Magela*

The Amor-Peixe Association was set up in 2003, in Corumbá, a Brazilian city on the banks of the Paraguay River, which forms the frontier between Brazil and Paraguay. With a lot of hard work and creativity, the women make use of fish skins that were formerly thrown away and turn them into beautiful handicraft objects such as belts, bags, wallets, diaries, clothing, bracelets and costume jewellery. The project not only brings in an income for the women but it enhances their self esteem and is an excellent example of making good use of waste materials.

Since 2003 WWF-Brazil has been supporting the association by providing environmental education and fostering social insertion. In 2007, the NGO ran a series of capacity building workshops designed to enable the group to re-organise its structure.

That work was coordinated by biologist Terezinha Martins of WWF-Brazil's Pantanal Programme and professor Josenildo Souza e Silva from the Federal University of Rondônia, a fisheries engineer and a specialist in participative methodologies.

The educators and the group established a work plan that included a series of live workshops and activities to be undertaken in the intervals between them. At the workshops they learned about design, associativism, entrepreneurship, environment, participative management and public policies.

The knowledge acquired in the capacity building courses and the other activities has helped these craftswomen to improve their organisation and produce objects that are more attractive to the market while at the same time valuing the Pantanal's regional culture and the environment. "Nowadays they receive invitations to participate in events like fairs and seminars and their work is widely recognised as an example of sustainable handicrafts", declares Terezinha.

The recycling work generates income and reinforces these Pantanal women's identities. In addition to the social and organisational aspect, the project has strongly emphasised environmental considerations. In the Amor-Peixe, nothing is thrown away. Everything is made use of. Even the fish scales are transformed into costume jewellery. […]

Available at: <http://www.wwf.org.br/?26703/Amor-Peixe-project-consolidated-as-an-example-of-sustainable-handicraft-production>. Accessed on: November 7, 2013.

---

3. Read the text above and decide if these eight statements are (T)rue or (F)alse.

a) The Amor-Peixe Association began in 2007. (   )
b) The women use fish bone to make handicraft objects. (   )
c) The handicraft items are a source of income for the women. (   )
d) WWF-Brazil helped the project by running workshops. (   )
e) The Pantanal's culture is valued by the work of the project. (   )
f) The project helped reinforce the women's identity. (   )
g) The project was coordinated by two engineers. (   )
h) The name of the author of this article suggests she is Brazilian. (   )

Workbook

B. GRAMMAR

1. Read two other fragments from the "Amor-Peixe project" text and circle the appropriate options. When you have finished, visit the website and check if your answers are correct.

"At the end of October, the Amor-Peixe Women's Association in Corumbá (Mato Grosso do Sul) and WWF-Brazil ran a capacity building course on associativism and handicraft production using tanned fish **skin's / skins** for new **members / members'** of the association. A meeting was also arranged with the new **partner's / partners** that will be supporting the women's group from now on. The workshop and the alliance of new **partners' / partners** marked the finalisation of the formal support WWF-Brazil has been giving to the project since 2003."

"Today Amor-Peixe has become an example of community organisation and is frequently called on to share its experience with other **groups / group's**. In the middle of November, the **association's / associations** president Joana Ferreira was invited to come to Brasília (**Brazil / Brazil's** capital) to take part in a workshop organised by the Ministry of Agrarian Development where she will make a presentation of the **association's / associations** experience to other groups."

Available at: <http://www.wwf.org.br/?26703/Amor-Peixe-project-consolidated-as-an-example-of-sustainable-handicraft-production>. Accessed on: November 7, 2013.

2. Observe the photos and captions. What are the people in line going to do in each situation?

Madonna's fans in front of L'Olympia City Hall, Paris, France, 2012.

People line up to buy tickets for a film festival in Berlin, Germany, 2012.

People line up to get on a bus on the Chang'an Avenue in Beijing, China, 2008.

Students selecting food items at a school cafeteria in Rotterdam, NY, USA, 2012.

Part 4 (Units 7 & 8)

C. VOCABULARY

1. Review some words related to handicrafts by completing this conceptual map with the materials you may use to produce handicraft work.

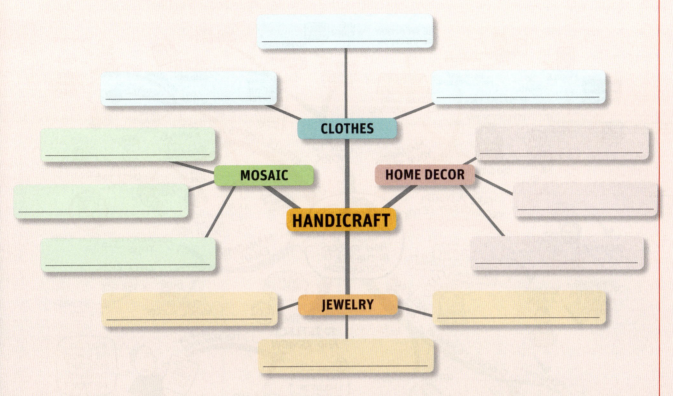

2. Complete this crossword puzzle related to festivals and parades.

Across
6. A very decorated platform used in Carnival festivals.

Down
1. A set of small paint buckets used for painting people's faces in festivals.
2. Mask traditionally used in Venice's Carnival balls.
3. Peculiar clothes associated to characters, nations, or groups of people.
4. Necklaces used by people in some festivals can be made of these round pieces of colored glass or acrylic.
5. A great number of people gathered to watch or take part in a festival.

Workbook

A. READING

1. Do you get distracted easily when you are using the Internet? _____

2. In your opinion, what are (or can be) the most distracting activities while you are online? _____

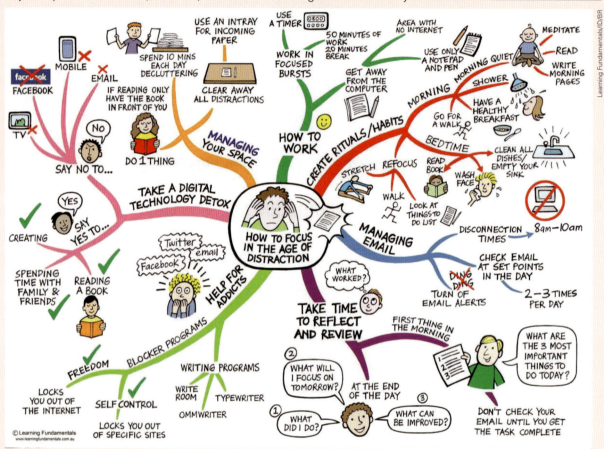

3. The text above mentions the expression "the age of distraction." Is the Internet the one to blame, or is it the way we deal with the new communication technologies?

_____

4. Based on the infographic above and on your knowledge, choose one of the options in parentheses to make appropriate recommendations for people to focus in the age of distraction. Write the word.

Managing your space

a) _____ (Do/Don't do) just one thing at a time.
b) _____ (Keep/Don't keep) distractions away from you.
c) _____ (Spend/Don't spend) ten minutes organizing your things.

Take a digital technology detox

d) _____ (Spend/Don't spend) time with your family and friends.
e) _____ (Use/Don't use) your cell phone, send e-mail, watch TV, or access Facebook.

Help for addicts

f) _____ (Use/Don't use) blocker programs or adopt an alternative to writing.

364

Part 5 (Units 9 & 10)

Take time to reflect and review

g) Early in the morning, _____ (*check/don't check*) your e-mail before you decide what the three most important things to be done are.

h) At the end of the day, _____ (*reflect/don't reflect*) on what you did during the day.

Managing e-mail

i) _____ (*Turn on/Don't turn on*) e-mail alerts.

j) _____ (*Keep/Don't keep*) your computer disconnected from 8am to 10am.

k) _____ (*Check/Don't check*) e-mail two or three times a day.

Create rituals/habits

l) _____ (*Have/Don't have*) a quiet morning: read, meditate, go for a walk.

m) Before bedtime, _____ (*wash/don't wash*) your face, clean the dishes, read a book.

How to work

n) _____ (*Stay/Don't stay*) away from the computer.

o) _____ (*Work/Don't work*) for fifty minutes and have a break for twenty minutes.

▌B. GRAMMAR

1. Use four verbs from the box to complete this description of a social network service. Remember to use the appropriate verb tense for this kind of text.

connect	be	consist	focus	share	chat

A social networking service _____ an online service, platform, or site that _____ on facilitating the building of social networks or social relations among people who, for example, _____ interests, activities, backgrounds, or real-life connections. A social network service _____ of a representation of each user (often a profile), his/her social links, and a variety of additional services. [...]

Available at: <http://mashable.com/follow/topics/social-networking/>. Accessed on: November 26, 2013.

2. Fill in the blanks with the verbs in parentheses. Decide if the actions are in progress or are routines/habits.

We _____ (live) in curious times. It's called the Age of Information, but in another light it can be called the Age of Distraction.

[...]

When we _____ (work), we _____ (have) distractions coming from every direction. In front of us _____ (be) the computer, with e-mail notifications and other notifications of all kinds. Then there's the addicting lure of the browser, which _____ (contain) not only an endless amount of reading material that can be a black hole into which we never _____ (escape), but unlimited opportunities for shopping, for chatting with other people, for gossip and news and lurid photos and so much more. [...]

Computers _____ (take over) our lives. And while I _____ (be) as pro-technology as the next guy (more so in many cases), I also _____ (think) we need to consider the consequences of this new lifestyle. [...]

Available at: <http://focusmanifesto.com/the-age-of-distraction/>. Accessed on: November 26, 2013.

Workbook

C. VOCABULARY

1. Do the crossword puzzle. Then check your answers with a classmate.

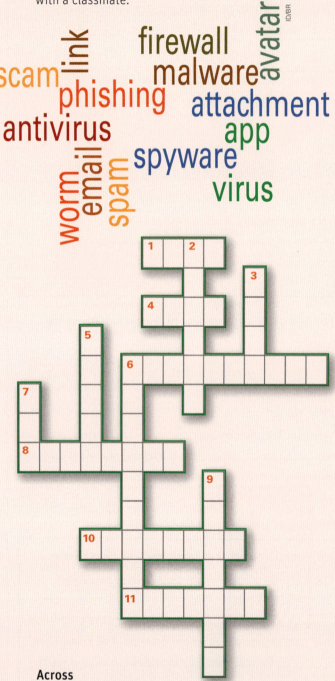

Across
1. An e-mail that is not wanted.
4. A dishonest way to make money by deceiving people.
6. A document or file that is sent with e-mail.
8. To request confidential information over the Internet under false pretenses in order to fraudulently obtain credit card numbers, passwords, or other personal data.
10. A technological barrier designed to prevent unauthorized or unwanted communications.
11. A computer software that secretly records information about the way you use your computer.

Down
2. An image or username that represents a person online within forums and social networks.
3. A computer virus that causes damage to computers connected to each other by a network.
5. A program that is designed to harm a computer by deleting data, ruining files, etc.
6. A protective software designed to defend your computer against malicious software.
7. An application; a computer program that performs a particular task.
9. A software designed to interfere with a computer's normal functioning.

2. *Come*, *connect*, *make*, or *send*? What are the verbs that go with these four groups of words?

_____ friends
              connections
              a mistake

_____ an e-mail
              a message
              an e-card

_____ to a solution
              to an agreement
              to a decision

_____ people
              roads
              places

3. Cross out the verb that does not go with the noun.
   a) describe, do, enjoy, have, share   AN EXPERIENCE
   b) receive, get, open, post, answer   E-MAILS
   c) join, participate in, start, make A WEB FORUM
   d) find, have, receive, look for, get A JOB
   e) write, start, send, read   A BLOG

Part 6 (Units 11 & 12)

A. READING

Read the following excerpt and answer the questions.

> An April 2009 survey by the Pew Research Center's Internet & American Life Project shows that 56% of adult Americans have accessed the Internet by wireless means, such as using a laptop, mobile device, game console, or MP3 player. The most prevalent way people get online using a wireless network is with a laptop computer; 39% of adults have done this.
>
> Adapted from: <http://www.pewinternet.org/Reports/2009/12-Wireless-Internet-Use.aspx>. Accessed on: December 4, 2013.

a) Who has accessed the Internet by wireless means?

_____

b) Does the text mention when the Internet was accessed?

_____

c) What does "this" in "39% of adults have done this" refer to? What is more important in this sentence: the fact itself or when it happened?

_____

d) Find in the text two sentences which refer to actions which happened at an unspecified time in the past. Which tense is used in these sentences?

_____

_____

e) Would you say these percentages are the same for Brazil and your community?

_____

f) How often do *you* use Wi-Fi Internet?

_____

B. GRAMMAR

1. Complete the sentences about the history of the radio with the correct form and tense of the verbs in parentheses.

   a) James Clerk Maxwell _____ (not/create) the first radio.
   b) He _____ (elaborate) the first radio-wave mathematical formula.
   c) In 1888, Heinrich Hertz _____ (test) Maxwell's assumption.
   d) Radio _____ (be) a subdivision of telecommunication.
   e) "When _____ Oliver Lodge _____ (name) the coherer?" "In 1894."
   f) In 1888, Temistocle Calzecchi-Onesti _____ (demonstrate) that a tube with iron filings conducted an electrical current.
   g) Radio communication _____ (involve) the transmission of electromagnetic waves.
   h) Before the 19th century, many scientists _____ (try) to invent something like the radio.
   i) Marconi _____ (notice) that electromagnetic waves _____ (travel) between two points separated by an obstacle.

367

Workbook

2. Complete this chart with other verbs according to the adequate spelling rule. Add two extra examples to each rule. Use the last line to explain the recurrent pattern in each category.

Simple Past Spelling Rules

1	2	3	4	5
E.g. dance *danced*	E.g. cut *cut*	E.g. stop *stopped*	E.g. play *played*	E.g. worry *worried*

3. Ask a classmate if she or he has ever done the actions suggested in the box below. Write the questions.

> text during a class   receive an unexpected call in the movies   access the Internet on a smartphone
> download apps through your cell phone   see someone texting while driving   exchange files via Bluetooth
> leave a message on voicemail   send pictures via SMS   film with a smartphone

a) _____
b) _____
c) _____
d) _____
e) _____
f) _____
g) _____
h) _____
i) _____

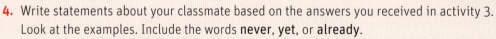

4. Write statements about your classmate based on the answers you received in activity 3. Look at the examples. Include the words **never**, **yet**, or **already**.

Paula has never texted during a class.
Paula hasn't texted during a class yet.
Paula has already texted during a class.

a) _____
b) _____
c) _____
d) _____
e) _____

Part 6 (Units 11 & 12)

5. Complete the groups below with irregular verbs. Consult the list of irregular verbs at the the end of the book.

All forms are the same CUT – CUT – CUT	2nd and 3rd forms are the same LOSE - LOST - LOST	All forms are different DRIVE - DROVE - DRIVEN

C. VOCABULARY

What do the seven symbols below refer to? Complete the crossword puzzle.

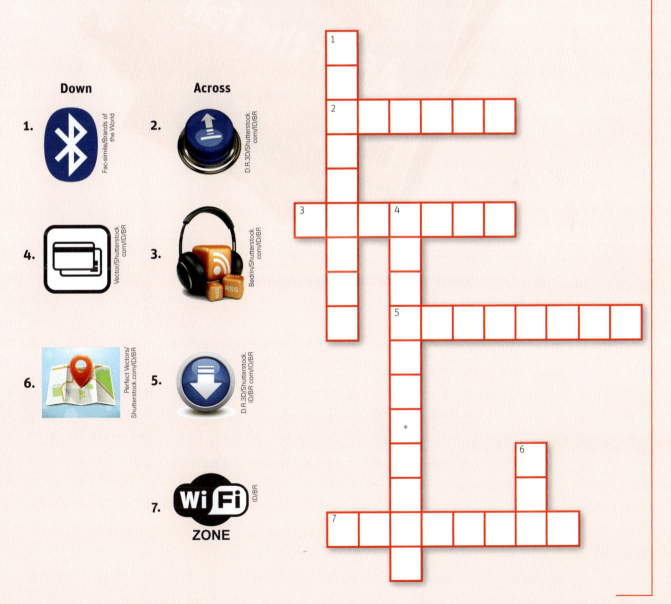

Workbook

A. READING

Take a look at this magazine cover and answer the questions.

Available at: <http://www.ritholtz.com/blog/2009/08/falling-home-price-magazine-cover/>. Accessed on: December 4, 2013.

a) What type of magazine is it? How do you know?

_____

b) The word "fall" can be interpreted literally and metaphorically. What are some of the possible interpretations? Use a dictionary to help you.

_____

_____

c) What does the falling object represent literally and metaphorically?

Literally: _____

Metaphorically: _____

d) Do you think the message portrayed on this cover is positive or negative? Explain.

_____

Part 7 (Units 13 & 14)

B. GRAMMAR

Digital consumption is usually big news in online newspapers. Examine the graph and say what the people from these countries were doing online at the time of the report.

Digital Consumption

For many Chinese digital consumers, the Internet is becoming a fixture in their lives. What's more? They are enthusiastically embracing social applications, and prefer instant messaging over e-mail.
Top online activities by percentage of digital consumers in each country (2009)

	Instant Messaging	Online Music	Reading News	Online Video	Search Engine	Online Gaming	Email	Blogging	Social Networking	E-Commerce
CHINA	87%	83%	80%	76%	69%	55%	53%	38%	33%	28%
INDIA	62%	60%	61%	53%	50%	54%	95%	N/A	23%	17%
BRAZIL	61%	49%	47%	49%	83%	44%	77%	17%	69%	17%
RUSSIA	56%	47%	65%	41%	81%	31%	78%	33%	15%	21%
U.S.A.	38%	34%	70%	68%	89%	35%	91%	11%	35%	71%
JAPAN	23%	25%	90%	49%	92%	16%	88%	32%	32%	46%

*Data gathered from the Boston Consulting Group report, "China's Digital Generations 2.0."

Available at: <http://marketingland.com/infographic-meet-the-chinese-facebook-twitter-youtube-4863>. Accessed on: December 4, 2013.

a) In China, they _____ (send) more messages than in the other countries.

b) The Japanese _____ (read) more news online than the other countries.

c) Chinese people _____ (send) more instant messages than e-mail.

d) People in India _____ (watch) more online videos than people in Brazil.

e) More than 90% of Indians _____ (send) e-mails.

f) A small percentage of Americans _____ (blog).

g) The country where people _____ (use) social networks the most was Brazil.

h) Most Japanese people _____ (use) search engines.

i) The United States is where people _____ (buy) online the most.

j) More people in Russia _____ (listen) to music online than in the United States.

371

Workbook

C. VOCABULARY

1. Complete the empty spaces below with the four parts of a news story.

Available at: <http://1.bp.blogspot.com/_9gn6KLa5xtY/Sqp82LVQhBI/AAAAAAAAE6c/F-Mfus9aBOE/s400/911NewYorkTimesFrontPageSept112001>. Accessed on: December 4, 2013.

2. Use the suffixes **-ion**, **-tion**, and **-ment** to transform these verbs into nouns.

communicate   entertain   empower   collect   classify   inform

_____ _____ _____ _____ _____ _____

3. Now use the suffixes **-ing** and **-ive** to transform these verbs into adjectives.

collect   perform   communicate   entertain   inform

_____ _____ _____ _____ _____

Part 8 (Units 15 & 16)

A. READING

Read the following text and answer the questions.

Testosterone TV: What Shows Are Most Watched By Men?

When they're not playing fantasy football, guys like shows that give them a competitive edge – and advertisers will pay more to reach them.

The television landscape has splintered, with niche networks now catering to every conceivable demographic and interest. But amid the clutter, there is one large yet elusive constituency that advertisers still pay a premium to reach: men, especially young men. That's because males still watch less television than females, making them more difficult for advertisers to locate.

In fact, most estimates put the TV-watching audience at about 60 percent women, and despite a seismic shift in gender roles, women are still at home – and in front of the television – much more often than men.

Available at: <http://www.hollywoodreporter.com/news/television-shows-men-watch-222356>. Accessed on: December 4, 2013.

a) What does the expression "testosterone TV" in the title above mean? Explain.

_____

b) According to the text, what kind of TV shows do men watch most?

_____

c) Why are men a difficult target for advertisers?

_____

d) What is a possible explanation for the prevalence of a female TV audience?

_____

e) This text is about the American TV audience. What do you think about the TV audience in your country?

_____

f) What do you think of the way women are represented in the text? Does it reflect the women in your community?

_____

Workbook

B. GRAMMAR

1. Take a look at the technology predictions released in the press that didn't come true. Complete them with the simple future tense of the verbs in parentheses.

a) "We _____ (never/make) a 32-bit operating system."
Bill Gates, 1989

b) "A rocket _____ (never/be) able to leave the Earth's atmosphere."
New York Times, 1936

c) "Television _____ (not/last). It's a flash in the pan."
Mary Somerville, pioneer of radio educational broadcasts, 1948

d) "To place a man in a multi-stage rocket and project him into the controlling gravitational field of the moon where the passengers can make scientific observations, perhaps land alive, and then return to earth – all that constitutes a wild dream worthy of Jules Verne. I am bold enough to say that such a man-made voyage _____ (never/occur) regardless of all future advances."
Lee DeForest, American radio pioneer and inventor of the vacuum tube, 1926

e) "When the Paris exhibition [of 1878] closes, electric light _____ (close) with it and no more will be heard of it."
Oxford professor Erasmus Wilson, 1878

Available at: <http://listverse.com/2007/10/28/top-30-failed-technology-predictions/>. Accessed on: December 4, 2013.

2. Read the excerpts about YouTube and choose the most adequate linking word.

a) YouTube occasionally receives requests from governments around the world to remove content from our site, and [?], YouTube may block specific content in order to comply with local laws in certain countries.
Available at: <http://www.infowars.com/government-orders-you-tube-to-censor-protest-videos/>. Accessed on: December 4, 2013.

( ) in addition   ( ) for example   ( ) as a result

b) In order to create a YouTube account, we require users to confirm that they are at least 13 years old. Users who enter any age younger than 13 will be prohibited from creating YouTube accounts. [?], if a user's video gets flagged and, upon review, we determine that the user has inaccurately stated their age during the account creation process, we will suspend their account.
Available at: <http://support.google.com/youtube/bin/answer.py?hl=en&answer=126289>. Accessed on: December 4, 2013.

( ) However   ( ) In addition   ( ) Such as

c) Of course, using YouTube for the classroom goes far beyond just playing movies in the classroom. You can also use YouTube to encourage interaction by students. [?], as an assignment, you can have students include videos as part of a research project. They can upload those videos to their YouTube account.
Available at: <http://www.educational-freeware.com/news/youtube-classroom.aspx>. Accessed on: December 4, 2013.

( ) For example   ( ) However   ( ) In conclusion

d) Proper use of music and sound can make or break your video or film production. [?], for those who use YouTube in a professional way, using *the right type* of music in your productions can make all the difference between a happy and a grumpy client.
Available at: <http://www.reelseo.com/royalty-free-music/>. Accessed on: December 4, 2013.

( ) Moreover   ( ) However   ( ) While

Part 8 (Units 15 & 16)

C. VOCABULARY

1. Complete this crossword puzzle with the name of the corresponding weather forecast symbol.

2. What is the "perfect" weather for you? Explain why.

_____

Workbook

A. READING

1. What is global warming? Do you know what causes it?

_____

_____

2. Read the comic strip below and answer the questions.

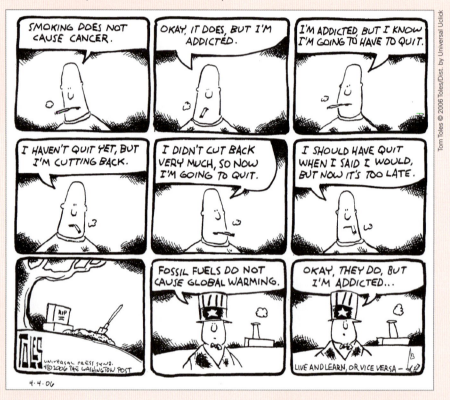

a) We can conclude that the first character   ( ) denied   ( ) ignored   ( ) criticized   the harms of smoking.

b) There is an implicit comparison in this comic strip. Read it again and complete the scheme below.

smoking	——— causes ———▶	
"is compared to"		"is compared to"
	——— causes ———▶	

c) The criticism of this comic strip is directed mainly to

     ( ) addicts.   ( ) industries.   ( ) managers.   ( ) smokers.

d) Do you think global warming really exists?

_____

e) What do you think we can do in order to stop or ease the harms of global warming?

_____

Part 9 (Units 17 & 18)

B. GRAMMAR

1. Read about some of the most amazing animals in the wild and decide if the adjectives in parentheses should be used in their superlative or comparative form.

a) The African Bush Elephant – Brute Strength

The king of the jungle is a title that still misleadingly belongs to the elephant, not the lion. Neither of them lives in any jungle in Africa. The African elephant is _____ (large) land animal on Earth and has zero natural predators (man doesn't count as natural). [...] Of course _____ (large) land animal is sure to be also _____ (powerful), and the elephant is, but it possesses an intelligence that may rival that of some primates. [...]

b) Sea Wasp Box Jellyfish – Most Lethally Venomous in the Sea

Everyone is always asking what animal packs _____ (deadly) venom in the world. [...] Sea life has abounded for about 3 billion years _____ (long) life on land, and the _____ (long) nature has to evolve its animals, the _____ (nasty), _____ (deadly), _____ (perfect) they get. There are many species of box jellies, but *Chironex fleckeri*, also called the sea wasp, is by far _____ (notorious). It can weigh up to 4 and half pounds (2 kgs), with a bell that can reach the size of a basketball, with 15 tentacles up to 10 feet long beneath. Its infamous venom was once thought to glow in the dark, but cannot. Instead, the venom absorbs and reflects _____ (slight) sunlight into and out from the tentacles, giving the jelly an ethereal glow even at twilight. Luckily, this enables you to see it coming. [...]

c) Amazonian Manatee (*Trichechus Inunguis*)

Is the Amazonian Manatee a lady or an ox? Her name comes from a Brazilian Indian word that means "Lady of the Water." [...] She is also referred to by some as the Amazon Ox Manatee. Whether an ox or a lady, the Amazonian Manatee is large, but is _____ (small) species of manatees. Amazonian Manatees can be found in the fresh waters of the Amazon River Basin throughout Brazil, Colombia, Peru and Ecuador. [...] West Indian and West African manatees have much _____ (rough) skin than the Amazonian Manatee, but they share the same gray color. The Amazonian Manatee sports a white or pinkish colored belly. [...] _____ (large) of this species measures from eight to ten meters in length.

Available at: <http://listverse.com/2012/06/18/top-10-deadliest-animals/> (a, b); <http://www.brazilianfauna.com/amazonianmanatee.php> (c). Both accessed on: December 12, 2013.

2. Add a tag question to each sentence below.

a) The elephant is the king of the jungle, _____

b) The elephant has no natural predators, _____

c) There are many species of box jellies, _____

d) The Sea Wasp Box Jellyfish can weigh up to 4 and half pounds, _____

e) The original name of the Brazilian Manatee came from an Indian name, _____

f) Amazonian Manatees can be found in the Amazon River, _____

Workbook

C. VOCABULARY

Complete this crossword puzzle with some environmental problems. Read the five clues below.

DOWN

1. The process of destroying a forest and replacing it with something else. The term is used today to refer to the destruction of forests by human beings and their replacement by agricultural systems.
2. An increase in the Earth's average atmospheric temperature that causes corresponding changes in climate and that may result from the greenhouse effect.
3. A long-term change in the Earth's climate, especially a change due to an increase in the average atmospheric temperature.

ACROSS

4. The trapping of the sun's warmth in a planet's lower atmosphere, due to the greater transparency of the atmosphere to visible radiation from the sun than to infrared radiation emitted from the planet's surface.
5. The introduction of harmful solutions or products into the environment.

Source: <http://dictionary.reference.com/> (1, 2, 3, 5) and <http://oxforddictionaries.com/definition/english/greenhouse%2Beffect> (4). Both accessed on: December 13, 2013.

Part 10 (Units 19 & 20)

A. READING

1. Read the two nutrition facts labels below. Then decide:

   Text ____ describes a hamburger; Text ____ describes a tuna fish sandwich.

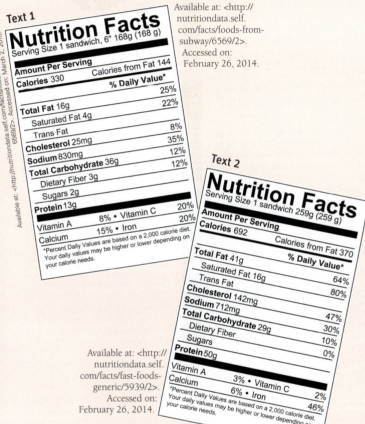

Text 1 — Available at: <http://nutritiondata.self.com/facts/foods-from-subway/6569/2>. Accessed on: February 26, 2014.

Text 2 — Available at: <http://nutritiondata.self.com/facts/fast-foods-generic/5939/2>. Accessed on: February 26, 2014.

2. What type of information in the labels above helped you answer the questions in activity 1?

   _____

   _____

3. Based on the nutrition facts labels above, which food is richer in the elements below? Write **H** for hamburger and **T** for tuna fish sandwich.

   ( ) calories   ( ) sugars
   ( ) saturated fat   ( ) protein
   ( ) cholesterol   ( ) vitamin A
   ( ) sodium   ( ) calcium
   ( ) carbohydrates   ( ) vitamin C
   ( ) dietary fiber   ( ) iron

4. Answer the questions based on this graph and the chart about eating disorders in the USA.

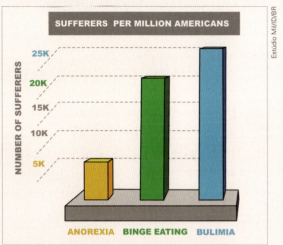

Adapted from: <http://www.mirror-mirror.org/graphs-on-eating-disorders.htm>. Accessed on: December 13, 2013.

Eating Disorders Comparison Chart (fragment)

	Anorexia	**Bulimia**	**Binge Eating Disorder**
Weight	Significantly underweight; BMI of less than 17.5	Varies, usually normal weight or overweight	Usually overweight
Eating habits	Takes in a few calories, may eat only a limited variety of foods and may have odd food rituals	Binges by eating large amounts of food in a short period of time, then purges by vomiting and/or abusing laxatives	Binges by eating large amounts of food in a short period of time, may restrict food in between binges

a) What is the most prevalent eating disorder in the US?

   _____

b) Does the graph show the percentage of people who suffer from anorexia?

   _____

c) What do bulimics normally do with the food they eat?

   _____

d) How many Americans, out of one million, suffer from binge eating?

   _____

379

Workbook

B. GRAMMAR

1. Match the items accordingly to make complete sentences.

   A. If you exercise regularly,

   B. Your risk of developing intestinal cancer is higher

   C. If you cook meat and poultry all the way through,

   D. If you eat fewer calories and burn more calories,

   E. Your body's metabolism will start to slow down in order to conserve calories

   ( ) pathogens die.

   ( ) your body will begin to use fat stores for energy and you will lose weight.

   ( ) you will prevent excess weight gain or help maintain weight.

   ( ) if you eat too little.

   ( ) if you consume red and processed meat regularly.

   Based on: <http://straighthealth.com/pages/five/not-losing-weight.html>. Accessed on: December 13, 2013.

2. Give advice to a person who asks you the following questions. Follow the example.

   a) What would happen if I ate only fast food sandwiches?

   If you ate only fast food sandwiches, you would gain a lot of weight.

   b) What would happen if I had a less idle life?

   _____

   _____

   c) What would happen if I ate too much sugar?

   _____

   _____

   d) What would happen if I lost some extra weight?

   _____

   _____

3. Use the Simple Past and the Past Perfect to contrast the events on this timeline.

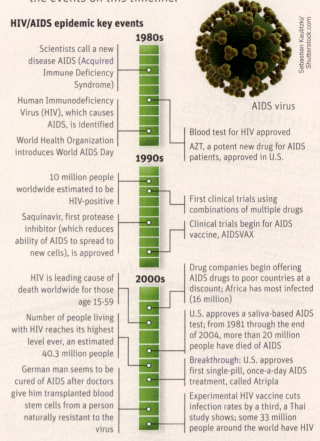

HIV/AIDS epidemic key events

1980s
- Scientists call a new disease AIDS (Acquired Immune Deficiency Syndrome)
- Human Immunodeficiency Virus (HIV), which causes AIDS, is identified
- World Health Organization introduces World AIDS Day
- Blood test for HIV approved
- AZT, a potent new drug for AIDS patients, approved in U.S.

1990s
- 10 million people worldwide estimated to be HIV-positive
- Saquinavir, first protease inhibitor (which reduces ability of AIDS to spread to new cells), is approved
- First clinical trials using combinations of multiple drugs
- Clinical trials begin for AIDS vaccine, AIDSVAX

2000s
- HIV is leading cause of death worldwide for those age 15-59
- Number of people living with HIV reaches its highest level ever, an estimated 40.3 million people
- German man seems to be cured of AIDS after doctors give him transplanted blood stem cells from a person naturally resistant to the virus
- Drug companies begin offering AIDS drugs to poor countries at a discount; Africa has most infected (16 million)
- U.S. approves a saliva-based AIDS test; from 1981 through the end of 2004, more than 20 million people have died of AIDS
- Breakthrough: U.S. approves first single-pill, once-a-day AIDS treatment, called Atripla
- Experimental HIV vaccine cuts infection rates by a third, a Thai study shows; some 33 million people around the world have HIV

AIDS virus

Sebastian Kaulitzki/Shutterstock.com

U.S. Food and Drug Administration, The Columbia Electronic Encyclopedia Graphic. Available at: <http://www.jameslogancourier.org/index.php?itemid=5436>. Accessed on: December 13, 2013.

a) When the World Health Organization _____ _____ (introduce) World AIDS Day, the U.S. _____ (approve) AZT.

b) When the clinical trials for the AIDS vaccine _____ (start), scientists _____ _____ (already approve) the first protease inhibitor.

c) When the U.S. _____ (approve) a saliva-based AIDS test, they _____ (approve – neg.) the first single-pill yet.

d) When the U.S. _____ (approve) the first single-pill for AIDS treatment, HIV ___ _____ (reach) its highest level ever (40.3 million people).

Part 10 (Units 19 & 20)

C. VOCABULARY

Match the following words to their categories in the chart.

MINERALS LEG OBESE OVERWEIGHT HEALTHY FRUITS SKIN ARTHRITIS MOUTH ANTIOXIDANTS TEETH HAIR WHOLE GRAINS VEGETABLES BIOTIN NUTS TUNA STOMACH CHICKEN TYPE 2 DIABETES VITAMINS HEART HIGH BLOOD PRESSURE ENERGETIC FIBER CANCER EGGS HEART DISEASE

ILLNESSES

WORDS THAT DESCRIBE A PERSON

NUTRIENTS

FOOD

PARTS OF THE BODY

Workbook

A. READING

1. What do you know about Martin Luther King, Jr.? Why is his name related to the theme "affirmative action?"

   _____

2. Read these biographical notes on the life of Martin Luther King, Jr. and complete the chart by writing the corresponding years.

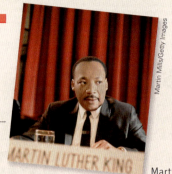

Martin Luther King, Jr., 1965.

Did you know...?

Words such as "negro" and "colored" are considered offensive today. The meaning of words change over time.

Martin Luther King, Jr., (January 15, 1929-April 4, 1968) was born Michael Luther King, Jr., but later had his name changed to Martin.

[…]

Always a strong worker for civil rights for members of his race, King was, by the year of 1954, a member of the executive committee of the National Association for the Advancement of Colored People, the leading organization of its kind in the nation. He was ready, then, early in December, 1955, to accept the leadership of the first great Negro nonviolent demonstration of contemporary times in the United States, the bus boycott. The boycott lasted 382 days. On December 21, 1956, after the Supreme Court of the United States had declared unconstitutional the laws requiring segregation on buses, Negroes and whites rode the buses as equals. During these days of boycott, King was arrested, his home was bombed, he was subjected to personal abuse, but at the same time he emerged as a Negro leader of the first rank.

[…]

In the eleven-year period between 1957 and 1968, King traveled over six million miles and spoke over twenty-five hundred times, appearing wherever there was injustice, protest, and action; he directed the peaceful march on Washington, D.C., of 250,000 people to whom he delivered his address, "I Have a Dream"; was named Man of the Year by *Time* magazine in 1963; and became not only the symbolic leader of American blacks but also a world figure.

[…]

On the evening of April 4, 1968, while standing on the balcony of his motel room in Memphis, Tennessee, where he was to lead a protest march in sympathy with striking garbage workers of that city, he was assassinated.

Adapted from: <http://www.nobelprize.org/nobel_prizes/peace/laureates/1964/king-bio.html>. Accessed on: December 13, 2013.

| 1929 | | | 1955 | 1956 | | 1968 |

1957 - 1968

	He is shot and killed.
	Martin Luther King, Jr. travels long distances fighting intensely for the cause of his community.
	Martin Luther King, Jr. is born.
	Black citizens are able to ride buses with white citizens "as equals."
	He takes over the leadership of the bus boycott, a significant event in the civil rights movements in the USA.

Part 11 (Units 21 & 22)

3. Does the text mention when Martin Luther King, Jr. had his name changed?

_____

4. Try to remember the names of other affirmative action leaders. Consider people in your own country and people from abroad.

_____

B. GRAMMAR

1. Imagine you read these pieces of news on the Internet and you want to report them to a friend. Finish the sentence about each headline appropriately. Pay attention to the verb form!

a)

> ## Indian Muslim Women Fight for Gender Equality in Marriage
>
> by Feminist Majority Foundation Blog on Apr 27, 2012

Available at: <http://feminist.org/blog/index.php/2012/04/27/indian-muslim-women-fight-for-gender-equality-in-marriage/>. Accessed on: December 13, 2013.

A website published that _____

_____

_____

b)

> ## US Supreme Court allows anti-gay funeral protests
>
> 2 March 2011 Last updated at 19:55 GMT

Available at: <http://www.bbc.co.uk/news/world-us-canada-12624539> Accessed on: December 13, 2013.

I found out that _____

_____

_____

c)

> ## Brazilian Supreme Court Approves Racial Quotas in University

Available at: <http://www.geledes.org.br/areas-de-atuacao/educacao/cotas-para-negros/13998-brazilian-supreme-court-approves-racial-quotas-in-university>. Accessed on: December 13, 2013.

I learned that _____

_____

_____

d)

> ## An end to male, pale and stale? Scottish parties promise action on equality
>
> Posted by Severin Carrell, Scotland correspondent 19.53 BST

Available at: <http://www.guardian.co.uk/uk/scotland-blog/2012/apr/19/scottish-parties-promise-equalities-action>. Accessed on: December 13, 2013.

I learned from _The Guardian_ that _____

_____

_____

2. Based on the different intelligences, write sentences about what you **can** and **can't** do well. You can mention the abilities of the _can do_ list of Unit 21 (_Lead-in_). Look at the example.

I can use different words to express myself,

but I can't remember pieces of music easily.

_____

_____

_____

_____

_____

_____

383

Workbook

C. VOCABULARY

1. Look at some actions related to multiple intelligences. Match the words in the box below to the actions in the illustration. Some answers are given for you. Write the numbers in the circles.

1	drum	15	map
2	reason	16	write
3	teach	17	dance
4	care for	18	talk
5	play	19	listen
6	draw	20	think critically
7	act	21	connect to living things
8	color		
9	visualize	22	reflect
10	explore	23	make authentic choices
11	interact		
12	touch	24	rap
13	collaborate	25	experiment
14	move		

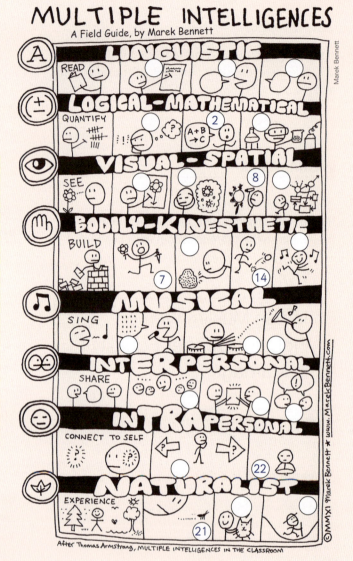

2. Odd one out. Cross out the word that **doesn't** belong in each group.

a) People whose primary intelligence is bodily-kinesthetic can more naturally
    move.   sing.   dance.   act.

b) People whose primary intelligence is visual can more naturally
    construct.   color.   map.   draw.

c) People whose primary intelligence is interpersonal can more naturally
    teach.   share.   collaborate.   reason.

d) People whose primary intelligence is linguistic can more naturally
    read.   quantify.   write.   listen.

e) People whose primary intelligence is logical-mathematical can more naturally
    reason.   experiment.   think critically.   compose.

f) People whose primary intelligence is musical can more naturally
    rap.   sing.   color.   chant.

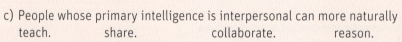

Part 12 (Units 23 & 24)

A. READING

Read the posters below and do the activities that follow.

Available at: <http://technabob.com/blog/2010/08/06/vintage-facebook-skype-and-youtube-posters/>. Accessed on: December 13, 2013.

a) The elements on the posters that remind the reader of old times are
   (   ) the characters' hairstyle.
   (   ) the clean furniture.
   (   ) the color of the posters.
   (   ) the computers' design.
   (   ) the wireless keyboard.
   (   ) the typefaces used.

b) What is the sign of "modernity" in each poster?
   _____

c) Consider the main message in each poster. Which words show the qualities of the digital tools?

Poster A: _____

Poster B: _____

d) Consider the small texts at the bottom of each poster. Make a list of the adjectives used.

Poster A: _____

Poster B: _____

e) Do these adjectives accurately describe Facebook and YouTube? _____
   _____

f) What adjectives would you use to describe these digital tools for a more serious text?
   _____

B. GRAMMAR

1. Read about some accidental inventions, according to a website. Then complete the statements based on this information.

   I. Saccharin, the sweetener in the pink packet, was discovered because chemist Constantin Fahlberg didn't wash his hands after a day at the office.

Available at: <http://www.educationalservice.net/2012/february/20120238_inventions.php>. Accessed on: December 13, 2013.

385

Workbook

II. There are many stories of accidentally invented food: the potato chip was born when cook George Crum (yes, really his name!) tried to silence a persnickety customer who kept sending French fries back to the kitchen for being soggy; popsicles were invented when Frank Epperson left a drink outside in the cold overnight; and ice-cream cones were invented at the 1904 World's Fair in St. Louis.

Available at: <http://www.sherpasoftware.com/blog/off-the-topic-accidental-inventions-that-changed-the-world/>. Accessed on: December 13, 2013.

III. Alexander Fleming didn't clean up his workstation before going on vacation one day in 1928. When he came back, Fleming noticed that there was a strange fungus on some of his cultures. Even stranger was that bacteria didn't seem to thrive near those cultures. Penicillin became the first and is still one of the most widely used antibiotics.

Available at: <http://www.sherpasoftware.com/blog/off-the-topic-accidental-inventions-that-changed-the-world/>. Accessed on: December 13, 2013.

a) Saccharin _____ by chemist _____.

b) The potato chip _____ by George Crum because one of his _____ kept sending soggy _____ back to the kitchen.

c) Popsicles _____ by _____ after he had left a drink outside in the cold overnight.

d) Ice-cream cones _____ in 1904.

e) Penicillin _____ by _____ because he had forgotten to clean his workstation before going on vacation in 1928.

2. Read about how chocolate is made. Complete the spaces with the appropriate form of the verbs in parentheses.

HOW CHOCOLATE IS MADE

- The first step is the harvesting of the cocoa pods containing the cocoa beans.
- The pods _____ (crush) and the beans and surrounding pulp extracted and fermented naturally for about six days, after which the beans _____ (dry).
- The finest chocolate _____ (produce) when the drying process _____ (do) naturally by the sun for seven days or more.
- The next process _____ (share) with coffee in that the beans _____ first _____ (grade), then roasted.
- Light crushing separates the kernel or "nib" from the shell or husk (like shelling a nut); the husk _____ then _____ (separate) or "winnowed" out and discarded.
- The nibs, which are very high in fat or cocoa butter, _____ then finely _____ (mill) and liquefy in the heat generated by the milling process to produce cocoa liquor.
- At this point the manufacturing process splits according to the final product. If the end product is chocolate, some of the cocoa liquor _____ (reserve); the rest _____ (press) to extract the cocoa butter, leaving a solid residue called press cake. Press cake _____ finely _____ (grind) to produce what is known to consumers as cocoa powder.
- The retained cocoa liquor and/or solid cocoa mass _____ (blend) with chocolate butter and other ingredients to produce the various types of chocolate.

Adapted from: <http://www.aphrodite-chocolates.co.uk/how_chocolate_made.htm>. Accessed on: December 13, 2013.

Part 12 (Units 23 & 24)

3. What would have happened if the car had never been invented? Read this incomplete excerpt once and check how much you understand. Then complete the spaces using the options from the box.

During the early 20th century, the dominant mode changed from rail to auto. In the 2nd half of the century, air travel became of major significance. Energy efficiency improved since the new modes were much more energy-efficient than the old rail mode was in 1900. Technological improvements (with setbacks at times) also helped. But ironically, if the auto and airplane _____ and most all travel was still by rail, fuel efficiency _____ even more, since government might have mandated energy-efficiency standards for rail like they did for autos. And without the convenience of the auto and the high speed of the airplane, there would have been far less travel. Thus far less energy _____. [...]

Some people erroneously think that a major reason for the high fuel consumption today is because we abandoned rail to opt for the auto and airplane. In other words, we are using the wrong modes. But if we continued to travel as much as we do now and did it all by rail, we _____ much energy either, since the energy efficiency of rail isn't much better than the auto. In reality, if rail _____ the only option for travel today, the volume of travel _____ due to the inconvenience of schedules and access. This would save a lot of energy, not because of rail but because of less travel.

Available at: <http://www.lafn.org/~dave/trans/energy/fuel-eff-20th-1.html>. Accessed on: December 13, 2013.

> would sharply decline ◆ would have been consumed ◆ wouldn't save ◆ were ◆
> hadn't been invented ◆ would have likely increased

C. VOCABULARY

Complete this word formation table. Then surf the Net and find examples in which these words are used.

WORD FORMATION		
VERB	**NOUN**	**ADJECTIVE**
invent	invention	
innovate		
	creation	
generate		
	information	
----	technology	technological
historicize		
----		technical
----	future	
	development	
		accomplishable

387

Glossary

A

achievement: realização
acquired: adquirido(a)
actually: realmente, de fato
addict: viciado(a)
addiction: vício
advantage: vantagem
advertising techniques: técnicas de publicidade e propaganda
advice: conselho, recomendação
affairs: assuntos
alongside: ao lado de
amazing: maravilhoso(a), extraordinário(a), incrível
apologize: pedir desculpas
arguably: indiscutivelmente
around: em volta de, ao redor de
array: série
arrested: preso(a), detido(a)
astonishing: surpreendente
at least: pelo menos
attorney: procurador(a), advogado(a)
award: prêmio
aware: consciente, ciente
awareness: consciência

B

backgrounds: experiências, históricos
battles: lutas, batalhas
behind the lens: atrás das lentes
belief: crença
believe: acreditar, crer
beware: tomar cuidado, precaver-se
bigness: grandeza (no sentido de corpulência)
blob: gota, pequena quantidade
bond: estabelecer vínculo, unir-se
boost: elevação, impulso, reforço
border: fronteira
both: ambos, ambas
bottle: garrafa
brain: cérebro
branch: ramo, segmento
brand-new: novo(a) em folha
breaking: break (estilo de dança de rua)
breakthrough: importante descoberta, avanço
breathe: respirar
breath-taking: de tirar o fôlego
bright: claro(a), resplandecente
bring: trazer
broken down: despedaçado(a), arrasado(a)
build equity: criar redes de relacionamento
burst onto: estourou
busy: ocupado(a), sobrecarregado(a)

C

can: poder, ser capaz de
carve: esculpir
catwalk: passarela (de desfile de moda)
caught: pego(a), capturado(a)
cave in: ceder a pressão
challenge: desafio
champion: campeã(o)
charge: cobrar
chart: gráfico, quadro
cheat: colar (em prova, exame)
clap hands: bater palmas
close: íntimo(a), próximo(a)
clown: palhaço(a)
clue: pista, dica
complaints: reclamações, queixas
confident: confiante, seguro(a)
cope with: lidar com
countless: incontáveis
craft: artesanato
crowned: coroado(a)

D

damage: dano, avaria
deal (with): lidar com
device: dispositivo
disease: doença, enfermidade
display: exibir, mostrar
dougie: dançar com estilo
dream: sonho
drop: perder, deixar cair
drowned: afogado(a)
dude: gíria cara "arrumadinho", rapaz
due to: devido a
duties: deveres, funções

E

earn: conquistar, ganhar
earrings: brincos
embellished: embelezado(a), decorado(a)
embroidery: bordado
endear: enaltecer, tornar importante
endorse: defender, apoiar
energetic: vigoroso(a), ativo(a)

388

engage: envolver-se
enhance: realçar
enough: suficiente
ensure: assegurar-se, garantir
entrepreneur: empresário(a)
exchange: trocar
eyeliner: delineador de olhos

F

fabric: tecido, pano
fad: tendência, moda
few: alguns, algumas (não muito)
fickle: inconstante
figure out: descobrir
fined: multado(a)
fix: consertar, arrumar
footsteps: passos
former: ex, anterior
fortunate: felizardo(a)
frame: moldura
fulfill: realizar, satisfazer
fulfillment: satisfação
fun: divertido(a)
fur: pelo de animal
furnish: mobiliar

G

gamut: gama
gap: lacuna, espaço
gather: reunir
gig opportunities: oportunidades de trabalho informal (bico); trabalhos no campo da música
glitzy: chamativo(a)
glue: cola
gold: ouro
graduated (from): formou-se (pela)
grasp: compreender
guess: adivinhar
guest: convidado(a)

H

half: metade
happen: acontecer, ocorrer
hard-driving: de pulso forte, "durão"
harmful: prejudicial
harness: aproveitar
harvesting: colheita
hazardous: perigoso(a), arriscado(a)
healthy: saudável
hectic: agitado(a)
hooked: fisgado(a), adepto(a)
hope: esperança
horde: multidão, horda

hose: mangueira (de regar)
huge: enorme
hurt: doer, machucar

I

illness: doença, enfermidade
increase: aumentar
indeed: realmente, sem dúvida
instead of: em vez de, ao invés de, no lugar de
internship: estágio, residência (para médicos)
invite: convidar
inviting: convidativo(a)
iron filings: limalha de ferro
issue: assunto, tema, matéria

J

jump: pular, saltar

K

keep: manter
kick: chutar
kill: matar
kind: tipo

L

landfill: aterro
landscape: paisagem
laughter: riso, gargalhada
launched: lançado
law school: faculdade de direito
law: lei, regulamentação
leafy vegetables: verduras cheias de folha
led (to): levou a, conduziu a
live: ao vivo
locking: estilo de dança funk
losing touch: perdendo contato
lowdown: fatos concretos
lump: caroço, inchaço

M

meaning: significado
measured: medido, calculado, avaliado
mercilessly: impiedosamente
missing: ausente, algo que falta
mold: modelo
mood: humor, estado de espírito, astral
mourned: velado(a), em situação de luto

Glossary

N
nomination: indicação
notice: aviso, lembrete
nowadays: hoje em dia, atualmente

O
often: frequentemente
ongoing: em andamento
open-minded: de mente aberta, liberal
otherwise: do contrário, caso contrário
overall: de maneira geral
overcome: superar, vencer, derrotar
overnight: da noite para o dia
overwhelming: irresistível, incontrolável
own: próprio, do(a) próprio(a)
owner: proprietário(a)

P
pay foward: pagar adiantado
perform: apresentar, atuar, representar
performance: desempenho
perv: abreviatura para perverted (pervertido[a])
pic: abreviatura para picture (foto)
pitch: sugestão de matéria a um jornal, revista, etc.
popping: estilo de dança de rua
poppy: papoula
pouts: caras e bocas
practice: consultório, clínica
praise: elogiar, enaltecer
predictor: indicador
prosecuted: processado(a) criminalmente
proud of: orgulhoso(a) de
pull out: tirar, sacar
pundit: perito, especialista
pursue: buscar, ir atrás de
push out (to a list): enviar, adicionar, incluir

Q
quickly: rapidamente

R
raise: criar, crescer, cultivar
rate: taxa
reach: atingir, alcançar
realize: perceber, notar
realm: esfera, domínio, reino
records: relatórios, históricos
referee: árbitro(a) de partida esportiva
refreshed: revigorado(a), reanimado(a)
regardless: independentemente de
released: divulgou
relish: apreciar, "curtir"

remarkable: notável
required: necessário, exigido
resentment: ressentimento, indignação
rights: direitos
ripped: rasgado(a)
role: papel, cargo
rope: corda
rub: esfregar
rules: regras

S
safe: seguro(a), fora de perigo
safer: mais seguro
sales: vendas
savvy: bem informado(a), conhecedor(a)
scratch: rabisco, arranhão
scrub: esfoliante
seam: costura
seek: procurar, buscar
seem: parecer
set: estabelecer, determinar
settle: estabelecer
shape: forma, formato
shortage: escassez, falta, insuficiência
shuffle: sacudir
sick: doente, enfermo(a)

sign-up sheet: formulário/ficha de inscrição
site: local, lugar, sítio
skills: habilidades
skin: pele
slightly: levemente
snack: lanche, refeição leve
sort: tipo, espécie
source: fonte, origem
spanning: abrangendo, abarcando
spark: fagulha, faísca
speech: fala, discurso
spent: gasto, utilizado
spin: girar
spoil: estragar, atrapalhar
stage: palco
stand: permanecer, ficar
stands: bancas de revista

starchy: (alimento) com amido
steal: roubar, furtar
stepdad: padastro
sticker: adesivo
stopwatch: cronômetro
straight: reto(a)
strength: força
stricken: atingido(a)
strict: rigoroso(a), severo(a)
striking: impressionante
stroll: passear, dar uma volta
suit: servir "direitinho", ajustar
suitable: adequado(a), apropriado(a)
surefire: infalível, certeiro(a)
surface: superfície
surroundings: arredores
sweat: suor, transpiração
swinging: balançando

T

tap: bater levemente (sapateado)
taste: provar, ter paladar
tasty: saboroso(a)
tepid: morno(a), pouco entusiasmado(a)
thigh: coxa
threats: ameaças, perigos
through: através de, por meio de
throughout: por toda parte
throw: jogar, lançar, arremessar
thunderstorm: tempestade de raios e trovões
toward: em direção a, para
track: rastrear, sondar
trapped: preso(a), capturado(a) em armadilha
truly: verdadeiramente
trustworthy: confiável
try: tentar
turn down: dispensar, rejeitar

U

unlike: ao contrário de, diferentemente de
unlikely: improvável
utterly: completamente

W

wading through: lidando com muitas informações
wait for: esperar, aguardar
ward off: precaver-se contra
wardrobe: guarda-roupa
waste: desperdiçar (verbo)
waste: lixo, resíduo (substantivo)
wave: onda
ways: maneiras, modos
weight: peso
wellness: bem-estar
whilst: enquanto
wide: grande, amplo(a)
wig: peruca
wildly popular: superpopular
will: determinação
wintry: de inverno, frio, gelado
wish: desejar
withdrawal: abstinência
worried: preocupado(a)

Y

yield: produção, rendimento
youth: juventude

391

Bibliography

ABREU-TARDELLI, L. S.; CRISTOVÃO, V. L. L. (Org.). *Linguagem e educação*: o ensino e a aprendizagem de gêneros textuais. Campinas: Mercado de Letras, 2009.

BAZERMAN, C. *Gênero, agência e escrita*. Trad. e adap. Judith Chambliss Hoffnagel. São Paulo: Cortez, 2006.

BORGES, E. F. V.; PAIVA, V. L. M. O. Por uma abordagem complexa de ensino de línguas. *Linguagem & Ensino*, Pelotas, v. 14, n. 2, p. 337-56, jul./dez. 2011.

BRASIL. *Ensino médio inovador*. Brasília: MEC/SEB, 2009. Disponível em: <http://portal.mec.gov.br/dmdocuments/ensino_medioinovador.pdf>. Acesso em: 27 jul. 2012.

_____. Lei n. 9.394, de 20 de dezembro de 1996. *Lex*: Leis de Diretrizes e Bases da Educação Brasileira (LDB). Brasília, 1996.

_____. *Orientações curriculares para o ensino médio*. Linguagens, códigos e suas tecnologias. Brasília: MEC/SEB, 2006. v. 1.

COPE, B.; KALANTZIS, M. Multiliteracies: The beginning of an idea. In: COPE, B.; KALANTZIS, M. (Ed.). *Multiliteracies*: Literacy learning and the design of social futures. London: Routledge, 2000. p. 3-8.

CRISTOVÃO, V. L. L.; NASCIMENTO, E. L. (Org.). *Gêneros textuais*: teoria e prática II. Palmas, União da Vitória: Kayguangue, 2005.

LARSEN-FREEMAN, D. Chaos/Complexity science and second language acquisition. *Applied Linguistics*, v. 18, n. 2, p. 141-65, 1997.

MARCUSCHI, Luiz Antônio. *Produção textual, análise de gêneros e compreensão*. São Paulo: Parábola Editorial, 2008.

MILLER, C. R. Rhetorical community: the cultural basis of genre. In: FREEDMAN, A.; MEDWAY, P. (Ed.). *Genre and the New Rhetoric*. London: Taylor and Francis, 1994. p. 23-42.

NOVAK, J. D.; GOWIN, D. B. *Learning How to Learn*. New York, NY: Cambridge University Press, 1984.

PAIVA, V. L. M. O. As habilidades orais nas narrativas de aprendizagem. *Trabalhos em Linguística Aplicada*, v. 46, n. 2, p. 165-179, 2007.

_____. Como o sujeito vê a aquisição de segunda língua. In: CORTINA, A.; NASSER, S. M. G. C. *Sujeito e linguagem*. São Paulo: Cultura Acadêmica, 2009.

_____. Modelo fractal de aquisição de línguas. In: BRUNO, F. C. (Org.). *Reflexão e Prática em ensino/aprendizagem de língua estrangeira*. São Paulo: Clara Luz, 2005. p. 23-36.

PALTRIDGE, B. *Genre and the Language Learning Classroom*. Ann Arbor, MI: The University of Michigan Press, 2004.

RAIMES, A. *Techniques in Teaching Writing*. New York, Oxford: Oxford University Press, 1983.

RICHARDS, J.; PLATT, J.; WEBER, H. *Longman Dictionary of Applied Linguistics*. Hong Kong: Longman, 1985.

SAUSSURE, F. *Curso de linguística geral*. Trad. Antônio Chelini, José Paulo Paes e Izidoro Blikstein. São Paulo: Cultrix, 1995.

SILVA, T. C. *Pronúncia do inglês*: para falantes do português brasileiro: os sons. Belo Horizonte: FALE/UFMG, 2005.

ZIMMER, M.; SILVEIRA, R.; ALVES, U. K. *Pronunciation Instruction for Brazilians*: Bringing theory and practice together. New Castle upon Tyne, UK: Cambridge Scholars Publishing, 2009.